European Democracies

Eighth Edition

MARKUS M. L. CREPAZ

The University of Georgia

JÜRG STEINER

*University of North Carolina – Chapel Hill
and University of Bern, Switzerland*

~~Hotel~~:
Narodni Trida 13
110 00 Praha 1

PEARSON

Boston   Columbus   Indianapolis   New York   San Francisco   Upper Saddle River
Amsterdam   Cape Town   Dubai   London   Madrid   Milan   Munich   Paris   Montreal   Toronto
Delhi   Mexico City   São Paulo   Sydney   Hong Kong   Seoul   Singapore   Taipei   Tokyo

Senior Acquisitions Editor: Vik Mukhija
Editorial Assistant: Isabel Schwab,
  Beverly Fong
Executive Marketing Manager:
  Wendy Gordon
Production Manager: Meghan DeMaio
Creative Director: Jayne Conte

Cover Designer: Karen Noferi
Cover Image: (c) AFP/Getty Images
Project Coordination, Text Design,
  and Electronic Page Makeup:
  Abinaya/Integra Software Services
Printer/Binder/Cover Printer:
  Courier Westford

Library of Congress Cataloging-in-Publication Data
Crepaz, Markus M. L.
  European democracies/Markus M.L. Crepaz, Jürg Steiner.—8th ed.
    p. cm.
  Includes bibliographical references and index.
  ISBN-13: 978-0-205-85478-3 (alk. paper)
  ISBN-10: 0-205-85478-8 (alk. paper)
  1. Europe—Politics and government—1945-   2. Democracy—Europe.
  I. Steiner, Jürg.   II. Title.
  JN94.A2C74 2013
  320.94—dc23
                                        2011042913

10 9 8 7 6 5 4 3 2 1— V013 —15 14 13 12

ISBN 10: 0-205-85478-8
ISBN 13: 978-0-205-85478-3

BRIEF CONTENTS

DETAILED CONTENTS

CHAPTER 3
"The Most Specific Manipulative Instrument of Politics": Electoral Systems and How Votes Are Turned into Seats   64

CHAPTER 4
From Legislative to Executive Authority: Cabinet Formation and Heads of State   91

CHAPTER 5
Courts   135

CHAPTER 6
Referenda   148

CHAPTER 7
Federalism   155

CHAPTER 8

Social Movements   162

CHAPTER 9

The State, Corporatism, the Great Meltdown of 2008, and the Greek Debt Crisis of 2011   178

PREFACE

Since the publication of the seventh edition of *European Democracies*, the big event is the severe continuation of the global financial and economic crisis, which is hitting Europe hard. European countries have to think anew the role of the state and the free market. How much should the state intervene to prevent dangerous bubbles in the free market? To what extent is the state responsible for creating a safety net for all its citizens with regard to old age, sickness, and unemployment? Should a safety net also be offered to poor refugees who enter Europe from war-torn countries in Africa, the Middle East, and elsewhere? All these questions force political parties in Europe to rethink their programs and election strategies. The continuation of the global financial and economic crisis has also had great influence on the programs and policies of the European Union. These are trying times for Europe as for the rest of the world.

NEW TO THIS EDITION

European Democracies features 15 topical chapters. There are now separate chapters for referenda and federalism, while the chapters on the end of the Cold War and transitions to democracy have been combined into a single chapter. For the new edition, we cover the following political developments:

- Foremost, we discuss the continuation of the global financial and economic crisis. We analyze the responses of the individual European countries and above all the European Union and compare these with the response of the United States.
- Greece, Portugal, Ireland, and even Spain and Italy have fallen into a deep debt crisis; the European Union and the International Monetary Fund have great difficulties in finding suitable ways to help.
- We show how the disruptions resulting from the global financial and economic crisis have made immigration, especially from Africa, an ever-bigger problem in Europe, leading to more nationalism and a strengthening of the extreme political right.
- In Great Britain, the 2010 elections brought a very unusual outcome, with no party gaining a majority in parliament. As a consequence, a coalition between Conservatives and Liberal Democrats was formed.
- Also in Great Britain, in 2011 a proposal to change the winner-take-all system giving more options to the voters was defeated in a national referendum.

- In France, the leader of the right-wing party Popular Front, the aging Jean-Marie Le Pen, has turned over the leadership to his daughter Marine. She pursues the anti immigration policy of her father, and with her youthful look and populist demeanor she may play the spoiler in the 2012 presidential elections.
- In Germany, the Greens gain increasing voter support, while the Free Democrats are in decline.
- In Italy, Prime Minister Silvio Berlusconi was increasingly plagued by tax, corruption, and sex scandals forcing him to resign as prime minister.
- Norway suffered a terrible massacre by an anti-Islamic fanatic.
- In the Netherlands, the anti-Islamic Freedom Party of Geert Wilders managed to become the third largest party.
- Spain suffers from very high unemployment, especially among young people who organize protests to draw attention to their plight.
- In Switzerland, it becomes increasingly difficult to form the traditional all-party governments.
- Croatia is preparing to become member of the European Union, but a national referendum is still needed.
- Tensions continue between Serbia and Kosovo, with the former not recognizing independence of the latter.
- In Bosnia-Herzegovina, the three ethnic groups of Serbs, Croats, and Bosnjaks do not come closer together so that the country continues to be on shaky ground.
- Hungary now has a government leaning to the right, stressing nationalistic themes, and endangering press freedom.
- Poland makes remarkable progress economically and also in how to practice democracy.

FEATURES

We are both European natives—Crepaz from Austria and Steiner from Switzerland. Both of us have many years of experience of teaching American undergraduate students on European politics; Crepaz at the University of Georgia at Athens, Steiner at the University of North Carolina at Chapel Hill. Although the book is written primarily for American students, it is also widely used in Europe and has been translated into Polish and Russian. The guiding principle in writing *European Democracies* was always that studying European politics should contribute to understanding political science at large. Therefore, the concepts and theories presented in this book have relevance for general political science. When we explain, for example, the workings of the European Court of Justice, we do not take a narrow European focus but use concepts and theories that are relevant to explain judicial behavior in other parts of the world. Or when we present the deliberative model of democracy, this model is grounded in the general literature of political philosophy. With this guiding principle, it was obvious to us that we needed a topical approach for the organization of the book.

If we had a country-by-country approach, we would have remained too much within the narrow European context. We use country material only to illustrate a theoretical point of the particular chapter. We use, for example, Sweden to illustrate the concept of minority cabinet, which means that under specific conditions a cabinet may survive although it does not enjoy a majority in parliament. If students, however, wish to write a case study about a particular country, our index should help in that it gives entries for each country with many subheadings.

With regard to pedagogical principles, we rely on the following three principles, which are firmly grounded in pedagogical research.

First, the material leads the student from known to unknown material, from easy to more difficult questions. If at all appropriate, for each new issue the text begins with the American situation and then asks how the European situation is both similar and different.

As a second pedagogical principle, we work with a few carefully chosen in-depth discussions to teach students more than broad surveys. Our goal is to teach students the major concepts of European politics. The text does not encourage students to memorize facts and names, but rather to understand the principles behind them. If a text tries to cover all European countries, the treatment of each country must necessarily be somewhat superficial. Limiting the discussion to the three or four largest European countries is also unsatisfactory, because some of the most exciting political questions arise in the smaller European countries.

As a third pedagogical principle, the text explicitly addresses why knowledge of other countries should matter to American students. When they have seen the many ways in which Europeans handle politics differently from Americans, they may ask: "So what? What does this mean for us? Should we act like Europeans, or should they act like us?" The discussion of each topic ends with such normative questions without trying to answer them in any definitive way. In teaching on both sides of the Atlantic, we have found it striking to note the different responses of American and European students for many normative political questions. Although American and European students need not share the same values, they should become more aware of how their values differ. In studying these normative questions, students ultimately will learn more about themselves and their values.

Thus, our third pedagogical principle leads back to the first one: The study of European politics not only should start at home but should also end at home. Having seen how Europe is different, American students may change some of their ideas about how a good democracy should function, while at the same time some of their old ideas may be reinforced.

One of the reviewers of the book suggested that we add a chapter on culture. We agree that culture is an important aspect for understanding European politics. But we still prefer to deal with this aspect in the individual chapters in which it is highly relevant. The index, however, has many entries under the heading of culture, so that students interested in this aspect have an easy way to find the respective information. In Chapter 1, we begin with a broad comparison of the United States and Europe with regard to history, geography, and culture. In Chapter 2, we deal with political parties. In any democracy, political parties are of great importance because they compete in elections and thus allow citizens to select their leaders. Chapters 3 through 7 present the institutions within which political parties operate. We will show the great influence that institutions have on the behavior of political parties and individual politicians. We will also show that because there is great variation in the institutional setting of European democracies, party systems vary greatly among European countries.

In Chapter 3, we will present how parliamentary elections are organized in Europe. American students may be surprised to learn that there is only a single country, the United Kingdom, using the winner-take-all system as practiced for congressional elections in the United States. All other countries use proportionality or a mix of winner-take-all and proportionality. Proportionality simply means that the percentage of parliamentary seats gained by a party corresponds to the percentage of its voter support.

Chapter 4 deals with the executive branch of government. In the United States, the head of the executive branch, the president, is elected by the people, and the cabinet members serve at his pleasure. This is called a presidential system. By contrast, most European countries have a parliamentary system in which the head of the executive branch, called the prime minister or chancellor, is appointed by parliament. Cabinet members have a much stronger position than in the United States, and the prime minister or chancellor functions more like a captain of a team.

Chapter 5 addresses the courts, which are less powerful in European countries than in the United States. Europeans are often surprised by the great power exercised by the U.S. Supreme Court. The chapter also covers the increasingly important European Court of Justice. Chapter 6 explains the use of the referendum in European democracies. The referendum is most heavily used in Switzerland, but other European countries are also using it more. Chapter 7 covers federalism, and we will see that there is great variation in this respect. Some countries, such as France, are very centralized, whereas other countries, such as Germany, have a federalist structure of government.

Chapters 8 and 9 introduce more actors in European politics. Chapter 8 describes social movements such as environmental movements, and Chapter 9 discusses economic interest groups such as business associations and labor unions. Although political parties are the classical actors in any democracy, social movements and economic interest groups have sometimes an even greater influence on policymaking in Europe. This is also the chapter where we take a more detailed look at the origins and consequences of the Greek sovereign debt crisis.

Having described the institutions and the actors operating within them, Chapter 10 then presents data about the policy outcomes in European democracies, for example, the level of taxes or governmental health-care expenditures. Students are encouraged to explain variations in such policy outcomes among European democracies and also in comparison with the United States, using the material learned in the previous chapters. This will make for interesting term papers written by students.

Chapter 11 describes how in 1989 Communism in the Soviet Union and Eastern Europe broke down, leading to the end of the Cold War. In order to understand the current situation in Europe, it is important to recall that after

1945 the continent was divided by the Iron Curtain for almost half a century. The enduring effect of this division is visible, for example, in the lesser economic development in Central and Eastern Europe. We explain how after 1989 the Central and Eastern European countries made the transition to democracy.

Despite the fact that fierce and extreme nationalism led to two world wars and all their devastating consequences, such nationalism is still a phenomenon to reckon with in Europe. It even led to a brutal war in the Balkans in the 1990s. We cover nationalism in Europe in Chapter 12.

When there are deep divisions in a society, power sharing among the various societal groups may help a country to reach some level of stability. As we will see in Chapter 13, with regard to Northern Ireland and Bosnia-Herzegovina, for example, power sharing is not easily implemented in a successful way.

Chapter 14 addresses what is perhaps the most important development in European politics since World War II: the creation and development of the European Union. The goal is not to arrive at a United States of Europe after the model of the United States of America. It is a new form of government with political authority divided among the European, the national, and the regional levels, with no level having ultimate priority. This new form of government may be called multilevel government.

Finally, in Chapter 15 we will put European politics into a global perspective and show to what extent European politics is influenced by what happens in the global setting, for example, with regard to international migration. Such migration, especially from third-world countries, has made Europe much more multicultural, which has led to challenging new problems, in particular with regard to the millions of immigrants of the Muslim faith. What the United States has been learning for a long time, Europe now learns the hard way—namely, that it is not easy for very different cultures to peacefully live together. As a country that has long been a destination for immigrants from around the world, the United States has perhaps found it easier to accommodate different cultures than Europe, which has a much longer cultural tradition of its own. Thus, globalization is a great challenge for Europe, not just in terms of immigration but also in other aspects such as the increased amount of economic competition on a global scale.

SUPPLEMENTS

Pearson is pleased to offer several resources to qualified adopters of *European Democracies* and their students that will make teaching and learning from this book even more effective and enjoyable. Several of the supplements for this book are available at the Instructor Resource Center (IRC), an online hub that allows instructors to quickly download book-specific supplements. Please visit the IRC welcome page at www.pearsonhighered.com/irc to register for access.

MySearchLab

For over 10 years, instructors and students have reported achieving better results and better grades when a Pearson MyLab has been integrated into the course. MySearchLab provides engaging experiences that personalize learning, and comes from a trusted partner with educational expertise and a deep commitment to helping students and instructors achieve their goals. *Writing & Research:* A wide range of writing, grammar, and research tools and access to a variety of academic journals, census data, Associated Press newsfeeds, and discipline-specific readings help you hone your writing and research skills. To order MySearchLab with the print text, use ISBN 0-205-85421-4.

Passport

Choose the resources you want from MyPoliSciLab and put links to them into your course management system. If there is assessment associated with those resources, it also can be uploaded, allowing the results to feed directly into your course management system's gradebook. With MyPoliSciLab assets like videos, mapping exercises, *Financial Times* newsfeeds, current events quizzes, politics blog, and much more, Passport is available for any Pearson political science book. To order Passport with the print book, use ISBN 0-205-85422-2.

Pearson MyTest

This powerful assessment generation program includes multiple-choice questions, true/false questions, and essay questions for each chapter. Questions and tests can be easily created, customized, saved online, and then printed, allowing flexibility to manage assessments anytime and anywhere. Available exclusively on the IRC.

ACKNOWLEDGMENTS

We would like to thank the reviewers of this edition for their valuable input: James Allan, Wittenberg University; Laurie Buonanno, Buffalo State College, SUNY; Martin Farrell, Ripon College; Teri Givens, University of Texas at Austin; Kema Irogbe, Claflin University; Zachary Irwin, Penn State University; Brian Kupfer, Tallahasee Community College; Shane Martin, Pennsylvania State University; Sydney Van Morgan, Cornell University; and Michelle Hale Williams, University of West Florida.

MARKUS M. L. CREPAZ
JÜRG STEINER

ABOUT THE AUTHORS

Markus M.L. Crepaz was born and raised in Austria. After attending the University of Salzburg from 1982 to 1986, he began his graduate study at the University of California, San Diego, where he completed his Ph.D. in 1992. He is a Professor of Political Science at the University of Georgia, and Associate Director of the Center for the Study of Global Issues (GLOBIS). He has published numerous articles on electoral engineering, European politics, corporatism, and the impact of political institutions on a host of policy outcomes. His current research focuses on the effects of increasing immigration on the willingness of European publics to continue funding the welfare state. His latest book is entitled *Trust beyond Borders: Immigration, Identity and the Welfare State in Modern Societies* and was published by the University of Michigan Press in 2007. From July 2009, he is also the Head of the Department of International Affairs within the School of Public and International Affairs (SPIA). Having lived in both worlds, the Old and the New, gives him a unique perspective from which to teach and research European politics in the United States.

Jürg Steiner is professor emeritus at the University of North Carolina at Chapel Hill and the University of Bern in Switzerland. He held a 2003–2004 chair position at the European University Institute in Florence, Italy. He is the winner of several teaching awards. His most recent publications is *Deliberative Politics in Action*, Cambridge University Press, 2004 and The *Foundations of Deliberative Democracy*, Cambridge University Press, 2012. Currently, he works on the potential for deliberative politics in deeply divided societies such as Belgium, Bosnia-Herzegovina, Colombia, Cyprus, Kosovo, Northern Ireland, and Turkey. Steiner is a Swiss citizen who for more than 30 years has divided his teaching time between the United States and Europe.

Becoming Modern in Europe and America: Different History, Different Politics

American tourists visiting European cities are invariably attracted to features in the landscape that Europeans take for granted, features utterly absent in the United States. Through the viewfinders and digital displays of their cameras they eagerly search for uniquely "European" features, and once they find them, they enthusiastically shoot away at the towering castles, impressive cathedrals, old town squares, and city walls. Much of contemporary European politics—such as the presence of Socialist parties, strong unions, secularism, and highly developed welfare states—is directly linked to these structures, for they attest to a time of drastic status differences between the rulers and the ruled whose origins go back to the Middle Ages. In an attempt to overcome these status differences, European history became intimately intertwined with revolutions, upheavals of sudden and violent changes of power structures that ultimately manifested themselves in the presence of strong Socialist parties, powerful unions, mostly secular societies, and a highly influential state apparatus. The ultimate prize of these struggles was the development of extensive welfare states in Europe, while the United States, lacking a "genuine revolutionary tradition,"[1] only developed a skeletal welfare state.

HOW DO WE KNOW THAT EUROPE IS DIFFERENT?

What exactly are the differences that set European and American politics and society apart? The following characteristics provide a place to begin:

- **Socialist parties** enjoy a massive presence in European legislatures, versus the total absence of Socialist parties in the American Congress.
- **The welfare state** in Europe is extensively developed—for example, it has not only income replacement programs that protect people in case

1

of accident, sickness, unemployment, and old age, but also programs that enable citizens to become active participants in the economic and social life of their country such as job training programs, stipends, subsidized transportation to work, and educational subsidies—whereas the welfare state in the United States exists in only skeletal form.

In 2007, the three "big spenders" in the European Union (EU) were France, Sweden, and Austria, which spent 28.4, 27.3, and 26.4 percent, respectively, of their gross domestic product (GDP) on social expenditures, while the United States spent just a little over 16 percent, as shown in Figure 1.1.

Even countries with a long authoritarian past and that joined the EU relatively recently, such as Greece and Spain, and Central and Eastern European countries such as Hungary and Poland, spend a higher percentage of their GDP on social expenditures than the United States.

The goal of such programs is to make people's survival independent of the action of market forces. Redistribution is mainly achieved through taxes and transfer payments such as retirement, disability, and health care payments. Welfare states have a high capacity to redistribute incomes.[2]

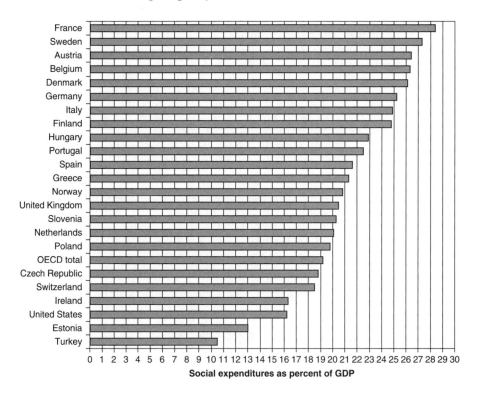

FIGURE 1.1

Social expenditures (old age, health, survivors, incapacity-related benefits, family benefits, and others) as percentage of gross domestic product in 2007.

Source: Organization for Economic Cooperation and Development. OECD Social Expenditures Database, in 2007.

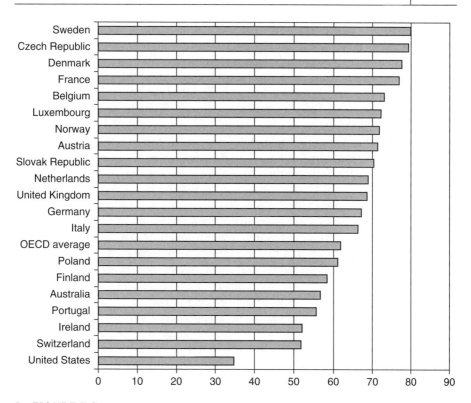

FIGURE 1.2

Effect of taxes and transfers (poverty reduction) measured in percentages on the entire population in the mid-2000s.

Source: OECD Factbook, 2009.

The "redistributive capacity of the state" captures the degree to which taxes and transfer payments lift people out of poverty (defined as people living with less than 50 percent of the median income). Figure 1.2 shows that the ability of taxes and transfer payments to lift Americans out of poverty is significantly smaller than it is in European countries. While taxes and transfers in Sweden reduce the number of people in poverty by 80 percent, in the United States the figure is only 35 percent.

■ **Unionization Rates** Most European countries have a highly unionized workforce. Although union density—the percentage of workers who are also members of unions—is declining almost everywhere in industrialized democracies, in 2003 the average union density in the 15 EU countries was around 43 percent, compared with 13 percent in the United States. Figure 9.1 shows the union density rates in countries in 2003, with Sweden indicating that almost 80 percent of its workforce is unionized, while for France that percentage is less than ten. Still, union density in the "old" 15 countries of the EU before 10 new countries were added in 2004 was more than three times higher than in the United States.[3]

■ **Paternalism** Europeans allow the state a much larger role to play in politics than Americans. The American proverb attributed to Thomas Paine sums it up succinctly: "That government is best that governs least"—or at least this is what most Americans thought until the economic crisis of 2008, which was triggered by the bursting of the housing bubble. Suddenly the "state" appeared as the only alternative to an economic system that was believed to be infallible. In January 2009, President Obama pushed through a $787 billion stimulus package to "prime the pump" of the economy, that is, to put money in people's hands in the hope of stirring up demand and thereby get the economy functioning again. On February 16, 2009, the widely read magazine *Newsweek* declared that "We are all Socialists now," suggesting that "…for the foreseeable future Americans will be more engaged with questions about how to manage a mixed economy than about whether we should have one."

Europeans, as opposed to Americans, do not have many qualms about state intervention in the economy. They see government not as an obstacle but as a facilitator that helps them to achieve their goals and as a protector against misfortune. In public opinion polls, Europeans time and again are ready to grant government a bigger role than Americans. In the 5th Wave of the World Values Survey taken in 2005–2006, on a scale of 1 to 10, 8.5 percent of Americans believed that the "government should take more responsibility to ensure that everyone is provided for" (1) while over 13 percent (10) believed that "people should take more responsibility to provide for themselves." In Germany, 12.5 percent of respondents believed the former, while only 2.5 percent believed the latter. If the question was asked whether "incomes should be made more equal" or whether "larger income differences are needed as incentives for individual effort," 4.8 percent of Americans believe that incomes should be made more equal while 8.2 percent of Germans believe this should be done. On the other end of the scale, the differences are even bigger: While 8.6 percent of Americans believe that large income differences are needed as incentives for individual effort, only 1.3 percent of Germans feel that way.[4]

It is not only in the perception of the public where the extensive role of the European state becomes evident. The constitutions of many European countries reveal a strong, perhaps even paternal, role of the state. For instance, article 19 of the Dutch constitution states that "It shall be the concern of the authorities to promote the provision of sufficient employment." According to article 20, "It shall be the concern of the authorities to secure the means of subsistence of the population and to achieve the distribution of wealth." Similarly, article 22 argues that "The authorities shall take steps to ensure the health of the population. It shall be the concern of the authorities to provide sufficient living accommodation." Finally, article 23 argues that "Education shall be the constant concern of the government." To enshrine such "concerns of the government" into the American constitution when it was created would have been unthinkable. It may be even more unrealistic today to expect that

▶ BOX 1.1 WE ARE ALL SOCIALISTS NOW

[...] There it was, just before the commercial: the S [Socialism] word, a favorite among conservatives since John McCain began using it during the presidential campaign. (Remember Joe the Plumber? Sadly, so do we.) But it seems strangely beside the point. The U.S. government has already—under a conservative Republican administration—effectively nationalized the banking and mortgage industries. That seems a stronger sign of socialism than $50 million for art. Whether we want to admit it or not—and many, especially Congressman Pence and [talk show host Sean] Hannity, do not—the America of 2009 is moving toward a modern European state. [...] We remain a center-right nation in many ways—particularly culturally, and our instinct, once the crisis passes, will be to try to revert to a more free-market style of capitalism—but it was, again, under a conservative GOP administration that we enacted the largest expansion of the welfare state in 30 years: prescription drugs for the elderly. People on the right and the left want government to invest in alternative energies in order to break our addiction to foreign oil. And it is unlikely that even the reddest of states will decline federal money for infrastructural improvements. [...] Bush brought the Age of Reagan to a close; now Obama has gone further, reversing Bill Clinton's end of big government. The story, as always, is complicated. Polls show that Americans don't trust government and still don't want big government. They do, however, want what government delivers, like health care and national defense and, now, protections from banking and housing failure. During the roughly three decades since Reagan made big government the enemy and "liberal" an epithet, government did not shrink. It grew. But the economy grew just as fast, so government as a percentage of GDP remained about the same.

Much of that economic growth was real, but for the past five years or so, it has borne a suspicious resemblance to Bernie Madoff's stock fund. Americans have been living high on borrowed money (the savings rate dropped from 7.6 percent in 1992 to less than zero in 2005) while financiers built castles in the air. [...] Now comes the reckoning. The answer may indeed be more government. In the short run, since neither consumers nor business is likely to do it, the government will have to stimulate the economy. And in the long run, an aging population and global warming and higher energy costs will demand more government taxing and spending. ■

Source: Newsweek, February 16, 2009.

such articles could be incorporated into the American constitution through the amendment process, as individualistic beliefs and deep-seated suspicions of the state are the predominant political attitudes in contemporary America.

■ **Class Matters**   Another significant difference between Europe and America centers on the importance of social **class**. Though waning, social class is still very important in Europe, while it is much less so in America. The identity of an individual in Europe is very much connected to whether one belongs to the "working class" or not. In Europe, the school system channels pupils very early into various class-based categories, either toward vocational training or higher learning. Those who make it to the elite universities can expect to be rewarded with top positions in government. One such school is the ENA (École nationale d'administration) in France.[5] To which social class one belongs is clearly demonstrated in people's accents, titles, and lifestyles. There is a defined class consciousness in Europe, both among the working class and the privileged.

In the United States, class does not play such a crucial role. Most people in America consider themselves to belong to the *middle class,* even though households may have drastic income differences ranging from $40,000 to $500,000. It is more useful to think of "Americanism" as a creed. American identity is less a matter of material conditions or education and more a matter of ideology. The American creed includes liberty, egalitarianism (equality of opportunity), individualism, populism, and laissez-faire. When immigrants arrived in the New World, they were a very disparate group whose identities were shaped by their primordial attachments—their nation, their "blood" relationships, their ethnic backgrounds. Until the middle of the eighteenth century, there was very little awareness of an "American" ideology. However, as Great Britain started to put heavier loads on its colonies in the New World, such as with the Stamp Act of 1765, a new "Americanism" began to grow. The American creed developed as a necessary element to distinguish the American settlers from the British once the relationship between the settlers and their British government began to decline. America needed to develop its own identity vis-à-vis its British counterpart and in so doing constructed the American creed. Precisely because the multitude of races, nationalities, and ethnicities made it impossible to forge a common identity on such primordial building blocks, Americans invented an identity on the basis of ideological principles. For this very reason, some behavior can be called "un-American," whereas there is no such thing as behaving, for example, in an "un-Swedish" way.

■ **Spirituality**   Religion plays a significant role in American society. Although European societies have become rather secular, religion in America is vibrant. The question item that reveals most dramatically the differences in the role of religion between Europe and America is the following statement: "Politicians who do not believe in God are unfit for public office." Remarkably, in 2005 a majority of 32 percent of Americans either "strongly agreed" or "agreed" with that statement, while only 12.5 percent of the Italians, and only, 3.3 percent of the Swedes either agreed or strongly agreed with that statement.[6]

Figure 1.3 shows two indicators as to the importance of religion in people's lives: one question taps an attitude and the other behavior. In the former people were asked whether they thought religion was important. In the latter people were asked if they were either "active," "inactive," or "not" members of churches or religious organizations. Along both dimensions, the United States clearly is at the top of the rankings; although when it comes to attitudes, the United States is closely followed by Italy. However, when it comes to behavior, again the United States leads the pack with almost 38 percent of Americans saying they are "active" members of a church or religious organization while only slightly over 9 percent of Italians and only 4.5 percent of French can make that claim. It is interesting to see the difference of the formerly "West" and "East" German states with nearly double the percentages of West Germans who say they are "active" members as compared to people living in the formerly East German states revealing the impact of 40 years of communist rule.

When it comes to spirituality, a clear picture emerges: The United States is the most spiritual of the modern societies, followed, with some distance, by Italy and Ireland. Religion tends to be the least important in Sweden, Denmark, and the Netherlands. What is most fascinating is that when it comes to poverty reduction, social assistance programs, and the generosity of the welfare state in general, the Nordic countries tend to be in the lead

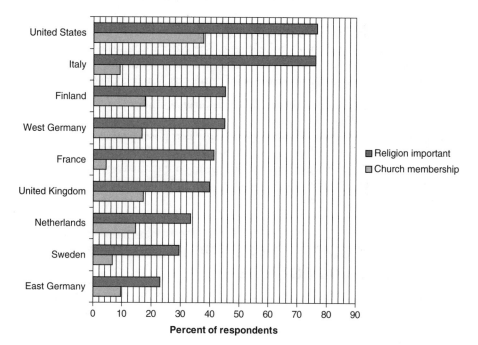

FIGURE 1.3

Percentages of respondents who indicated that religion is either "very important" or "rather important" in their lives ordered from highest to lowest in 2005. The "church membership" question asked respondents whether they were "active, inactive, or not a member of a church or religious organizations," also in 2005. The figure shows the percentage of those who said they were "active" members. "West Germany" and "East Germany" refer to those German states that were once the western and eastern part, respectively, of the unified Germany during the Cold War until 1989.

Source: World Values Survey, 5th wave, ICPSR, 2005, Ann Arbor, MI: The University of Michigan.

BOX 1.2 FINN'S SPEED FINE IS A BIT RICH

One of Finland's richest men has been handed a record 170,000-euro (over 200,000 U.S. dollars) speeding ticket, thanks to the country's policy of relating the fine to your income. Jussi Salonoja, the 27-year-old heir to a family-owned sausage empire, was given the £116,000 ticket after being caught driving 80 km/h in a 40 km/h zone. Helsinki police came up with the figure after tax office data showed that Mr. Salonoja earned close to £7 million in 2002. If his penalty stands it will beat the previous record of almost 80,000 euros. That figure (£54,000) was paid in 2000 by Finnish Internet millionaire Jaakko Rytsola, when he was caught speeding. Yet Mr. Salonoja could get his penalty reduced, as was the case with Nokia executive Anssi Vanjoki. In 2002, Mr. Vanjoki's 116,000-euro fine was reduced by no less than 95 percent due to his drop in income following a downturn in the mobile phone maker's profits. ■

Source: BBC News, February 2, 2004.

while the United States is at the bottom. When it comes to religion, the United States is at the top of the league. The Nordic countries are generous with social programs and not very religious; the United States is very religious, but not generous with social programs. What is the explanation?

This last point highlights the massive differences between European and American politics. The burning question, of course, is how can these differences be explained? Where do they come from? How is it possible that someone who drives at twice the speed limit can get a fine of over $200,000 in Finland, as shown in Box 1.2? Why is it that most European countries favor "equality" over "liberty" while the opposite is the case in America? We find the answers to these questions in the next section.

EXPLAINING DIFFERENCES: THE IMPACT OF HISTORY, GEOGRAPHY, AND CULTURE

It is remarkable that American politics is so different from European politics given that America was largely founded by European immigrants. Clues as to why European politics is different can partly be found in those monuments and features Americans love to visit when in Europe: the castles, cathedrals, city walls, and market squares that are conspicuously absent in America. These features significantly affected the process of what is called "modernization" or "nation building." It proved to be a wrenching process for all modern nations as major conflicts arose over the future identity of the nation, the legitimacy of rule, the capacity of the state to penetrate every nook and cranny of the new territory by its laws, and how to distribute the pieces of the economic pie. Many attempts have been made at explaining the "exceptional" nature of American politics. The following explanations highlight some of the most important, but definitely not all, reasons why there is such a remarkable difference between European and American politics.

Absence of Feudalism in America The castles, cathedrals, old town squares, and city walls that still dot the European landscape originated in the period of the Middle Ages when nobles controlled their realm from their castle, typically perched upon a hill. The motto of **feudalism**—the social relations between lords and vassals—could be described as "to serve and protect." The lord would protect his "subjects" from attacks from neighboring lords; in turn, the peasants had to serve the lord by relinquishing a part of the fruits of their labor known as *tithe*, the root word for "tax," or through the widely despised *corvée*, the unpaid compulsory labor demanded by a lord or king. The respective social positions of peasants were "ascribed"; in other words, a peasant could never rise above his or her station. This established an extremely rigid class structure that continued throughout the Industrial Revolution, when many of the peasants became industrial workers and the nobility either morphed into captains of industry or became part of the landed aristocracy, such as the *Junkers* in Germany in the nineteenth and early twentieth centuries.[7]

America, on the other hand, has no feudal residues. It was born modern.[8] It was bourgeois from the beginning. When immigrants arrived on the shores of America, they started with a clean slate. The sense of hierarchy that so permeated European society was significantly flattened when immigrants came to the New World. In America there was a much less developed social pecking order. As a result, class consciousness never developed to the same extent as in Europe. This meant that the sense of class, of exploitation over hundreds of years of peasants and workers upon which European Marxists could build their revolutionary theory and practice, never had any traction in America. As so powerfully summed up by Werner Sombart: "No feudalism—no socialism."[9]

Relative Early Affluence Another explanation dealing with the American exception highlights the **relative early affluence** of American workers compared to their European counterparts. According to Karl Marx, immiseration and impoverishment of the working class is what kindles the fires of revolution. Comparing the fate of the workers in Germany with those in the United States in the nineteenth century, Sombart finds that American workers earned about two to three times more than German workers at roughly the same cost of living. Hence, American workers had less of a reason to storm the barricades. Again, in the memorable words of Sombart: "All socialist utopias come to grief with roast beef and apple pie."[10]

The Disintegrative Forces of Immigration The ethnic diversity of immigrants proved to be particularly corrosive when it came to establishing unions and Socialist parties in the United States. Different waves of immigrants of varying nationalities and religions coming into the United States created an extraordinarily diverse labor force. Socialists appealed to workers along class lines, while Democrats and Republicans exploited the ethnic differences in appealing to members.

The craft unions in the American Federation of Labor (AFL) were organized along ethnic lines, which aggravated the problems faced by the Socialists—particularly after the 1890s when the largest streams of immigrants were no longer the "old immigrants," the British, Germans, and northern Europeans who were skilled and assimilated rather quickly into the larger society, but immigrants from Southern, Central, and Eastern Europe, who had fewer skills, spoke poor English, and were discriminated against by the earlier immigrants who blended more easily with the native-born whites.[11]

In addition, immigrants themselves were ideologically quite distinct. The most radical immigrants were the Germans, who brought with them experiences of the failed democratic revolutions of 1848 and the persecution of Socialists under Bismarck in the 1870s. These immigrants also had firsthand experience with the strains of industrial production. On the other hand, many immigrants were actually quite conservative and ready to absorb the reigning ideology of their new homeland. Because many experienced life to be so much better in the New World than in their old homeland, they, "with the enthusiasm of converts, praised the Republic and the material blessings it offered."[12] Moreover, given the sectarian, fundamentalist character of the Socialist Party, many Catholic immigrants could not find an ideological home in this party. In the words of Lipset and Marks, "Vigorous Catholic opposition to socialism can hardly be exaggerated as a reason for the failure of the Socialist party."[13] Finally, even the Socialists succumbed to racism, allowing **immigration** only for Northern Europeans and excluding Catholics, and Southern, Central, and Eastern Europeans. Obviously, the American experience in organizing for labor was very different from the European experience. Because European nations were relatively homogeneous, it was possible for "class" to become a salient issue. Only on the basis of ethnic homogeneity could class become a most powerful vector in European politics—a vector that ultimately pointed in the direction of the welfare state.

Frederick Jackson Turner's Frontier Thesis Turner, who was a historian, delivered a speech in Chicago in 1893 titled "The Significance of the Frontier in American History." By "**frontier**" he meant the tip of the spear of westward expansion from the East Coast to the Pacific by settlers who claimed "free" land on which to build their livelihood. In Turner's words, "So long as free land exists, the opportunity for a competency exists, and economic power secures political power."[14] The opportunity to expand westward functioned very much like a safety valve insofar as it took the revolutionary winds out of the sails during periods of worker unrest in the industrial cities of New York, Boston, and Chicago. Many workers, instead of fighting it out with the industrial bosses, chose to move west, claim land, and in essence, become capitalists themselves. European workers did not have that option. European industrial cities were teeming with disgruntled workers who were ready to take on the fight with their bosses for fairer wages and better working conditions. According to Turner, however, the frontier, with its vast lands to the west, turned out to be "the line of most rapid and effective Americanization,"[15] while this very same process spelled doom for the Native Americans.

American Sectarianism   Americans are some of the most religious people in the world while at the same time belonging to one of the most advanced nations in the world. This makes America quite distinct, as the typical pattern of development suggests that as economic development increases, adherence to traditional values (such as churchgoing) should decrease. This pattern clearly holds true in Europe, which is very secular. In the United States, most believers adhere to *sects*—such as the Baptists, Presbyterians, or Methodists, and many others— rather than *churches,* as is the case in Europe. European churches were always closely connected to the state. They were state financed, hierarchical, claimed to be the arbiter between the individual and God, and were actively engaged in political affairs, particularly as far as the alleviation of the plight of the poor was concerned. The close intertwining of God and politics can clearly be seen in such documents of the Catholic Church as *Rerum Novarum* (1891, Pope Leo XIII), *Quadragesimo Anno* (1931, Pius XI), and its *Catechism*. They speak to the wretched living conditions of the poor, the inhumane working conditions of laborers, and the need for a "just wage." The church presented itself as an agent of social reform and asked for active support from the people. In the view of the Catholic Church, the plight of the working class had to be seen as part of an organic whole where the whole community would be affected if workers were treated unjustly.

On the other hand, American sects never emphasized community. Rather, they highlighted individuality and the lone relation between God and the believer. Max Weber described the Protestant work ethic as being based on competitive, rational, individualistic behavior, which encouraged entrepreneurial achievement. The religious tradition of Protestant "dissent" has called on believers to follow their own interpretation of the scriptures, undiluted by formal religious institutions. In most Protestant sects, there is no agent or mediator between the believer and God as in Catholicism, where the church plays this role. In Weber's interpretation, responsibility for leading a virtuous life rests with the individual who stands alone before God, as committed sins cannot be absolved through confession. This puts a heavy burden upon a Protestant believer, for when the day of reckoning comes, all deeds will be added up cumulatively.[16] The consequence of this religious doctrine is that Americans are uniquely moralistic. They tend to see things in black and white—people of other countries are either "good" or "bad," behavior is either "right" or "wrong." In the words of Seymour Martin Lipset, "Americans are utopian moralists who press hard to institutionalize virtue, to destroy evil people, and eliminate wicked institutions and practices."[17] This dichotomous, almost fundamentalist, worldview is revealed clearly in the rhetoric of foreign policymaking, from Ronald Reagan's aim to destroy the "evil empire" to George W. Bush's single-minded pursuit to smoke out the "evildoers" and the widespread references to scriptures that punctuated his speeches: "To endorse a war and call on people to kill others and die for the country, Americans must define their role in a conflict as being on God's side against Satan, for morality against evil."[18]

In addition, the congregational nature of American sects fostered egalitarian, individualistic, and populist values that located the purpose of religious organization not in arguing for social reform but in the spiritual satisfaction of the individual. This led to a shift in focus away from the community to the individual, from objective social conditions to the piety of the individual and what the individual could do to improve himself or herself. Indeed, Americans are workaholics. Statistics indicate that Americans are in the top three (together with Japan and Australia) in terms of hours worked per year.[19]

Racial Heterogeneity in America The creation and expansion of the welfare state in the nineteenth and twentieth centuries in Europe was underpinned by a sense of community and social solidarity of citizens toward each other. The basic premise on which the state could extract large sums of money through taxation and distribute it in the form of benefits was that most people believed that the recipients of public funds were people like themselves, facing difficulties that they themselves might face one day.[20] This organicist notion of the welfare state was founded on widely held concepts of community and feelings of mutual obligation toward fellow citizens. In the classic study *Citizenship and Social Class*, T. H. Marshall explains the foundations on which social citizenship rests: "Citizenship requires…a direct sense of community membership based on loyalty to a civilization which is a common possession."[21]

In other words, the sacrifices citizens engage in by voluntarily giving up a significant portion of their income in order to finance the welfare state are easier to come by if the recipients of such assistance look and behave similarly to those who provide the assistance. If, however, there is a perception that taxes are paid by one type of people and received by another, the willingness to support such redistributive schemes is reduced. This is the major finding of a study by Alberto Alesina et al., who argue that the reason why the American welfare state is less developed is because "…racial animosity in the United States makes redistribution to the poor, who are disproportionately black, unappealing to many voters."[22] In other words, people are more likely to support welfare if they see it received by people of their own race, but are less supportive if they see it received by people of another race.

Europe is not immune from such stereotypes as it confronts for the first time increased diversity as a result of massive immigration. As more and more immigrants stream into European countries, will Europeans be willing to continue funding the welfare state as the likely recipients of welfare become increasingly very different from them in terms of race, religion, ethnicity, and language? One of the authors (Markus M. L. Crepaz) has further researched this question and concludes that increased immigration will not lead to an Americanization of the European welfare state for two main reasons: First, the European welfare state became fully developed *before* widespread immigration occurred, in contrast to what took place in America. Second, the presence of an encompassing welfare state affects the levels of social trust in society, thus reducing resentment toward foreigners.[23]

This is not a complete list of explanations for the exceptional or deviant politics of America. However, this list can shed light on many differences between European and American politics. The attentive reader of this book will notice many such differences discussed in the following chapters, particularly in Chapters 2 through 9. These differences represent the ultimate causes as to why we observe variations in, for example, income inequality, voter turnout, poverty, and "life chances" between America and Europe.

STRUCTURE OF THE BOOK

Having seen in this first chapter how the history and politics in Europe are in important ways different from the United States, we turn in the following chapters to specific aspects of European democracies. However, we keep making comparisons with the United States in the individual chapters. We will also not limit ourselves to the present time, but, as in this chapter, we will give historical depth to our analysis.

Political scientists try not only to describe political phenomena but also to establish causal relations among important political phenomena. This is called *theory building*. In this theoretical spirit, we will not only describe political phenomena, but we will also address the question of the preconditions and consequences of particular phenomena. In this process of theory building, logically sound hypotheses need to be formulated and then tested with empirical data. It is often not easy to establish in a convincing way whether the data support a particular hypothesis or not. Different scholars may come to different conclusions, and this contributes to vigorous and stimulating scholarly discussions.[24]

We begin in Chapter 2 with political parties. In any democracy, political parties are of great importance because they compete in elections and thus allow citizens to select their leaders. Chapters 3 through 7 present the institutions within which political parties operate. We will show the great influence that institutions have on the behavior of political parties and individual politicians. We will also show that because there is great variation in the institutional setting of European democracies, the party systems vary greatly among European countries.

In Chapter 3 we will present how parliamentary elections are organized in Europe. American students may be surprised that there is only a single country, the United Kingdom, using the winner-take-all system with one ballot as practiced for congressional elections in the United States. All other countries use winner-take-all with two ballots, proportionality, or a mix of winner-take-all and proportionality. Proportionality simply means that the percentage of parliamentary seats gained by a party corresponds to the percentage of its voter support.

Chapter 4 deals with the executive branch of government. In the United States, the head of the executive branch, the president, is elected by the people, and the cabinet members serve at his pleasure. This is called a presidential system. By contrast, most European countries have a parliamentary system, in which the head of the executive branch, called the prime minister or chancellor, is appointed by parliament. Cabinet members have a much stronger position than in the United States, and the prime minister or chancellor functions more like a captain of a team.

Chapter 5 addresses the courts, which are less powerful in European countries than in the United States. Europeans are often surprised by the great power exercised by the U.S. Supreme Court. Chapter 6 explains the use of the referendum in European democracies. The referendum is most heavily used in Switzerland, but other European countries also increasingly use the referendum. In Chapter 7 we will see that there is great variation with respect to federalism. Some countries are very centralized, such as France, whereas other countries, such as Germany, have a federalist structure of government.

Chapters 8 and 9 introduce more actors in European politics. Chapter 8 describes social movements such as environmental movements, and Chapter 9 discusses economic interest groups such as business associations and labor unions. Although political parties are the classical actors in any democracy, social movements and economic interest groups have sometimes an even greater influence on policymaking in Europe.

Having described the institutions and the actors operating within these institutions, Chapter 10 then presents data about the policy outcomes in European democracies—for example, the level of taxes or governmental health-care expenditures. Students are encouraged to explain variation in such policy outcomes among European democracies and also in comparison with the United States using the material learned in the previous chapters. This will make for interesting term papers written by students.

Chapter 11 describes how in 1989 Communism in the Soviet Union and Central and Eastern Europe broke down, leading to the end of the Cold War. In order to understand the current situation in Europe, it is important to recall that the continent was divided by the Iron Curtain after 1945 for almost half a century. The enduring effect of this division is visible, for example, in the lesser economic development in Central and Eastern Europe.

Chapter 12 further explains how after 1989 the Central and Eastern European countries made the transition to democracy. In this chapter, we will also see how Germany and Italy, after their defeat in World War II, made the transition to democracy. We will also cover the transition to democracy in Spain in the 1970s.

Despite the fact that fierce and extreme nationalism led to two world wars and all their devastating consequences, fierce nationalism is still a phenomenon to reckon with in Europe. It even led to a brutal war in the Balkans in the 1990s. We cover nationalism in Europe in Chapter 12.

When there are deep divisions in a society, power sharing among the various societal groups may help to reach some level of stability. As we will see in Chapter 13, with regard to Northern Ireland and Bosnia-Herzegovina, for example, power sharing is not easily implemented in a successful way.

Chapter 14 addresses perhaps the most important development in European politics since World War II—the creation and development of the EU. The goal is not to arrive at a United States of Europe after the model of the United States of America. It is a new form of government that may be called multilevel government.

Finally, in Chapter 15 we will put European politics in a global perspective and show to what extent European politics is influenced by what happens in the global setting, for example, with regard to international migration. Such migration, especially from Third World countries, has made Europe much more multicultural, which has led to challenging new problems, in particular with regard to the millions of immigrants of Muslim faith. What the United States has been learning for a long time, Europe now learns in a hard way—namely, that it is not easy for very different cultures to peacefully live together. As a typical immigration country, the United States has perhaps found it easier to accommodate different cultures than Europe, which has a much longer cultural tradition of its own. Thus, globalization is a great challenge not only for Europe, but also in other aspects such as the increased level of economic competition on a global scale.

KEY TERMS

class   5
feudalism   9
frontier   10
immigration   10
paternalism   4

racial
   heterogeneity   12
relative early
   affluence   9
sectarianism   11

Socialist
   parties   1
spirituality   6
the welfare state   1
unionization rates   3

DISCUSSION QUESTIONS

1. What other differences, than those highlighted previously, exist between American and European politics?
2. For those of you who have traveled to Europe, what places have you visited and why?
3. In most European countries, "equality" is considered to be prior to "freedom," whereas the opposite is the case in the United States. Is it possible to have both a highly egalitarian and a highly free society?
4. Is "class" an important concept in America? If yes, what "classes" can you identify and how do you draw the lines between them?
5. How does religion influence American and European politics? In which of the two places is the influence of religion on politics more extensive?
6. Does "freedom" include the right to organize in the form of unions?
7. As mentioned earlier, in international statistics on hours worked per person, the United States tends to be at the top. Why do Europeans work less?
8. How do the differences in American and European politics and society manifest themselves in policy outcomes?

NOTES

1. Louis Hartz. *Liberal Tradition in America: An Interpretation of American Political Thought Since the Revolution* (New York: Harcourt Brace, 55).
2. Markus M. L. Crepaz. Veto Players, Globalization and the Redistributive Capacity of the State: A Panel Study of 15 OECD Countries. *Journal of Public Policy* 21 (2000): 1–22.
3. European Industrial Relations Observatory (EIROnline). Available online at http://www.eurofound.europa.eu/areas/industrialrelations/dictionary/definitions/european industrialrelationsobservatory.htm
4. *World Values Survey*, 5th Wave. International Consortium for Political Science Research (ICPSR). (Ann Arbor, MI: The University of Michigan, 2000).

5. The French Elite: In ENA We Trust. *The Economist,* July 21, 2005.
6. *World Values Survey.* International Consortium for Political Science Research (ICPSR). (Ann Arbor, MI: The University of Michigan, 2005).
7. Seymour Martin Lipset. *American Exceptionalism: A Double Edged Sword* (New York: Norton, 1996).
8. Barrington Moore. *Social Origins of Dictatorship and Democracy: Lord and Peasant in the Making of the Modern World* (Boston, MA: Beacon Press, 1966).
9. Werner Sombart. *Why Is There No Socialism in the United States?* (White Plains, NY: International Arts and Sciences Press, 1976). First published in German in 1906.
10. Ibid., 26.
11. Seymour Martin Lipset and Gary Wolfe Marks. *It Didn't Happen Here: Why Socialism Failed in the United States* (New York: Norton, 2000).
12. Marcus Lee Hansen. *The Immigrant in American History* (New York: Harper Publishers, 1964, 96).
13. Lipset and Marks, *It Didn't Happen Here,* 154.
14. Frederick Jackson Turner. *The Frontier in American History* (New York: Henry Holt and Company, 1920, 13).
15. Ibid., 3.
16. Max Weber. *The Protestant Ethic and the Spirit of Capitalism* (New York: Routledge, 1999). Originally published 1904/1905.
17. Lipset, *American Exceptionalism,* 63.
18. Ibid., 20.
19. For statistics, see http://www.nationmaster.com/graph-T/lab_hou_wor.
20. David Willets quoted in "Discomfort of Strangers," by David Goodhart. *The Guardian,* February 24, 2004.
21. Thomas Humphrey Marshall. *Citizenship and Social Class* (London: Pluto Press, 1950, 24).
22. Alberto Alesina, Edward Glaeser and Bruce Sacerdote. *Why Doesn't the US Have a European-Style Welfare State?* (Cambridge, MA: Institute of Economic Research, 2001, 1).
23. Markus M. L. Crepaz. *Trust beyond Borders: Immigration, the Welfare State and Identity in Modern Societies* (Ann Arbor, MI: The University of Michigan Press, 2007).
24. Jelle Visser and Anton Hemerijck. *A Dutch Miracle: Job Growth, Welfare Reform and Corporatism in the Netherlands* (Amsterdam, Netherlands: Amsterdam University Press, 1997).

Political Parties

In any democracy, political parties are essential because they compete in elections, allowing citizens to elect their leaders. Without political parties, democracy is not possible, an argument that has been made in a classical way by Seymour Martin Lipset and Stein Rokkan.[1] Therefore, it seems appropriate to begin our study with political parties. At the beginning of the chapter, we discuss the role of political parties in democracies in general and then turn to the specific parties in European democracies. We begin with the Socialist Party, which is difficult to explain to an American audience because Americans often identify European socialism with the old Soviet Union. This is a misguided comparison, as European Socialists are very much democratically oriented. We then turn to the *Liberals,* a term that is used very differently in Europe than in the United States; European Liberals are strongly free-market oriented. Next come Conservatives, Christian Democrats, the New Radical Right, Greens, and country-specific regional parties. We will see that a simple dimension from left to right is not sufficient to locate European parties in a meaningful way. Rather, we need a multidimensional space to locate European political parties. Understanding the concept of multidimensional space is crucial to understanding this chapter.

The United States has only two viable political parties, although sometimes efforts are made to create a third party. European democracies, by contrast, have a multitude of political parties. Another difference is that political parties play a much bigger role in Europe than in the United States. This is true, in particular, for parliamentary elections and the formation of cabinets, as we will see in Chapters 3 and 4. Thus, it is appropriate to devote this second chapter to the description of the political parties in European politics. They do not differ simply on a dimension from left to right, and one may even ask whether the terms *left* and *right* have not become too vague to describe clearly enough the political parties in Europe. As noted, we will see that the European political parties are located in a multidimensional political space, which is the key concept of the chapter. As we go along, we will show the relationships among the various parties, making it increasingly clear what is meant by a multidimensional political space. Before we do this, we need to examine the origins of political parties, the functions they serve, the difference between parties and interest groups, and how parties change over time.

POLITICAL PARTIES—THE "CHILDREN OF DEMOCRACY"

The development of political parties is closely linked with the process of democratization, particularly with the extension of mass suffrage. Most European countries completed this process by the early 1920s. Before the establishment of general **voting rights**, there existed only groups of notables who congregated in small "clubs" or "caucuses." They used their means and influence to make themselves or their protegés available as candidates to be elected. Membership in such "clubs" was tightly controlled and kept at very low numbers. Such clubs, cliques, or caucuses did not seek expansion of their members as do modern parties. They did not open their doors to anyone who wanted to become a member. Only "qualified" members of society—that is, those who could bring influence to bear on the interests of the groups—could join these illustrious caucuses. For conservative groupings in late nineteenth-century Europe, this meant that the members of such **cliques** or clubs were made up of aristocrats, industrial magnates, bankers, wealthy businessmen, and even influential clerics. This system of privileged access became outmoded once mass suffrage was extended.

The introduction of universal or near-**universal suffrage** in the early twentieth century had two significant consequences: It led to the rise of Socialist parties and it expanded the role of parliaments. At the beginning of World War I, membership in the German Social Democratic Party numbered more than a million, and the party enjoyed a high annual budget of more than 2 million German marks.[2] The universal right to vote combined with an explosive membership turned Socialist parties into the first mass political parties. Mass membership in the Socialist parties also led to an equalization vis-à-vis the much smaller but well-endowed conservative caucuses, which were made up of a few wealthy individuals. Socialist parties relying on collective financing could field candidates for election to parliaments without needing the support of conservative-leaning capitalists. With a strong party structure and public financing, Socialist parties could now afford to print their own newspapers and support political campaigns, thus opening the door for the development of mass parties as we understand them today. The contrast between the highly disciplined, publicly financed, and tightly organized mass parties and the "cliques" made up of men of privilege is stark. As explained by Max Weber,

> Now then, the most modern forms of party organizations stand in sharp contrast to this idyllic state in which circles of notables and, above all, members of parliament rule. These modern forms are the children of democracy, of mass franchise, of the necessity to woo and organize the masses and develop the utmost unity of direction and strictest discipline.[3]

FUNCTIONS OF POLITICAL PARTIES

What do political parties do? It seems difficult to conceive of politics without reference to political parties. Yet, for the public, the term *political party* generally has negative connotations, in the sense that parties are simply seen as vehicles for individuals to rise to power, or that they are the realm in which corruption unfolds, as exemplified by the party machines in the United States at the turn of the twentieth century. The German term *Parteibuchwirtschaft* and the Italian term *Partitocrazia* highlight the corrosive character of political parties. Both terms refer to the tendency of political parties to act as **patrons** and see individuals as **clients**. There are numerous examples of such behaviors— for example, when citizens attempt to get access to public housing, having the right "party book" might help them to be selected over others without such an affiliation. In addition, party affiliation may aid in getting a job as a civil servant, receiving public contracts, and so on. As a result, people, particularly in tough economic times, will join political parties not out of conviction but out of necessity. The acronym of Mussolini's fascist party was PNF (*Partito Nazionale Fascista*). Many people joined that party not for reasons of conviction but for what the Italians called *per necessità famigliare* (for family reasons), which carries, of course, the same acronym. Today commentators often urge politicians to rise above "party politics."

Political scientists, on the other hand, have a much more positive view of political parties. They argue that the modern representative democracy is not possible without political parties. The main functions of political parties are as follows:

- **Parties Structure the Popular Vote** Political parties are the crystallization point of the multitude of political demands. They reduce the people's varied standpoints to a few manageable ones, thereby aggregating diverse interests. Parties represent the main cleavages in society—the main lines of political contention, such as socioeconomic, regional, linguistic, or religious differences. The party labels function in most cases as signals for citizens that indicate where the various parties stand and help reduce the complexity of the issues at hand.
- **Parties Recruit Leaders for Public Office** In premodern times, leaders inherited their positions as kings, dukes, or barons, for example. With political parties in place, leaders emerge in such structures as a result

of what amounts to an apprenticeship that unfolds over a long period of time. Many leaders of parties start out at the lowest political rungs and work their way to the top. Parties thus act as a recruiting vessel in which activists develop over time the skills necessary to take on leadership positions.

■ **Parties Formulate Public Policy** The perennial question in politics of "what is to be done" is generally spelled out in so-called party manifestos. Parties usually spend a large amount of time and effort on the creation of these manifestos because they represent the codified convictions and intentions of the respective political parties. Public policy typically emerges from these manifestos, oftentimes as a result of compromises with other parties that share political power through coalitions. In the United States one speaks of party platforms, which have much less importance than European party manifestos. As we will see in Chapters 3 and 4, this difference between European countries and the United States is largely due to differences in parliamentary election systems and cabinet formation.

■ **Parties Organize the Flow of Power** In most parliamentary democracies, people vote primarily for parties, not for individuals. Thus, parties act as an intermediary between the public and the state. Parties connect voters to the political world. Also, across most European democracies, the party with the highest popular vote is asked to form a government. Members of European parties in the legislature tend to display stronger coherence, with less wiggle room to vote differently than what their party advocates, compared to their American counterparts. Thus, political power is inseparably connected to political parties.

The American political scientist Elmer Schattschneider remarked in 1942, "It should be flatly stated that the political parties created democracy and that modern democracy is unthinkable, save in terms of parties."[4]

DIFFERENCES BETWEEN POLITICAL PARTIES AND INTEREST GROUPS

In modern polities based on popular sovereignty and mass suffrage, two paths—one formal and the other informal—toward making policy exist. The formal path is via political parties and other constitutionally recognized methods, such as referenda and plebiscites. The informal path is through interest groups, sometimes referred to as "pressure groups," which lobby lawmakers to engage in policies that are favorable to their cause. While at first glance political parties and private interest groups may look similar, they are in fact quite different. The three main differences between political parties and interest groups are as follows:

■ **Political Parties' Concerns Are Public in Nature** This stands in contrast to private interest groups, which tend to approach the government in order to gain advantage for their generally small numbers of supporters.

This is typically the case for economic interest groups such as the labor unions in the United Kingdom (e.g., TUC—Trades Union Congress) or the American Medical Association (AMA) in the United States. The large-scale public concern of political parties is evident in the so-called "catch-all" parties, that is, parties that appeal to basically every strata in society. The advantages that accrue as a result of interest group activity, on the other hand, tend to flow to only a very small slice of society.

■ **Political Parties' Candidates Run for Election**   This is another significant difference between political parties and interest groups. Although it is true that in many countries voters vote for parties rather than individuals, it is very clear in each circumstance who the party leader will be, even before the election. Each party will offer a clear choice as to who would become prime minister, the leader of the opposition, or who would head various ministries, even before the election. Interest group politics is much less transparent; much happens in the lobbies of parliaments or Congress that is not exposed to public scrutiny, and lobbyists do not have to face the public in the same way as party leaders. Party leaders must mobilize enough people to vote or not vote for them, while this check of accountability is absent in the realm of interest groups. Interest groups do not attempt to achieve their goals by electing leaders from among their own ranks to government office.

■ **Parties Are Publicly Financed; Interest Groups Are Not**   This statement is not entirely true. Parties do receive some support from members, just as interest groups do. Parties also receive support from interest groups, but both of these sources of income are significantly smaller than what parties receive through public financing. Most European parties receive benefits in kind, such as free broadcasting time before elections, free mass mailings, and even grants to parliamentary groups to cover their operating expenses. In many European countries political parties receive public funds in proportion of the share of votes received. Financing of interest groups is a wholly private affair and is mostly generated by member contributions. In the United States, there is no public funding of political parties.

SOCIALISTS

The term *Socialist* is derived from the Latin root word *socius*—a comrade or fellow. Socialists claim that they want to extend help to all needy members of society as if they were comrades or fellows. In the United States, *Socialist* tends to have a very negative connotation, which goes back to the time of the Cold War. The official name of the Soviet Union at that time was the Union of Soviet Socialist Republics (USSR). In that instance, the term *Socialist* referred to the dictatorial phase following the proletarian revolution, as we will see in Chapter 11. The Soviets claimed they were still in this phase because capitalism had not yet been defeated worldwide. In European democracies, however, Socialist parties are firmly committed to democracy. Nonetheless, after the Soviet Union began to crumble, Socialist leaders were worried that the name of their party would be

◣ BOX 2.1 SOCIALISTS PONDER A CHANGED WORLD

New York

Buoyed by the collapse of one of its oldest foes, the Communist movement, but uncertain about its own role in the post-cold-war world, the Socialist International gathered in New York this week to set a course for the future. Willy Brandt, the former West German Chancellor who has been president of the Socialist International since 1976, chaired the two-day meeting at the Waldorf-Astoria. Mr. Brandt suggested that Socialism is a victim of semantics. "Let's face it," he said, "Socialism has been discredited by the mess created in the so-called 'socialist countries.'"

"Our traditional role has not changed," said Pierre Mauroy, former Prime Minister of France and First Secretary of the French Socialist Party. "As the countries of Eastern Europe move towards a market economy, Social Democracy will continue to serve as a strong counter-balance to the excesses of laissez-faire." ◼

Source: New York Times, October 11, 1990.

tainted. Thus, the late Willy Brandt, former West German chancellor, addressing the Socialist International in October 1990, said, "Let's face it. Socialism has been discredited by the mess created in the so-called 'socialist countries'" (see Box 2.1).

In Box 2.1, reference is made to social democracy. Is there a difference between a Socialist and a Social Democrat? Yes and no. The difference is certainly not in the sense that Social Democrats support democracy more than Socialists. The precise party label depends on the country and is relatively inconsequential. In France the party is called Socialist and in Germany it is called Social Democratic, but this difference in name does not mean the French party supports democratic principles any less so than does the German party. Particular national circumstances also explain why in Great Britain and the Netherlands, for example, the Socialists are called the Labour Party. For the remainder of the book, the term *Socialist* is used unless there is a need to make a differentiation.

How do Socialists view the world? What are their goals and strategies? Essentially, they see the gap between rich and poor as too great. A major goal of Socialist policy is to narrow this gap. Socialists argue that the fruits of democracy can be enjoyed only by people who have a sufficient level of economic security. As the German dramatist Bertolt Brecht wrote in the famous *Threepenny Opera*, people first must eat.[5] Individuals who must worry constantly about what to eat, where to find shelter, and what to do in case of illness and in old age are not truly free. They are unable to participate in political life, which, therefore, tends to be dominated by the more affluent and, as a result, is not really democratic.

According to Socialist thinking, the state must intervene in the economy if more **equality** in society is to be achieved. If market forces have free play, the gap between rich and poor will only widen. It is only the state that has the necessary authority to redistribute income from the rich to the poor. For Socialists, state intervention in the economy is not an obstacle but a precondition for an effective democracy. Thus, what we see here are fundamentally different definitions of democracy. From the perspective of a free market, a democracy should give everyone the freedom to profit from given opportunities. From a Socialist perspective, a democracy can function only if the state corrects the distribution of wealth arrived at by market forces. Although Socialists agree among themselves on the necessity for the state to redistribute income, there is wide disagreement in the Socialist ranks about the specifics of this intervention. One option is to nationalize private companies. If business belonged to the state, the rich could not get richer through the accumulation of profits, because the profits would go to the community as a whole. Nationalization was, for a long time, popular among many Socialists. When Socialist François Mitterrand became president of France in 1981, key sectors of the economy—including almost all banks and large pharmaceutical companies—were nationalized. These measures, however, were less dramatic than they may appear to an American observer. First, prior to the emergence of the Socialist movement there was a century-long French tradition of a strong state role in the economy. Thus, long before Mitterrand took office, many banks already belonged to the state. Second, the state under Mitterrand did not take over small businesses such as the corner bakery. Socialists, too, believed that the quality of the famous French bread would be better if a multitude of private bakers competed with one another. Thus, French Socialists were not, in principle, against competition. In fact, part of their justification for nationalizing big companies was that under state control, these companies could compete more successfully in the world market.

During their time in office, French Socialists became more critical of nationalization, and they even began a program of denationalization. A key reason for this change in policy was that the Socialists had to accept the fact that financial investors were worried about nationalization and withdrew large amounts of capital from France during the time Socialists were in office. At about the same time, the British Labour Party, too, moved away from a policy of nationalization. It had been the opposition party for a long time and feared that continuing to insist on nationalization would frighten investors, which, in turn, would make voters reluctant to support the Labour Party.

Socialists in other countries had turned away earlier from the concept of nationalization. Thus, Helmut Schmidt, the Social Democratic West German chancellor from 1974 to 1982, never tried to implement a program of nationalization. Socialists such as Schmidt preferred more indirect state intervention through tax laws, social programs, and so forth. They accepted private ownership of big companies as long as the companies' power was sufficiently checked through governmental regulation.

With the outbreak of the global financial and economic crisis in 2008, nationalization of major banks and other large companies not only suddenly became once again a topic of debate among European Socialists, but also became a general political issue in Europe and even in the United States. One could speak at least of partial nationalizations in the sense that big banks and companies received great amounts of governmental monies in order to survive.

In Chapter 10, "Policy Outcomes," we will describe what forms these partial nationalizations took in various European countries and how these policies compared with what was undertaken in the United States. In the present context, it is important to note that even Socialists did not wish to go back to their earlier doctrines of full nationalizations but considered the financial and economic crisis as an extraordinary event that demanded extraordinary measures, including some partial nationalizations. In former times, European Socialists agreed that economic growth was good, provided that the fruits of this growth were not unfairly distributed in society. The main controversy centered on the question of whether the state should intervene directly, through nationalization, or whether redistribution of income could be achieved better through more indirect state measures. Today, a more fundamental question is discussed among Socialists, namely, whether the side effects of economic growth are so negative that, ultimately, they may place the survival of the human race in jeopardy. Such side effects often are referred to by the technical economic term *external costs*. The debate about the external costs of economic growth has split the Socialists severely. On one side are blue-collar workers who wish to profit through higher wages from continued economic growth. They tend to support, for example, the expansion of nuclear power to prevent energy shortages. On the other side is a new breed of more intellectually oriented Socialists—teachers, social workers, and so on. For them, limits must be imposed on economic growth; otherwise, our natural environment eventually will be destroyed. As a prime example, these new Socialists cite global warming with its potentially disastrous effects. They also point out that current economic life puts too much stress on working people, leading to all sorts of health problems. These Socialists see dangers not only in an unrestricted free market but also in large and often anonymous state bureaucracies. They advocate a simpler lifestyle and a more decentralized government structure with extensive self-administration at the local level. Instead of producing more cars to commute to increasingly distant workplaces, people should bicycle to work in their own, relatively self-sustained, small communities.

Such an interpretation of Socialist thought leads to a search for new political allies. Traditionally, the Socialist parties were confronted only with the choice of alliances to the left or to the middle. They could try to forge a coalition with the Communists, or they could keep their distance from the Communists and seek partners from the middle of the party spectrum. The new breed of Socialists sees political life less in terms of left and right. For them, the important question is whether someone uncritically supports more economic growth or whether one is willing to reconsider the concept of growth and seek alternative life-styles. Here Socialists find allies among environmentalists and, in particular, the Green Party, which is described later in this chapter. Members of the women's movement, the youth movement, the peace movement, and oppressed minorities such as foreign workers and homosexuals also are seen as potential allies. As a consequence of these developments, Socialist voters are less and less blue-collar working-class people, many of whom now support parties of the New Radical Right. As political scientist Herbert Kitschelt states, "In most countries the class structuring of the (Socialist) vote has progressively declined over time, though with a different pace and rhythm."[6] Increasingly, the Socialists get their support from people working in education, health care, social work, counseling, communication, and the arts.

As a result, Socialist parties are scrambling to find a new identity. The two most vocal early proponents of this new orientation were Prime Minister Tony Blair of the United Kingdom and Chancellor Gerhard Schröder of Germany. On June 8, 1999, they signed a document titled "Europe: The **Third Way**." What does "third way" mean, and how has it changed the policies of Social Democratic parties? It meant to come to grips with some of the excesses of state intervention. For example, the document highlighted that in the past, the "means of achieving social justice became identified with ever higher levels of public spending regardless of what they achieved," that "rights were elevated above responsibilities," that the "balance between the individual and the collective was distorted. Values that are important to citizens, such as personal achievement and success, entrepreneurial spirit, individual responsibility and community spirit, were too often subordinated to universal social safeguards," and that "the ability of national governments to fine-tune the economy in order to secure growth and jobs has been exaggerated."[7]

These are remarkable admissions of the failures of social democracy in the past and read more like a critique by conservatives who are shouting, "I told you so." The policies of the "third way" include, among others, the following (for a detailed discussion of the third way, see an excellent paper by Dutch political scientist Hans Keman[8]):

- Embracing globalization and scientific changes by establishing an environment in which businesses can prosper and adapt and new businesses can be set up and grow.
- Flexible adaptation of workers to changing demands in the workplace, meaning that wages should move up or down in proportion to demand and that it should be easier for employers to hire and fire workers.
- Reconciling environmental responsibility with a modern, market-based approach. Public expenditures as a proportion of national income have reached their limits of acceptability. The public sector needs to be radically modernized, and public services need to be reformed to achieve better value for the money. Concepts of efficiency, competition, and high performance must be emphasized.
- Tax policies to promote sustainable growth by cutting corporate tax rates, rewarding "hard work" through a reduction of personal and corporate tax rates, and simplifying the tax code.
- Establishing an active labor market policy for the Left by ensuring that the state is an active agent for change. This means reforming welfare systems that put limits on an individual's ability to find a job by transforming the safety net of entitlements into a springboard to personal responsibility.

The leader who probably went the furthest in implementing elements of the "third way" was Schröder. Facing high unemployment rates in excess of 10 percent and intent on making the German economy more competitive by reducing the tax rates on businesses, Schröder engaged in what some describe as a major attack on the generous German welfare system. Germany has some of the highest labor costs of the European countries.

Why would reducing the welfare state be advantageous for the German economy? The argument is as follows: In order to maintain the extensive German welfare state, high taxation levels are necessary, making it difficult for German companies to compete against countries with more limited welfare states and lower taxes. By cutting back the welfare state, taxes can be lowered, which in turn should make Germany economically more competitive by creating higher profits that could then be plowed back into human and investment capital.

For a Social Democrat such policies are difficult to swallow. Indeed, largely as a result of these policies, Schröder lost the election in 2005 (Chapter 4). Not surprisingly, given his positive view of the market, after his electoral defeat he became a successful international businessman.

The German case highlights the boundaries to which political leaders can push their parties before voters will reign them in. Parties do change, but they are also "sticky" in the sense that parties have, over time, built up constituencies who expect various goodies from their parties. Leaders who attempt to engage in change too quickly and too radically will be punished at the ballot box—a lesson that Chancellor Schröder had to learn the hard way.

In Great Britain, Tony Blair had to take early retirement in 2007, not over his market-oriented domestic policies but over Iraq (see Chapter 4). His successor, Gordon Brown, continued in domestic affairs the "third way" of Blair. When Brown was made prime minister by his party in June 2007, he exclaimed:

> If people think we will achieve our goals in the future by retreating to failed approaches of the past, then they have not learned the lesson I have learned from the last ten years.... I believe in a British economy founded on dynamic, flexible markets and open competition.[9]

Brown, however, was not successful in implementing his third way and lost the elections in 2010 (see Chapter 3). In the 2007 French presidential elections, the Socialist candidate Ségolène Royal took a position rather to the center with regard to the importance of the market and was quite successful, gaining 47 percent of the vote but still losing to Nicolas Sarkozy (see also Chapter 4). We must also note that in the French Socialist party there are still strong leftist tendencies in opposition to the more centrist course of Royal. For Germany, it is remarkable that in 2007 a new party to the left was founded that is in opposition to the centrist economic policies of the traditional Social Democrats. The new party is simply called The Left (*Die Linke*). It emphasizes the limits of market principles for a just society. According to The Left, the profit principle has become much too dominant.

In conclusion, there is great variation among Socialists from country to country and also within individual countries. The outbreak of the severe global financial and economic crisis in 2008 was a great challenge for the Socialists in terms of which direction to go with regard to their position to the free market: to continue with the third way or to go back to a more traditional leftist position. It has not been not easy for European Socialists to decide how to handle this challenge and has led to much internal conflict. Electorally, Socialists are in a downswing. The elections to the European Parliament always give a good picture of where political parties are going, although these elections have somewhat unique characteristics, in particular a low voter turnout (see Chapter 14). In the June 2009 elections, in all 27 EU countries, Socialists went down to 22 percent from 28 percent five years before.

LIBERALS

For Americans it may be surprising to learn that in European countries there are political parties that call themselves Liberal parties but are in important aspects the very opposite of American liberals. European Liberals are the most free-market-oriented among European political parties, whereas in the American political spectrum, liberals are the most critical of market forces. As in the previous section, we have here another case where political labels have very different meanings in Europe and the United States. The term *liberal* is derived from the Latin root word *libertas,* meaning freedom. Thus, it is natural that in some European countries the Liberals include the term *free* as part of their official name. In Germany, for example, the Liberals are called Free Democrats. In the United States, *liberal* designates a position to the left and *freedom* a position to the right—for example, the conservative organization Young Americans for Freedom. In Europe, *liberal* and *free* are used as synonyms.

European Liberals emphasize the importance of **individual freedom** in every aspect of life. Economically, this leads to a strong preference for free markets, both domestically and internationally, but European Liberals advocate a "free market" for moral issues, too. They wish to leave the choice on issues such as abortion and divorce primarily to the individual, who should take personal responsibility. They do not like the state and its bureaucrats to intrude into the private lives of citizens. The free and autonomous decisions of individuals are at the core of liberal thinking. Large organizations are viewed with skepticism because Liberals believe that they tend to limit individual freedom. This applies not only to the state but also to other large organizations, such as trade unions and churches.

The historical roots of European liberalism go back to early modern Europe—the fifteenth to eighteenth centuries. In medieval times, the individual was seen primarily as member of a group or community. People were strongly embedded in their towns, guilds, monasteries, universities, and so on. They defined themselves, to a large extent, as members of such groups, and these definitions gave meaning to their lives. Individuals were like members of a body. Just as a leg has meaning only as a part of the entire body, a medieval baker, for example, had meaning only as a member of his guild.

Given this medieval perception of the individual, it was a true revolution when the individual emerged as a private human being with his or her own worth independent of all group memberships. In early modern Europe, the individual began to stand for himself or herself. The individual was allowed and even encouraged to think for himself or herself, to make his or her own life plans. This stress on the individual was linked with the emerging industrial and commercial capitalism, which in turn caused individualism to grow further. Migration, urbanization, and technological change opened a new range of occupational choice, and these new opportunities required new skills. The capacity to achieve and perform in new roles acquired great importance. The individual stood much more for himself or herself than in medieval times. Individual self-fulfillment and individual happiness became goals in themselves. These are, in a nutshell, the historical roots of the Liberal parties in Europe. They emphasize individual autonomy and individual freedom above all—both in economic and moral aspects. The individual should make his or her own choices and live with the consequences, for better or for worse.

According to Liberal thinking in the European sense, the less state intervention, the better. This does not mean, however, that Liberals do not see some useful role for the state. Thus, European Liberals believe the state has certain responsibilities for helping the unemployed, the handicapped, and the old, although Liberal social programs are more limited than those advocated by Socialists. Liberals in Europe also acknowledge that some regulations for moral behavior are necessary, in particular for adolescents. They also support governmental programs to fight drug abuse, although many Liberals are willing to legalize "soft" drugs.

The exact role European Liberals see for the state is a constant topic for internal party discussion, and great differences usually exist among the varying positions within each party. Indeed, internal differences are a major characteristic of European Liberals, which is understandable given their heavy emphasis on individual autonomy. In parliamentary debates, the Liberals are usually those with the least amount of voting discipline. The German Free Democrats are a good example of a Liberal party with much internal dissent. Some in the party stress individual freedom with regard to social issues, whereas other German Free Democrats put the emphasis on unleashing **market forces** in the economy. Depending on which side has the upper hand, the party enters different cabinet coalitions, either more to the left or more to the right (see Chapter 3). Electorally, Liberals are a middle-sized party in Europe. In the June 2009 elections of the European Parliament, they reached 11 percent, down from 13 percent five years before.

Returning to the United States, it is interesting to ponder who in American politics is liberal in the European sense. In the United States one tends to call such politicians conservative on economic issues and liberal on social issues. Do any names of such American politicians come to mind who are Liberals in the European sense? Is Barack Obama more a Socialist or a Liberal in the European sense, or does neither of these labels neatly apply to him?

CONSERVATIVES

The meaning of European liberalism can be further clarified by comparing it to European conservatism. The term *conservative* is derived from the verb *conserve,* which, according to the *Oxford English Dictionary,* means "keep from decay or change or destruction." What do Conservatives wish to keep from decay, change, or destruction? Above all, the structure of authority in society. Conservatives believe that individuals are lost if they are not embedded in a firm **structure of authority**. Conservatives have a very different view of the individual than Liberals. According to Conservative thinking, individuals are by nature weak and need guidance. If left alone, they are likely to mess up. They must be guided by authorities such as the state, the church, and the family. Conservatives worry that these authorities may decay. Therefore, it is the primary goal of Conservative policy to preserve the structure of authority in society. This does not mean Conservatives object to all change, but change should not be sudden and abrupt.

The major difference between Conservatives and Liberals concerns the extent to which moral decisions should be left to the individual. Unlike Liberals, Conservatives advocate relatively strict guidance in such matters as abortion and drug use. This guidance can come through governmental regulation, as well as from such institutions as the church and the family. Thus, it is only logical that Conservatives support measures to strengthen the church and the family. Another difference between Conservatives and Liberals concerns attachment to symbols of the state. For Liberals, state symbols—such as the national flag and the national anthem—are not rejected, but they do not have great emotional value. Liberals are too individualistic to enjoy marching with others behind a flag. Conservatives, on the other hand, claim that the state needs strong symbols to maintain its authority. According to Conservative thinking, the state must be based not only on rational utility but also on emotions. Therefore, Conservatives revere state symbols and are offended when others do not.

In economic questions, both parties share a preference for free-market solutions and are therefore natural allies in this respect. If differences between the two parties occur, it is usually because Liberals defend the principle of free competition even more consistently than Conservatives. This can be explained by the different ways Conservatives and Liberals justify the free market. For Liberals, free-market competition encourages individuals to develop their potential to the fullest extent. Thus, the free market finds its justification in the needs of the individual. Conservatives share this view to a large extent, but they also refer to the **natural order of society** to justify the free market. According to Conservative thinking, a hierarchical structure of society corresponds to a law of nature. As in the animal world, among human beings there are always some who are naturally stronger and more successful than others. Conservatives applaud biologists such as Konrad Lorenz who have discovered that there are natural leaders in the animal world and believe that analogies can be made with the human race. Some people will always be economically more successful than others, and this should be considered as natural. To try to redistribute income to achieve economic equality goes against nature. The economically successful should be allowed to keep most of the fruits of their success. Given their emphasis on order, it becomes understandable why Conservatives are sometimes afraid of too much competition. To be sure, in their rhetoric Conservatives are always very much for the free market. But if bankruptcy of a large company threatens the economic and political stability of an entire region, Conservatives are likely to be more willing than Liberals to bail out the company with governmental monies. This is again visible in the global financial and economic crisis that began in 2008. In Germany, for example, Free Democrats are much more reluctant than the conservative Christian Democrats to bail out companies with taxpayers' monies.

The economic crisis also highlights intriguing differences between European and American conservatives. While European Conservatives indeed favor a more market-oriented society than European Socialists, compared to conservatives in the United States they see a significant role for the state when it comes to redistribution and the nurturing of community. In October 2008, the Conservative chancellor of Germany, Angela Merkel, after introducing a law designed to stabilize the financial markets, declared that "With this piece of legislation we will be taking extensive, far-reaching, and drastic measures in order to put in place the structures needed to ensure a 21st century market economy 'with a human face.'"[10]

Similarly, the Conservative French president Nicolas Sarkozy was unsparing in his verdict of unregulated capitalism. He called the speculative, financial capitalism "an immoral system" that has "perverted the logic of capitalism." According to Sarkozy, "It's a system where wealth goes to the wealthy, where work is devalued, where production is devalued, where entrepreneurial spirit is devalued. [...] In capitalism of the 21st century, there is room for the state."[11]

In this context, it is also interesting to refer to an episode in the drafting of the Reform Treaty for the EU in 2007 (Chapter 14). The issue was how to formulate

▶ BOX 2.2 LESSONS FROM A CRISIS

European *Schadenfreude* over the ills of American capitalism does not signify a dramatic move away from the free market.

One by one, European leaders have lined up to hail the triumph of welfare over Wall Street. "The idea that markets are always right was a mad idea," declared the French president Nicolas Sarkozy. America's laissez-faire ideology as practiced during the subprime crisis "was as simplistic as it was dangerous," chipped in Peer Steinbrück, the German finance minister. He added that America would lose its role as "financial superpower." [...] Even left wing editorialists in France, quick to sneer at degenerate American capitalism, have tempered their glee. "There would be something comical, even pleasurable, in watching the frenetic agitation of the banking world," wrote Laurent Joffrin, editor of the *Libération* newspaper, "if millions of jobs were not at stake, not to mention the economic balance of the planet."

A common thread can nonetheless be detected in European responses to America's troubles. It goes as follows: We always knew that unbridled free markets were a mistake, yet we were derided for saying this; now we are all paying the price for your excesses. In the face of popular consternation at capitalist decadence, the activist state is back in fashion—and we Europeans are taking credit for it. ■

Source: The Economist, October 4, 2008.

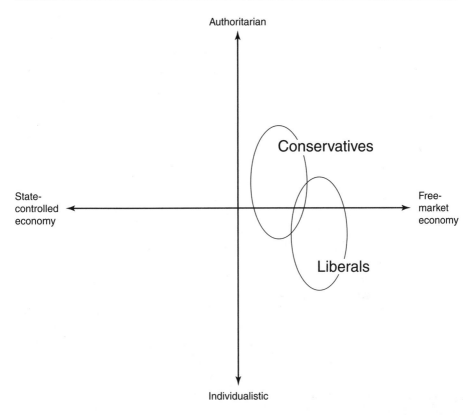

FIGURE 2.1

Location of Liberals and Conservatives on a dimension from state-controlled economy to free-market economy and on a dimension from authoritarian to individualistic.

the goal of a free market among the member countries of the EU. Gordon Brown of the Labour Party, the British prime minister, did put more emphasis on the competitive aspect of the market than Conservative French president Nicolas Sarkozy. This episode indicates that the distinctions among the various European parties are often not clear-cut, especially because the individual parties often vary greatly from country to country in their orientation. In Great Britain, with Tony Blair and now with Gordon Brown, Socialists have become quite market oriented. In France there was always a tradition, also among conservatives, to give a strong role to the state in the economy. This solves the puzzle of why the Socialist Brown is more a supporter of a competitive market than the Conservative Sarkozy.

If we rely only on the terms of the political left and the political right, it is virtually impossible to differentiate Liberals and Conservatives in the European context. If we use the two-dimensional space shown in Figure 2.1, the two parties become quite distinct. In this figure we avoid the terms *left* and *right* altogether, because they are too vague. They were introduced into the political vocabulary during the French Revolution. When the French National Assembly gathered in 1789, the deputies advocating change happened to sit to the left of the chairman, and those defending the status quo sat to his right. The chairman began to refer to them as the "left" and the "right." Thus, the two terms emerged in an accidental way. Still, they were quite useful because European history after the French Revolution was for a long time a battle between the forces of the old privileges and those advocating change. In today's Europe, however, politics has become so complex that we need more than a single dimension of differentiation.

In Figure 2.1, the horizontal axis goes from a state-controlled to a free-market economy. The farther left a party is located, the more it supports state intervention to redistribute income from rich to poor. The farther right it is located, the more it supports free play for market forces. The figure indicates a position toward the right for both Liberals and Conservatives. Liberals support free economic competition somewhat more consistently than Conservatives, for the reasons just noted. But overall, the two parties are very close together on the horizontal axis. The vertical axis goes from authoritarian to individualistic. An authoritarian position emphasizes the importance of authority in society, whereas an individualistic position stresses individual autonomy. Here Conservatives and Liberals are much more clearly distinguished, although some overlap also exists on this dimension. More so than Socialists and Liberals, Conservatives vary a great deal from country to country, which is clearly visible in the variety of labels used for Conservative parties. In Great Britain the party with the conservative orientation is simply called the Conservative Party. In most other European countries, however, Conservatives carry other party labels; in Sweden, for example, they are called the Moderate Unity party; in Greece, New Democracy; in Spain, Popular Alliance.

Why does such variety exist among Conservatives from country to country? By their very nature, Conservatives stress the importance of national identity. As a consequence, each party has emerged from its specific national context without much international influence. Socialists and Liberals, on the other hand, have more universal messages, so it was more natural for them to cooperate at an international level. The lack of international unity among Conservatives is shown in their difficulty in organizing as a single party in the European Parliament (Chapter 14).

CHRISTIAN DEMOCRATS

In some countries, such as Germany, Poland, Hungary, Italy, the Netherlands, and Switzerland, there are parties with the label "Christian Democrat." These parties are usually quite Conservative in orientation, but also emphasize **social programs** based on Christian doctrines. According to Christian thinking, it has always been important to help the poor. Great emphasis is also put on the need to help families. Although social programs are important for Christian Democrats, they put much less emphasis on governmental programs. They rely much more on the principle of subsidiarity, which means that matters should be handled in the least centralized ways, by local communities, the churches, and voluntary organizations of civil society. Although Christian Democrats are often lumped together with Conservative parties, with regard to social and family programs they have distinctive features. In Italy, the Netherlands, and Switzerland,

Christian Democrats stress the need for social and family programs so much that they are not considered to be parties of the political right but are thought of as center parties. Although Christian Democratic parties have the label "Christian" in their name, its voters are less religious than typical Christians in the United States. The secular trend described in Chapter 1 can also be seen among Christian Democratic voters. The closeness of Conservatives and Christian Democrats is most clearly visible by the fact that in the European Parliament, they form together a single political group. In the June 2009 elections of the European Parliament, this group was by far the leader with 36 percent of the votes, only 1 percent less than five years before.

NEW RADICAL RIGHT

The New Radical Right has a much less coherent program than the Socialists, Liberals, Conservatives, or Christian Democrats. Each of the latter parties is based on ideas that can be traced to a particular philosophical tradition. One can identify the philosophers who laid the groundwork for the ideologies of these parties. The New Radical Right, by contrast, is much more amorphous in its ideas. It is primarily defined by what it is against; in this sense, it is to a large extent a protest party. Given this orientation, the New Radical Right is able to attract a great variety of voters who mainly have in common the fact that they are dissatisfied with the established political parties.[12]

The New Radical Right is in some ways a continuation of the Fascism of the first half of the twentieth century. To emphasize this element of continuity, the New Radical Right is sometimes called Neofascist. There are, however, important differences between Fascism and the New Radical Right, so it may be better to reserve the term *Fascism* for the earlier historical period. Fascism was introduced by Benito Mussolini in Italy during the early 1920s. The term is derived from the Latin *fasces*, which means a bundle of sticks tightly held together—a symbol of strength in ancient Rome. In Germany, Adolf Hitler founded the National Socialist Party, which was also Fascist in orientation. The main characteristic of Fascism was its extreme nationalism and militarism. The total identification with one's own nation had, as a corollary, the rejection of everything that was alien to that nation. Under Hitler, this led to the atrocious attempt to exterminate Jews in concentration camps. Other groups, such as Gypsies, also were considered undesirable and suffered the same fate.

With regard to the role of the state in the economy, Hitler and Mussolini had an ambivalent attitude. Mussolini was a militant Socialist before founding his Fascist movement, and Hitler included the term *Socialist* in the name of his party. The Fascists' main objection to the political left was its international orientation. Fascists found it unpatriotic that Communists and Socialists looked for allies in other countries. The call for workers of all countries to unite was diametrically opposed to Fascist thinking, which saw one's own nation as the sacred community to which all allegiance was owed. In this context, it is an interesting historical detail that Mussolini was expelled from the Socialist Party because of his vehement support for the entry of Italy into World War I.

Rejecting Communists and Socialists for their lack of nationalistic feeling did not mean that Fascists had no reservations about the free market, however. The notion of competition was too disorderly for them. Fascists advocated a strong state that would show leadership in economic matters. Simply working for profits was not proper for Fascists, who felt only disdain for the capitalist mentality. Hitler had a very stormy relationship with the business community. On the one hand, he needed its support, but on the other hand, he hated the business world.

How different is the New Radical Right of today from the Fascism of Hitler and Mussolini? First, the New Radical Right has chosen other party labels, such as Freedom Party in Austria, National Front in France, Republicans in Germany, Progress Party in Norway, and New Democracy in Sweden. Second, the New Radical Right claims that its distinction from fascism is not only in labels, but also in democratic orientation. It is true that in contrast to Hitler and Mussolini, the leaders of the New Radical Right in their speeches support the notion of democracy. However, in today's Europe, the value of democracy is so commonly accepted that it would be political suicide to take an antidemocratic position. Thus, the leaders of the New Radical Right do not object to democracy at all; on the contrary, they often criticize the ruling political elites for not being sufficiently democratic in listening to the voice of the common people. Whether the New Radical Right itself would behave in a democratic way if alone in power is untested and remains an open question. Third, economically the New Radical Right is more for the free market than the Fascists were. It argues, in particular, against high taxes, wasteful welfare programs, and arrogant state bureaucrats.

In Figure 2.2, we locate the New Radical Right on the same two dimensions used in Figure 2.1. On the vertical dimension, the New Radical Right is at the authoritarian pole. Strength and discipline are emphasized in its ranks. Typically, parties of the New Radical Right have a strong leader; for example, Jean-Marie Le Pen of the National Front in France. Law and order are important values for supporters of the New Radical Right. Part of authoritarianism is also nationalism, and the voters of the New Radical Right are very nationalistic, which is particularly expressed by their demand that the number of foreign workers and refugees be kept as low as possible. With regard to the horizontal economic dimension, we have already seen that the New Radical Right takes a strong position against wasteful government spending; it objects, in particular, to welfare benefits for "outsiders" in society, such as immigrants, the homeless, drug addicts, homosexuals, unwed mothers, and abstract modern artists. The free-market position of the New Radical Right is not derived from broad economic and philosophical principles but from the wish not to pay high taxes. Hans-George Betz emphasizes the same point:

> The radical populist right's neo-liberal program is only secondarily an economic program. Primarily, it is a political weapon against the established political institutions and their alleged monopolization of political power which hampers economic progress and suppresses true democracy.[13]

Why the name *New Radical Right?* The terms *new* and *radical* help to differentiate the New Radical Right from the Old Moderate Right. If we refer

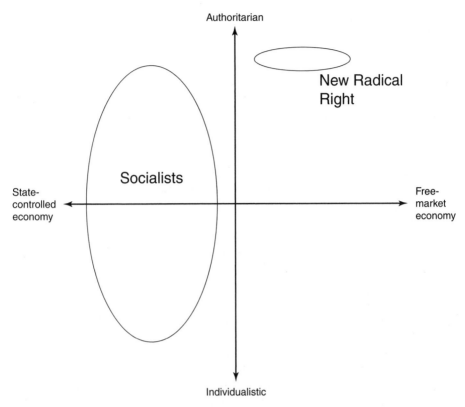

FIGURE 2.2
Location of the New Radical Right and Socialists on a dimension from state-controlled economy to free-market economy and on a dimension from authoritarian to individualistic.

back to Figure 2.1, the Old Moderate Right is the authoritarian wing of the Conservatives. When we compare Figures 2.1 and 2.2, we see how the line between the New Radical Right and the Old Moderate Right is blurred. It is, therefore, easy for the New Radical Right to pull support from dissatisfied voters of the Old Moderate Right, particularly during hard economic times. The voters floating between Conservatives and the New Radical Right are mostly middle class. On the one hand, there are people of the old middle class—shopkeepers, craftspeople, farmers—who fear for their economic future and are attracted by the antitax rhetoric of the New Radical Right. On the other hand, there are also voters of the new middle class—computer experts, media consultants, financial analysts, and so on—who find the government-off-your-back message of the New Radical Right appealing. As Betz puts it, these highly educated people "accept the market as the ultimate arbiter over individual life chances and...are well-prepared to play the game of individual effort, self-promotion, and self-advertisement."[14] Figure 2.2 shows that the New Radical Right may pull support also from Socialists, who are widely dispersed on the individualistic–authoritarian dimension. Toward the authoritarian pole, one finds mainly blue-collar, working-class Socialists who may be attracted by the antiwelfare message of the New Radical Right because they tend to resent welfare programs for people whom they consider unworthy.

We now have identified the two core groups from which the New Radical Right pulls its support: the middle class and blue-collar workers. As Herbert Kitschelt puts it: "[T]he secret of the New Right's success is the combination of the two electorates in a single right-authoritarian message...: Racism serves as glue between the economic and social agenda of the authoritarian Right."[15] Betz summarizes the essence of the New Radical Right as follows:

> Radical right-wing populist parties are radical in their rejection of the established sociocultural and sociopolitical system and their advocacy of individual achievement, a free marketplace, and a drastic reduction of the role of the state. They are right-wing in their rejection of individual and social equality, in their opposition to the social integration of marginalized groups, and in their appeal to xenophobia, if not overt racism. They are populist in their instrumentalization of sentiments of anxiety and disenchantment and their appeal to the common man and his allegedly superior common sense.[16]

The National Front in France, with its past leader Jean-Marie Le Pen, perhaps typifies best the phenomenon of the New Radical Right. In 2011 he was replaced by his daughter Marine Le Pen who pursues the same policies as her father. Le Pen was a **populist** who knew how to mobilize the masses. As described by Pierre Bréchon and Subrata Kumar Mitra, Le Pen criticizes the ruling political elites of France as being too soft to provide effective solutions for contemporary problems, in particular with regard to immigration:

> The National Front has risen to national prominence because it has succeeded in giving concrete political expression to a latent xenophobia, reinforced by the problem of immigration. It has succeeded in placing this latent xenophobic fear in the context of a general ideology of the extreme right, based on a rejection of established political parties and distrust of democracy. Essentially an able populist politician, Le Pen mobilizes opinion against the political elite, whom he presents as far too soft to provide effective solutions for contemporary problems. By expressing it politically, the National Front has given both reinforcement and legitimacy to xenophobia.[17]

Le Pen was always shrewd in how he chose his words. He claimed not to be anti-Semitic, but at the same time he trivialized the Nazi gas chambers; he claimed not to have any ill feelings against foreigners, but already had warned in 1988 that "France will become an Islamic republic" when Islam was not yet a hot topic in Europe.[18] He speaks of "inequality of the races," but puts this statement in seemingly scientific terms in claiming that history has demonstrated that the races "do not have the same evolutionary capacity."[19] In the first round of the French presidential elections on April 21, 2002, Le Pen scored his biggest victory by serving a humiliating defeat to Socialist Lionel Jospin and coming in second behind Jacques Chirac. Chirac received 20 percent of the vote, Le Pen a little over 17 percent, and Jospin a little over 16 percent. This result sent shockwaves through France and Europe and virtually guaranteed victory to Chirac a week later in the second round of elections, which consists of a run-off between the two leading candidates. For the overwhelming number of French voters, Le Pen was an unacceptable candidate. In the 2007 presidential elections, Le Pen was down to 10 percent of the vote, to the great relief of many people in France and abroad. His age of 79 may have played against him. More importantly, the winning candidate, Nicolas Sarkozy, took a harsh position against immigrants and thus took votes away from Le Pen. Therefore, despite the relatively poor showing of Le Pen, France still has a large voter potential at the radical Right. With her youthful looks and populist demeanor Marine Le Pen may be able to mobilize voters on the right fringe even better than her father.

In Austria, the former leader of the Freedom Party, Jörg Haider, was even shrewder in hiding a xenophobic message behind relatively moderate language. As he exclaimed in one of his speeches, "We have not led wars in past centuries against the Turks so that they now fill our school classes."[20] His audience understood the message and exploded in frenetic applause. In 2008 Haider was killed in a car accident, which made him even more popular in elections following his death.

In Central and Eastern Europe, parties of the New Radical Right have also made great inroads. In Poland, for example, the League of Polish Families is a typical party of the New Radical Right. Its policy position is very nationalistic; it opposes Polish membership in the European Union and the selling of land to foreigners. It advocates the introduction of the death penalty, which is against the norms of the European Union and led to protests from Brussels (Chapter 14). The League of Polish Families also takes a strong position against any gay and lesbian rights and is very anti-Jewish, anti-Roma, and anti-German.

Two new studies systematically investigate what messages most help the New Radical Right to mobilize voters. Both studies come to the conclusion that it is the immigration issue. As Elisabeth Ivarsflaten puts it, "This study shows that mobilization of grievances over economic changes and political elitism and corruption play a less consistent part in the electoral performance of populist right wing parties across countries than do grievances over immigration."[21] Jens Rydgren goes further, investigating which specific immigration problems help the New Radical Right the most. He looks at the following four potential problems caused by immigration: (1) threat to national identity, (2) criminality and social unrest, (3) cause of unemployment, and (4) abuse of the welfare system. Although all four issues can be exploited by the New Radical Right, according to Rydgren, "Frames linking immigration to criminality and to social unrest are particularly effective discursive strategies to mobilize voter support for the radical right."[22]

In this section, we have seen that the New Radical Right has a very amorphous message that is nevertheless well understood by its supporters. They may not agree among themselves on many issues, but they find something in the message of the New Radical Right that appeals to them—be it the call for tax cuts and the expulsion of foreign workers, the criticism of state bureaucrats, the demand for law and order, or the antifeminist position. With the beginning of the global financial and economic crisis in 2008, the New Radical Right has been able to increase its voter potential. The general economic uncertainties and the failures of many leaders, especially in the banking sector, is fertile ground for the messages of the New Radical Right. In the June 2009 elections of the European Parliament, the New Radical Right increased its voting strength in many countries. In Great Britain, for example, the British National Party, which accepts only whites as members, won 6 percent of the votes. In Hungary, The Movement for a Better Hungary received 15 percent of the votes. Its motto, "Hungary Belongs to Hungarians," sounds harmless but is clearly directed against Jews, Roma, and nonwhites. It organizes military-style marches with flags and uniforms.

In the 2010 national legislative elections, the Freedom Party of Geert Wilders won 15.5 percent of the vote making his party the third largest in the Dutch Parliament. Most impressive what the vote of over 9 percent over the previous election result indicating that his tough stance on immigration from Muslim countries and anti-Islamic sentiments are finding resonance with a growing number of Dutch citizens. In the Dutch newspaper *De Volkskrant,* he opined in an open letter that the Qur'an is a "fascist book" inciting violence and should therefore be outlawed.[23] Of course, Wilders likes to provoke, but his provocations go so far beyond freedom of expression that a film of his was not shown on Dutch television, and for a period of time he was considered an "undesirable person" in Great Britain. In June 2011 he was acquitted of inciting hatred against Muslims. The court in Amsterdam relied on a supreme court law arguing that offensive statements of someone's religion does not constitute a criminal act. In Chapters 3 and 4 we will see how Wilders has become an important political force in the Netherlands.

Immigration and the attendant political challenges have led to the rise of radical right-wing parties in other, hitherto considered "liberal" countries such as Denmark, Sweden, Finland, and Norway. In Denmark, the Danish People's Party under the leadership of Pia Kjarsgaard has garnered almost 14 percent of the vote in the 2007 legislative elections making this party the third largest in Denmark. The Danish People's Party is against Muslim immigration, rejects multiculturalism, opposes Islamization, and favors strict assimilation of immigrants already living in Denmark. While not in a governing coalition, the party is influential in shaping policies of the conservative–liberal coalition such as the recent law passed overwhelmingly (97 yes, 7 no) by the Danish Parliament that immigrants who committed a crime will be deported after serving their sentence. Similarly, in May 2011, Denmark unilaterally introduced border controls undermining the EU-wide Schengen Agreement which abolished internal borders questioning the vaunted principles of the "four freedoms" in the European Union: freedom of movement of people, services, goods, and capital.

Even in Sweden did a far-right-wing party gain representation with 5.7 percent of the popular vote and 20 seats in the Riksdag, the Swedish parliament. As in Denmark, a tough antiimmigration and antimulticulturalism stance, as well as a stern law and order orientation, and deportation of immigrants who have committed crimes characterize the platform of the Swedish Democrats.

In the 2011 legislative elections in Finland, another new populist party exploded onto the scene, called the "True Finns," garnering almost 20 percent of the vote which translated in to 39 seats in the Eduskunta, the Finnish Parliament, making it the third largest party. While not as centered on immigration issues as some of their Scandinavian neighbors, the moniker "True Finns" reveals a nativist turn, not just vis-à-vis Muslim newcomers, but even including abolition of Swedish curriculum in Finish schools, limits on immigration and family unification, as well as deporting immigrants who have run afoul of the law.

Not even Norway, the richest European country on a per capita basis, and the one with the highest Human Development Index in the World—that is, the most developed country in the world based on measures of health, education, and income—is immune from the rise of radical right-wing parties.[24] On July 22, Anders Behring Breivik, a blond, blue-eyed, 32-year-old Norwegian committed the "biggest massacre by a single human being in modern times" by murdering 76 people.[25] He set off a massive bomb in front of government buildings in Oslo, the capital of Norway, then moved to a nearby island, and systematically shot scores of young people who were participating in a political youth camp of the Labour Party. This party received 35 percent of the vote in the 2009 national election and forms a governing coalition with its junior partner, the Centre Party. The Labour Party favors multiculturalism, diversity, tolerance, and protecting the achievements of the social welfare state and takes a relatively liberal stance toward refugees and asylum seekers, which, presumably, was the reason why Breivik singled them out.

From the late 1990s to 2006 Breivik was a member of the Progress Party whose ideology is centered on reducing immigration and asylum seekers, highlighting the strains immigration places on Norway's welfare state, more law and order, defense of Christian values, and a promarket, low-taxes approach to the economy. In the 2009 national elections, the Progress Party, or the Fremskrittspartiet as it is known in Norway, received almost 23 percent of the vote, making it the second largest party in Norway.

When interrogated about his motives, Breivik argued that he was trying to "save Norway and western Europe from 'cultural Marxism' and a 'Muslim takeover.'"[26] He believed that further Muslim immigration and multiculturalist policies are destroying European civilization. In a rambling 1,500-page manifesto, entitled "2083 A European Declaration of Independence," he claims, among other things, to have been "ordinated as the 8th Justiciar Knight Commander for [the] Knights Templar Europe" with the goal to "stop the ongoing Islamisation of Europe" drawing parallels to the crusaders of the fourteenth and fifteenth century.

This massacre sent shockwaves not only through Norway, the country which bestows the Nobel Peace Prize, but across a number of European countries where radical right-wing parties are on the rise.

One should also note, however, that the rise of the New Radical Right was not uniform in the elections of the European Parliament. Thus, in Germany, the Republicans, once seen as a danger to German democracy, obtained only a dismal 1.3 percent of the votes. For an excellent book on the theoretical understanding of the rise of radical right-wing parties, see Cas Mudde (2007).[27]

BOX 2.3 NORWAY ATTACKS:WE CAN NO LONGER IGNORE THE FAR-RIGHT THREAT

Breivik is not a Norwegian oddity, but symptomatic of a growing culture of politically motivated violence across Europe.

The *tragedy in Norway* this weekend may prove to be a watershed moment in terms of how we approach far-right followers, groups, and their ideology. Until now, European democracies and their security services had focused almost exclusively on the threat from al-Qaida-inspired terrorism. Right-wing extremist groups and their more violent affiliates were dismissed as a disorganized, fragmented, and irrelevant movement.

This conventional wisdom, however, ignored wider evidence of a more violent and confrontational mood that was emerging within *European far-right circles*.This shift may have been a response to the arrival of al-Qaida-inspired terrorism, or a sense that far-right political parties in Europe (such as the *Norwegian Progress Party* of which the attacker was once a member) were not having enough influence on issues such as immigration.

Two years ago, antiterrorism officers in Britain *warned of a growing threat* from right-wing "lone wolves." At the same time, the U.S. department of homeland security warned of the way in which the wider economic climate and election of the first African American president could result in confrontations between right-wing extremists and government authorities "similar to those in the past." These past events included the *bombing of a federal building in Oklahoma* that killed 168 people.

The events over the weekend directly challenged the idea that right-wing extremism is only a minor security threat. According to Norwegian police, the perpetrator—32-year-old Anders Behring Breivik—has confirmed that he worked alone on planning and carrying out the two attacks.

The sources of his ideological influences have started to become clear. He was far from what we might term a traditional right-wing extremist. While he was profoundly concerned about the effects of immigration, multiculturalism, Islam, and the growth of settled Muslim communities, he was also dismissive of crude racial supremacist and neo-Nazi ideas and the parties that espoused these ideas, naming—for example, the *British National Party (BNP)*.[...]

Through websites, literature, and meetings (all of which, it seems, Breivik was exposed to), this movement cultivates several narratives among its followers: the belief that they are engaged in a battle for racial or cultural survival; that their racial, religious, or cultural group is threatened by imminent extinction; that existing political options are incapable of responding to this threat; that urgent and radical action is required to respond to these threats in society; and that they must fulfill this duty in order to leave a legacy for their children and grandchildren.

These motives provide followers of far-right and fundamentalist groups with a compelling and convincing rationale for getting actively involved. Foremost, these citizens perceive that a wider community is under threat, whether from al-Qaida, supranational organizations such as the EU or UN, or the immigration of Muslims or growth of settled Muslim communities.

(Continued)

> ### ▶ BOX 2.3 CONTINUED
>
> Furthermore, they also contend that this threat is cultural rather than economic. It is not simply about jobs or social housing. It is a profound sense of concern that a set of values, way of life, and wider community are under threat, and that only the most radical forms of action can remove this threat.
>
> I recently reviewed an academic book that ended with the prediction that the next wave of terrorism in Europe will come not from al-Qaida-inspired groups, but rather right-wing groups that want to respond to this threat and reassert the position of their wider group. It is far too early to tell whether Breivik's actions will inspire copycat attacks, but one thing remains clear: the threat from right-wing extremist groups and ideas deserves far greater attention. ■
>
> *Source:* Matthew Goodwin, Guardian.co.uk. July 24, 2011.

GREENS

The environmental Green Party made its appearance on the European political scene during the late 1970s and early 1980s. A third dimension is necessary to define the political position of the Greens. This dimension ranges from **material** to **postmaterial** and was introduced by the political scientist Ronald Inglehart.[28] The material end of the dimension means a conventional support for economic growth. This position is based on the assumption that bigger is better: The more goods and services a society produces, the better off are the members of that society. At the postmaterial end of the dimension, limits to **economic growth** are advocated in order to save the environment and increase the quality of life. We encountered this postmaterial position earlier in this chapter when discussing the emergence of a new wing in the Socialist Party. (See also discussion of the environmental movement in Chapter 8.)

A postmaterial orientation means that material goods no longer have first priority and that people seek fulfillment primarily of their spiritual, ethical, and aesthetic needs. Self-actualization is a key postmaterial concept. Great emphasis is also put on cooperation and communal living. According to the Greens, it is time for societies to move from a material to a postmaterial stage. In their view, this is the only way to save ourselves and our natural environment. The implication of this thinking is a completely new orientation toward work. We must again find fulfillment in our daily work. This is impossible if we are merely small wheels in large bureaucratic organizations, whether public or private. The desired situation is work more at a local level. The Greens acknowledge that this is not the most efficient way to organize the economy, but they challenge the usual definition of economic efficiency measured in the increase of the gross domestic product (GDP). The GDP does not reflect, for example, stress on human beings and the destruction of nature. According to the Greens, the crucial criterion for work must be how much it contributes to the quality of life for human beings, as well as for animals and plants. Nature must be brought back into **equilibrium**. With this philosophy,

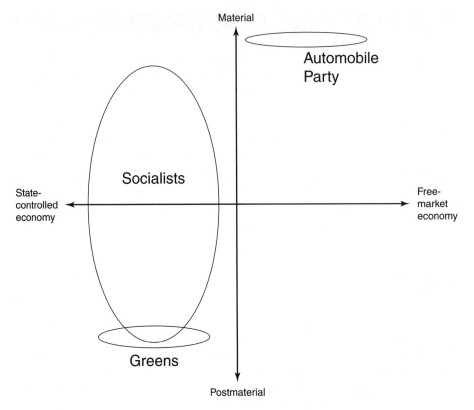

FIGURE 2.3

Location of Greens, Socialists, and Automobile Party on a dimension from state-controlled economy to free-market economy and on a dimension from material to postmaterial.

the Greens also have developed a strong interest in world peace and the fate of third-world countries.

In Figure 2.3 the horizontal dimension from state-controlled economy to free-market economy remains the same as in Figures 2.1 and 2.2. The vertical dimension now goes from postmaterial to material. If we were to add the dimension from individualistic to authoritarian, we would arrive at a three-dimensional political space. As we remember from geometry, it is possible to plot three dimensions on a two-dimensional sheet of paper, although the graph may lose clarity. In the current context, the depicted two dimensions in Figure 2.3 are sufficient, as the dimension from individualistic to authoritarian is relatively unimportant for the location of the Greens.

Although Greens are united in their emphasis on postmaterial values, they are more dispersed on economic questions. Generally, they tend toward the left, and many Greens, indeed, come from a Socialist or even a Communist background. Other Greens, however, see more merits in market mechanisms. Disagreements about the relative importance of the free market and state intervention have led to a great deal of tension among the Greens and occasionally have even caused them to split into separate parties. Thus, in Switzerland a Green-Liberal Party with a free-market program split from the Greens and is quite successful in elections. In the Czech Republic and the Republic of Ireland, the Greens became part of government coalitions of the Right (see Chapter 4). In Germany, on the other hand, the Greens place themselves on most issues to the left of the Social Democrats. These examples show how individual Green parties have quite different orientations from country to country.

Figure 2.3 also shows the position of the Swiss Automobile Party, which is the pure opposite of the Greens and helps clarify further the Green perspective. The Automobile Party has changed its name to Freedom Party, but colloquially it is still mostly referred to by its original name. It takes the material position to an extreme. The car, which is considered to be the ultimate material good, has to be protected against government interventions by all means. A slogan of the Automobile Party is "Unrestricted Driving for the Free Citizen." The supporters of the party protest whenever efforts are made to limit driving for environmental reasons. Such limiting measures include higher gasoline taxes, lower speed limits on highways, traffic-free streets in the inner cities, more stoplights, and less parking space. The Freedom Party considers such measures to be unnecessary restraints on the enjoyment of driving a car. This view is diametrically opposed to what is dear to Green supporters. Emotions are high between the two sets of values; as an illustration one may think of a chaotic traffic situation in which a Green supporter on a bike and a supporter of the Automobile Party in a fancy car begin to argue with each other. The Swiss Automobile Party is an extreme illustration of a free-market material party. There are other parties in Europe that come close to this extreme position in Figure 2.3, for example the Forza Italia in Italy.[29] It was founded by Silvio Berlusconi, the richest Italian, who as a successful entrepreneur stresses the free market and who in his personal lifestyle emphasizes material goods with luxury villas, cars, boats, airplanes, and so on.

The Greens are unusual not only because they do not fit the traditional patterns of party conflict in Europe, but also in the sense that they wish to be a completely different type of party. According to their views, the leaders of the established parties form an oligarchy and have lost touch with ordinary citizens. The Greens demand a fundamental democratization of political life and try to implement this principle first in their own ranks. Ideally, the Greens would like to have no leadership but rather equal participation by all members. To move toward this ideal, the Greens initially developed unusual party rules, particularly in Germany. There, the Greens at first did not allow their members of parliament to have incomes higher than those of blue-collar workers; the surplus had to be contributed to the party. After two years in office, Green members of parliament also were expected to rotate their seats to others in the party. These rules led to a great deal of acrimony in the German Green Party; they have often been violated, and in the meantime many of the rules have been abolished or at least relaxed. Power battles have become common in the Green Party as in all other parties, sometimes even in a harsher way. Thus, in March 2009 the Czech Green Party expelled four leading members, including two members of parliament, over the programmatic orientation of the party. The four expelled members had criticized that the party leadership sacrificed environmental issues for the sake of keeping political power.[30]

Who are the Green supporters? Much research has focused on this question, resulting in a high consensus on who votes for the Greens. According to the succinct summary by Herbert Kitschelt, they are "younger, educated, urban, secular members of the new middle classes."[31] They tend to work overproportionally in the public-service sector—in particular, in education, health, and social work. The Greens also attract many feminists, gays, and lesbians.

What specific policies do the Greens propose? In Germany, they have a lengthy and very detailed program,[32] containing, for example, a new energy tax and cuts in the workweek. According to the Greens, these two proposals offer the best hope for protecting the environment and reducing the country's persistent high unemployment. A so-called **eco-tax** would be imposed on atomic and hydroelectric power, as well as on fossil fuels—but not on renewable energy sources such as solar power. This eco-tax would be so stiff that energy consumption would significantly drop, which in turn would substantially cut pollution. The revenue produced by the eco-tax would be used to strengthen the welfare system. Job creation would be spurred by cutting the work week to 30 hours and abolishing overtime. As the spokesperson of the Greens claimed, these policies are meant as an alternative to what is called in German an *Ellbogengesellschaft*—literally an "elbow society," where everyone is aggressively using his or her elbows to get ahead.

Are the Greens likely to be a short-term phenomenon, or are they likely to endure as a political party? This is a widely discussed question that is addressed in a sophisticated way by political scientists Mark N. Franklin and Wolfgang Rüdig.[33] In their view, a necessary condition for the Greens to endure is "their ability to maintain a functioning and well-resourced party organization."[34] On these grounds, there were initially many doubts because the organization of the party was chaotic, which made a bad impression on many potential supporters, but in recent times, this has greatly improved. In their best result ever in any European country, the Greens got 24 percent of the votes in 2011 in the German Land of Baden-Württenberg, profiting from the concern about the nuclear catastrophe in Japan.

With regard to the social base of the Greens, Franklin and Rüdig arrive at the conclusion that it is very volatile. There is not yet much party loyalty, so the Greens must "mobilize many of their supporters afresh for each election."[35] The environment as the major issue of the Greens is also taken up by the Socialists, as we have seen earlier in the chapter. Environmentalists may also vote for a variety of other parties, as Oddbjorn Knutsen found out in a study of the party systems in the Scandinavian countries.[36] Thus, the Greens have no monopoly on environmental issues; voters with environmental concerns may easily move among several parties. The social base of the Greens may become more stable if a broadly based network of Green supporters develops. This stability was already visible in the two most recent elections of the European Parliament, in which the Greens managed to increase their voter strength from 5 percent in 2004 to 7 percent in 2009.

BOX 2.4   GERMANY: NUCLEAR POWER PLANTS TO CLOSE BY 2022

Germany's coalition government has announced a reversal of policy that will see all the country's nuclear power plants phased out by 2022. The decision makes Germany the biggest industrial power to announce plans to give up nuclear energy.... There have been mass antinuclear protests across Germany in the wake of March's Fukushima crisis, triggered by an earthquake and tsunami.... Mrs Merkel's centre-right Christian Democrats met their junior partners on Sunday after the ethics panel had delivered its conclusions.

Before the meeting she said: "I think we're on a good path but very, very many questions have to be considered." "If you want to exit something, you also have to prove how the change will work and how we can enter into a durable and sustainable energy provision."

The previous German government—a coalition of the centre-left Social Democrats (SPD) and the Greens—decided to shut down Germany's nuclear power stations by 2021. However, last September Chancellor Angela Merkel's coalition scrapped those plans—announcing it would extend the life of the country's nuclear reactors byan average of 12 years.

Ministers said they needed to keep nuclear energy as a "bridging technology" to a greener future. The decision to extend was unpopular in Germany even before the radioactive leaks at the Fukushima plant. But following Fukushima, Mrs Merkel promptly scrapped her extension plan, and announced a review... Before March's moratorium on the older power plants, Germany relied on nuclear power for 23 percent of its energy.

The anti-nuclear drive boosted Germany's Green party, which took control of the Christian Democrat stronghold of Baden-Wuerttemberg, in late March. Shaun Burnie, nuclear adviser for environmental campaign group Greenpeace International, told the BBC World Service that Germany had already invested heavily in renewable energy.

"The various studies from the Intergovernmental Panel on Climate Change show that renewables could deliver, basically, global electricity by 2050," he said. "Germany is going to be ahead of the game on that and it is going to make a lot of money, so the message to Germany's industrial competitors is that you can base your energy policy not on nuclear, not on coal, but on renewables." Shares in German nuclear utilities RWE and E. On fell on the news, though it had been widely expected. But it was good news for manufacturers of renewable energy infrustructure. German solar manufacturer, Solarworld, was up 7.6 percent whilst Danish wind turbine maker Vestas gained more than 3 percent. ■

Source: BBC News, Europe, May 30, 2011.

In the United States the environmental movement is quite strong, but the Green Party hardly exists. Why is this so? In Chapter 3, we will see that it may have to do with the particular American election system, which disadvantages smaller parties.

REGIONAL PARTIES

To locate regional parties, we have to introduce still another dimension of party space, the center–periphery dimension. If we take a typical regional party, such as the Scottish National Party, it is not possible to locate it on a left–right dimension, nor are the authoritarian–individualistic and material–postmaterial dimensions of much help.[37] Regional parties defend the interests of a periphery against the interests of the center of a country. Most political parties look at political life from the perspective of the national capital, where they have their headquarters and the focus of their daily activities. From this center perspective, the interests of **peripheral regions** often are neglected. It is against such neglect that regional parties try to fight. They look at politics from the vantage point of their regions. This center–periphery dimension was introduced into the literature by the late and highly respected Norwegian political scientist Stein Rokkan.[38]

In recent years, the importance of regional parties in Europe has increased rather than decreased. With societies becoming increasingly more modern, one may perhaps have expected the opposite trend: With fewer people in farming, higher levels of education, more geographical mobility, more travel, and more exposure to mass media, one might have thought that attachment to one's region would become less important. However, there is obviously a need in the modern world for roots, and the region is, for many, an entity that gives roots to the past and a feeling of solidarity to people with similar traditions and values. We will deal further with the question of regionalism in Chapter 7 on federalism, in Chapter 12 on nationalism and ethnicity, and in Chapter 14 on the European Union. This extensive treatment of the issue will show how important regionalism is in today's Europe. In addition to the Scottish National Party, the United Kingdom also has regional parties in Wales and Northern Ireland. In Spain, there are parties representing, in particular, the Basque, Catalan, Andalusian, Galician, Aragonese, and Valencian regions. Belgium is the European country where regionalism is most strongly expressed in the party system. Not only are there special regional parties for the Flemish and Walloon regions, more importantly, the major parties have special organizations for the two regions. Thus, there is a Francophone Socialist Party for Wallonia and a Flemish Socialist Party.

A regional party that needs special explanation is the Northern League in Italy. Its appeal has also to do with the fact that it expresses views close to the New Radical Right. This is another example showing how European political parties are often hard to classify in mutually exclusive categories. At the core of the Northern League is the Lombardy League (Lega Lombarda), which was founded during the early 1980s by the charismatic leader Umberto Bossi. For electoral purposes, the Lombardy League united with other regional leagues in northern Italy to form the Northern League. Some of Bossi's rhetoric is quite close to that of the New Radical Right; for example, when he accuses the established parties of wanting to transform Italy into a "multiracial, multiethnic, and multireligious society" that "comes closer to hell than to paradise."[39] Bossi exploits resentment not only against foreigners but also against the economically less developed Italians from the south. He promotes nationalism within the north of Italy, even playing with the idea that one day northern Italy could form a nation of its own.

COMMUNIST PARTIES

After the end of the Cold War in 1989, Communist parties were greatly weakened in Europe. But they still exist to some extent, either under the old name and, more often, under new labels. In order to understand European politics of today, it is important to consider that Communism was an important force in the quite recent past. As we will see in Chapter 11, in the countries in Central and Eastern Europe Communism was imposed by the Soviet Union and these countries had to live like in a large prison behind the Iron Curtain. Western Europe, Italy and France in particular, had large Communist parties, and it was unclear how strong the Soviet influence was on these parties. Communist ideology is based on Marxism. Who was Karl Marx, the man who had such a great influence on the Communist movement? A German philosopher, Marx was born in 1818 in Trier, in southwestern Germany, and he died in 1883 in exile in London. Among his famous publications are *Das Kapital* and, together with Friedrich Engels, *The Communist Manifesto*. What are the assumptions on which the philosophy of Marx is based? The most basic axiom is that human thinking and behavior are determined by **economic factors**. Marx speaks of an economic infrastructure and a noneconomic superstructure. Therefore, all meaningful explanations must begin with the economy of a society: its infrastructure. Causality begins with the material aspects of human life. All other aspects, such as politics, religion, education, and the arts, belong to the superstructure. These superstructural aspects can be understood only on the basis of their economic infrastructure. Thus, in the Marxist view, religious beliefs can be understood only on the basis of the society's economic infrastructure.

The economy is a broad concept, so which characteristics of economic life are of particular importance according to Marx? Here we come to a second basic assumption: The ownership of the means of production is the crucial factor. Marx distinguishes three means of production: land, capital, and labor. The basic distinction in society is whether someone owns land and capital or can offer only his or her labor. In industrial societies, the former are capitalists and the latter proletarians. During the early period of industrialization, when Marx wrote, many people could not clearly be classified as belonging to one of these two social classes. A baker, for example, who worked with his family and perhaps an apprentice, was neither a capitalist nor a proletarian. Marx predicted that such intermediate cases would become less and less frequent and that society would increasingly be divided into only the two classes, capitalists and proletarians. This prediction corresponded to what was to him a historical law, one he thought he had discovered in studying the industrialization of his time. With the increased costs of new technologies, companies needed to become bigger and bigger to survive. If the baker wanted to remain competitive, he had to transform his family bakery into a big factory. If he was not successful, he would become a laborer in such a factory. Land and capital would accumulate in the hands of fewer and fewer capitalists, and these capitalists would become richer and richer. But competition among capitalists would remain fierce, and to finance their expansion they would need a lot of money. The place where they can easily get this money is the proletariat. In this context, Marx coined the concept of **surplus value of labor**. This is the value of work done by the proletarians that is not returned to them in the form of wages, but is kept by the capitalists in the form of profits. According to Marx, this surplus value of labor would steadily increase so that less and less would remain for the proletarians, who would sink more and more deeply into poverty. This is what Marx meant when he called the capitalists *exploiters* and the proletarians *exploitees*.

Marx argued that the frustrations of the proletariat would eventually lead to a revolution that would overthrow the capitalists and bring the proletariat to power. Following the historical laws that Marx thought he had discovered, this revolution would occur by necessity. The only question was where and when it would happen. According to Marx, it was also certain that the revolution ultimately would be successful. After the revolution, the proletariat would establish a dictatorship. Marx called this the Socialist phase. This dictatorship was necessary to prevent a counterrevolution of the capitalists, who were also likely to operate from foreign countries. Consequently, it was necessary to bring the proletarian revolution to the entire world. The capitalists, with their selfish orientation toward profits, must be defeated everywhere, and until this was achieved, the proletariat would have to maintain its dictatorship.

The transition from the Socialist to the Communist phase could occur only when the capitalist mentality had been eliminated from the world. At this point, the dictatorship of the proletariat would no longer be necessary. All people would have been educated to think in an altruistic, unselfish way instead of in the earlier egotistical way. With this new orientation, all people would take from society only what they needed, and they would contribute everything that was within their capabilities. As a consequence, there would be no more scarcities, only a happy situation of plenty. Under these circumstances, the state would fade away. It would have become unnecessary. Because everyone would be morally pure, no police, no military, and no courts would be needed. And taxes would not even have to be collected because all members of society would contribute on a voluntary basis—all having become altruists.

How would people actually live in this final Communist phase? Marx, writing together with Friedrich Engels, claimed that Communist society would make it "possible for me to do one thing today and another tomorrow, to hunt in the morning, fish in the afternoon, rear cattle in the evening, criticize after dinner."[40] As political scientist William James Booth correctly argues, "Marx does not raise the issue of whether, for example, hunting is to be preferred to philosophy or, in general, of what the good life is. It is sufficient, for Marx, that…the individual be free of constraint."[41]

Given this vision of no constraints and ultimate salvation, Marxism may be interpreted as a religion or, at least, as a substitute for a religion. This is the way the French writer Albert Camus interprets Marx.[42] In Communism, as in a religion, the promise of one day reaching a utopian land of no evil encourages people to sacrifice in the present. The uncertainties of the present can be overcome by the certainties of the future. The sociologist Daniel Bell also interprets Marxism as a religion:

> What were the attractions of revolutionary Marxism that drew so many passionate intellectuals to its flag? What was the faith that, like that of the first-century Christian martyrs, summoned many to die for a cause? In one respect, the answer is simple: What once had appealed in the name of God crossed over to the banner of History. The belief remained in an eschatology that would end a divided consciousness, which placed men in a state of alienation. Marxism was a secular religion.[43]

Are Camus and Bell on the right track in interpreting Marxism as a religion? Or is it blasphemy to see Marxism in these terms? After all, Marx declared religion as the opiate of the masses. By the 1950s, Marxism had become intellectually out of favor. It seemed that its sociological class analysis was completely wrong. Instead of having an increasingly two-class system in highly industrialized societies, a broad **middle class** seemed to emerge. Thus, the potential for a proletarian revolution outside the Soviet bloc appeared increasingly remote. The arguments raised at the time against a Marxist class analysis were as follows:

1. Workers in capitalist societies have not sunk into an impoverished proletarian situation. Compared with the nineteenth century, when Marx wrote, they have been able to improve their standard of living, and today many of them enjoy a considerable wealth of consumer goods, although there are still large pockets of poverty.
2. Stocks are not concentrated in the hands of fewer and fewer individuals. On the contrary, more and more people participate in the stock market, in particular through new means such as mutual funds.
3. Business decisions are influenced not only by those who own stocks but also by a wide range of managers with special skills in law, engineering, economics, and so on.
4. Class structure is flexible, and there are many people who, thanks to their energy and intelligence, move from the bottom to the top in their own lifetime. On the other hand, there is also downward mobility.
5. There is a growing public sector of teachers, police, civil servants, and so on for whom the distinction between capitalists and proletarians does not apply.
6. There is a growing service sector in the private economy of health-care workers, hotel and restaurant workers, and so on, and people working in this sector are hard to organize in trade unions because they do not perceive themselves as workers in the classical sense.
7. Since the time Marx wrote, democratic forms of government have become more prevalent in highly developed capitalistic countries. In democratic elections everyone has one vote without regard for ownership of land and capital, although more affluent people have a higher chance to influence the election campaign.
8. Besides the difference between social classes, there are other important social distinctions, for example, those based on religion, race, language, and region. Important substantive issues such as abortion also cut across social classes.

All of these arguments against the class analysis of Marx add up to a **pluralistic** view of society. This view does not deny the fact that some people are very rich and others are very poor. Most people, however, are somewhere in the middle—some a little higher, others a little lower.

By the 1960s and 1970s, however, a new brand of Marxist scholars—neo-Marxists—gave new vigor to class analysis. Their analyses often differed in details, but their overall conclusion was always the same: Highly developed capitalist countries basically have a two-class structure of capitalists and proletarians. Their position was roughly as follows:

1. To give the workers access to consumer goods has a double advantage for the capitalists. First, it helps to pacify the workers. If they have cars for traveling and television sets for watching sports, they lose their revolutionary zeal. But to possess consumer goods does not mean the workers have gained any control over the important economic decisions in society; it only means they forget that they have no real economic influence at all. The workers have moved into a state of false class consciousness. Blinded by the richness of consumer goods, they think subjectively that they are no longer exploited, whereas objectively they still are. Second, giving consumer goods to the workers keeps the capitalist system going. Capitalists are aware of the danger of an impoverished proletariat that is not able to buy the increasing number of goods produced by the capitalist system. To prevent this danger, the capitalists are willing to increase the workers' wages. Although these wage increases marginally diminish the profits of the capitalists in the short run, their long-term profits will soar as a result of higher production levels. Overall, giving consumer goods to the workers in no way threatens the powerful position of those who own land and capital.

2. What about the argument that today many workers are themselves owners of stocks? Cannot these workers exercise power in shareholders' annual meetings? Not really, say neo-Marxists. To have true power in a company, one must own a large block of its stocks, not just a token few. With five or ten shares, workers get some dividends, and perhaps a nice meal at the shareholders' meeting, but have no real economic influence. The major effect is a reinforcement of their **false class consciousness**. With the possession of a few shares of stock, or participation in mutual funds, workers think of themselves as members of the middle class. Hoping to share in the profits, they now support the capitalist system. Thus, the dominant position of the capitalists is strengthened if they disperse stocks broadly among the population, as long as they keep the majority of the stocks in their own hands.

3. How do neo-Marxists handle the argument that many important business decisions are influenced not by shareholders but by managers, most of whom count themselves among the middle classes? A neo-Marxist would respond that one must distinguish between top managers on the one hand and middle- and lower-level managers on the other. The latter are merely useful tools in the hands of the capitalists. They help to control

the workers, which does not mean they have any broad-based economic power. Although they are not aware of it, these middle- and lower-level managers are just as exploited as the workers, in many ways even more so, because they have fewer opportunities to escape the pressures of work. The top managers, on the other hand, belong to the capitalist class, with which they share the same social background and values. Quite often, these top managers also own a high number of stocks.

4. Are there not many top managers who have advanced their careers through hard work and intelligence? Neo-Marxists do not deny the existence of such upward mobility, but they insist that such cases are rare and do not threaten the capitalist system. Before someone is allowed to reach the top level of a company, that person is carefully scrutinized to make sure that he or she accepts the basic values of capitalism. Therefore, such upwardly mobile people constitute no threat to the existing class structure. Their success stories even help to reinforce this structure by giving it the appearance of flexibility. Here neo-Marxists allude to the tendencies of the mass media to publicize the life stories of people who move from the bottom to the top. However, these stories are always of a few rare cases, and the fact that the overwhelming majority of proletarians never have a chance to enter the capitalist class does not change. Yet, seeing others move up, proletarians begin to attribute their own failure to personal shortcomings instead of the objective characteristics of the existing class structure. Such a perception further diminishes the class consciousness of the proletariat.

5. How does the increasing number of public employees fit into the neo-Marxist distinction between capitalists and proletarians? Just as in the private sector, a distinction is made between top public employees and those in middle and lower levels. The top bureaucrats belong to the capitalist class, with which they share the same social background and values. Whenever a basic conflict between the social classes arises, the top bureaucrats virtually always take the procapitalist position. Specifically, this means the top bureaucrats defend the concept of private property. If in rare cases they do not do so, they may lose their jobs or at least their promotion chances. In this sense, business has a privileged position to influence basic decisions of top civil servants. Top bureaucrats only remain neutral in conflicts between two property rights, such as between two automobile companies. Middle- and lower-level public employees are merely useful tools in the hands of the top bureaucrats. Teachers in the public schools help to socialize the children to the values of the capitalist system. To support this argument, neo-Marxists refer to textbooks that teach children in subtle ways how the profit motive contributes to the betterment of society. The police help the capitalists to control the proletariat, and tax collectors extract money from the lower class. Although teachers, police officers, tax collectors, and other public employees in similar positions are probably not aware of it, objectively they are in an exploited proletarian situation.

6. Employees in the service sector of the private economy are just as powerless and exploited as workers in the manufacturing sector. A hairdresser working for a wage is not in a different situation than a mechanic getting wages from an automobile company. The kind of clothing one wears for work does not make a difference, although workers in the service sector often think so.

7. Does not the principle of one person, one vote, in democratic elections contribute to some extent to equality among all citizens? Again, neo-Marxists disagree with this contention. First, decisions made by politicians are relatively unimportant compared with the decisions made in the boardrooms of the big multinational corporations. The main function of the political game is to entertain the public while diverting its attention from the more important business decisions. Second, to the extent that elections have any importance, they are manipulated by capitalist money that buys influence over nearly all parties and candidates. To understand the outcome of elections, it is important to know that newspapers, television, and radio are all directly or indirectly controlled by capital. Third, even if parties of the Left win elections, these parties merely do useful repair work for the capitalistic system without changing it in any fundamental way. Capitalists may sometimes even be glad when the Left wins, because a prime minister or a president of the Left may further help to cover up the real power structure in society, in the sense that leftist voters may get the wrong impression that they exercise real political power.

8. It may be true that there is an important social distinction between the superrich and everyone else. However, are other social differences also important? Not according to neo-Marxists. These other distinctions either reinforce the class difference or are merely superficial. The former situation is said to exist in the conflict between whites and blacks in the United States, where the capitalist class is almost exclusively white and most blacks have proletarian status. This does not mean, of course, that there are not masses of white proletarians, only that nearly all capital-ists are white. In the view of neo-Marxists, the race element helps to hide the real class structure. Capitalists are defended by white proletarians who are not aware of their real class interest, which, objectively, would be with the proletarians, regardless of race. Differences other than those based on social class can also be purely superficial, such as the language divisions in Switzerland, where capitalists come from all three major linguistic areas. Large banks are located in German-speaking Zürich, French-speaking Geneva, and Italian-speaking Lugano. Objectively, the proletariat from all three linguistic groups has the same class interest. To play one linguistic group against another is merely a surface conflict that helps to divert attention from the real class conflict. The same would be true, according to the neo-Marxist argument, for conflicts over issues such as abortion, which are only a means to divert attention from the class conflict.

In the 1960s and 1970s, neo-Marxist analysis had great intellectual appeal in Western Europe's academic circles, and also among intellectuals in other parts of the world such as Latin America, but much less so in the United States. Communists in Western Europe during the Cold War were certainly supported in many different ways by the Soviets, but they were not simply Soviet agents; they had their own reasons to be Communists. For Americans, who tend to identify Communism with the Soviet Union, it is not easy to understand why during the Cold War a fairly large number of Western Europeans chose to vote for Communist parties. Communism in Western Europe was referred to as **Eurocommunism.**

It is important to note that Eurocommunists had strong internal disagreements, which indicates that they did not simply execute orders from Moscow. Heated debates ensued about exactly what Marx meant by the concept of revolution and how he would interpret this concept under Western European conditions. The terrorist Left argued that violence needed to be used to overthrow the existing class system, whereas the official Communist parties took the position that revolutionary change could be caused through participation in the electoral process.

The terrorist Left was particularly active in the 1970s and the early 1980s. Estimates are difficult to make, but probably no more than a few thousand people in all of Western Europe were ever active in the terrorist Left. It consisted of no single organization, but was split into a large number of groups that often were in fierce competition with one another. Well known were the **Red Brigades** in Italy, the **Red Army Faction** in West Germany, and **Direct Action** in France.

Through kidnapping, assassinations, and other spectacular terrorist acts, the terrorist Left attracted worldwide attention to their cause. Just exactly what was this cause? What were they fighting for? The terrorist Left in Western Europe believed that capitalism could only be overcome through violence. But because most proletarians had lost their class consciousness, the violent overthrow of capitalism had become difficult. According to Marx, before a successful revolution can take place, the proletariat must be stripped of its false consciousness so that it can recognize the extent of its exploitation by the capitalists. How can this be demonstrated with sufficient clarity and vividness? The answer of the terrorist Left was to provoke the capitalists so they would be forced to show their "real face." If you shoot them in the knees and kill a few, they will bring out their military and police forces, and the brutality of their regime will become visible. The eyes of the proletarians will be opened to their true class situation. It turned out that the terrorist Left strategy failed. Instead of turning against the authorities, most workers turned against the terrorists.

Who were the terrorists? Were they the poorest of the poor in society, acting out of desperation? Not at all. Most terrorists came from affluent families and attended good schools. Women were heavily involved in the terrorist Left. Originally, many of these people had high ideals—a vision of a utopian, classless society with happiness for all. But, once engaged in terrorist activity, they were so busy hiding, robbing, and acquiring weapons that they no longer had the time and leisure to reflect on what this classless society might look like.

The Communist parties in Western Europe tried to organize politically and to participate in elections. The Communists had their greatest success in Italy. In that country's first parliamentary election after World War II in 1946, the Communists received 19 percent of the votes. Their share then steadily increased from election to election, to a high point of 34 percent in 1976. Afterward, a slow decline occurred with the party receiving 27 percent of the vote in 1987, the last election before the end of the Cold War. The other country where for a long time the Communists had substantial electoral support was France. After World War II and until the mid-1950s, the French Communist Party received about 25 percent of the votes at each election. Their voter share then decreased to around 20 percent, and stayed at this level until the end of the 1970s. A further decline occurred in the 1980s, to about 10 percent of the votes. There were no other Western European countries where the Communists had as much electoral success as in Italy and France. But in four countries—Finland, Greece, Portugal, and Spain—the Communists received, at least for some elections, two-digit support.

During the Cold War, Americans could easily understand how Communism had a grip on the satellite countries of the Soviet Union in Central and Eastern Europe, and how the terrorist Left tried to destabilize the democracies in Western Europe. But most Americans had difficulty understanding what the Communist parties in Western Europe were up to. Were they not steered by the Soviet Union, and would they not ultimately band together with the terrorist Left? Was participation in elections not just another means to destabilize the West? The Communist parties in Western Europe always declared that they were not involved in any terrorist activities and that they respected basic democratic principles. Increasingly they began to criticize the Soviet Union, for example, over the invasion of Czechoslovakia and Afghanistan and the existence of concentration camps in Siberia. The Italian Communist Party was particularly vocal in its criticism of the Soviet Union; the French Communists much less so. In their election campaigns, the Eurocommunists promised to bring more justice to the societies of Western Europe. They advocated stiffer taxes on the rich and more generous social programs for the poor.

How do we evaluate the rhetoric of the Western European Communist parties during the Cold War? Was it all a well-orchestrated campaign of disinformation, or did some Communists in Western Europe really believe in democratic principles? It is hard to distrust completely the sincerity of such statements.

In Italy and France, many local communities had Communist parties in power for a long time. How was this power exercised? Were basic civil liberties curtailed? The answer is clearly no. A well-known example is the Italian city of Bologna, which has been ruled for many years by the Communists and has enjoyed a good local administration. Do such examples prove that the Communists had accepted democratic principles? Not necessarily. Local communities are subordinated to the national governmental authorities, who are obliged to intervene if local communities violate basic democratic principles.

During a brief period following World War II, France had some Communist cabinet ministers. More important, from 1981 to 1984, the French cabinet was formed by Socialists and Communists (see Chapter 4). Did the Communist Party misuse this power to limit democratic freedoms? Again the answer is no. But, again, this is not proof that the Communists had accepted democracy as a form of government, because they were merely the junior coalition partner and thus had only limited power. At one time or another, Communists also exercised national executive power in Finland, Portugal, and Greece but, as in France, only as junior partners, so the question remains open as to how the Communist Party would have acted if it had gained full governmental control in a Western European country.

Whether a party is internally democratic should be an indication of whether it accepts democracy as a general principle for society at large. This is a severe test, because most non-Communist parties also violate to some extent the principles of internal democracy. It is widely documented that some internal debate took place, in particular, in the Italian Communist Party. Skeptics may object that such debates were merely organized to project the image of internal democracy. Other Communist parties, such as in France, tolerated much less internal debate than the Italian party.

From these indicators, no definite conclusion can be drawn about how Communists would have behaved if, during the Cold War, they had gotten full political control in a Western European democracy. So we will never know for sure what would have happened if, for example, the Italian Communists had won a majority in a parliamentary election.

What happened to the Western European Communist parties after the end of the Cold War? The Italian Communist Party made a vigorous effort to adapt to the new situation. It changed its name to the "Democratic Party of the Left" and cast itself in the Western European Socialist tradition. Nearly a third of the delegates, however, opposed the changes and walked out of the convention hall to form a group of their own, the Reform Communists. In 2007, the Democratic Party of the Left merged with a party more to the right to become simply the Democratic Party (Chapter 4). In France, the Communists have kept their name and were quite slow to change. In the first parliamentary elections after the end of the Cold War, French Communists were down to 9.2 percent and in 2007 to as low as 4.3 percent.

Are there still any prospects for Communism in Europe at all? One conclusion is firm: Communism in its **Stalinist** version is dead. There is no longer any support at all for the belief that the Communist Party has a right to a monopoly on power. The notion of a dictatorship of the proletariat is no longer tenable.

The political death of Stalinism does not mean that Karl Marx is dead as an intellectual force. After all, he was a philosopher of the nineteenth century, and it is not altogether clear how he would have reacted to the developments in the Soviet Union. One could very well argue that he would not have approved at all. As we saw earlier in this chapter, Marx used the concept of revolution in a rather abstract form and left ambivalent the matter of whether violence should be part of the revolution. The lasting contribution of Marx is his economic interpretation of society, and in this sense Marx will continue to have an intellectual influence on the European Left. At the same time, it must also be said that the influence of Marx has greatly diminished since the heydays of the 1960s and 1970s; for new issues of the Left, such as ecology and feminism, Marxism is no longer seen as relevant. With the outbreak of the global financial and economic crisis, however, the influence of Marx as a sociological analyst may again increase. After all, he had warned of unfettered capitalism based only on profit maximization. This analytical side of Marx must be clearly distinguished from his utopian view of an ultimate classless society, a view that has lost much of its appeal.

Although Marx will continue to have an influence, the European Left should not be identified with Marxism alone. In the past 200 years, there has been a great diversity of ideas on the Left, and this diversity has again become more apparent. Thus, there was always a tradition of the Left warning against the dangers of too much centralization and demanding more autonomy for small groups, in particular workers at their workplace and local communities.

A MULTIDIMENSIONAL POLITICAL SPACE

We have now located the political parties of Europe in a complex **multidimensional political space**, using four different dimensions. One may add still other dimensions; for example, a religious–secular or an urban–rural dimension. The reader should be aware that these dimensions are theoretical constructs that were developed so that we can better understand the ideological position of the various parties—but these constructs should not be seen as representing in any way an objective reality. As any other construct, these constructs have a subjective character rooted in the cognitive frameworks of the researchers who have proposed them. Reality can always be constructed in different ways, and there are certainly other ways to categorize the ideologies of the political parties in Europe. The four-dimensional space presented here is merely one possibility to make sense of the variations among the parties. In research about American politics, a multidimensional space is often used for the location of presidential candidates.

However we categorize the European political parties, there is no doubt that it has become more complicated to categorize them in an adequate way. This is true not only for foreign observers but also for Europeans themselves. The labels of the various political parties can no longer easily be identified with specific policy positions. This is different from traditional European politics, which was largely dominated by a single left–right dimension defined in economic terms. Now, other dimensions have equal and sometimes even more importance. To be sure, economic issues are still salient, such as taxes, social security, unemployment compensation, and financing of health care. But these economic issues are often of a very technical nature, so they do not raise much emotion in the general public. Other issues often create more controversy, such as how to regulate or deregulate drugs or whether to limit private automobile traffic. Such issues have little to do with the traditional left–right dimension.

Party competition may take place along specific dimensions, but in a multidimensional space there are many other possibilities of party competition.

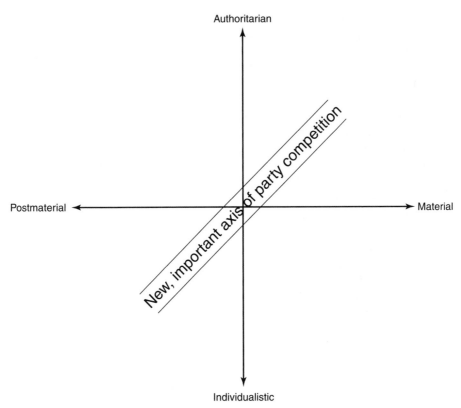

FIGURE 2.4
New, important axis of party competition.

Let us call axes the battle lines among the political parties. As an illustration, Figure 2.4 presents a new and important axis of party competition that cuts across two dimensions: the authoritarian–individualistic and the material–postmaterial. Of the four quadrants, only two are heavily populated in current European politics: the authoritarian–material and the individualistic–postmaterial quadrants. The battles on this axis are very emotional, the issues clear-cut and highly visible. Either one legalizes drugs, or one does not; either private automobiles are blocked from the inner city, or they are not; either refugees are accepted, or they are not; and so on.

The three traditional European parties—the Socialists, the Liberals, and the Conservatives—have difficulties in defining their positions on this axis. If the Socialists move too much toward the individualistic–postmaterial end, they risk losing their blue-collar, working-class supporters to the New Radical Right. If the Socialists move too much away from the individualistic–postmaterial end, they risk losing their newly gained supporters in the service sector to the Greens and other left-libertarian parties. The situation is no better for the Conservatives. If they move too far away from the authoritarian–material end, they lose voters to the New Radical Right; if they move too close in this direction, they lose voters at the center of the axis. The Liberals feel most comfortable in the individualistic–material quadrant; many of their supporters are upper-middle-class people who are individualistic on matters such as abortion but wish to enjoy their material consumer goods. If the political battles rage on the new axis, Liberals can either stay away, making their party irrelevant, or they can take a position on the new axis and risk being internally torn apart, with some of their supporters going to the Conservatives and others to the Socialists. Most comfortable on the new axis are the New Radical Right and the Greens. Being at both ends, they can easily define the nature of the political game, putting the other parties in an uncomfortable defensive position. This discussion illustrates the importance of how the battle lines are defined in a multidimensional space. To be successful, a party has to be able to define the political axes in such a way that it is located at a strategically advantageous location. The Free Democrats, for example, are well off if party competition in Figure 2.4 takes place either along the horizontal or the vertical axes because then they can take a clear offensive position.

Have the terms *left* and *right* become useless if one wishes to understand party competition in Europe? Yes and no. For scholarly analyses in political science, the two terms have become so vague that scholars are better off not using them at all and relying instead on more clearly defined terms, such as *postmaterial* and *individualistic,* but European politicians and voters still think in terms of left and right, and because we as political scientists need to understand their thinking we still have to be concerned with the terms *left* and *right.* What is meant by these two terms in current European politics? Oddbjorn Knutsen has studied this question for the voters in several European countries and has come up with a double conclusion.[44] On the one hand, the terms *left* and *right* continue to be identified by the public with the traditional economic dimension of state-controlled economy versus the free market. On the other hand, to be at the Left increasingly is also identified with postmaterial values, to be at the Right with material values. As Knutsen writes, "the new meanings of left and right are added to the old meanings." Therefore, we have now a left–right dimension "incorporating many types of conflict lines, and with different meanings to different people."[45] As argued earlier, such a broad dimension has lost its usefulness for analytical purposes, but it continues to be used by European voters and politicians to understand political life. In this sense the left–right dimension remains important in European politics.

A spatial term often used in European politics is the term *center,* and one speaks frequently of center parties. In Scandinavia there are political parties that explicitly call themselves center parties. Whatever their specific names, center parties are located at the median or close to it on all important dimensions. New research on center parties stems from Hans Keman[46] and Reuven Y. Hazan.[47] Keman calls the center parties "pivot parties in West European party systems…the linchpin for parliamentary democratic practice in multiparty systems…many of these parties have been remarkably successful in electoral terms as well as in gaining and keeping office."[48] Hazan agrees with Keman that center parties have great political influence in many European democracies; he goes a step further in also researching "the effect that the center has on the other parties in the system."[49] His conclusion is that a strong center party causes other parties to take more extreme positions than they would otherwise.

MEMBERSHIP IN POLITICAL PARTIES

Membership in a European political party is quite different from party membership in the United States. Americans reveal their party identification by registering, voting in general elections, and answering opinion surveys, but they do not formally join a party as they would a professional association or a service club, by paying annual dues and carrying a membership card. Europeans do precisely that when they join a political party: Membership in a political party is applied for, and the party has the right to reject applicants and to expel existing members, as we have seen earlier in the chapter for the Green Party in the Czech Republic.

What percentage of European voters are members of a political party? Figures vary strongly from country to country; usually membership is below 10 percent, and in some places as low as 5 percent or even less. There is also quite a bit of rotation, with many people moving in and out of parties. In Norway, for example, Per Selle and Lars Svasand found that in each of two 4-year periods they studied, "More people moved in or out of parties than were stable members."[50] Although it is common in Europe to give up membership in a political party, it is rare to change membership from one party to another. In the Norwegian study by Selle and Svasand, only 3 percent and 1 percent, respectively, did so in each of the two 4-year periods. It is one thing to quit a party but quite another thing to join another party. The latter is considered by many Europeans as disloyal.

There is much debate about whether party membership in Europe is in decline, and there are indeed some countries and individual parties where such a decline has been registered. In their careful study, Selle and Svasand come to a more nuanced conclusion. They find that in Great Britain, the Netherlands, and Denmark, party membership has decreased, but that it has increased in Belgium, Austria, Ireland, Germany, and Finland. In other countries, they find no clear trend. It is also interesting that the same party may gain members in one country but lose members in another country.

What are party members doing in their parties? For many, the answer is "not much." Various studies have found that merely about 10 to 20 percent of members are really active in their party organizations. Even for many of these members, the emphasis of their party activities is less on political discussions than on leisure and entertainment. To attract members, political parties organize all kinds of nonpolitical activities such as dances, hikes, picnics, and so on. The single most important political function of parties is to nominate candidates for political offices, an aspect to which we turn in the next chapter.

People outside a political party still may display party loyalty, but for some reason they decide against becoming formal party members. Bradley M. Richardson has found that for Great Britain, the Netherlands, and Germany, between 50 percent and 70 percent of all voters are "stable psychological partisans." His analysis demonstrates that "many voters' long-term party ties are buttressed by stable views toward long-term party principles and/or stable party images; many voters' loyalties are further fortified by negative views of opposing parties. This constrained structure of responses to parties makes European partisanship resemble an affect-laden schema."[51] Thus, we should distinguish carefully between party membership and party loyalty. Although, in general, party members show greater party loyalty than nonmembers, there is also some overlap in the sense that party loyalty may be higher among some nonmembers than among some members. Such members may simply forget to cancel their party membership but are no longer emotionally attached to the party. In this context, it is important to note that membership dues are not very high, in most cases below $100 annually.

STABILITY AND CHANGE OF PARTIES AND PARTY SYSTEMS

So far we have described individual parties. The term **party system**, however, does not refer to any individual party but rather to a set of parties and their relationship to each other. In the first section of this chapter, we argued that the origins of parties were directly connected to establishment of the mass franchise achieved in most countries by the early 1920s. As a result, once voters were allowed to give expression to their political desires by voting for their preferred party, the party system became "frozen" in time.[52] Indeed, party systems remained relatively stable until the late 1970s and early 1980s. However, in the 1960s social movements began to stir, which would manifest themselves eventually as new parties in the 1980s.

The rise of new parties such as the Greens can partly be explained as a result of increased education, the satisfaction of material demands, and socialization during a period of economic well-being. Some parties, such as radical right-wing parties, emerge as a result of new political issues such as immigration. Other parties form partly as a result of splitting off from established parties, such as in Germany the so-called Linke (Left Party), which split from the Social Democrats and merged with the successor party to the Communist Party in the former German Democratic Republic.

Despite these changes to the party landscape over the past three decades, it is also true that the basic Socialist/Conservative divide has remained rather stable with core blocs of voters providing continued support. Although there is certainly change occurring in European party systems, there are also continuities observable, particularly as far as the established parties are concerned.

The perhaps most disconcerting development over the last two decades has been the degree to which **voter turnout** has declined in many European democracies. The party of "nonvoters" has become one of the largest parties in many European countries, such as in France, where in the 2002 presidential election, more than 40 percent of the voting-age population did not participate. Five years later in 2007, however, participation in French presidential elections strongly increased again, with over 80 percent turnout in both rounds. Compared with American presidential elections this was a very high turnout.

We are now familiar with the wide range of political parties in Europe. We have learned the need to think in terms of a multidimensional space in order to understand the location of the various political parties. In the remainder of the book, we will learn about the institutions and the culture in which European political parties operate, and we will also see how the number and the kind of parties depend very much on the institutional and cultural setting of the respective country. We will discuss the national party systems, in particular, of the United Kingdom, France, Germany, Italy, Spain, the Czech Republic, Hungary, Poland, Ukraine, Bosnia-Herzegovina, Kosovo, Macedonia, Austria, Belgium, the Netherlands, Ireland, Switzerland, and Sweden. The book's detailed index easily refers readers to the respective countries.

KEY TERMS

clients   19
Cliques   18
Direct Action   53
economic factors   47
economic growth   41
eco-tax   44
equality   22
equilibrium   41
Eurocommunism   53
false class
   consciousness   50
individual freedom   27

market forces   28
material   41
middle class   49
multidimensional political
   space   56
natural order
   of society   29
party system   60
patrons   19
peripheral regions   46
pluralistic   50
populist   36

postmaterial   41
Red Army Faction   53
Red Brigades   53
social programs   32
Stalinist   55
structure
   of authority   29
surplus value of labor   48
Third Way   25
universal suffrage   18
voter turnout   60
voting rights   18

DISCUSSION QUESTIONS

1. Why does the term *liberal* mean something very different in the European political context as compared to the American political context?
2. Why are parties crucial for modern, democratic politics?
3. Why are there no Socialist parties in the United States?
4. Many European countries have postmaterial parties represented in their legislatures. Why are there no postmaterial parties in the American Congress?
5. Do the fall of the Berlin wall and the collapse of the Soviet Union mean that Marxism as a political philosophy is also finished?
6. Why was communism such an attractive ideology right after WWII in Europe, particularly in Italy?
7. Are there politicians in the United States who would fit into the New Radical Right in Europe? Who are they?
8. Why was it that the United States was much less receptive to Marxist ideology than some European or Latin American countries?
9. What do you think were the main reasons why Communism failed?
10. What is the advantage of perceiving the political space in a multidimensional fashion as opposed to the traditional left–right spectrum?

NOTES

1. Seymour Martin Lipset and Stein Rokkan. *Party Systems and Voter Alignments: Cross-National Perspectives* (New York: The Free Press, 1967).
2. Ibid.
3. Max Weber. [1919]. Politics as a Vocation. In Hans Heinrich Gerth and Charles Wright Mills, eds., *From Max Weber: Essays in Sociology* (New York: Oxford University Press, 1946, 102).
4. Elmer E. Schattschneider. *Party Government* (New York: Rinehart, 1942, 1).
5. Bertolt Brecht. *Threepenny Opera* (New York: Grove, 1949, 66–67).
6. Herbert Kitschelt. Class Structure and Social Democratic Party Strategy. *British Journal of Political Science* 23 (July 1993): 319. See also Herbert Kitschelt. *The Transformation of European Social Democracy* (New York: Cambridge University Press, 1994).
7. The complete document can be accessed online at http://www.socialdemocrats.org/blairandschroeder6-8-99.html.
8. Hans Keman. Third Ways and Social Democracy: The Right Way to Go? *British Journal of Political Science* 41, no. 3 (published online December 21, 2010): 671–680.
9. http://www.labour.org.uk, June 24, 2007.
10. See the official of website of the German government at http://www.bundesregierung.e/nn_6562/Content/EN/Artikel/2008/10/2008-10-15-merkel-bundestag__en.html.
11. Merkel, Sarkozy. Blair Call for New Capitalism. *CNBC*, January 8, 2009. http://www.cnbc.com/id/28557738.
12. For an explanation of the variation of the strength of the New Radical Right in Western European countries, see Kai Arzheimer. Contextual Factors and the Extreme Right Vote in Western Europe. *American Journal of Political Science* 53 (April 2009): 259–275.
13. Hans-George Betz. The New Politics of Resentment: Radical Right-Wing Populist Parties in Western Europe. *Comparative Politics* 25 (July 1993): 418.
14. Ibid., 423.
15. Herbert Kitschelt. Left-Libertarians and Right-Authoritarians: Is the New Right a Response to the New Left in European Politics? (Paper presented at the Western European Area Studies Center, University of Minnesota, November 1991, 15, 23).
16. Betz. The New Politics of Resentment, 413.
17. Pierre Bréchon and Subrata Kumar Mitra. The National Front in France: The Emergence of an Extreme Right Protest Movement. *Comparative Politics* 25 (October 1992): 80.
18. *New York Times*, March 29, 1988.
19. *New York Times*, October 2, 1996.
20. *Tages-Anzeiger*, Fernausgabe, February 2, 1993 (translation Jürg Steiner).
21. Elisabeth Ivarsflaten. What Unites Right-Wing Populists in Western Europe? Re-Examining Grievance Mobilization Models in Seven Successful Cases. *Comparative Political Studies* 41 (January 2008): 18.
22. Jens Rydgren. Immigration Sceptics, Xenophobes or Racists? Radical Right-Wing voting in Six West European Countries. *European Journal of Political Research* 47 (October 2008): 739.
23. *De Volkskrant*, August 8, 2008.
24. Human Development Report, United Nations Development Program, 2011.
25. Roger Cohen. *The New York Times*, July 25, 2011.
26. *BBC News Europe*, July 25, 2011.

27. Cas Mudde. *Populist Radical Right Parties in Europe* (Cambridge, MA: Cambridge University Press, 2007).

28. Ronald Inglehart. *The Silent Revolution: Changing Values and Political Styles among Western Publics* (Princeton, NJ: Princeton University Press, 1977).

29. In 2009, Forza Italia merged with Alleanza Nationale into Popolo della Libertà.

30. Neue Zürcher Zeitung, March 11, 2009.

31. Herbert Kitschelt. Left-Libertarian Parties: Explaining Innovation in Competitive Party Systems. *World Politics* 40 (January 1988): 194–234.

32. http://www.gruene.de.

33. Mark N. Franklin and Wolfgang Rüdig. On the Durability of Green Politics. *Comparative Political Studies* 28 (October 1995): 409–439.

34. Ibid., 434.

35. Ibid.

36. Oddbjorn Knutsen. The Materialist/Postmaterialist Value Dimension as a Party Cleavage in the Nordic Countries. *West European Politics* 13 (April 1990): 258–274.

37. For the voter support of the Scottish National Party, see Robert Johns, James Mitchell, David Denver, and Charles Pattie. Valence Politics in Scotland: Towards an Explanation of the 2007 Elections. *Political Studies* 57 (March 2009): 207–233.

38. Stein Rokkan. *Citizens, Elections, Parties: Approaches to the Comparative Study of the Process of Development* (Oslo, Norway: Universitetsforlaget, 1970). See also special issue on Stein Rokkan, *Historical Social Research* 20, no. 2 (1995): 88–118.

39. Quoted in Betz, The New Politics of Resentment, 417.

40. Karl Marx and Frederick Engels. *The German Ideology in Collected Works*, vol. 5 (New York: International Publishers, 1976, 47).

41. William James Booth. The New Household Economy. *American Political Science Review* 85 (March 1991): 71.

42. Evelyne Pisier and Pierre Bouretz. Camus et le Marxisme. *Revue Française de Science Politique* 35 (December 1985): 1056.

43. Daniel Bell. The Fight for the 20th Century: Raymond Aron versus Jean-Paul Sartre. *New York Times Book Review* (February 18, 1990): 3.

44. Oddbjorn Knutsen. Value Orientation, Political Conflicts and Left-Right Identification: A Comparative Study. *European Journal of Political Research* 28 (1995): 63–93.

45. Ibid., 87.

46. Hans Keman. The Search for the Center: Pivot Parties in West European Party Systems. *West European Politics* 17 (October 1994): 124–148.

47. Reuven Y. Hazan. Center Parties and Systemic Polarization. An Exploration of Recent Trends in Western Europe. *Journal of Theoretical Politics* 7, no. 4 (1995): 421–445.

48. Keman. The Search for the Center, 124, 145–146.

49. Hazan. Center Parties and Systemic Polarization, 436.

50. Per Selle and Lars Svasand. Membership in Party Organizations and the Problem of Decline of Parties. *Comparative Political Studies* 23 (January 1991): 463.

51. Bradley M. Richardson. European Party Loyalties Revisited. *American Political Science Review* 85 (September 1991): 751, 766.

52. Lipset and Rokkan. *Party Systems and Voter Alignments*.

"The Most Specific Manipulative Instrument of Politics":
Electoral Systems and How Votes Are Turned into Seats

Most people think that democracy means free and fair elections. While such election procedures are certainly an important element, it is just as important to examine how various countries allocate seats after the people have spoken and their votes are in. Across European democracies there are very different systems in place that significantly shape how the will of the people is transformed into actual political outcomes. Different rules means different political behavior among voters and party elites, the enactment of different policies, and even difference in the length and survivability of governments. This is why Giovanni Sartori described electoral systems as "the most specific manipulative instrument of politics."[1]

Our discussion now turns to the institutions within which political parties operate, and in the current chapter we deal with parliamentary election systems. By this we mean the formal rules according to which elections of parliament are organized, which vary widely among European democracies. Students should learn how election rules affect the success of political parties, both positively and negatively. Election rules, like any rules, are never neutral. We discuss in detail Great Britain, the Netherlands, Switzerland, Ireland, Germany, France, and Italy. Each of these countries has special features in its election rules, thus illustrating the wide range of possibilities available for organizing parliamentary elections. In Chapter 11, we will also see how Hungary and Poland chose an election system after the fall of Communism in 1989.

Americans are accustomed to simple rules for parliamentary elections. For the U.S. Senate, whoever receives the most votes in his or her state is elected. The same rule applies to the U.S. House of Representatives: Whoever wins the most votes in his or her congressional district is elected. For both the Senate and the House, a single ballot is needed. In Europe, the simple **winner-take-all** system with a single ballot is used only in Great Britain, where it is called "first-past-the-post." This system may also be called single-member district (SMD) plurality, meaning that only one member of parliament is elected per district and that it is sufficient to reach a **plurality** of the votes (not a majority in the sense of 50% + 1) in order to get the seat. Other European countries use a wide variety of rules to elect their parliaments. Election rules are not interesting for their own sake, but because they influence the way the political game is played. The connection between the rules of the game and the game itself is well known from sports. Changes in the rules of a sport often influence the kinds of players who are able to make the team. As we see in this chapter, the same holds true for politics. A politician or a political party who is successful under one set of rules may not be successful under another. French political scientist Maurice Duverger was the one who has formulated this argument in a classical way.[2]

Generally speaking, European politicians depend for their electoral success to parliament much more on their political parties than their American colleagues. For U.S. congressional elections, each candidate has pretty much to fight for himself or herself to be elected. This means in particular to organize a very personalized election campaign and to collect the necessary money. As a consequence, money is much more important for electoral success in the United States than in Europe. Parliamentary elections in Europe are also less costly since there are more restrictions on campaign expenditures. For example, in many countries, political advertising on radio and television is not allowed.

WINNER-TAKE-ALL WITH SINGLE BALLOT: GREAT BRITAIN

Both the House of Commons and the House of Lords meet in Westminster Palace on the river Thames. From about 1340, parliament began to meet in Westminster, which can be considered the birthplace of modern parliaments. In 1941, during World War II, the chamber of the House of Commons was destroyed by German air attacks. After the war, the chamber was rebuilt based on the old designs. Buildings can be an important part of the tradition of institutions, and this was well understood when Westminster was rebuilt according to the old plans.

The House of Lords formerly consisted of hundreds of members of the hereditary nobility and some members who received titles merely for their lifetime. However, the House of Lords Act (1999) fundamentally changed the character of the House of Lords by removing hereditary peerage. The first line of the new law is explicit: "No-one shall be a member of the House of Lords by virtue of hereditary peerage." However, to make this fundamental constitutional change possible, a compromise was reached, allowing 90 hereditary peers to remain in the House of Lords on a temporary basis. The House of Commons is democratically elected on the basis of one person, one vote. In former times, the House of Lords had more prestige and power, hence the term *upper house*. Over the centuries, the House of Commons, the "lower" house, became more and more important, and today it is the dominant chamber. Thus, contrary to what one may logically expect, the term *lower* connotes more power than *upper*.

For the election of the members of the House of Commons, Great Britain is divided into as many **electoral districts** as there are parliamentary seats—currently 655—and in each district the candidate who has the most votes wins the seat. The winner gets everything, the loser nothing. As in the United States, there is no requirement that the winner reach an absolute majority of 50 percent + 1; a mere plurality of the votes is sufficient. Thus, with three candidates in a district, the winner may receive only 40 percent of the vote, with perhaps the two other candidates each getting 30 percent.

The winner-take-all system is strongly biased in favor of the two largest parties in a country. In the U.S. Congress, no third parties have been represented to any significant extent in recent times. Is this due to the electoral system? Yes, most likely, but U.S. third parties get so few votes in congressional elections that at first glance it may not be clear how their lack of success could possibly be due to the electoral system. This chapter should make clear that under a different electoral system, U.S. third parties would have a better chance of representation in Congress. In presidential elections circumstances are somewhat different, so third-party candidates have a better chance, as the candidacy of Ross Perot in the 1992 election illustrates. In this chapter, however, we are concerned only with parliamentary, not presidential, elections.

In British parliamentary elections, third parties are numerically much stronger than in American congressional elections. As a consequence, and paradoxically, it is easier to demonstrate with the British case how a winner-take-all system works against third parties. If third parties get a fair amount of voter support, it is easier to see how this support fails to translate into parliamentary representation. The discrimination against third parties can best be illustrated with the 1983 general election, in which third parties received particularly high voter support but little parliamentary representation. The Conservatives, while only winning a plurality of the vote (42.4 percent), won a landslide 61.1 percent of parliamentary seats.

This large victory occurred because the opposition was badly divided. Shortly before the election, moderate Labour members had split from their party to form their own centrist Social Democratic Party (SDP). The SDP entered into the so-called Alliance with the Liberals, which meant that the two parties agreed to have only one candidate in each district, either a Social Democrat or a Liberal. Before the 1983 election, the Liberals were the perennial third party in British electoral history. They achieved sizable voter support but hardly any seats because they were first-past-the-post in only a few districts. In the 1974 election, for example, the Liberals won a substantial share of voter support (18.6 percent) but managed to win only 13 seats (2.0 percent). Uniting their forces in 1983 in the Alliance, Liberals and Social Democrats hoped to win not only voters but also seats. However, this hope was disappointed; their voter support of 25.4 percent translated into a mere 3.5 percent of the seats. The Alliance was punished by an electoral system in which only winning matters, and a good showing in second or third place counts for nothing.

With only a slightly higher voter support of 27.6 percent, Labour won nearly 10 times as many parliamentary seats (32.3 percent) as the Alliance. The reason was that Labour voters were concentrated in working-class districts where, in many cases, the party was able to come in first. The Alliance voters, in contrast, were spread more evenly over all districts. This distribution made for a good showing overall in Great Britain but resulted in very few district victories. And with the winner-take-all system, only victories count.

To understand fully the winner-take-all system, we also must consider **anticipatory effects**. Many voters do not like to "waste" their vote on a party that is expected to have no chance of victory. In the 1983 election, this mechanism worked strongly against the Alliance. Many voters seriously considered voting for it but, according to a study by Ivor Crewe, eventually did not, because they anticipated that the Alliance candidates had no chance of winning their district.[3] The British case also should help us understand that election rules are not simply a given but are themselves an outcome of the political game. Because it was at a serious disadvantage under the winner-take-all system, the Alliance advocated a change to proportional representation. But Conservatives and Labour, which both greatly profited from the existing system, were opposed to such a change, and, given the distribution of the seats in the House of Commons, the Alliance had no chance to have its way.

The reason why neither of the two large parties in Great Britain wants to change the electoral system is also shown in the results of the 2005 elections. This time it was the Labour Party that profited from the distortionary effects of the electoral system. In that particular election, only 3 percentage points in the popular vote separated Labour from the Conservatives. Yet this small margin in popular votes translated into 25 percent more seats for Labour than for the Conservatives. With only a little over 35 percent of the voters choosing Labour, the lowest percentage of popular votes for a winning party ever, Labour could still claim a majority in the House of Commons of over 55 percent of seats.

The Liberal Democrats received over 22 percent of public support, yet this translated into merely 9.6 percent of all seats.

The 2010 elections brought a very unusual outcome for Great Britain, a hung parliament, the first time that such an outcome occurred since 1974. A hung parliament means that no party gets a majority of the seats in parliament. In this election, Conservatives got 36 percent of the popular vote, Labour 29 percent, and Liberal Democrats 23 percent, with the remaining 12 percent going to minor parties. As we have seen above, in the preceding elections in

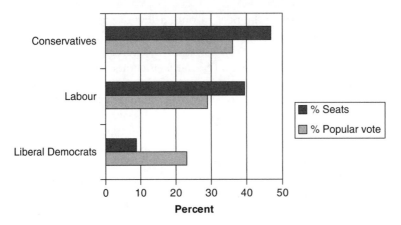

FIGURE 3.1

Voter support and percentage of parliamentary seats in the 2010 general election to the British House of Commons.

Source: BBC News, June 10, 2010

2005 Labour got about the same popular vote as Conservatives this time. But while Labour then got a majority of the parliamentary seats, Conservatives this time got only 306 seats, short of a majority in the 655-member House of Commons. How can this be?

The answer has to be seen in the intricacies of the election system. What counts is only winning electoral districts. It just happened that Conservatives did quite well in many districts, but often just barely lost against another party. It very much depends on how the popular vote is distributed among the electoral district, how the popular vote translates into parliamentary seats. In 2010, Conservatives had tough luck that as the leading party with 36 percent of the popular vote they reached only 47 percent of the parliamentary seats. Labour received 40 percent of the parliamentary seats, and Liberal Democrats 9 percent. We will see in the next chapter how a cabinet could be formed under these unusual circumstances of a hung parliament. There, we will also see that a change of the election system in the direction of more proportionality was defeated in a national referendum May 5, 2011.

Until now, we have focused on the negative effects on smaller parties of the winner-take-all system. On a more positive note, one also could argue that this type of electoral system helps to prevent the entry of extremist parties to parliament, thus making governance easier. The British case supports this argument, as extremist parties are very little or not at all represented in the country's legislature. This moderating effect, however, is likely to occur only for a **unimodal distribution** of voter preferences, where most voters are in the middle and few are at the extremes so that their distribution has a bell-shaped curve. The United States and Great Britain have, by and large, such unimodal distributions of voter preferences on most important dimensions and, therefore, approximate the situation depicted in Figure 3.2. Under these conditions,

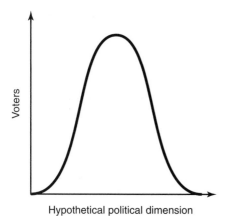

FIGURE 3.2

Unimodal distribution of voter preferences on a hypothetical political dimension.

we would indeed expect a moderating effect, because to take an extreme position would lead nowhere. After all, most voters are located in the middle.

Figure 3.3 represents an extremist distribution of voter preferences, with the highest number of voters at the two extremes. We can easily see that in such a situation a moderate position has little appeal. Let us assume that the voters at the left of our political dimension in Figure 3.3 are Catholics and those at the right are Protestants, with the two groups far apart on all important issues. With a winner-take-all system, one candidate is likely to appeal to Catholics, the other, to Protestants. The election then corresponds more to a census, in the sense that the size of the two groups is counted. The campaign will have a polarizing effect, because each candidate will do everything to *mobilize* the members of

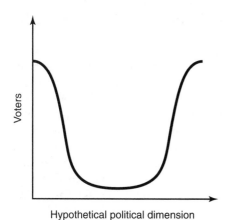

FIGURE 3.3

Extremist distribution of voter preferences on a hypothetical political dimension.

his or her group. This is basically the situation in Northern Ireland. The only difference between that situation and the situation represented in Figure 3.3 is that one group in Northern Ireland, the Protestants, is numerically stronger than the Catholics, which further exacerbates the problem, because in most districts Catholics have no chance of winning. London is slowly beginning to recognize the unfairness of the winner-take-all system under these circumstances and has imposed proportionality rules for local elections in Northern Ireland and for elections of Northern Ireland representatives to the European Parliament. For the crucial elections to the House of Commons, however, Northern Ireland continues to use the winner-take-all system. (More on the troubles in Northern Ireland in Chapters 12 and 13. There we will see that Protestants can best be characterized as British Unionists and Catholics as Irish Nationalists.)

PARTY LIST PROPORTIONAL REPRESENTATION: THE NETHERLANDS

The basic principle of party list **proportional representation** (hereafter PR) is simple: A party receives parliamentary seats in proportion to its share of the total vote. If a parliament has 100 seats and a party wins 10 percent of the total vote, then that party will be awarded 10 parliamentary seats. If the party wins 1 percent of the vote, it receives one seat. What if a party in this situation wins 1.5 percent of the vote? Will it receive one or two seats? This will depend on what fractions of seats the other parties get. Mathematically this is not an easy problem, and there are different formulas to find a solution. Together with the mathematician Hans Riedwyl, one of us (Steiner) has dealt with this problem at the crossroads of political science and mathematics in the journal *Comparative Politics*.[4] Jay K. Dow could demonstrate that the more proportionate an election system, the greater the ideological dispersion of parties.[5]

The Netherlands uses party list PR in its most simple form. The Dutch parliament has 150 members who are elected from a single, nationwide electoral district. The political parties submit lists of their candidates, and the voters simply choose one of these lists.[6] The votes are tallied in a two-step process. First, the number of votes nationwide for each party is counted and then converted into a percentage of the total vote cast. In the 2010 election, the People's Party for Freedom and Democracy received the most votes (20.5 percent), the Labour Party came second (19.6 percent), the Party for Freedom third (15.5 percent), the Christian Democratic Appeal fourth (13.6 percent), and the Socialist Party fifth (9.8 percent). According to the PR system, the People's Party for Freedom and Democracy received 31 seats, the Labour Party 30, the Party for Freedom 24, the Christian Democratic Appeal 21, and the Socialist Party 15. The other 29 seats were awarded to five smaller parties. The smallest party receiving parliamentary representation, the Party for the Animals, was awarded two seats for its 1.3 percent of votes cast. Just imagine how impossible it would be for such a party to get any representation in the U.S. Congress, not because Americans are not protective of animals, but because in the winner-take-all election system, such a party would have no chance to get any representation.

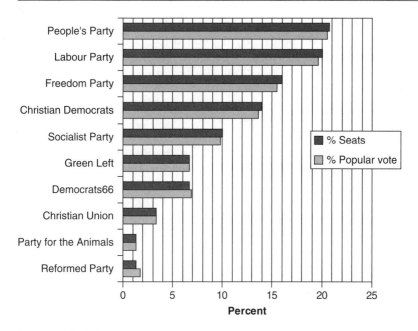

FIGURE 3.4

Voter support and percentage of parliamentary seats in the 2010 parliamentary election to the Dutch parliament (Tweede Kamer)

Source: Time World, June 10, 2011

Figure 3.4 clearly shows how closely the percentage of popular votes per party and its corresponding percentage of seats track each other. There are very small differences between the two bars, indicating the high proportionality of that electoral system.

We now know how the first step of the Dutch electoral system—the distribution of parliamentary seats to the political parties—works. The second step is to consider how the individual parties determine which of their candidates will be elected. Each party lists its candidates in the order in which they will be awarded the seats won by the party. For example, the Labour Party's first 30 ranked candidates became its parliamentary representatives. This system of having the parties rank their own candidates provides an important means of controlling the behavior of party members.

How is the ranking done? Who gets the favorable ranks at the top? Who would be so foolish as to enter the race last on a list? A small group, such as the party's executive committee, usually prepares the **party list**. A party convention then approves the list, usually without making major changes. A young party member beginning his or her career would feel honored just to be placed on the list, even if the actual rank gave absolutely no chance of election. By working hard for the party, a candidate expects to move up the list to finally receive a rank that assures him or her of election to a parliamentary seat. Prominent party leaders and successful members of parliament are usually given places on the list that virtually guarantee reelection to parliament. This system strengthens the parties by giving them the opportunity to reward loyal party members with good rankings and punish less loyal ones with bad rankings.

Some parties have now begun to have internal elections among party members to establish the rankings. This shows that the Dutch system leaves it to the individual parties on how to establish the ranking of their candidates. We must add a rule that currently has very little practical importance but is still interesting for American readers because it brings a personalized element to the Dutch system. Voters may, if they wish, give a personal preference to a single candidate on their party list. Usually such preference votes go to the top candidates on the lists who are elected, thanks to their good rankings. If a candidate, however, reaches a certain quota of preference votes, he or she is elected even if he or she is not high enough in the party rankings. This happened in the 2006 elections for one candidate, Fatma Koser Kaya of Democrats 66. She was only sixth in her party rankings, and her party received three seats. She is of Turkish origin and received much support from Turkish organizations with 34,564 personal preference votes, many more than the required quota of 16,397 votes. She was, therefore, declared elected, and the third candidate on the list had to yield. If Dutch voters would give their personal preference votes to lower-ranked candidates more often, this obscure rule would become more important. The Turkish organizations knew how to use this rule to their advantage. Rules of the game are important, but one must know how to use them. This is the case not only in sports but also in politics.

The Dutch system of party ranking stands in sharp contrast to American practice. An American candidate need only receive the most votes in a district. This voter support often depends only slightly on the candidate's party loyalty, and sometimes it is even advantageous for an American candidate to demonstrate some independence from the official platform of his or her party.

The lack of party discipline in the United States, however, cannot be due solely to the system of election, because Great Britain combines the same winner-take-all system with a fairly high party discipline. Although it is certainly true that party list PR as practiced in the Netherlands contributes to strong party discipline, it is not true that strong party discipline is impossible under a winner-take-all system. Whether party discipline is strong or weak in a winner-take-all system also depends on other factors—in particular, on whether a country has a presidential or a parliamentary system of government. As noted, Great Britain has a parliamentary system, and in such systems the formation of a government and the vote of confidence in parliament strengthen party discipline, as we will see in Chapter 4. In the absence of a parliamentary system, the United States can afford low party discipline. Thus, the winner-take-all electoral system, in combination with the absence of a parliamentary system, explains to a large extent why American political parties have low party discipline.

In the Netherlands, party list PR has contributed to a diverse **multiparty system**, because small fringe parties have a chance of winning parliamentary representation. As we will see in Chapter 11, the first free Polish election organized according to pure proportionality led to an even more diverse party system than in the Netherlands. In this context, we can report an interesting research finding by Lawrence Ezrow.[7] If we look at the average policy position in a party system with proportionality, this position is usually quite close to the center. To be sure, there may be some extreme parties, but most parties take a position quite close to the center. Therefore, taking all parties together, it is wrong to say that proportionality necessarily leads to extremisms in politics. Emphasizing that this is not true, Ezrow has in the title of his paper the phrase "the dog that didn't bark."

With an electoral system of pure proportionality, in the United States any group receiving as little as 0.25 percent of votes cast would win a seat in the U.S. House of Representatives (1 out of 435 seats). How many groups could receive at least so much support? How many votes could a party win stressing environmental issues, as the Green Party does?

The introduction of party list PR in the United States might allow the election of representatives from a great variety of parties. Under such a system, congressional membership would more closely reflect the diversity of the American population, and many voters would find a party closer to their preferences than under the current two-party system of Democrats and Republicans. What would be the major disadvantages of using a PR system for American congressional elections? Americans often say they would miss voting for a particular candidate whom they know personally and consider to be their own representative. This weakness, however, can be remedied without abandoning the principle of proportionality. Party list PR as practiced in the Netherlands is not the only way to implement the principle of proportionality. More personalized forms of proportionality are also feasible. We turn next to Switzerland, Ireland, and Germany as illustrations of more personalized systems of PR.

PERSONALIZED PROPORTIONAL REPRESENTATION: SWITZERLAND, IRELAND, AND GERMANY

Switzerland

For the election of the National Council, the lower house of parliament, the Swiss modify party list PR in two important ways. Both modifications have the consequence of personalizing relations between voters and candidates. The first Swiss modification is that rather than a single, national electoral district, they have 26 electoral districts corresponding to the 26 Swiss Cantons. The 200 National Council seats are divided among the Cantons according to population. The largest Canton, Zürich, elects 34 representatives and the smallest Canton only one. The parties submit candidate lists in each Canton containing the names of their candidates for that Canton's seats. The results are counted separately for each Canton.

Having 26 electoral districts instead of a single national district works against the smaller parties. If Switzerland were treated as a single electoral district, only one-half of 1 percent of the vote would be needed to win 1 of the 200 National Council seats. With elections taking place in 26 separate districts, however, a higher percentage of votes is needed to win. In Zürich, a party must win about 3 percent of the vote to win 1 of the Canton's 34 seats. In a Canton with 10 seats, 10 percent is necessary to receive 1 seat. In the small Cantons with only one seat, the party with the most votes wins the seat. Thus, if the number of seats per district is reduced to one, the proportionality system becomes a system of winner-take-all.

If this system were applied to the United States, the 50 states could be the electoral districts, and within each state the congressional delegation would be elected according to PR. In this way, some of the disadvantages of pure PR could be alleviated. Very small parties would be able to win seats only in the largest states, such as California and New York.

The second Swiss modification is that the voters, not the parties, rank the candidates. The parties merely submit a list of names without rank. The voters do not actually rank the candidates in the sense of first rank, second rank, third rank, and so on. They can merely decide for each candidate whether (1) to leave the candidate unchanged a single time on the list, (2) to put the candidate on the list a second time, or (3) to drop the candidate from the list. The only condition is that the overall number of names on the list of each voter is not greater than the number of seats to be elected from the Canton. A voter also can decide to make no changes at all to the list. In this case, no preference is given to any of the candidates, but the ballot counts for the number of seats attributed to the party.

Voters may further complicate their list by writing in candidates from other parties. Thus, a Socialist voter may put a Free Democratic candidate on his or her list, either once or twice. With this write-in possibility, computation of the results becomes complicated. In the example just given, the Free Democratic **write-in candidate** counts for the Free Democratic Party and detracts from the Socialist Party's strength; the voter has split his or her vote between the two parties. Voters can go even further and write in candidates from as many parties as they wish, but again, the total number of names on their list is not allowed to exceed the number of seats in the Canton. Given this election system, candidates like to be put on the top of their party lists, but the reason is different from the Netherlands (see the previous section). If Swiss voters must drop candidates from the lists because they have written in other candidates twice, they have a tendency to cut candidates at the end of the lists. Therefore, candidates at the top of the lists have a certain advantage.

The computation of the results proceeds, in principle, in the same manner as in the Netherlands. First, for each Canton, the number of seats each party receives is determined. Second, candidates win these seats in order of their ranking. This ranking is based on the number of times a candidate's name appears on all the lists, including write-ins on other parties' lists.

The freedom of choice that the voter has in the Swiss system weakens the party's control over its candidates, and thus party discipline is as low as in the United States. Although a Swiss party still controls whether or not a candidate gets listed, it cannot influence a candidate's chances of election through rank on the list. Once candidates are listed, they are on their own and must try to get a maximum number of voters to write them in twice and a minimum to cross them out. Although this system gives great power to the electorate, it also increases the influence of interest groups. These groups inform their members about the candidates who favor their interests and for whom two votes should be cast, as well as about candidates who should be crossed out because they do not favor the group's interests. A teachers' group, for example, will inform its members which candidates are sympathetic to teachers' needs and which are not. Letters are sent out by a large number of groups ranging from businesspeople to fishing workers. Candidates depend on political parties only for getting listed on the ballot; to be elected, they then must obtain the support of a large number of different interest groups.

The Swiss still vote for party lists, but their electoral system allows them to express preferences for and against particular candidates. The election also takes place in relatively small districts, where voters feel more at home than in a single national district. These factors together personalize the relations between voters and candidates. We discuss the party structure in the Swiss parliament in the next chapter in connection with cabinet formation in Switzerland.

Ireland

Personalized PR also can be attained through the **single transferable vote** (STV) system, as practiced in the Republic of Ireland. Although Ireland is the only European country using this system, it is worth discussing because some local U.S. communities use the system, and there are efforts to use it more widely in the United States (see the end of this section). The reason this electoral system is called STV should become clear as we proceed. Ireland's parliament, with a total of 166 seats, is elected from 43 districts, with the number of seats per district ranging from three to five. In each district, voters rank the candidates in order of preference, for example, candidate A rank number 1, candidate B rank number 2, and so on. To be elected, a candidate needs a quota of the total votes according to the so-called Droop formula:

$$\frac{\text{total valid votes}}{\text{seats} + 1} + 1 = \text{quota}$$

With four seats in a district and 100,000 valid votes, the required quota is 100,000 divided by 5 + 1 = 20,001. When the counting of the ballots begins, at first only the first rankings on the ballots are considered. Let us assume that based on these first rankings only candidate A reaches the quota. He or she is, therefore, already declared elected. In the further counting, still only first rankings are considered. What happens with the ballots on which candidate A ranks number 1? Obviously he or she does not need these ballots anymore, so they are transferred to the second-ranked candidates on the respective ballots. Let us now assume that thanks to such transfers candidate B reached the quota, too, and is, therefore, declared elected. In the further counting there are ballots on which candidates A and B take the first two ranks and, of course, they do not need these ballots anymore. According to the logic of STV, these ballots are transferred to the third-ranked candidates. As the counting continues further, candidate C also reaches the quota and is declared elected. If the district has four seats to allocate, the counting continues and the ballots with candidates A, B, and C in the top positions go to the fourth-ranked candidate. If the fourth seat cannot be allocated in this way, the candidate with the lowest number of votes is eliminated and his or her votes are transferred to the candidate highest on the respective ballot. If the fourth seat is still not allocated, the candidate with the second-lowest number of votes is eliminated and his or her votes are transferred, and so on.

A practical example of the 2007 elections in the district of Dublin Central shall illustrate the system. Four seats were to be filled, and there were 13 candidates running. The prime minister, Bertie Ahern, was running in this district and had the most first preferences with 12,734 voters ranking him in first place, and since the quota according to the Droop formula for this district was 6,928, Ahern was declared elected. No other candidate reached the quota in the first counting. Tony Gregory had 4,649 first preferences, and Joe Costello 4,353. In the further counting, both reached the quota thanks to transfers, and they, too, were declared elected. The fourth seat went to Cyprian Brady, who was only ninth with regard to first preferences since a mere 939 voters ranked him first. But Brady had so many voters ranking him second, third, and so on that he was still elected. His case illustrates nicely how with the STV system not only first ranks count. Ahern and Brady are both of Fianna Fáil party, Costello is an independent, and Gregory is of the Labour party. Thus, not only two parties are competitive.

The system works like runoffs, in which voters are called to the ballot a second time. With STV, however, voters make their choices in a single ballot, hence the term *single* transferable vote. One problem still remains—namely, the potential for abuse in the sense that the election officials could count the ballots in an order so that the votes for particular candidates are transferred. Different rules exist to prevent such abuse and to make the system work as randomly as possible, but the potential for abuse nevertheless exists.

What are the optimal strategies for candidates within an STV system? The electoral game is certainly much more complex and subtle than with winner-take-all, where one simply needs more votes than any other candidate. With STV a candidate may do well even if he or she is not the first choice of many voters but is ranked second or third—perhaps even fourth or fifth—by a large number of people. On the other hand, candidates are likely to attain a bad election result if, other than a core of dedicated supporters, candidates do not have many other voters willing to rank them. As Michael Gallagher summarizes, "A candidate with relatively little first-preference support but with wide acceptability to many voters may fare better in terms of seats than one with more hard-core support but with little ability to attract lower preferences from supporters of other parties or candidates."[8]

Figure 3.5 shows that for the 2011 election the STV had a proportional effect on the distribution of seats, in the sense that the smaller parties also

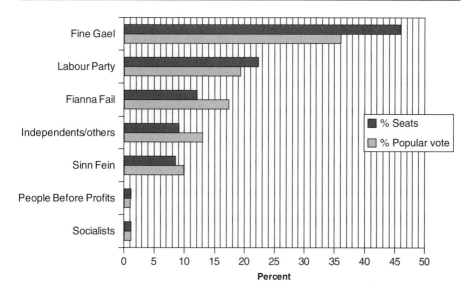

FIGURE 3.5

Voter support and percentage of parliamentary seats in the 2011 general elections to the Irish parliament (Dail Eireann).

Source: Electionsireland.org, February 25, 2011.

received representation. Even candidates running as Independents received 13 seats. Thus, although candidate-centered, STV does not work as much against smaller parties as the winner-take-all system. Fianna Fáil and Fine Gael have both grown out of the Irish struggle for independence and are both conservative in orientation. Fianna Fáil was for a long time the leading party but was severely punished in the 2011 election for mishandling the financial crisis, going down from 78 to merely 20 seats. The STV system has strong supporters. Election expert Enid Lakeman states, "STV will force [the voter] to recognize that there are degrees of excellence among the candidates of his preferred party and will further invite him to consider candidates of other parties and indicate any with whom he has a measure of agreement."[9] With regard to the United States, experts on electoral systems agree that a change from the current winner-take-all system to the principle of proportionality would only be possible if the new system were based not on party lists but on the STV system. An advocate of STV for America, George H. Hallett Jr., argues that "it can transform our legislative elections from contests to win all the spoils of victory for one group and keep other people out to invitations to all citizens to come in and take part in a great cooperative democracy."[10] Hallett even expects that STV eventually may be required by the courts in the United States, because it gives adequate representation to such minorities as Hispanics and African Americans. The STV system is not unknown in the United States. In New York City, for example, the local school boards are elected according to this system; in Cambridge, Massachusetts, the city council is elected in this manner.

Germany

Germany uses yet another system of **personalized proportional representation**. Its main feature is that each German voter has two votes on his or her ballot—the so-called first and second vote. The first vote is according to winner-take-all in single districts; the second for party list proportionality. Surveys indicate that most German voters do not fully understand how their complicated electoral system operates. Whether or not it is understood, however, the system's results have been reasonable compared to the extreme party fragmentation of the pre-Hitler Weimar Republic. In the Bundestag, the lower house of parliament, there are two major parties, the Christian Democrats and the Social Democrats, but some smaller parties also have representation. Very tiny parties, however, are excluded from parliamentary representation. As we will see in Chapter 11, Hungarian voters have two votes, as in Germany: one according to winner-take-all in single districts and the other for party list proportionality. In Hungary the votes are counted independently of each other, whereas in Germany the counting of the two votes is linked in a complex way that needs some explanation.

When the constitution of the Federal Republic of Germany—then West Germany—was written in 1949, the Western powers, especially Great Britain and the United States, urged the adoption of a winner-take-all system that they hoped would prevent severe party fragmentation. Many German leaders argued, however, that a winner-take-all system could not adequately represent the political diversity of the country. As political scientist Kathleen Bawn argues, there were also strong domestic political pressures against a winner-take-all system.[11] The Social Democrats had, at the time, slightly less voter support than the Christian Democrats and feared that a winner-take-all system would allow the Christian Democrats to win an absolute majority in parliament and to govern alone. To prevent such an outcome, the Social Democrats enlisted the support of the Free Democrats and other smaller parties, which, out of self-interest, were also against the winner-take-all system. In the crucial vote in the body enacting the electoral law, the winner-take-all system was defeated 36:28 against the opposition of the Christian Democrats. As Bawn comments, the selection of the German election system shows "that the political aspect of institutional choice is important.... Electoral systems can be explained as a social choice, affected by the interests of the participants and by the institutions that structure the choice"[12]

The solution enacted was to elect one-half of the Bundestag by the winner-take-all system and the other half by PR. Each voter votes twice, once in the winner-take-all election and once in the PR election. The former is called the voter's first vote; the latter, his or her second vote. Both votes are cast the same day, on the same ballot. For the first, or winner-take-all, vote the country is divided into small electoral districts that correspond in number to half of the parliamentary seats. In each district the candidate with the most votes is elected. For the proportional part of the election, the Germans use party list PR, with the candidate ranking done by the parties. The electoral districts are the individual German *Länder* (states), such as Hamburg, Bavaria, and Saxony.

Voters are allowed to split their two votes. In the winner-take-all election, they may vote for one party and in the party list PR election, for another. This provision creates the opportunity for highly sophisticated voting behavior. Supporters of the small Free Democratic Party might cast their first vote for a candidate of one of the two large parties, knowing that their own candidate has virtually no chance of winning the winner-take-all election, but they can still cast their second vote for their own *party* list. Supporters of a large party may return the favor, voting with their second vote for the party list of a minor party, especially if the two parties plan to enter a governmental coalition after the elections. Such strategic voting is empirically demonstrated in a recent study by Thomas Gschwend.[13] The crucial point of the system is that only the second vote determines the total number of seats a party gets in parliament. Each party receives the same proportion of seats as its nationwide proportion of second votes, making the German system very proportional. With the first vote, the voters merely determine which candidate should represent their specific district. The elected candidates are then subtracted from the total number of seats a party has gained, and the remaining seats are filled from the top of the party lists in the individual states. A hypothetical example is as follows: A party gains 33 percent of the second votes nationwide and therefore receives 33 percent of the 672 seats in the Bundestag—224 seats. The party wins 100 single districts, and the remaining 124 seats are filled from the top of the party lists in the individual states.

The fact that German voters are allowed to split their votes has the consequence that a party may win more single-district seats in a state (*Land*) than it is entitled to in this state on the basis of its support in the second votes. In such cases, the strict principle of proportionality is broken, in the sense that the party can keep as surplus mandates (*Überhangmandate*) the additional seats won in single districts. In the electoral history of Germany, the number of surplus mandates has ranged from 1 to 24, so the issue may appear to be a technicality with little significance. Max Kaase, however, makes the interesting comment that "If two parties in a coalition advise their supporters to strategically split their ballots between the two partners, or if one large party were to formally split into two parties, then a large number of surplus mandates could be artificially created." For Kaase, the issue of surplus seats "points to a definite deficiency, a fault in the present electoral system that could be used for a manipulation of the electoral outcome because it allows for different weights of individual voters."[14]

The German system also contains a provision for an **electoral threshold** against tiny parties. This threshold denies parliamentary representation to parties that win less than 5 percent of the second votes nationwide and are also unable to win three single districts. To get any parliamentary seats, one of these two criteria must be met. The threshold is defended on the grounds that parties failing to cross it are so tiny that they have no real parliamentary legitimacy. The actual electoral disadvantage for tiny parties is even greater, because voters do not expect them to cross the threshold and, therefore, tend to vote for other parties that they know will win seats. In the 2009 election, the radical right-wing party, National Democratic Party (NPD), attained only 1.8 percent of the second votes and was unable to win any single district. Therefore, it received no parliamentary representation. Tiny parties may still get representation if they are regionally concentrated. This happened in 2005 to the Party of Democratic Socialism, the former Communists in East Germany, who received their support mostly in eastern Germany. Although they did not receive 5 percent nationwide, they had three direct seats qualifying them for parliamentary representation. (The 2009 election will be analyzed in Chapter 4 in connection with cabinet formation in Germany.)

CHANGING THE ELECTORAL SYSTEM: FRANCE AND ITALY

As Kathleen Bawn has argued with the German example, electoral systems "are bargained over by parties and individuals with conflicting interests."[15] The logic of this argument is that parties and individuals may attempt to change electoral systems that no longer serve their interests. In the United States, there is occasionally talk of changing the way Congress is elected, but, practically speaking, no changes are likely to occur anytime soon. So it is interesting for American readers to see how electoral systems are actually changed. We use in this chapter France and Italy as illustrations. In Chapter 11, we will describe how Poland in the early 1990s, following the German model, introduced a 5 percent threshold in its election system of proportionality; as a consequence of this change in the election rules, the number of parties in its parliament could be reduced from 29 to 6.

France

In 1985 the French changed their double-ballot system to the principle of proportionality, but in 1986 they changed back to the **double-ballot system**. Before the 1993 election, there was talk of a renewed change to proportionality, although this time no change occurred. These events illustrate that electoral systems are not a given but are the result of the political game.

France practiced PR under its Fourth Republic (1946–1958). With the change to the Fifth Republic in 1958, General Charles de Gaulle and his supporters introduced a system whose most visible feature is that two separate elections take place a week apart; hence it is called the two-ballot system. For the purpose of parliamentary elections, France is divided into the same number of electoral districts as there are seats in the National Assembly, the lower house of the French parliament, which meets in the Palais Bourbon on the left bank of the river Seine. To be elected on the first ballot, a candidate has to receive an absolute majority (50 percent + 1) of votes cast in his or her district. In addition, a candidate's share of the vote has to constitute no less than one-fourth of registered voters. Because the first ballot usually lists candidates from several parties, there are relatively few districts where a candidate receives the votes necessary to win the election at that point. In the 2002 elections, this was the case for 58 out of 577 districts; in the 2007 elections 110 out of the same number of districts. If a second ballot is necessary, only candidates who appeared on the first ballot can be listed on the second ballot, and all candidates who receive less than 12.5 percent of the first ballot are eliminated.

At the time of the two changes to the electoral system in 1985 and 1986, the main parties of the Left were the Socialists and the Communists, and the parties of the Right were the Union for French Democracy (UDF) and the Rally for the Republic (RPR). The normal pattern in the first ballot was that candidates from all four major parties plus, in many districts, those from several minor parties also enter the competition. The main function of the first ballot is to check the voting strength of each individual party. Thus, the first ballot functions in some ways like an American primary. The main competition occurs on the one hand within the Left and on the other hand within the Right. On the Left, the question was whether the Socialist or the Communist candidate received more votes. Similarly, UDF and RPR candidates competed for the first place on the Right.

For the second ballot, the usual situation was that the weaker candidates on both the Left and the Right withdrew. The purpose of withdrawing was to increase the chance that one's side of the spectrum would win. If, for example, the UDF candidate in a district received 30 percent on the first ballot and the RPR candidate 25 percent, the chance of the Right to win could be increased if their forces were combined so that only the stronger candidate remained in competition. If the Right united behind the UDF candidate, it would be suicidal for the Left to continue the race with both a Communist and a Socialist candidate. The logic of the electoral system was for the Left, too, to withdraw its weaker candidate.

This device of voluntary withdrawals works best if, in the country as a whole, both parties on either side have about equal strength. Thus, if the RPR candidate withdrew in the previous example, this could easily be compensated for by the withdrawal of a UDF candidate in another district. The situation is more complicated when one party is clearly stronger than the other party of the same side. In the history of the Fifth Republic, this was often the situation of the Socialists vis-à-vis the Communists. In the 1981 parliamentary election, for example, the Socialists received nationally 37.8 percent voter support on the first ballot; the Communists received a mere 16.1 percent. If the Communist candidate had been required to withdraw in every district where the Socialist candidate was stronger on the first ballot, there would have been very few districts where the Communist candidate could have represented the Left on the second ballot. Recognizing this difficulty, and in an effort to ensure maximum Communist voter turnout on the second ballot, the Socialists withdrew some of their own first-ballot candidates, even though these candidates ran ahead of the Communist candidates. With the support of the Socialist voters, the Communist candidates in these districts then had a chance to win the second ballot. Which candidate withdrew in a particular district was decided in negotiations between national and local party headquarters. The goal of this political maneuvering was to ensure that both sides got parliamentary seats in approximately the same proportion as their national strength on the first ballot.

Sometimes, however, this goal was not attained because voters did not follow the recommendations of their party leaders. This was especially a problem for the Communist Party, which was considered by many Socialist voters as too extreme. As a consequence, such voters often did not follow their party leaders' recommendations and abstained on the second ballot or even voted for the candidate of the Right. This mechanism can be demonstrated by comparing the seats received by the Communist Party in the 1981 election with its voter support in the first ballot. Although the voter support was 16.1 percent, the party received only 9.1 percent of the seats. For Domenico Fisichella, "The general conclusion that emerges from the French experience is that its Communist party is always—and almost always to a marked extent—underrepresented under the double-ballot system."[16] The Socialists, on the other hand, profited from the Communist support in the second ballot and received 59.3 percent of the seats, although their voter support in the first ballot was "only" 37.8 percent. This discussion shows that the French double-ballot system demands a great amount of skill on the part of the political parties and their leaders. The game has to be played very differently on the two ballots. On the first ballot, the main competition is within the coalition of the Left and within the coalition of the Right; on the second ballot, the competition changes to a battle between the Left and the Right.

Why did the French change in 1985 from the double-ballot system to proportionality? It was the Socialist Party—in particular its leader, François Mitterrand—who pushed for the change. Why did the Socialists replace an electoral system from which they so obviously had benefited? The answer is that the electoral situation had greatly changed since 1981, and the Socialists feared that they would be hurt by the double-ballot system in the 1986 election. Opinion surveys and local elections had revealed such a loss of voter support for both Socialists and Communists that the parties of the Right were expected to take over control of the National Assembly. This situation would be difficult for Mitterrand, whose first term as president did not end until 1988. As we will see in Chapter 4, a French president under the Fifth Republic has much power, and Mitterrand used this power to pass the change in the electoral system in parliament.

Mitterrand hoped that PR would increase the number of parties in the National Assembly, thus making the parliamentary situation more fluid and allowing him and his party more room to maneuver. This is exactly what happened in the March 1986 election. Splinter parties of the Right distracted so much voter strength from the RPR and the UDF that the two parties' combined seats fell short of an absolute majority in the National Assembly. The two parties were particularly hurt by the entry of 35 members of the right-wing National Front to parliament. Immediately after the 1986 election, the newly elected parliament changed the electoral rules back to the double-ballot system. This time, the push came from the RPR and the UDF. They did not like the fact that the National Front could challenge them at the extreme Right. Returning to the double-ballot system was anticipated to weaken the National Front, which indeed it did. When, after the 1988 presidential election, early parliamentary elections were called, the National Front virtually disappeared from parliament, although it remained at about the same level in voter strength. In the 1988 election, the Socialists had recovered their 1981 voter strength, but before the 1993 election they were back in deep electoral trouble. Once again, there was talk that Mitterrand might change the electoral system back to proportionality. But this time no change occurred, mainly because, contrary to 1985, the Socialists had no majority in the National Assembly to ram through a change in the electoral law. The 1993 elections were then a real catastrophe for the Socialists. Not only did their voter support in the first ballot drop from 37.6 percent to 17.6 percent but also their parliamentary representation had nearly a free fall from 280 to 53 seats. This severe drop in seats was clearly a result of the double-ballot system. Had the electoral system been changed to proportionality, the Socialists also would have lost many seats, but with 17.6 percent voter support they still would have kept about 100 seats (17.6 percent of 577 seats). A useful measure of **electoral distortion** might be simply the difference between the percentages of seats minus the popular vote percentages. The larger that number, the larger the electoral distortion. France in the 1980s and early 1990s has given us a nice illustration of how changes in electoral rules influence election results. In recent years, France has stayed with the double-ballot system. We will discuss the recent results for parliamentary elections in connection with presidential elections in Chapter 4.

Italy

Italy changed its electoral system in 1993 from party list proportionality to a mixed system, with 75 percent of the members of parliament being elected by winner-take-all in single districts and 25 percent by party list proportionality in regional districts. In 2005, the electoral system was changed back to proportionality. What was behind these changes, and did they have the desired effects? After the Fascist dictatorship under Benito Mussolini, Italy established a democracy but did not manage to arrive at much governmental stability, as we will see in Chapter 4. Part of the problem was the large number of parties that emerged under the electoral system of PR. In the last election before the end of the Cold War, 14 parties were represented in the Chamber of Deputies, the lower house of parliament.

The end of the Cold War changed Italian politics in a fundamental way. Gone was the fear of a Soviet-inspired Communist takeover. The Italian Communist Party changed its name to Democratic Party of the Left, but a faction split and created its own Reform Communist Party. In the 1992 parliamentary election, the Democratic Party of the Left received 16.1 percent of the votes, and the Reform Communists received 5.6 percent (Figure 3.6). Combined, this was 21.7 percent, down from the 26.6 percent that the old Communist Party received in the 1987 election. The Christian Democrats were also down from 34.3 percent to 29.7 percent. Down also were the Socialists as the third-largest party, from 14.3 percent to 13.6 percent. The great winner of 1992 was the Northern League, a merger of the Lombard

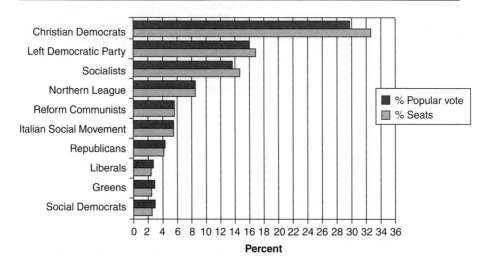

FIGURE 3.6

Voter support and percent of parliamentary seats in the 1992 election to the Italian Chamber of Deputies.

Source: Keesing's Record of World Events 38 [London: Longman, 1992, page 38870].

League and other Leagues in the north of Italy. It increased its voter support from 0.5 percent to 8.7 percent. Although a regional party of the north, it is also a protest party with some closeness to the New Radical Right (discussed in Chapter 2).

After the 1992 elections, government instability continued in the usual manner. This lack of positive change, combined with the discovery of several bribery scandals involving the highest levels of Italian politics, began to shake up the situation. In this shake-up the instrument of the popular referendum was of key importance. Reform-minded men and women, under the leadership of Mario Segni, who had left his Christian Democratic Party, collected enough signatures to put several changes in the Italian political system to a popular vote. The most important proposal was to change the electoral rules for the Senate, the upper house of parliament. Seventy-five percent of the senators would be elected by winner-take-all, while for the remaining 25 percent, party list proportionality would continue to be used. The expectation was that linking the senators closer to the voters would cut down on corruption because voters could more easily vote corrupt politicians out of office. It was also hoped that the new electoral system would cut down on the number of parties in the Senate. The change in the electoral rules was overwhelmingly accepted in the referendum, with 82 percent voting yes. After the results were in, there were celebrations in the streets. Commentators spoke of a new beginning, the end of the old Italian Republic, and the beginning of a Second Republic (see Box 3.1).

After the referendum, parliament extended the new electoral system to the Chamber of Deputies, and new elections for both houses of parliament were

BOX 3.1 ITALIANS GIVE BIG SUPPORT TO NEW WAY OF POLITICS

ROME—In a striking repudiation of the political order, Italy's voters gave overwhelming support Monday to plans to dismantle the postwar electoral system that many Italians blame for chronic corruption and a succession of weak and unstable governments.

After two days of voting in a landmark referendum, Italians demonstrated their desire for profound change by approving the direct election of most senators and a ban on government financing of political parties. They also voted to abolish ministries for state industry, tourism and agriculture, which in recent years had become notorious havens of patronage ... "This result shows the country's enormous will for change," said Mario Segni, the maverick Christian Democrat who broke with his party and organized the referendum. ■

Source: International Herald Tribune, April 20, 1993.

held in March 1994. Each voter had two votes, one for the winner-take-all part of the election, the other for the proportionality part.

In the weeks before the national elections, the Italian party system was in real turmoil. The Christian Democrats changed their name to Italian Popular Party. New parties were created, some parties merged, and others split. Mario Segni, the key organizer of the referenda on political reforms, initiated a party called Pact for Italy. Silvio Berlusconi, a wealthy businessman and owner of the famous soccer club A.C. Milano, founded the party Forza Italia, the expression used to cheer on Italian national sports teams ("go Italy, go!"). The Italian Social Movement also renamed itself as the National Alliance. Among all parties there was great uncertainty about how best to compete under the new election system. For the winner-take-all part, electoral alliances had to be formed in order to increase the chances of winning districts. But with whom and with what exact commitments? There was still one-quarter of the seats to be filled by proportionality, and for this part of the election, strategies other than those used for the winner-take-all part had to be used.

Let us begin the analysis of the election results with the proportionality part for the Chamber of Deputies. Here, a threshold of 4 percent of the votes had been introduced as necessary in order to receive any representation at all. Seven parties were able to cross this threshold: Forza Italia with 21 percent, Democratic Party of the Left with 20.4 percent, National Alliance with 13.5 percent, Popular Party with 11.1 percent, Northern League with 8.4 percent, Reform Communists with 6 percent, and Pact for Italy with 4.6 percent. The newcomer, Forza Italia, only two months old, was the big winner. Another big winner was the National Alliance, which increased its voter share since the previous election from 5.6 to 13.5 percent. The Democratic Party of the Left and the Reform Communists, the two descendants of the Communist Party, both slightly increased their share of the votes—the Democratic Party of the Left from 16.1 percent to 20.4 percent, the Reform Communists from 5.6 percent to 6.0 percent. Thus, together the former Communists reached 26.4 percent, again coming close to their best results in the past. The Northern League stagnated and dropped slightly from 8.7 percent to 8.4 percent. The Pact for Italy of Mario Segni attained a disappointing 4.6 percent of the votes. The big losers were the former Christian Democrats who, despite their name change to Popular Party, dropped from 29.7 percent to 11.1 percent. The Socialists of former prime minister Bettino Craxi, now under indictment, did not even reach the threshold of 4 percent.

If the elections had been held according to proportionality entirely, as in all previous elections since World War II, the story would end here. Under the new election law, three-quarters of the deputies were elected in single districts according to the winner-take-all principle. For this part of the elections quite a different game was played. Whereas each party campaigned for itself in the proportionality part, the winner-take-all part necessitated electoral alliances. Because in single districts only winning counts and there are no rewards for being second, third, and so on, the Italian parties tried to form broad-based electoral alliances. Three such alliances emerged, one each at the Left, the Center, and the Right. The electoral alliance of the Left consisted of the Democratic Party of the Left, the Reform Communists, the Greens, and some other leftist parties. The electoral alliance of the Center brought together the Popular Party and Pact for Italy. At the Right, an electoral alliance was forged among Forza Italia, the Northern League, the National Alliance, and some other rightist parties.

The purpose of the electoral alliances was to unite behind a single candidate in each district and thus increase the chances of winning the district. The Right, for example, would have a candidate of Forza Italia in one district, of the Northern League in another district, of the National Alliance in a third district. The distribution of the districts within each electoral alliance led to much bickering. The electoral alliances were also unable or unwilling to establish common programs. It is important to understand that the three alliances were formed for purely tactical electoral purposes and lacked internal unity.

It is clear that the new electoral system did not have the desired effect of reducing the number of parties in parliament. As a columnist for the Italian newspaper *La Stampa* put it the day after the elections: "Behind the great change, there was to be seen the usual Italian political uncertainty, unstable if not ungovernable, seeking only cease-fires or revenge."[17] In Italy, the great fragmentation of the party system was too much ingrained for a change in the electoral system to have any significant influence on the number of parties.

In the wake of the 2001 elections, a certain simplification in the party system took place in the sense that two moderate blocs emerged. At the center-right is the "House of Freedoms" (Casa delle Libertà) consisting of Forza Italia, the National Alliance, the Christian Democratic Center, and the Northern League. At the center-left is the "Olive Tree Alliance" consisting of the Democrats of the Left, the Daisy Democracy, the Italian Democratic Socialists and Greens, the Party of the Italian Communists, and the New Socialist Party of Italy.

The Reformed Communists and two regional parties belonged to neither of the two blocs.

If the intent of changing the electoral law was to reduce the number of parties, that goal was only partly achieved. The number of parties winning more than 4 percent in the proportionality part of the election was indeed reduced to five as compared to eight in the 1996 election. Nevertheless, given that 75 percent of the seats are allocated on the basis of winner-take-all, it is remarkable that there were still 12 parties represented in the Italian Chamber of Deputies.

This highlights an important issue: The number of parties, while often-times driven by the electoral system, is not necessarily *only* driven by it. It also depends on the number of cleavages in a society. A society with many cleavages might have many parties in parliament even though the electoral system is winner-take-all. Conversely, it is possible that a country with PR might be divided only along one dimension. As a result, there might only be two or three parties represented even though PR is in force. A prime example of such a society is Austria after World War II and throughout the mid-1980s.

In the French case, we have seen how politicians attempt to change the electoral system in order to maximize their chances to win the next election. Italy can now also be added to this list. In the fall of 2005, seven months before the next general election, the ruling Center-Right coalition, under the leadership of Silvio Berlusconi, pushed through a plan to change the current electoral system (75 percent of seats based on SMD, and 25 percent based on PR). On October 14, the lower house of parliament, in which the Center-Right coalition had an absolute majority, supported Berlusconi's bill to introduce an electoral system in which 100 percent of the seats are allocated on the basis of PR. With passage of this bill into law, Italy came full circle from having an electoral system based on 100 percent PR for all seats until 1994, when the first national elections were held under the then-new electoral system (75 percent of seats based on SMD, 25 percent on proportionality). Now, 11 years later, Berlusconi had managed to change the electoral system back to 100 percent PR, to the bitter dismay of opposition parties, in an obvious attempt to win the next election (see Box 3.2). Since 2005 Italy has stayed with proportionality. We will discuss the country's most recent election results in Chapter 4 in the context of cabinet formation.

The cases of France and Italy have raised the question of whether it is proper for politicians to change electoral rules in their favor. In sports it is certainly not allowed to change rules during a game. Who should have the authority to change electoral rules—parliament, the voters, the courts, a combination of the three? Is a political game ever over like a sports game, so that one can change the rules for future games, or is politics an ever-continuing game? Should the new rules come into effect only when the politicians making the new rules have left office? Or should there be a waiting period of, say, 10 years until the new rules take effect? France and Italy provide fertile ground on which to discuss these questions.

BOX 3.2   SILVIO BERLUSCONI'S PARLIAMENTARY GAMES

What to do when polls show you might lose the next election? If you're Italian Prime Minister Silvio Berlusconi, you just change the rules. He's on a legislative rampage and more changes are just around the corner. . . . On October 13, his coalition passed a major electoral reform which critics say was intended to improve Berlusconi's chances in April [2006]. Under the bill, the next elections, slated for next spring, would be based on a system of proportional representation. This would mean voters would choose party lists rather than individual candidates. Essentially, it reverses a 1993 change to the electoral system which sought to fix an Italian democratic state which saw 51 government changes in 47 postwar years. . . . Berlusconi was lukewarm about the legislation at first, agreeing to it only to save his coalition. But then the prime minister had his market researchers check out their computer programs and data bases. After testing various models, they concluded that Berlusconi's only chance to capture a majority in next year's elections would be under electoral laws heavily based on proportional representation. ∎

Source: Spiegel Online, October 21, 2005.

VOTER TURNOUT

Voter turnout in Europe is generally much higher than in the United States, usually in the 70, 80, or even 90 percent range. Why is there so much more interest in parliamentary elections in Europe than in the United States? Many factors come into play, such as differences in the system for voter registration, size of the countries, and education. In the context of the present chapter, it is interesting to discuss the possible influence of electoral rules on voter turnout. Generally speaking, electoral rules as used in Europe give the voter more influence on the outcome of parliamentary elections than in the United States. In many U.S. congressional districts, the incumbent is so firmly established that a challenger has little chance to win. Often, competition works only when there is no incumbent or for a first-term incumbent. Even if a district is truly contested, voters with somewhat extreme views may feel left out because both the Democratic and Republican candidates tend to run on a platform that is pretty much in the middle. If a voter has a Green preference, for example, he or she may not feel represented by either candidate and may stay home.

In parliamentary elections in Europe, it is not so unrealistic that a few dozen votes may make a difference. In a proportional election system, getting just a small number of extra votes may secure an additional seat for a party. Why do the British have a much higher turnout than the Americans, although both practice the winner-take-all in single districts? Contrary to the United States, Great Britain has a parliamentary, not presidential, system for selecting its executive. As a consequence, as we see in the next chapter, party discipline in parliament is much more important, and this, in turn, helps to mobilize voters on election day. In this chapter we have seen how voter preferences are translated into parliamentary seats, and we have encountered a wide variety of electoral rules. Such variation does not occur randomly but has to be seen in a historical context. Those who make the rules have the power. Rules are also important once a parliament is elected and begins to operate. In the next chapter, we turn to these internal operations of European parliaments and, in particular, to the selection of cabinets out of their midst. There is evidence that PR systems tend to buoy voter turnout. Peter Selb has found "overwhelming evidence" that proportionality helps voter turnout. He then goes further and asks why this is so, testing two hypotheses.[18] One argument is that proportionality leads to a higher number of parties, which in turn helps voter turnout. Empirical data reject this hypothesis, and a high number of parties even has the tendency to depress voter turnout. By contrast, the hypothesis is holding up that safe seats in winner-take-all systems give few incentives for voters to turn out, an argument that we have already made at the beginning of this section with regard to the United States.

This chapter contained a lot of technical information about parliamentary election systems in Europe. This information should not be memorized for its own sake. Students should be challenged to understand how election systems are man-made and can be changed with different impacts on the party systems.

KEY TERMS

anticipatory effects   67
double-ballot system   80
electoral distortion   83
electoral districts   66
electoral threshold   79
multiparty systems   72

party list   71
personalized proportional
   representation   78
plurality   65
proportional
   representation   70

single transferable
   vote   75
unimodal
   distribution   68
winner-take-all   65
write-in candidate   74

DISCUSSION QUESTIONS

1. Calculate the index of "electoral distortion" (percent of popular votes minus percent of seats) for the largest parties in the Netherlands. Is it higher or lower than in the United Kingdom or France? Why? Electoral rules such as the difference between PR and winner-take-all raise fundamental issues of what "representation" actually means. Which of the two systems do you think is more representative? In single-member districts, how can a voter's views be represented if he or she does not share the ideology of the lone representative? Conversely, how can somebody in a PR system be responsive to the needs of individuals in a particular area if that individual ended up in parliament by virtue of having been listed high on the party list?

2. Designing electoral rules raises the crucial question of what "representation" should mean? What do you think "representation" actually means?

3. Which system, proportional representation (PR) or single-member district (SMD), contributes more to what you understand by "representation"?

4. In SMD, how can a voter's view be represented if he or she does not share the ideology of the lone incumbent?

NOTES

1. Giovanni Sartori. *Parties and Party Systems* (Cambridge, MA: Cambridge University Press, 1976).
2. Maurice Duverger. *Political Parties. Their Organization and Activities in the Modern State* (London: Wiley, 1965).
3. Ivor Crewe. Why Labour Lost the British Election. *Public Opinion* 6 (June/July 1983): 60.
4. Hans Riedwyl and Jürg Steiner. What Is Proportionality Anyhow? *Comparative Politics* 27 (April 1995): 357–369.
5. Jay K. Dow. Party-System Extremism in Majoritarian and Proportional Election Systems. *British Journal of Political Science* 41 (2011): 3441–3461.
6. Parties submit different lists in different administrative districts. These lists are then linked at the national level.
7. Lawrence Ezrow. Parties' Policy Programmes and the Dog that Didn't Bark: No Evidence that Proportional Systems Promote Extreme Party Positions. *British Journal of Political Science* 38 (July 2008): 479–497.
8. Michael Gallagher. Comparing Proportional Representation Electoral Systems: Quotas, Thresholds, Paradoxes and Majorities. *British Journal of Political Science* 22 (October 1992): 480.
9. Enid Lakeman. The Case for Proportional Representation. In Arend Lijphart and Bernard Grofman, eds, *Choosing an Electoral System: Issues and Alternatives* (New York: Praeger, 1984, 49).
10. George H. Hallett. Jr. Proportional Representation with the Single Transferable Vote: A Basic Requirement for Legislative Elections. In Arend Lijphart and Bernard Grofman, eds, *Choosing an Electoral System* (New York: Praeger, 1984, 125).
11. Kathleen Bawn. The Logic of Institutional Preferences: German Electoral Law as a Social Choice Outcome. *American Journal of Political Science* 37 (November 1993): 965–989.
12. Ibid., 987–988.
13. Thomas Gschwend. Ticket-splitting and Strategic Voting under Mixed Electoral Rules: Evidence from Germany. *European Journal of Political Research* 46, no. 1 (January 2007): 1–23.
14. Ibid., 163–164.
15. Bawn, The Logic of Institutional Preferences: German Electrical Law as a Social Science Outcome, 965.
16. Domenico Fisichella. The Double-Ballot System as a Weapon against Anti-System Parties. In Arend Lijphart and Bernard Grofman, eds, *Choosing an Electoral System* (New York: Praeger, 1984, 183).
17. Quoted in the *New York Times,* March 30, 1994.
18. Peter Selb. A Deeper Look at the Proportionality-Turnout Nexus. *Comparative Political Studies* 42, no. 4 (April 2009): 527–548.

From Legislative to Executive Authority: Cabinet Formation and Heads of State

So, free and fair elections have happened, the votes went through the strainer of various electoral systems, and parties have received various numbers of seats. However, no government has been formed yet. At this point, all we have are allocations of seats to various parties in the respective houses of parliament, that is, the legislators or lawmakers. The crucial question that emerges at this point is, How do we move from legislative authority to executive authority, which is what governments are? In other words, how are governments made? Having described in Chapter 3 how parliaments are elected and how they work, we turn now to the rules for cabinet formation. We need to understand that most European democracies have a **parliamentary system** in which the cabinet with a **prime minister** or chancellor at its head is appointed by the parliament. Besides the prime minister or chancellor, there are individual cabinet members responsible for foreign affairs, national defense, education, agriculture, and so on. There are also some **semipresidential systems** with a president elected by the people and a prime minister appointed by parliament. We will illustrate such systems with the case of France. At the level of the European Union (EU), we have neither a parliamentary nor a semipresidential system but a very complex interplay among the European Parliament, the European Commission, the European Council, and the Council of Ministers, all to be explained in Chapter 14.

Sometimes parliamentary systems are unstable, but we will show that this is by far not always the case. In fact, cabinet formation may take many different forms, and we will illustrate this with examples from Great Britain, Germany, Switzerland, Sweden, Italy, and France. In the United States, the president, as head of the executive branch, holds also the symbolic role of head of state. In Europe this is different—the prime minister or chancellor is not head of state; this role belongs to a monarch or a civilian president.

In the United States, the relationship between the legislative and executive branches of government is characterized by a system of checks and balances. The president, as chief executive, is elected not by Congress but directly by the people—if we disregard the aspect of the Electoral College. Congress cannot oust the president with a vote of no-confidence. The only exception, impeachment, is very different from a vote of no-confidence. On the other hand, the president cannot dissolve Congress and call for early elections.

Most European democracies have a parliamentary system with rules that are fundamentally different from those of the American presidential system. The most important characteristic of the parliamentary system is that the executive is selected by the parliament and depends on the confidence of parliament for survival. The voters elect their parliament, which is, therefore, the sole body that can claim to represent the will of the people in a direct way. The ways in which presidential and parliamentary systems relate voters to the legislative and executive branches of government are presented in Figure 4.1.

The executive branch in a European parliamentary system is the **cabinet,** which is headed by a prime minister whose role is very different from that of the U.S. president. (Depending on the country, the prime minister may have the title of *chancellor.*) In the United States, cabinet members are appointed by the president and serve at his pleasure. Some cabinet members may come from the Congress; however, if they accept a cabinet position, they must give up their seat in Congress.

In a parliamentary system, leading members of parliament form the cabinet. The prime minister is merely the first of the team—hence the term *prime* minister, or in Latin *primus inter pares* (first among equals). The rule is that the prime minister and the other ministers retain their seats and voting rights in parliament while serving in the cabinet. There are, however, a few exceptions to this rule.

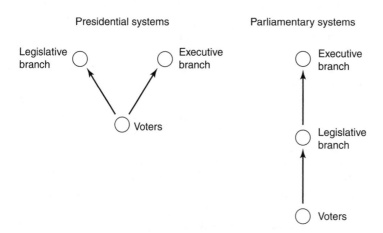

FIGURE 4.1

Relations between voters and the legislative and executive branches of government in presidential and parliamentary systems.

In Switzerland, Norway, and the Netherlands, cabinet members are required to give up their parliamentary seats. There are also exceptions to the rule that cabinet members are selected from the parliament. Especially in crisis situations, it may happen that persons with high reputations from outside parliament are asked to serve in the cabinet. This was, for example, the case in Italy during a severe crisis in 1993, when the president of Italy's central bank was called in as prime minister.

Within any particular cabinet, the prime minister's role may be stronger or weaker, depending on the individual's personality and the overall political circumstances. Legal authority also plays a role. In Germany, for example, the chancellor is particularly strong because he or she has the legal authority to give directives to other cabinet members. This authority is not available in many other countries, where the prime minister must rely on more informal means to exert influence.

A new cabinet must win a vote of confidence in parliament. In some countries an explicit vote of confidence is not necessary. In such cases, the cabinet is formally appointed by the head of state—for example, by the queen in Great Britain—and it is assumed that the cabinet has the **confidence of parliament** unless the latter explicitly expresses its lack of confidence. This technicality does not change the basic fact that the cabinet depends on the confidence of parliament. In a vote of confidence, party discipline is imposed. If a member of parliament breaks party discipline in a vote of confidence, this is likely to lead to severe sanctions and, in some cases, even expulsion from the party. To understand the vote of confidence, we must understand that the relevant actors are not individual members of parliament, but the parties. The question is not how individual X, but how party X, will vote.

Just as parliament gives its confidence to the cabinet, it may withdraw this confidence at any time. The only formality required is a **vote of no-confidence**, which is a political act and does not imply that the cabinet has done something improper or illegal. Thus, a vote of no-confidence is very different from impeachment in the United States. An impeached and convicted U.S. president leaves political life in disgrace, whereas a prime minister whose cabinet loses a vote of confidence usually stays on as a member of parliament. He or she even may continue to play a leadership role, for example, as head of the opposition. How parliaments handle votes of confidence and no-confidence varies greatly from country to country. The most influential factor is whether a single party controls a majority in parliament and is thus able to form a cabinet of its own.

Before we begin our overview, a clarification is necessary for Americans who wish to read European newspapers. In Europe the cabinet is often called the "government"; in Great Britain, for example, one speaks of the government of Gordon Brown. In French the term is *gouvernement*. In the United States, by contrast, the term *government* has a much broader meaning, referring not only to the executive branch, but also to all three branches together. When Americans mean "government" in the European sense, they often speak of the **administration**, such as the Obama administration. When Europeans speak of the administration, they mean the state bureaucracy. These semantic differences show that often it is not easy for either Americans or Europeans to read newspapers from the other side of the Atlantic.

SINGLE-PARTY–MAJORITY CABINETS

In this section we discuss situations in which a single party possesses an absolute majority (50 percent + 1) in parliament and forms the cabinet alone. Great Britain is the classic example of this situation, and we use it as our illustration. In Great Britain, general elections usually give an absolute majority of seats in the House of Commons to either the Labour Party or the Conservative Party. In 2010, however, as we have seen in Chapter 3, no party received a majority of seats in the House of Commons, so that we have a hung parliament. Before we deal with this exceptional situation for Great Britain, we look first at its usual pattern of cabinet formation.

If one party has an absolute majority in the House of Commons, cabinet formation is straightforward because **party discipline** is imposed: The majority party simply forms a cabinet. This can be well illustrated by the events following the 2005 election, when Labour won 356 of the 646 seats (see Table 4.1). After this victory, it was clear that Labour would form the cabinet. Who would be the prime minister and the other cabinet members? For this question, we must distinguish between two situations: Either the winning party was already in power before the election, or it was in opposition. In 2005, Labour had been in power since 1997. In accordance with the idea of never changing a winning team, most members of the old cabinet, including the prime minister, Tony Blair, retained their positions. The second situation was illustrated in 1979, when the Conservatives, under the leadership of Margaret Thatcher, won the elections as the opposition party. In such cases, the concept of a **shadow cabinet** is important. During the period of opposition, a party announces the names of members who would fill the various cabinet positions in the case of electoral victory. This cabinet-in-waiting is called the shadow cabinet. Its members act as spokespersons of their party in parliamentary debates. The shadow foreign minister, for example, confronts the actual foreign minister in debates on foreign affairs. This is a good training

---

TABLE 4.1

Voter support and parliamentary seats in the 2005 general election to the British House of Commons

Party	Voter Support (%)	Seats %	Seats N
Labour	35.3	55.1	356
Conservatives	32.3	30.6	198
Liberal Democrats	22.1	9.6	62
Others	10.3	4.7	30
Total	100.0	100.0	646

Source: BBC News, Election 2005.

ground, because it gives the shadow foreign minister experience in foreign affairs should his or her party win the next election.

How can a member of parliament advance in the party to become a member of the cabinet or the shadow cabinet? Because the House of Commons is very large, with more than 600 members, there will always be many more ordinary members than leaders. The leaders sit on the front benches to either side of the aisle—the government on the right side of the speaker and the opposition on the left side. The distance between the front benches is two swords plus one foot, a reminder of the long tradition of the House of Commons. The nonleaders must sit at the back and are therefore called backbenchers. How do backbenchers become leaders? They must prove themselves to their peers in parliament. If this is done successfully, they may one day rise to a cabinet position and, ultimately, perhaps even to the prime ministership.

In order to become prime minister, one must first be party leader. The two major parties have different rules of how they elect their leaders. These internal party rules are changed quite often. The current rules for the Conservatives are that as a first step there is a nominating process among the Conservative members of parliament (MPs), whereby two candidates are nominated. In a second step these two names are submitted to ordinary party members. In contrast to American parties, British parties have members who formally enroll in the party and pay an annual fee (see Chapter 3), as is done when joining any club or association. Whoever of the two candidates wins the most votes among party members is elected party leader. If the party is in government, the party leader becomes prime minister; if the party is in opposition, the party leader becomes leader of the opposition.

Labour also has a two-step election process. As for the Conservatives, for Labour, too, the nominating process begins in the parliamentary group. To be nominated, however, the rules are different. It is sufficient for a nomination to get the support of 12.5 percent of the Labour MPs. Thus, it is mathematically possible to have more than two nominations. In the second step, ordinary party members have one-third of the votes, another third goes to affiliated trade unions, and the last third to all Labour members of the House of Commons and the European Parliament (for the latter see Chapter 14). As we see, the selection process for the British prime minister is quite different from the one for the American president. What are the main differences? Are there also similarities? What are the advantages and disadvantages of the two selection processes?

If we compare the career path of a British prime minister with the usual path to the American White House, the differences are striking. Of the last six presidents, four became presidents without any prior Washington experience: Jimmy Carter, Ronald Reagan, Bill Clinton, and George W. Bush. All four, in fact, made beneficial use of the argument that they were not part of the Washington establishment. The elder Bush had much Washington experience before becoming president—for example, as head of the Central Intelligence Agency (CIA)—but he had been in Congress for only a short period of time. Barack Obama was merely a first-term senator. Thus, none of the last six presidents had established a long and distinguished career in Congress. British prime ministers, by contrast, complete a long apprenticeship in the House of Commons before entering office. Which career path is preferable? An American president who comes from outside may have the advantage of bringing a "fresh wind" and a new outlook, but this advantage is countered by a lack of experience, which can be seen as a real disadvantage. As former German chancellor Helmut Schmidt notes:

> It remains a pity that the process of nominating and electing [an American] President does not pay any attention to their foreign political expertise or experience or ability. They have never been tested in it, whereas in a parliamentary system, people who make it to the top have been tested first.[1]

Although a British prime minister first needs the support of his or her party colleagues in parliament, broader support is also needed. A successful candidate must appeal to ordinary party members and, in the time of television, increasingly to the public at large. The latter aspect means that a British prime minister is becoming increasingly similar to the American president with regard to leadership style. Both have to be able to communicate well with the general public. Blair was very adept in this respect, while Brown is less charismatic as a public figure.

Differences between Great Britain and the United States are also striking with regard to the role of the opposition. In Great Britain, as long as the government party does not lose its majority through defections or losses in elections for vacant seats (by-elections), it can pursue whatever policies it chooses. In the Falkland Islands crisis of 1982, for example, the Labour Party had no means of impeding the war policy of the governing Conservatives. When the government decided to send warships to liberate the Falkland Islands from Argentine occupation, there was nothing that the opposition could do about it. Under the British system, the majority cabinet governs with an absolute mandate. This mandate is buttressed by the norm of **collective responsibility**, which is a uniquely British doctrine. It states that all members of the cabinet must support the official government line. If not, they must be willing to resign their posts. The purpose of this doctrine is to signal to the people the unity of the government. One of the most spectacular resignations occurred during the buildup to the Iraq war when the leader of the House of Commons, Robin Cook, resigned from the cabinet on March 17, 2003, stating that he "cannot accept collective responsibility for the decision to commit Britain now to military action in Iraq without international agreement or military support."[2] The prime minister can also dismiss cabinet members. This process was studied by Anthony King and Nicholas Allen, who found that it is not easy for a prime minister to dismiss powerful cabinet colleagues; Margaret Thatcher, the Iron Lady, was most successful in the recent past to do so.[3]

The function of a motion of no-confidence submitted by the opposition needs clarification. As long as the governing party controls an absolute majority of the parliamentary seats, such a motion has no chance of success. The governing party has enough votes to defeat such a motion, which will be supported only by the opposition. So why submit a motion of no-confidence to begin with? The purpose is not to topple the government but to give the opposition the opportunity to say what it finds wrong with the policies of the government and what it would do instead. The government, in turn, has the opportunity to defend its policies. In this way, the voters see the differences between the governing and the opposition parties. On election day the choices are thus clear: The voters can opt either for a continuation of the existing policies or for a change to the policies advocated by the opposition.

In order to understand why, in a vote of no-confidence, members of parliament vote strictly along party lines, one has to understand the role of the so-called **whip**. Whips are members of parliament who exercise supervisory functions. Headed by a chief whip, the whips must make sure that all their colleagues are present for an important vote, particularly for a motion of no-confidence. Because voting is public, they also see to it that everyone is following the party line. Both the governing party and the opposition have whips. The expression entered into the parliamentary vocabulary during the eighteenth century. It was taken from fox hunting, which was very popular at the time in the British upper class but is now illegal. The "whipper-in" had the task of keeping the hounds in the pack. The highest level of required party discipline is the three-line-whip, where the agenda point to be voted on in the House of Commons is, in a literal sense, underlined three times. MPs rarely deviate from the party line in order to take a position on an issue that is particularly popular in their district. Giacomo Benedetto and Simon Hix have investigated who the most likely party rebels are and whether their number has increased.[4] The main finding is that former cabinet ministers and backbenchers without hope for promotion are most likely to vote against their party. These two groups are least likely to fear sanctions from the party leadership. Since the 1960s, the magnitude of internal party revolts has increased, although overall such revolts are still rare.

By contrast, in the United States, a congressperson's first interest is his or her **constituency**, not his or her party. It is electoral success in the constituency that ensures political viability, not party loyalty. As a result, congresspersons have a tendency to first ensure the support of their constituency, oftentimes through inefficient, so-called pork-barrel projects (e.g., when a congressperson attaches a rider consisting of a post office, a bridge, or a highway to be built in her constituency to an omnibus bill) rather than by displaying party loyalty.

In the United States the distinction between governing and opposition parties is much less clear than in Great Britain. Prior to the 1996 American presidential elections, the Democrats controlled the White House and the Republicans controlled Congress, so that in the election campaign it was often unclear who could take credit and who was to blame for governmental policies. This situation of divided government happened again after the 2006 midterm elections, this time with a Republican president confronting a Democratic Congress. In Great Britain, the governing party must take full responsibility for all government policies. As a consequence, the voters have a clear choice: continue with the governing party or oust it. Americans prefer to check and balance governmental power. Which system is more democratic, and what is the meaning of the term *democratic* in this context?

Although the executive branch in Great Britain, when compared to that in the United States, has more leeway to pursue long-term policies, its power should not be exaggerated. First, it must contend with powerful interest groups outside the House of Commons. Second, the British cabinet also must consider the wishes of its backbenchers; otherwise it might suddenly be faced with serious internal party rebellion. A good illustration is the ousting of Margaret Thatcher as prime minister in November 1990 after she had been in office since 1979. Thatcher was increasingly seen in her own party as arrogant and autocratic. As we have seen, British prime ministers are also leaders of their parties. They need to be reappointed on a yearly basis for this position, although this is usually a formality for a sitting prime minister. In November of 1990, however, Thatcher was challenged by her former defense minister, Michael Heseltine, who had been dismissed by Thatcher from his job in the cabinet and forced to take a seat on the backbenches. From there he began to organize an effective campaign against the leadership of Margaret Thatcher and stood as candidate against her. At the time, the Conservatives had the rule that the selection process was limited to its parliamentary group. In the first ballot Heseltine lost, but only narrowly, so that Thatcher did not reach the number of votes required by the party rules. She was still confident that she would win the second ballot, for which fewer votes were necessary to win. However, when important cabinet members told her that she might not have the necessary votes or even that they would personally vote against her, she withdrew her candidacy. In the second ballot, two other powerful party members entered the race: the foreign minister, Douglas Hurd, and the finance minister (the chancellor of the exchequer), John Major. Again there was no winner, but Major was very close, so the two other candidates withdrew in his favor and no third ballot was necessary. Thatcher was bitter, accepted from the queen the title of nobility "Lady," and moved to the House of Lords.

Another example of the limited power of a British prime minister is of how Tony Blair was forced to resign in 2007. Blair was the strongest European supporter of the war in Iraq and was often ridiculed as a poodle of Bush. Blair came increasingly under attack from his own Labour Party, especially from its left wing. He was in a far more uncomfortable position than Bush who, after his reelection in 2004, could not be removed from office short of impeachment. Since Blair's position as prime minister was based on his position as party leader, he risked being removed from his leadership position in the party as had happened to Thatcher. Blair found a more elegant way to leave office. In the fall of 2006, he announced that he would leave office within a year as party leader and, therefore, as prime minister. On May 10, 2007, Blair followed up on this promise and set June 27 as the date he would leave office. Thanks to this prolonged retirement phase, Blair was able to bring about substantial progress to the situation in Northern Ireland (Chapter 13) and to attain some other successes so that he could leave office in relatively good standing. To make his announcement on May 10, 2007, Blair went to his electoral district where he had begun his career and which he still represented in the House of Commons. To great applause, he declared:

> So, I've come back here to Sedgefield, to my constituency, where my political journey began and where it's fitting that it should end. Today I announce my decision to stand down from the leadership of the Labour Party. The party will now select a new leader. On the 27th June I will tender my resignation from the office of Prime Minister to the Queen. I've been Prime Minister of this country for just over 10 years. In this job, in the world of today, I think that's long enough for me, but more especially for the country. And sometimes the only way to conquer the pull of power is to set it down.[5]

In contrast to the situation after Thatcher's ousting, there was little competition after Blair. The chancellor of the exchequer (finance minister), Gordon Brown, had for a long time been the favorite to succeed Blair. Therefore, the succession process was more of a formality. There was only one other candidate, John McDonnell of the left wing of the Labour Party. Brown stood domestically pretty much where Blair stood, stressing more free market elements than the left wing of the party (Chapter 3). With regard to Iraq, however, Brown took his distance from Blair, calling the heavy involvement of Britain in the war an error. Brown, born in 1951, has a PhD from Edinburgh University. After some university teaching, he entered the House of Commons at the relatively young age of 32. He is the author of several scholarly books, including a book titled *Values, Visions, and Voices*.

As we have seen previously, to be nominated in the Labour Party as candidate for party leader, 12.5 percent of all Labour MPs are needed; in this situation, this meant 45 votes. Brown reached a superb result with 313 votes, while McDonnell attained a mere 29 votes and was therefore not nominated as candidate. Thus, Brown was the only candidate, but he still had to go through the second phase of the election process. Six candidates made the nomination as candidates for deputy party leader, so that the second phase still had some suspense. In the following weeks, Brown and the six candidates for deputy party leader had to confront ordinary party members in so-called hustings in various places in the United Kingdom. *Hustings* is an old-fashioned word for election platform; its usage shows the love of the British for traditions. Party members could ask questions in advance and, as a sign of modernity this time, on the Internet. At the hustings in Coventry on May 20, 2007, for example, a Robert Smith of Nottingham asked the following pertinent question: "How will you insure that Labour reconnects with voters who were lost as a result of the decision to go to war in Iraq?"

At a party convention in Manchester on Sunday, June 24, 2007, Gordon Brown was officially made party leader amid much warm applause. He accepted the election with the following statement: "It is with humility, pride and a great sense of duty that I accept the privilege and the great responsibility of leading our party and changing the country."[6] Brown expressed his basic political values as follows:

> I am a conviction politician. My conviction that everyone deserves a fair chance in life. My conviction that each of us has a responsibility to each other. And my conviction that when the strong help the weak, it makes us all stronger.

With regard to Iraq, Brown cautiously distanced himself from Blair in stating that "We will meet our international obligations," but pointedly adding that "we will learn lessons that need to be learned." Domestically, Brown pledged to continue the moderate centrist course of Blair. On the one hand, he stated, "I believe in a British economy founded on dynamic, flexible markets and open competition.... If people think we will achieve our goals in the future by retreating to failed approaches of the past, then they have not learned the lessons I have learned from the past ten years." On the other hand, Brown stressed that he will look out for the poor, in particular with regard to health care, education, and housing, exclaiming, "As a party we have always known that we succeed best when we reach out to and engage the whole community. So here I stand proud of our Labour party but determined that we reach out to all people who can be persuaded to share our values and who would like to be part of building a more just society." Exactly as scheduled and mentioned above, three days later, on June 27, Brown took over as prime minister from Tony Blair.

The cases of Thatcher and Blair show that the power of a British prime minister is not unlimited, even if she or he has a majority in parliament. The real challenge comes not from the opposition party but from within her or his own party. It is interesting to note that during the November 1990 crisis, the Labour opposition submitted a motion of no-confidence against the government. As expected, according to the British rules of the game, party discipline among the Conservatives worked, and the motion was defeated. Submitting the motion gave Labour the chance to criticize the disarray of the government. Labour did not, however, expect to win the motion of no-confidence.

Typically in the British cabinet, there is an open, frank discussion concerning decisions to be made in which every cabinet member is heard, but the prime minister has the right to sum up the discussion. Votes are virtually never taken. Patrick Gordon Walker, a former member of the cabinet, describes an imaginary cabinet meeting. After a lengthy discussion, the prime minister sums up and concludes as follows: "Is the cabinet agreed with my summing up and the additional points made by the chancellor? (Silence, with a few muttered 'agreed')."[7] This summing up gives quite a bit of power to the prime minister.

Finally, we must address the question of how the government party and the opposition party compete with each other in the British system. The normal pattern is that they both take a moderate position in the middle, where there are the most voters, as Great Britain has a unimodal distribution of the electorate, as depicted in Figure 3.2. Margaret Thatcher was a notable exception to this rule because she pursued very conservative policies. She had the ambition not simply to appeal to the preferences of the voters but to change these preferences. As we remember from Chapter 3, she was never able to attract a majority of the voters; she became prime minister only because the opposition was so badly split.

The Labour Party, too, at times, tried not simply to appeal to the existing preferences of the voters but to change these preferences. When in opposition after 1979, Labour advocated very leftist policies, insisting in particular on a strongly state-controlled economy. However, the party came to acknowledge that the financial "markets remained nervous about the possibility of a Labour victory . . . Labour did moderate its policies in an attempt to reassure markets."[8] At the forefront of these changes was Tony Blair, who took over as leader of the party in 1994. Under his leadership, Labour abandoned its commitments to nationalization and dropped from its program the demand for "common ownership of the means of production, distribution and exchange." Blair hailed the day of this decision as "a day of destiny for our party and our country."[9] Blair also took up traditional Conservative values such as fighting crime. After his speech at the party convention in September of 1996, the British Union Jack was projected on the wall behind him, which emphasized that Labour was no longer willing to leave the theme of patriotism to the Conservatives.

A year after taking office, Gordon Brown was confronted with the global financial and economic crisis, which made it difficult for him to find the best policy position for the Labour government. On the one hand, he tried to stay with the third way in the middle; on the other hand, he had to intervene more often in the economy than he had promised when he took office. He was not successful with this balancing act and as a consequence lost more and more of his initial popularity. There was also a scandal of many MPs charging inappropriate personal expenses to taxpayers, a scandal that Brown did not handle well. In June 2009, in elections to the European Parliament, Brown's Labour party suffered an embarrassing defeat, falling to 16 percent of voter support. The BBC had the headline: "Labour slumps to historic defeat." A few cabinet ministers resigned and asked Brown to do the same, and this call came also from a fair number of Labour backbenchers. Brown, nevertheless, managed to survive. He reshuffled the cabinet, bringing in new cabinet members loyal to him. The rebellion in the backbenches was also not strong enough to topple him.

All this did not augur well for Labour when new elections took place in 2010. They lost their majority in the 650-member House of Commons, going down from 356 seats to 258. But as we have seen in Chapter 3, Conservatives did not either gain a majority of seats, with 306 seats being short of the required majority of 326 seats. Now Liberal Democrats as the party in the middle were courted by both Labour and Conservatives to form a coalition cabinet. Labour lost the battle, Brown retired as party leader and was replaced by Ed Miliband, who at age 41 pledged to represent a new generation. He won the leadership position against his older brother David. In the new cabinet of Conservatives and Liberal Democrats, the leader of the Conservatives, David Cameron, became prime minister, while the leader of the Liberal Democrats, Nick Clegg, became deputy prime minister.

As we have seen in the previous chapter, Liberal Democrats as the third largest party were always disadvantaged by the winner-take-all parliamentary election system. As a condition for joining the cabinet, they got from the Conservatives the concession that a referendum will be held on a change of the election system to the so-called *alternative vote system*. Thereby, the voters in their single district would not only vote for one candidate as in the existing system, but they could rank all candidates according to preferences. If a candidate reaches 50 percent of first choices, then he or she is elected. If no candidate reaches this level, the candidate with the lowest first votes is eliminated and his or her backers' second choices are redistributed to the other candidates, and this procedure is repeated until one candidate reaches 50 percent. With this system, Liberal Democrats would get a better chance to gain parliamentary seats because they would appear on many ballots as second or third choices. The two large parties rejected a change to such a system, so it was no surprise that when the referendum was held, May 5, 2011, the change was overwhelmingly defeated, with only 32 percent voting in favor.

MINIMAL-WINNING CABINETS

In a parliamentary system, when no party controls a majority in parliament, the process of cabinet formation is very different from that in Great Britain. One possibility is the formation of minimal-winning cabinets, where as many political parties as are necessary form a coalition to attain a majority in parliament. In other words, all coalition partners are necessary to form the cabinet; there are no surplus members in the coalition. Should we not expect all cabinet coalitions to be of a minimal-winning size? What is a rationale for adding more parties than are necessary to win?[10] Why include, say, a third party in a coalition if two parties have enough votes for a majority in parliament? As we will see in the next section, such oversized coalitions can and do occur.

Germany, since 1969, is a good illustration of how minimal-winning cabinets are formed. In the 1969 election to the Bundestag, the Christian Democrats (CDU/CSU)[11] received 242 seats, the Social Democrats (SPD) 224, and the Free Democrats (FDP) 30. The CDU/CSU felt that they had won the election, and they pondered the question of whether they should enter into a coalition with the SDP or with the FDP. They were shocked when late on the night of the election the SPD and the FDP announced that they had made a deal. With a combined 254 seats, these two parties were just above the necessary majority of 249, so they could win a vote of confidence in parliament. Legally, everything was in order, but a public debate began over whether the procedure followed on election night was in accordance with the spirit of basic democratic principles. The question was raised whether excluding the party with the most votes from the cabinet violated the will of the electorate. The counterargument was that more voters had supported the SPD and the FDP together than the CDU/CSU alone, so the new cabinet was, in fact, based on the majority will of the people. What emerged from this debate was the informal rule that the voters should be informed of the coalition intentions of the various parties before the election. It should not be left to a few leaders to decide on election night what coalition is to be formed. In many other European democracies, however, such an informal rule does not exist; thus, the composition of the cabinet may still be decided by a few key leaders on election night.

In Germany, with the Greens emerging in the 1980s and maturing in the 1990s, it has not only become more difficult to say with whom a coalition will be formed but what the outcome of an election will be. For example, it was widely assumed that for the 1998 election, the CDU/CSU and SDP would form a **grand coalition**, until the actual results were in and the SDP and the Greens proved to be stronger than expected. This election result led to a rethinking of possible coalition partners and, having a numerical majority for a possible "red-green" coalition, momentum grew for the formation of such a coalition *after* the election. Indeed, such a coalition was promptly installed.

Similarly, during the short campaign in the summer of 2005, and particularly after the formation of the *Linkspartei* (Left Party), which consisted of a more leftist part that split off from the SPD and combined with the PDS (the Communist Party of former East Germany), it was assumed that the CDU/CSU would form a coalition with the FDP. Again, actual election results interfered with coalition plans made before the election: The CDU/CSU disappointed bitterly and even together with the FDP would not have had a majority of seats in the German Bundestag, obliterating all promises to form a CDU/CSU and FDP coalition. Finally, a grand coalition of the CDU/CSU and the SPD formed, and because the CDU/CSU was slightly larger than the SPD the chancellorship went to the former, with Angela Merkel of the CDU as chancellor. Since the late 1960s, the German party landscape has become much more variegated, making it very difficult to tell voters before an election takes place with whom large parties will form a coalition. For the September 2009 election, however, the old informal rule again applied. Before the election, the CDU/CSU and the FDP announced that they would form a coalition if together they would have enough votes. They indeed received together a majority, and, as announced, formed a coalition.

Another informal rule regarding cabinet formation developed from an episode in the fall of 1982 in the middle of a legislative period. The coalition of the SDP and the FDP was still in office, but there were increasing strains between the two coalition partners, especially over economic matters. Under the strong influence of its economics minister, the FDP advocated more free-market solutions, broke its coalition with the SPD, and entered into a coalition with the CDU/CSU. Social Democrat Helmut Schmidt was thus replaced as chancellor[12] by Christian Democrat Helmut Kohl in a parliamentary vote. The reason Schmidt was ousted was not his unpopularity; on the contrary, opinion surveys indicated that Schmidt was more popular than Kohl at that time. The reason was that the FDP changed coalition partners. A public debate began as to whether a small party should have the power to replace the chancellor in this way; after all, the FDP had campaigned in the parliamentary election of 1980 with the promise to continue their coalition with the SDP. Was this promise valid for the entire legislative period? Was it a betrayal of the voters to change coalition midcourse? The argument was made that a cabinet had been formed without due input by the voters. Early elections were demanded for such situations so the voters could decide. Kohl took this demand seriously, and in the spring of 1983 early elections took place. The coalition of the CDU/CSU and the FDP won and thus had a direct mandate from the voters. It seems likely that in the future, changes of coalitions will no longer occur without a prior election. This would be an informal rule supplanting the formal rule of the "constructive vote of no-confidence." This is a special German feature that we do not find in any of the other countries discussed in this chapter. The constructive vote of no-confidence means a cabinet can be overthrown only if, with the same vote, a new cabinet is selected. Thus, a vote of no-confidence cannot merely be negative regarding the current cabinet, but also must be "constructive" in forming a new cabinet. This rule was applied in the 1982 change from the Schmidt to the Kohl cabinet. What the new informal rule seems to say is that for a change in cabinet, new parliamentary elections are preferred to the instrument of the constructive vote of no-confidence. This happened again in 2005 when the coalition of the SPD and the Greens was so weakened by the emergence of the Left Party that the coalition was no longer viable to govern in an effective way. The SPD/Green coalition was replaced, as noted, by a coalition of the CDU/CSU and the SPD—not with a constructive vote of no-confidence, but rather after early elections. The development of a set of widely accepted, informal rules for the process of cabinet formation was important for the stability of Germany. This contrasts with the **Weimar Republic**, before Hitler's takeover, when deep disagreements existed about the very rules for cabinet formation. Today, the political elites by and large agree on how the game should be played.

One of the central features of parliamentary systems is that executive authority not only emerges from legislative authority, but that executive authority is also responsible to it. The vehicle by which this responsibility is carried out is enshrined in Article 68 of the German Basic Law (Grundgesetz), which allows for the chancellor to call for a vote of confidence. If it fails, the president can dissolve parliament and call for new elections. In the spring of 2005, Schröder lost on purpose a vote of confidence so that early elections could be called. The reason he asked members of his own party and the members of the Green Party to withdraw their support for his government was occasioned by the SPD's defeat in the Land elections of North Rhine-Westphalia. Losing this election also meant that Schröder lost majority support in the German upper house, the Bundesrat. He lost this election due to the unwillingness of many voters in that region to go along with his plans to revamp the German welfare system, known as Agenda 2010, which would involve painful cuts in Germany's hitherto generous welfare system. Using Article 68 of the Basic Law raised serious constitutional issues insofar as it was argued that losing a Land election does not constitute a sufficient reason to force a dissolution of parliament. After all, his government still had a majority in the Bundestag, Germany's lower house. In effect, Schröder asked members of his own ruling coalition to vote against him to ensure losing the vote of no-confidence, thereby forcing new elections. Some constitutional theorists were concerned about this "insincere" use of Article 68. Nevertheless, the German Supreme Court eventually concurred with the decision of parliament, and the German president, Horst Köhler (see later in this chapter), also gave a green light for new elections to take place on September 18, 2005.

Once the seats were tallied, it was clear that five parties gained representation in the German parliament. None of the "expected" combinations such as between the SPD and the Greens or between the CSU/CSU and the FDP gained enough seats to form a coalition based on a majority of seats. In the ensuing coalition negotiations, various options were entertained, such as a "traffic light" coalition (Red [SPD], Yellow [FDP], Greens), or a "Jamaica" coalition (Black [CDU/CSU], Yellow, Green—the colors of the flag of Jamaica). The central problem of such negotiations is not only the need to find a combination that ensures a majority, but also a majority of parties that can actually work together. Oftentimes, this automatically excludes particular combinations, such as a red-red-green combination. Neither of the two "red" parties (the SPD and the Linkspartei) was willing to share executive power with the other, as they had split up over major policy differences just a few months before the election.

Eventually, on October 10, 2005, three weeks after the election, negotiations over the formation of a grand coalition with the first female chancellor in German history, Angela Merkel, were initiated. In the tradition of parliamentary systems that the party with the highest vote share also gets to determine who becomes chancellor, for the CSU/CSU this meant yielding many important ministries to the SDP.

The grand coalition of the CDU/CSU and the SPD had to deal with the severe recession beginning in 2009, not a task that helped their popularity with voters. Both governing parties lost votes in the September 2009 election, SPD much more so than the CDU/CSU (see Table 4.2). The voter support for the SPD dropped from 34.2 to 23.0 percent, for the CDU/CSU from 35.2 percent to 33.8 percent. The big winner was the FDP increasing its voter support from 9.8 percent to 14.6 percent. As already mentioned, this allowed the formation of a CDU/CSU and FDP coalition as desired by both sides. A majority in the Bundestag, however, was only reached because the CDU/CSU got 24 surplus seats, while none of the other parties got any (for the concept of surplus seats see Chapter 3). As the CDU/CSU was again the larger party in the coalition, Angela Merkel stayed on as chancellor. At the left, the big story was the catastrophic defeat of the SPD while the Left Party and the Greens won 3 percent and 2 percent respectively. One reason for the severe defeat of the SPD was the drop

---

▶ TABLE 4.2

Voter support and parliamentary seats in the 2009 general election to the German Bundestag

Party	Voter Support (%)	Seats %	Seats N
Conservatives (CDU/CSU)	33.8	38.3	239
Social Democrats	23.0	23.5	146
Free Democrats	14.6	15.0	93
Left Party	11.9	12.2	76
The Greens	10.7	11.0	68
Others	6.0	0	0
Total	100.0	100.0	622

Source: Psephos, Adam Carr's Election Archive, 2011.

in voter turnout from 77.7 percent to 70.8 percent. Many former SPD voters stayed home, frustrated by the economic performance of their party in the grand coalition. Other former SPD voters turned to the more radical Left Party and the Greens, neither of which had any government responsibilities. The losses of the CDU/CSU were less severe because Chancellor Merkel was personally popular, taking a centrist position on many issues and projecting a motherly image. With the FDP as her new coalition partner, she had to move more to the right for economic matters.

We have seen in this section that with a higher number of parties gaining representation, cabinet formation becomes more complex. One option is to form **minimal-winning coalitions** with just enough parties to win but not more. Germany is a good illustration for this option. There has never been a coalition with surplus coalition partners. Minimal winning can also be understood in a stricter way in the sense that a coalition includes only as many individual members of parliament as are necessary to win. With this definition, the grand coalition of the CSU/CSU and SDP from 2005 to 2009 was not minimal winning. To be sure, both parties were necessary to reach a majority in parliament. The coalition, however, included many more members of parliament than 50 percent + 1. By contrast, the 1969 coalition of the SDP and the FDP was not only minimal winning with regard to the number of parties but almost also with regard to the number of members of parliament since it included 254 members, barely above the required majority of 249. Another classical minimal-winning coalition in both senses was formed in Ireland after the 2007 elections. Fianna Fáil with 78 seats and the Greens with 6 seats formed a coalition. With 84 seats together, they had just enough votes to control an absolute majority in the 166-member Irish parliament.

OVERSIZED CABINETS

Although they do not occur often, certain circumstances encourage the formation of oversized coalition cabinets. Oversized cabinets include more coalition partners than are necessary to attain a majority in parliament. Switzerland shall help to illustrate the concept of **oversized coalitions**. Switzerland is the only system in Europe where once a government (called the Federal Council) is set up by the legislature, the legislature cannot dissolve it. The members of the government are elected individually by the legislature for the entire legislative period of four years. Thus, in Switzerland, unlike in a regular parliamentary system, the government is *not* responsible to the legislature, at least not in a formal way. Thus, the term of responsible government as previously explained does not apply to Switzerland. Of course, in order to pass legislation, the government still depends on the support of the legislature, but the legislature has no way to withdraw the confidence from the government and thus topple it.

The cabinet is elected in a joint session of both houses of parliament. The lower house, called the National Council, has 200 members, each Canton being represented according to its population. The upper house, the Council of States, has 46 members, 2 from each Canton.[13] When modern Switzerland was founded in 1848, the United States was taken as a model for the Swiss bicameral system, with the National Council corresponding to the House of Representatives and the Council of States to the Senate. The size of the Swiss cabinet—seven members—is unusually small. That size is fixed by the Swiss constitution. Another specifically Swiss feature is that all seven cabinet members are of equal rank, and no one carries the title of prime minister. There is merely a rotating chair on a yearly basis strictly according to seniority.

A full-fledged grand coalition was created in 1959. The three largest parties, the Free Democrats, the Christian Democrats, and the Social Democrats, each had two seats in the Federal Council. The Swiss People's Party as the fourth-largest party got the remaining seat. Until the elections of 1999, the Swiss People's Party remained in fourth place, and the three other parties stayed in the top three positions so that the Federal Council kept the same formula, 2:2:2:1, for the distribution of the seven seats. The elections of 1999, however, brought a change in the ranking of the top four parties: The Swiss People's Party was able to over-take the Christian Democrats, who fell to fourth place. The mathematical logic would have been that the Swiss People's Party would have gotten a second seat at the cost of the Christian Democrats. The composition of the Swiss Federal Council, however, is not merely a function of mathematical formulas. Parliament in 1999 decided that the Swiss People's Party had first to demonstrate that its position among the three largest parties would not be a short-lived phenomenon. Thus, the party remained for the time being with a single seat in the Federal Council. By 2003, the Swiss People's Party was now definitively among the largest three parties, while the Christian Democrats stayed on fourth place. As a conse-quence, the Christian Democrats lost their second seat to the Swiss People's Party.

The October 2007 parliamentary elections kept the same ranking of the four top parties. Therefore, the expectation was that the party composition of the Federal Council would remain the same: two Swiss People's Party members, two Social Democrats, two Free Democrats, and one Christian Democrat. But things did not go according to the traditional Swiss playbook. The Swiss People's Party has a very charismatic leader in the person of Christoph Blocher, who four years ago was elected to the Federal Council. This time, parliament preferred another member of the Swiss People's Party, Eveline Widmer-Schlumpf, and Blocher lost his seat. This was only the fourth time in modern Swiss history since 1848 that a sitting Federal Councilor was ousted.

What happened? The Swiss People's Party is at the right wing of the Swiss party spectrum, taking an especially hard line on restrictions on immigration. For the parliamentary elections, the party had a poster with three white sheep kicking a black sheep out of Switzerland. This poster was severely criticized both in Switzerland and abroad for being racist and xenophobic. Blocher had played a crucial role in the election campaign, although it is Swiss tradition that federal councilors should stay as much as possible above the partisan fray. Blocher often used demeaning language against political opponents, which is considered as unbecoming for a federal councilor. All these factors allowed the Social Democrats, the Greens, the Christian Democrats, and some Free Democrats to oust Blocher and to replace him with the more moderate and conciliatory Widmer-Schlumpf.

The leadership of the Swiss People's Party had announced in advance that it would not tolerate Blocher's replacement with another member of the party. In such a case, the elected candidate would either not accept the election or, if he or she did, would be expelled from the party. This is exactly what happened. Widmer-Schlumpf accepted her election and was, therefore, expelled from the party.

Samuel Schmid, also of the Swiss People's Party, ran for reelection and won. The party, however, had decided to give up his seat out of protest should Blocher not be reelected. Since Schmid was not willing to give up his seat, he too was expelled from the party. Widmer-Schlumpf and Schmid helped to create a new party, the small Bourgeois Democratic Party. Therefore, the grand coalition of the four largest parties no longer existed since the Swiss People's Party was now in opposition. One year later, however, Schmid resigned over a scandal in his department and was replaced with Ueli Maurer, a true representative of the Swiss People's Party since he had been for a long time its successful president. The Swiss People's Party wants to be back with a second seat in the Federal Council, and if this happens, the disruption of the grand coalition will have been a short interlude.

After the parliamentary election of October 2011, the grand coalition was not yet re-established. The Swiss People's Party lost 2.3 percent of its support but remained the strongest party. Yet, its effort to gain again two seats in the Federal Council failed. It was not able to oust Eveline Widmer-Schlumpf, who was easily re-elected. She received the support of the parties of the center-left, the coalition that had already elected her four years earlier. Two factors were important for the re-appointment of Widmer-Schlumpf. First, and most importantly, she had done a good job and had gained much respect as minister of finance in a troubled economic environment. Second, there is a great reluctance in Switzerland to oust sitting Federal Councilors: as we have seen above, in the long history of modern Switzerland, this has happened only four times.

Numerically, for the time being, we can no longer speak of a grand coalition in Switzerland. The political party of Widmer-Schlumpf, the Bourgeois Democratic Party, did remarkably well in the parliamentary election, gaining 5.4 percent of the votes. For a new party this was a good result, but it did not entitle it to a seat in the seven-member Federal Council. Therefore, Switzerland is currently in an exceptional situation. The claim of the Swiss People's Party for a second seat is in principle recognized by the other parties, but the party would have to wait for a more favorable situation, presumably the retirement of Widmer-Schlumpf. The Swiss People's Party, however, does not take this delay in strides, but protested vehemently that it did not yet get its fair numerical share in the Federal Council. It announced that it will take a stance of opposition forcing popular referenda on many issues.

Are the Swiss by nature more cooperative than others? This hypothesis must be rejected, because there was a time when the Swiss played the game of cabinet formation very competitively. For many centuries after its foundation in 1291, Switzerland was a loose, mainly military federation of independent Cantons. The country lacked a common executive at the national level. During the first half of the nineteenth century, Switzerland experienced a bitter fight over the issue of centralization of power. The Free Democrats advocated more centralization, while the Christian Democrats, at that time called Conservatives, fought any attempt to create a central executive. This conflict led to a short civil war in 1847, won by the Free Democrats. As the winners, the Free Democrats established a constitution in 1848 that provided for a national executive: the seven-member cabinet. For parliamentary elections, the winner-take-all system was chosen. In the first elections, the Free Democrats received a parliamentary majority and used this majority to form a cabinet consisting only of members from their own party, a single-party majority cabinet as is the custom in Great Britain. In election after election, they renewed their majority in parliament and each time filled the cabinet posts with their own people.

A turning point came in 1891, after nearly a half-century, when the Free Democrats still had a majority in parliament but offered one of the seven seats to the Conservatives. In 1918, the Conservatives received a second seat, with the Free Democrats still controlling the other five seats. In the same year, the winner-take-all system for parliamentary elections was changed to the current system of proportionality. The same development—from confrontation to cooperation—happened with regard to the Social Democrats, who began to gain parliamentary strength early in the twentieth century. Initially, the Social Democrats had been treated as outcasts. When they organized a general strike in 1918, the cabinet intervened with troops. This resulted in bloody clashes, and on several subsequent occasions parliament refused to accept any Social Democrats in the cabinet. The turning point here came during World War II, when the first Social Democrat was allowed to join the cabinet. In 1959, the Social Democrats received a second seat and thus had representation corresponding to their electoral strength. The principle of proportionality is applied not only to political parties but also to the linguistic groups in Switzerland. The country has four official languages, with 63.7 percent of the population speaking German, 20.4 percent French, 6.5 percent Italian, and 0.5 percent Romansh—a language spoken only in Switzerland. A variety of other languages are spoken in Switzerland, mainly by foreigners, but none of them has official status. The French and Italian speakers together always have two or three seats in the cabinet, corresponding to their proportion in the population. These rules of proportionality in cabinet formation are not written down in the constitution or in special laws but are based on informal, mutual understandings.

The logic of the Swiss grand coalition is not that the major parties agree on a common program but rather that the major parties should all be represented when the Federal Council makes its decisions. Often no consensus is reached in the Council such that a decision is made by majority vote. Such votes should in principle be kept confidential, but sometimes they are leaked to the media. As the recent events described above indicate, working together in the Federal Council has become more difficult. Some political scientists have proposed a change to minimal-winning coalitions as explained in the previous section. But the idea of grand coalitions is so ingrained in Swiss culture that no such change is likely any time soon.

Oversized coalitions are not unique to Switzerland. Even Great Britain, the classic example of a competitive democracy, went through a period of an oversized coalition during World War II, when Conservatives, Labour, and Liberals together formed the cabinet. If an oversized coalition includes all major groups of a country, one also uses the concept of power sharing. This concept is often discussed as a solution for multicultural societies, and we will come back to it in Chapter 13.

MINORITY CABINETS

We speak of **minority cabinets** when the party (or parties) forming the cabinet does not possess a majority of the seats in parliament. Sweden offers good illustrations of why minority cabinets form and how they operate. An episode that occurred in April of 1996 illustrates how the Social Democratic cabinet managed to govern despite its minority status. It negotiated with the Center Party a package of measures to reduce the budget deficit. This package included, among others, cuts in aid for developing countries and an increase in energy taxes. As the leader of the Center Party emphasized, his party was not part of the cabinet and wished to keep its independence for other parts of the budget.[14] In the same way, the Social Democratic minority cabinet sought on a case-by-case basis support from other parties.

The Social Democrats again formed a minority cabinet after the 2002 election, where they received only 144 out of 349 seats (41.2 percent). After some initial wrangling they secured the cooperation of the Left Party and the Greens to support their policies on a case-by-case basis. Such arrangements may be described as "contract parliamentarism," which regulates the roles and functions between the governing parties and the support parties. Such a contract is typically of a written nature, is public, extends beyond any specific legislative deal, and includes members of the support parties to serve at high levels, but not cabinet-level positions.[15] The two support parties, the Left Party and the Greens, were allowed to place functionaries into several ministries but were not able to secure any ministries for themselves.

The September 2006 elections allowed Sweden to have a cabinet with a majority in parliament. The four parties of the right—the Moderates, the Liberals, the Christian Democrats, and the Center—together attained 178 of the 349 seats, which was a majority allowing Fredrik Reinfeldt, leader of the Moderates, the largest of the four parties, to become prime minister of a four-party coalition. The Social Democrats with 130 seats were still the largest party, but since the four parties of the Right controlled a majority in parliament, the Social Democrats had to give up power. In the 2009 election, the four parties of the Right again won a majority and could continue to govern.

Sweden illustrates how there can be quite different reasons why political parties do not enter a cabinet yet are willing to support cabinet policies on a case-by-case basis. It is especially noteworthy that a party may prefer to be outside rather than inside the cabinet. Joaquín Artés and Antonio Bustos show this in an excellent study of a Catalonian nationalist party in Spain, the Convergencia I Unió (CiU). The two largest Spanish parties, the Popular Party on the right and the Socialist Party on the left, sometimes formed minority cabinets supported from the outside by the CiU. This small party of the Catalan region found that it was to its advantage to stay outside the cabinets but to support the cabinets both of the Left and the Right on a case-by-case basis. Under these conditions, the cabinets depended more on the CiU than if it had been in the cabinet. As Artés and Bustos conclude from their study, "Collaboration with the governing parties was beneficial for a relatively small nationalistic party like CiU in terms of programme fulfillment."[16]

Minority cabinets are not unique to Sweden and Spain. It should be clear by now that chaos will not necessarily result if a majority coalition cannot be formed in a parliamentary system. With minority cabinets, governmental life can continue in an orderly way for quite a while.[17] Minority cabinets, however, are also vulnerable to be overthrown at any time in parliament. An example is the Socialist minority cabinet of José Sócrates in Portugal that in March 2011 was overthrown over its austerity program. The other political parties did not agree with the program and united to withdraw confidence from the Socialist minority cabinet. As we will see in the next section, chaos did still not result since Sócrates continued as head of a caretaker cabinet and immediately headed for Brussels for an important meeting of the European Union.

CARETAKER CABINETS

After parliamentary elections it takes sometimes quite a long time until a coalition cabinet can be put together. Who governs during this time? It is simply the old cabinet that stays in office as caretaker cabinet. It handles everyday business but cannot take major initiatives. This is illustrated in Belgium, where caretaker cabinets often have to operate for many months—for example, after the 2010 election—because it was so difficult to form a government coalition across the deep divide between Flemish and Walloon political parties. Sona N. Golder studied for European democracies the factors contributing to delays in cabinet formation and found that polarization of the parties and uncertainties about their bargaining positions contribute to delays.[18]

CABINET INSTABILITY

We have now discussed four European democracies in which the executive cabinet is selected by the parliament: Great Britain, Germany, Switzerland, and Sweden. In each of these countries different rules govern the process of cabinet formation, yet all four countries have relatively stable executives. This finding should lead us to reject the hypothesis that selection of the executive by parliament necessarily leads to instability. Indeed, it seems that stability is possible under widely differing circumstances. By the same token, there is no guarantee that a parliamentary system leads to cabinet stability. Italy offers the prototypical example of high cabinet instability under a parliamentary system. We will also briefly describe an episode of cabinet instability in the Czech Republic.

Ever since the end of World War II, the Italian parliament has had a large number of parties, but so does the Swiss parliament, and we have seen how much cabinet stability Switzerland enjoys. In contrast to Switzerland, however, Italy always had strong parties at the extremes, the Neofascist Italian Social Movement on the Right and the Communists on the Left. Until the end of the cold war, these two parties were always excluded from cabinet positions. The argument for their exclusion was that they did not accept basic democratic principles. Cabinet formation, therefore, was always limited to the moderate parties in the middle: Christian Democrats, Liberals, Republicans, Social Democrats, and Socialists. Immediately after World War II, the Christian Democrats had close to, and at one time even slightly above, a majority in parliament. They developed into *the* governing party; without their participation, no cabinet could be formed. The prime minister and other key ministers were always selected from the ranks of the Christian Democrats.

The dominant position of the Christian Democrats turned out to be a basic weakness of the system. In a democracy, voters should have a realistic possibility of ousting a party from power. But in Italy, there was simply no numerical alternative to a cabinet led by the Christian Democrats, because cabinet participation of Communists and Neofascists was out of the question. Whatever the election results, until the early 1980s, the prime minister was always a Christian Democrat. It might be expected that the dominant position of the Christian Democrats at least had the advantage of leading to cabinet stability, but the opposite was true. Cabinets were usually short-lived, and Christian Democratic prime ministers succeeded one another at brief intervals. This occurred in part because the Christian Democratic Party was in fact a loose federation of several independent factions. Each faction was identified with a particular leader and had a strong organization of its own.

During the time of Christian Democratic dominance, cabinet formation was mainly a result of infighting among these various factions. If a faction was excluded from important cabinet posts, it maneuvered to overthrow the cabinet and replace it with a cabinet dominated by its own people. As a consequence, Italy had frequent cabinet crises despite the fact that the prime minister was always a Christian Democrat. The composition of the cabinet constantly changed, but the game was always played among the same few politicians. They were mostly Christian Democrats but also included some members of the smaller parties of the middle. A key actor might have been prime minister in one cabinet, absent from the next one, then foreign minister, and prime minister again in still another cabinet. An extreme case was Christian Democrat Giulio Andreotti, who held posts in 36 cabinets, including seven turns as prime minister. As Carol Mershon aptly characterizes the situation, "Cabinets in Italy both changed and remained the same."[19] Because of this basic stability it was not costly to overthrow a cabinet, because the politicians responsible for a cabinet crisis could be surely predicted to participate again in future cabinets.

The end of the cold war changed Italian politics in a fundamental way, but cabinet instability continued. As we have seen in Chapter 3, the fear of a Communist takeover in Italy had gone; the Communist Party changed its name to Democratic Party of the Left and hence became a potential coalition partner to form a cabinet. Another important development was the discovery of major political corruption scandals involving virtually all political parties and key sectors of the business community. We have also seen in Chapter 3 how the electoral system in Italy was changed through a popular referendum from proportionality to a mixed system, where three-quarters of the members of parliament are elected by winner-take-all and the remaining quarter by proportionality. In March 1994, the first election under the new system brought great changes among the political parties. The Christian Democrats suffered heavy losses although they had changed their name to Popular Party; the Northern League was greatly strengthened; the Italian Social Movement changed its name to National Alliance and also had a great electoral success; and finally, a new party, Forza Italia founded by Silvio Berlusconi, immediately became an important player in Italian politics.

Forza Italia, the National Alliance, and the Northern League together had a majority in parliament, and they tried to form a cabinet, but there were great ideological differences among the three parties. The Northern League wanted to decentralize the country, whereas the National Alliance favored a strong central authority. Umberto Bossi, the leader of the Northern League, raised questions of whether the National Alliance was too authoritarian to participate in the government. The leader of the National Alliance, Gianfranco Fini, made every effort to project the image of a modern and respectable party. He repeatedly described the Holocaust as an error that led to horror, but for many this was too weak a condemnation of the Fascist past. It was disturbing that at the victory celebration of the National Alliance at Rome's Piazza del Popolo, hundreds of youth in the crowd gave straight-arm Fascist salutes and chanted "Duce! Duce!" as was the custom during the regime of Benito Mussolini. It was also a worrisome sign that one of the seats of the National Alliance was won by Alessandra Mussolini, the dictator's granddaughter. She declared before the elections: "Fascism was a very important part of history that can no longer be demonized or canceled out. But it's history, and no one is thinking of introducing it again."[20] After the elections, many newspapers in other European countries expressed great worries that the Neofascists would participate in a future Italian government.[21]

But what about Forza Italia and its leader Silvio Berlusconi, who was to be prime minister of the new cabinet? Would he be able to hold the parties of the Right together and to make sure that the National Alliance would not gain too much influence? What was his program? He attracted voters mainly by his smooth personality and much less by any specific program. To be sure, he advocated tax cuts and more free-market policies, but when, after the elections, he described the goals of the future government, it all sounded very vague. He postulated the need for "all types of freedom: the family, the individual, business, the free market, competition, profit, solidarity, Christian traditions, respect and tolerance toward all, even our adversaries."[22] The *New York Times* called Berlusconi "Italy's Knight in Teflon. With his business empire and his 70-room villa outside Milan, and with his sense of personal style, Mr. Berlusconi has packaged himself as the Italian dream."[23]

It was only after six weeks of arduous negotiations that, in May 1994, Berlusconi was able to put together a cabinet of his Forza Italia, the National Alliance, and the Northern League. But in December of the same year Berlusconi resigned. There were major defections in his coalition; furthermore, his brother received a suspended jail sentence for corruption charges, and Silvio Berlusconi himself was interrogated about his business dealings. Because it was not possible to put together a new coalition among the parties represented in parliament, a banker without political affiliation, Lamberto Dini, formed a caretaker cabinet of so-called technicians. This cabinet was able to survive for about a year, but then early parliamentary elections were called for in April 1996.

These elections ended with a victory of the Center–Left. The Democratic Party of the Left, the Popular Party, the Greens, and some smaller Center–Left parties had put together an electoral alliance called the Olive Tree, which gained the most parliamentary seats, although not quite an absolute majority. In the vote of confidence, the Reform Communists supported the government of the Olive Tree, which was headed by Romano Prodi of the Popular Party, a respected university professor of economics. Despite their support of the vote of confidence, the Reform Communists refused to be represented in the government, which, therefore, had a minority status. It was an indication of the delicate position of the Reform Communists that one of their members voted against the government and in protest left the party. The Prodi government was the fifty-fifth since World War II, but Prodi promised that it would be an exceptional government in the sense that it would survive the entire legislative period. It did not.

In 1998 the Reform Communists withdrew their support from the Prodi government, considering it not enough to the left. Then Massimo D'Alema of the Democratic Party of the Left could again get the support of the Reform Communists although not their entry into the government. D'Alema was prime minister for two years but resigned in 2000 after a severe defeat of the Left in regional elections. For the remainder of the legislative period in 2001, Socialist Giuliano Amato headed still another cabinet of the Left. In the legislative elections of 2001, the Right won a majority, and it was once again Berlusconi who became prime minister. He stayed in office the entire legislative period from 2001 to 2006, a first in Italy since World War II. This did not mean that Italy was no longer plagued by instability—there was constant infighting among the coalition partners of the Right. At one point Berlusconi was even forced to resign as prime minister, only to succeed himself.

For the April 2006 general elections, Berlusconi, a master of staging political spectacles, vowed to stay in power. In February of that year, he declared himself to be the "Jesus Christ of Italian politics," who sacrifices himself for everyone. Earlier, he also compared himself to Napoleon in describing his achievements during the past five years in office.[24] Berlusconi, the richest man in Italy, controls significant elements of the Italian media. He directly controls two private television channels and, as prime minister, indirectly controls three public TV channels. In addition, as explained in Chapter 3, he pushed through a change in the electoral law, making it 100 percent proportional in the hope that would help him win the election.

Berlusconi's challenger was again Romano Prodi, an economics professor, former Italian prime minister, and former president of the European Commission (Chapter 14). In terms of personality, Berlusconi and Prodi could not have been more different. Berlusconi was the flashy, populist showman and former cruise ship crooner, and Prodi was the bookish, dull, technocratic professor. Predictably, the campaign leading up to the April 10, 2006, election was one of the most bitter in recent Italian history.

It also proved to be one of the closest elections. For the lower house, Prodi's Center–Left coalition won 49.8 percent of the popular vote while Berlusconi's Center–Right coalition won 49.7 percent, a difference of only 25,000 votes compared to the 38 million votes cast. In the upper house, it first appeared that

Berlusconi had won, but after the votes of the Italian expatriates were counted, the Prodi coalition also won a thin majority of 158 seats over 156 seats for the Berlusconi coalition.

Despite the extremely close outcome, based on proportional representation, Prodi had a comfortable majority in the lower house in terms of seats. How can this be? The distribution of votes for the lower house was based on a single nationwide district, with the proviso that the party coalition that wins a plurality in terms of votes will get at least 340 out of 630 seats (54 percent), the so-called "majority bonus." The idea of this quirky law was to ensure solid majorities, thus increasing the effectiveness of lawmakers to pass legislation. It is ironic that the author of this law was Silvio Berlusconi himself, who was now hurt by this majority bonus clause. Sometimes politicians try to be too smart!

The majority bonus ensured that while only 25,000 votes separated the two major coalitions, Prodi's coalition had 74 seats more than Berlusconi's coalition in the lower house. Another change that backfired for Berlusconi was to allow Italian expatriates to vote in these elections for the first time, because he assumed that they would vote for him. However, not only did they not vote for him, but the expatriates' votes were the ones that broke his political back. Six Senate seats were allocated for Italian expatriates in four gigantic global districts: Europe (two seats); Asia/Africa, Oceania, Antarctica (one seat); North/Central America (one seat); and South America (two seats). Of the six seats, four went to Prodi's coalition, one to Berlusconi's, and one to an independent party.

With a very slight majority in the Senate, it was difficult for Prodi to put together a stable coalition. In contrast to the first Prodi cabinet in the 1990s, this time the Reform Communists were willing to enter the cabinet. Its leader, Fausto Bertinotti, got the important and prestigious job as president of the Chamber of Deputies. It was quite a sight to see someone who still called himself a Communist preside over the debates in the lower house of parliament. In 2007, Democrats of the Left and the Daisy Democracy merged into a single party called the Democratic Party. Some at the left wing of Democrats of the Left, however, objected to the merger and joined more leftist parties. The major problem of the Prodi cabinet was that it depended on several splinter parties at the extreme left. Indeed, at one point Prodi lost a crucial vote in the Senate, which forced him to resign. But as Berlusconi did in a similar situation (see previously), Prodi followed himself, having been able to put his coalition again together. The end of Prodi as prime minister, however, came in January 2008 when a small party left his cabinet so that there were no longer enough votes in parliament for Prodi to win a vote of confidence. In April 2008 early elections were called, which brought the parties of the right back to power, once again with Berlusconi as prime minister. He attempted to merge all parties of the right into a single party, but the Northern League refused, showing once again the shaky nature not only of the left but also of the right. Berlusconi managed, however, to merge his Forza Italia with the National Alliance of Gianfranco Fini into a new party, Popolo della Libertà (People of Liberty). Although since 2001 Italy has had only two prime ministers, Berlusconi and Prodi, the country is still plagued by great instability because both the Right and the Left are internally badly split. As Italian political scientist Paolo Bellucci puts it, "The Italian party system is still unstable . . . in a constant state of flux."[25] To understand Italian politics has not become easier—on the contrary. A further unpleasant element came into play when in 2009 Berlusconi was increasingly criticized as being too flirtatious with beautiful young women, leading his wife to publicly ask for a divorce. Italian politics may be colorful but not necessarily efficient. Things got even worse for Berlusconi when in October 2009 Italy's highest court overturned a law that had given Berlusconi and a few other high office holders immunity from prosecution while in office. This ruling means that Berlusconi has to appear in court for several corruption charges. He reacted with great anger, claiming that the judges were of the political left and were thus out to get him. He ended the press conference with a defiant "Viva Italia, viva Berlusconi." In 2010, things got even worse for Berlusconi when Gianfranco Fini, deputy chairman of the new party People of Liberty, began to increasingly criticize Berlusconi over his policies, and even more damaging, over his lifestyle. Berlusconi reacted in kicking Fini out of the party, who, in turn, created a new party, Futuro e Libertà (Future and Liberty). Fini then supported a vote of no-confidence of the Left hoping to overthrow Berlusconi, but was not successful, Berlusconi being able to keep just enough votes on his side. A new low point for Berlusconi came in 2011 when he was brought to court for having had sex with a minor. Berlusconi denies all allegations, and the court case may be prolonged for a long time by Berlusconi's defense team. Italy is indeed an illustration of political instability. Italian citizens are fed up with their politicians and all their complicated power games. Finally, November 2011, Berlusconi had lost so much support in his coalition and even in his own party that he was forced to submit his resignation as prime minister.

BOX 4.1 BERLUSCONI AFFAIRS TEST PATIENCE OF FEMALE LOYALISTS

By Jean Di Marino

Some Italian women say their PM is undermining their dignity—and hope to see him jailed. My hairdresser, Flavia, calls herself a "Berlusconiana." She voted for Italy's Prime Minister, Silvio Berlusconi, when he first came to power in 1994, and has supported him ever since. She's ideally placed to sum up the range of Italian women's attitudes to Il Cavaliere (the knight), as he is widely known, in the run-up to his trial on allegations of paying for sex with an under-age prostitute.

According to Flavia, her clients are divided equally between those who love and those who loathe the premier. But recent events have not made her alter her own stance. "Everything they're saying about Berlusconi has been invented," she says. "The reports that he's going with under-age girls are all gossip." We still have to see if it's true. "They do everything to try to put him in a bad light. But in the end, they never succeed."

(Continued)

▶ BOX 4.1 CONTINUED

Political scientist James Walston, from the American University of Rome, says Mr Berlusconi's most faithful supporters are less educated and older women, who watch a lot of television. "What seems to be the case is that many of those are still with him." He says television is the reason. Mr Berlusconi's family controls Mediaset, which operates the country's top three private channels. As head of government, he also has indirect authority over the state-owned broadcaster, Radiotelevisione Italiana (Rai).

Lorella Zanardo, who co-directed a documentary called *Women's Bodies*, critiquing depictions of women on Italian television, agrees. "For 80% of people who watch television in Italy, television is their only source of information. And the television is owned by Berlusconi," she says. "So the information you receive is what he wants us to know."

Nevertheless, allegations about the prime minister's escapades have inspired some change in attitude. Florence city councillor Bianca Maria Giocoli says they triggered her decision, last year, to leave Mr. Berlusconi's People of Freedom party (PdL). She joined the new Future and Freedom party (FLI), formed by one-time Berlusconi ally, Speaker Gianfranco Fini. "I was a convinced Berlusconiana and I am disappointed," says Ms. Giocoli, a 54-year-old lawyer.

"It's like when you're in love and you discover that the person you've been with for a long time is completely different." Italy has traditions. "We have so many poets and artists, quite apart from the workers who work so hard every day. Why throw this all away? Truly it's a sin."

"There was a certain fascination . . . for Berlusconi. That's finished," says Annamaria Tagliavini, a director at a major feminist organization, the Centro di Documentazione delle Donne, in Bologna. Hundreds of thousands of women were of similar mind, rallying in Rome and other cities in February this year, saying the most recent sex scandal, involving the aspiring model Kahrima El Mahroug (nicknamed Ruby, and then 17 years old), had disgraced Italy.

James Walston says the protests were significant because women of many different classes, levels of education, and age took part. "You had older women, girls, professionals and workers who were saying: 'This is enough! This is not what women's liberation meant 30 years ago and it's not what it means now'."

Annamaria Tagliavini believes the protests were a watershed. "We've finished an era, in which there was a certain relationship of fascination—among women of a certain social group—for Berlusconi," Ms. Tagliavini says. "This sort of feeling has finished."

"With the situation getting worse from day to day—with more revelations about the premier's private life—I believe that this women's movement will become stronger and stronger. It's difficult to go back from this." But while some of his female supporters have been swayed, others are sticking to their views.

"Sure Berlusconi has parties, inviting girls to his place," hairdresser Flavia says. "It's true a public person has to take more care—but it's still his private life. When the people went out to vote, he won. The will of the people must be respected. The important thing is that he's working for the country. Now he has to govern and that's all." ■

Source: BBC News, Europe, 4. April, 2011

In the new democracies in Central and Eastern Europe, cabinet instability is oftentimes similar to that in Italy. A particularly difficult situation arose in the Czech Republic after the June 2006 parliamentary elections. In the country's 200-member parliament, both the parties of the left and the parties of the right had exactly 100 seats. This situation resulted in a severe deadlock. In September 2006, the Civic Democratic Party, a party of the right, attempted to rule with a minority cabinet; within a month, however, it lost a vote of no-confidence and had to resign. In January 2007, three members of the leftist Social Democrats defected from their side by abstaining or being absent in a crucial vote of confidence. This allowed a coalition of the right with the Civic Democratic Party, the Christian Democrats, and the Greens to win the vote of confidence 100:97. As we have seen in Chapter 2, it is noteworthy that the Greens, in Europe usually a party of the left, were willing to participate in a coalition of the right. Instability continued, and the Left attempted several times to overthrow the cabinet with a vote of no-confidence. Finally, in March 2009 four members of the Right defected and supported a vote of non-confidence of the Left, which succeeded with exactly the necessary 101 votes. In this crisis situation, a transitory cabinet of nonpartisan experts was formed with the director of the National Statistical Office as prime minister. All this shows how cabinet stability can be endangered if there is a risk of defections. Cabinet stability depends very much on party discipline within the coalition partners.

SEMIPRESIDENTIAL SYSTEMS

In semipresidential systems, there is a president elected by the people and a prime minister elected by parliament. We use France to illustrate the workings of such systems. In Central and Eastern Europe, semipresidential systems have become quite frequent, in particular in Finland, Poland, Slovakia, Romania, Bulgaria, Croatia, and Lithuania.

The semipresidential system in France was established with a new constitution in 1958 at the beginning of the Fifth Republic. (France numbers each new democratic period in its history; the First Republic was during the French Revolution.) The Fourth Republic (1946–1958) had a parliamentary form of government, and—much like Italy today—was very unstable and had frequent cabinet crises. The country also suffered from internal conflict over its involvement in colonial wars in Indochina and Algeria. In 1958, the turmoil was so great that the parties in parliament were no longer able to form a viable cabinet. Charles de Gaulle stepped in; in 1940, he had escaped the German occupation by going to London, where he organized the Resistance movement. Returning to France in triumph in 1944, he served briefly as head of the government, but soon, disgusted by the bickering among the many parties, he retreated to his rural hometown to await the hour when he could emerge as the savior of France.

Unlike other strong leaders in French history, de Gaulle did not establish a dictatorship. However, he changed the political institutions so much that his coming to power in 1958 was counted as the beginning of another Republic. He built a political system that was a combination of a presidential and a parliamentary system, with both a president and a prime minister. Since the retirement of de Gaulle, the relation between president and prime minister has changed greatly, but let us first see what the relation was under de Gaulle himself. As president, he liked to handle the big questions, leaving the routine day-to-day work to the prime minister. The president was elected by an electoral college and, after 1962, directly by the people. To be elected directly by the people corresponded to de Gaulle's leadership style. He did not want to depend on the goodwill of professional politicians, whom he detested for their selfish maneuvers. De Gaulle liked to enter into a dialogue directly with the French people, who in his view had more common sense than the politicians. De Gaulle saw himself as France's father figure: If he explained what had to be done in the higher national interest to the men and women of France, he was sure they would trust and follow him. De Gaulle believed that his personal mission was to restore the historical greatness of France. At the end of his speeches, he used to intone the national anthem and exclaim with a grandiose gesture of his arms, "Vive la France!"

De Gaulle held office from 1958 to 1969, and during those years he acted in many ways like a powerful monarch. Many important decisions were made by him alone, and critics raised the question of whether France was still a genuine democracy. A bothersome issue was the fact that the president was elected for a very long term—seven years—and could run for reelection as many times as he wished. Another distinguishing characteristic was the importance attached to the popular referendum. At first sight, this seems to have increased the democratic quality of the regime. Indeed, in Chapter 6 we see how in some European countries, the referendum is used to strengthen the political role of the people. But, under the rules of the Fifth Republic, the referendum strengthens the president by allowing him to bypass parliament and appeal directly to the people.

Still another issue that raised questions about the democratic nature of the Fifth Republic was that in its early years parliament had virtually no power. In contrast to the system of the Fourth Republic, the prime minister was not selected by parliament but was appointed by the president. Under de Gaulle, the prime minister served completely at the pleasure of the president, who could dismiss him at any time. The role of parliament was very limited. Sometimes a new cabinet sought the approval of parliament, but such approval was not necessary. Under de Gaulle, parliament also had few legislative powers, because the president often ruled by executive decrees. With regard to the relationship between the president and the prime minister, all essential power lay with the former. The prime minister had to do whatever the president did not wish to do himself. This system was tailored to the personal needs of de Gaulle, who, as already mentioned, saw himself as a world leader and liked to concentrate his attention on the big questions of foreign policy and defense. He left the day-to-day business, and especially contact with parliament, to the prime minister.

During the first years of the Fifth Republic, de Gaulle was very popular and much admired. The French people were grateful that he saved the country from the chaos of the Fourth Republic and restored order. De Gaulle fulfilled the longing for a strong leader—as had Napoléon I after the French Revolution, Napoléon III after the revolution of 1848, and Marshal Pétain after France's defeat in 1940. But unlike his predecessors, de Gaulle was ultimately not a dictator. To be sure, he eliminated many checks and balances from the political system of France. He felt responsible only to his beloved French people. Some feared that this was empty rhetoric and that de Gaulle would secure his reelection by manipulation, but this fear was unjustified. When his first term was over, de Gaulle sought reelection in a free and open competition. His main adversary was Socialist François Mitterrand, later himself president of France.

Mitterrand forced de Gaulle into a runoff, which de Gaulle won only narrowly; afterwards, much of his charismatic attraction was lost. In May of 1968, he was challenged by a massive student revolt. In the following year, he tried to restore his prestige with a referendum on regional reform and reorganization of the Senate, the upper house of parliament. De Gaulle hoped that these reforms would be popular and that an overwhelming approval by the people would again enhance the legitimacy of his regime, but he was disappointed when the referendum was defeated by a majority of 53 percent. De Gaulle had seen enough, and although he legally was not required to do so, he resigned from the presidency and retired to his small hometown, deeply hurt.

The United States had a stormy relationship with de Gaulle, who took no orders at all from Washington. He withdrew French troops from the North Atlantic Treaty Organization (NATO) command, although formally France remained a member of the alliance. (As we will see at the end of the section, in 2009 France came back as a full member of NATO). In later years, American opinion has become more positive toward de Gaulle. In the early 1990s, a survey among political scientists at American universities showed strong support for the view that de Gaulle was a figure of great historical consequence and that he brought "authority and stability" back to France.[26] This positive evaluation in retrospect is due to the fact that the institutions of the Fifth Republic were able to survive de Gaulle. Initially, it was feared that the constitution of the Fifth Republic was tailored too much to the personal needs of de Gaulle. But since 1969, France has had five presidents, and the Fifth Republic is still intact. The presidency is still the most powerful institution in France, although not as much as in the early years of de Gaulle. Since de Gaulle's resignation, other institutions, in particular parliament and the prime ministership, have been strengthened so that today the system has more checks and balances than when de Gaulle was at the height of his power.

A major constitutional change came into effect in 2000 that limits the term of the president to five years. What has also been reduced since the time of de Gaulle is the plebiscitary nature of the presidency. The immediate successor of de Gaulle, Georges Pompidou, organized a referendum in 1972. But then there was no referendum for 20 years, and it was only in 1992 that Mitterrand used the referendum in the hope of strengthening his political standing. The issue was the ratification of the Maastricht treaty for further European integration (see Chapter 14). Opinion surveys indicated strong public support for the treaty, and

Mitterrand hoped to reverse his decreasing popularity with a clear victory in the referendum. But as the day of the referendum approached, public support dwindled and the referendum passed only by the narrowest margin. As in the case of de Gaulle in 1969, Mitterrand learned that the French president could no longer use the referendum for his own purposes, as was the case in the early years of the Fifth Republic. In 2005, President Jacques Chirac submitted the new constitution of the EU (see Chapter 14) to a referendum, and to the embarrassment of Chirac the French people voted against it.

The most ambivalent feature of the Fifth Republic is the status of the prime minister. What happens if parliament is of a different political orientation than the president? To whom is the prime minister responsible—to parliament or to the president? This was no problem up to 1981 because both the president and the majority in parliament were always of the Right.

Therefore, the selection of the prime minister by presidents de Gaulle, Pompidou, and Valéry Giscard d'Estaing, who were all of the Right, did not encounter opposition in parliament. In 1981, Socialist Mitterrand won the presidency. Confronted with a parliament dominated by the Right, he immediately called early parliamentary elections, which the Socialists won. It was no problem, therefore, for Mitterrand to appoint a Socialist as prime minister. The dominance of the Socialists came to an end with their defeat in the parliamentary election of March 1986. Confronted with this situation, Mitterrand chose to invite Chirac, a leader of the Right and later president himself, to form the new cabinet. This was the first time in the history of the Fifth Republic that the president and the prime minister had come from opposite ends of the party spectrum. This system of a president of one side of the political spectrum and a prime minister of the other side is called *cohabitation*. Although there were fears of a constitutional crisis and even of a breakdown of the Fifth Republic, cohabitation worked relatively smoothly. It came to an end in 1988 when Mitterrand was reelected to a second term as president. He immediately called early parliamentary elections, which brought losses for the Right but not enough gains for the Left to reach a majority.

In this situation Mitterrand selected Socialist Michel Rocard as prime minister, who formed a minority cabinet. We have already dealt with the concept of a minority cabinet in the Swedish, Spanish, and Italian contexts; the Rocard cabinet serves as another illustration of how minority cabinets can survive. By the spring of 1991, as a result of defeats in by-elections for vacant seats, the Socialists were down to 274 seats in the National Assembly, 15 short of an absolute majority. Where could they find the necessary votes? There were 21 deputies who belonged to no party; the Rocard government could rely on, at most, 14 of these independents to support its policies. Thus, in the best of cases, it still needed at least one defection from either the Communists on the Left or the Christian Democratic Union at the Center. A good illustration of how Rocard could put together a winning coalition was the bill to reform local government that came to a vote in April of 1991. One deputy of the Christian Democratic Union voted with the government; of the independent deputies, 11 did likewise, and 3 abstained. Because not all deputies were present, the bill could pass by one vote. Sometimes, however, the Rocard government was unable to put together such winning coalitions. But in such cases it could resort to Article 49–3 of the French constitution, which allows the government to engage its survival to depend on the passage of a bill. This constitutional article is formulated in such a way that for the government to fall, the opposition needs a majority of the *total* membership of the National Assembly—not only of those voting. This is a more difficult requirement for the opposition than in Sweden, Spain, and Italy, where a majority of those voting is sufficient to bring down a government. At first glance such nuances in voting rules may seem trivial and dull, but the case of the Rocard government shows that details of voting rules may be of crucial importance for the survival of a government.

After his second term ended in 1995, Mitterrand retired and died soon afterward. The next president was Jacques Chirac of the Right, whom we have met previously as prime minister during the time of cohabitation with Mitterrand. After his first term of seven years ended, he gained reelection, but now according to the new rule only for five years. For the 2007 presidential elections, there were speculations that Chirac would run again, which would have been possible since France has no term limits. But given his age of 74, he decided against it. His favorite candidate was his prime minister, Dominique de Villepin. However, an outsider, Nicolas Sarkozy, was able to get the nomination. Sarkozy's crucial step was when he managed to win the leadership position of the Union for the Presidential Majority (UMP), the major party of the Right and Chirac's own party. Having reached this position, Sarkozy easily obtained the nomination at the party convention. He had proven what a shrewd politician he was in outmaneuvering Chirac and Villepin.

The Left entered the race with Ségolène Royal, the first time that France had a woman as a serious candidate for president. Jean-Marie Le Pen of the radical Right ran again despite his age of almost 80. The race became more lively and also more unpredictable when François Bayrou entered the race as candidate of the Center. His party was the Union for French Democracy (UDF). Traditionally, French politics pits the Left against the Right so it was something quite new to have a serious candidate at the center. French people were very interested in the race. Some election events in soccer stadiums attracted more than 40,000 people; in both rounds of the elections turnout was more than 80 percent (compare this with turnout in American presidential elections). Voter turnout in France is helped by the fact that the entire country is a single electoral district so that every vote really counts. In the United States, by contrast, there are always only a few contested states, so-called swing states.

Just as for parliamentary elections (see Chapter 3), for presidential elections, too, there are two ballots, one week apart. To be elected in the first ballot, a candidate would need an absolute majority (50 percent + 1). Given that there are always numerous candidates, there is no chance that a candidate is elected in the first ballot. The two top vote getters of the first ballot then enter the second ballot. In the first ballot of the 2007 elections, the four main candidates reached the following percentages of the votes (the remaining 13.9 percent went to eight minor candidates).

Nicolas Sarkozy	31.2
Ségolène Royal	25.9
François Bayrou	18.6
Jean-Marie Le Pen	10.4

On the basis of these results, Sarkozy and Royal could enter the second ballot, where the main battle was for the centrist voters of Bayrou. Since the UDF is traditionally more a party of the right, Sarkozy was more successful with the former Bayrou voters than Royal. Sarkozy could also get many Le Pen voters, although Le Pen had told his voters to vote for neither candidate in the second ballot. What all major opinion polls had predicted, then happened, a clear victory for Sarkozy with 53.1 percent of the votes.

Sarkozy had a good and fast start, and within a few weeks two-thirds of the French people were pleased with how he began his presidency. After he had courted in the election campaign Le Pen voters at the right, he moved now quickly to the center and even to the left; he made a prominent Socialist, Bernard Kouchner, his foreign minister. Kouchner is very popular in France as the founder of the organization Doctors Without Borders. Socialists got so upset with Kouchner that they immediately expulsed him from the party. It was a great coup of Sarkozy to pull away Kouchner from the Socialists. Sarkozy was not less successful with the UDF, making one of their prominent members, Hervé Morin, the defense minister. Most importantly from a symbolic perspective, Sarkozy appointed Rachida Dati as justice minister. She was only 41 years old, had grown up with 11 siblings in a North African ghetto of a small French town, and her father was from Morocco and her mother from Algeria. In the cabinet of 15 members, seven were women. The average age of the cabinet members was very low for French politics: only 52, the same age as Sarkozy. All this sounded like a fresh start for many French people.

François Fillon, politically close to Sarkozy, became prime minister. He had written a book in which he argued for a strengthening of the presidency. This view fit well with the ambition of Sarkozy, who wanted himself to make all important decisions, both domestically and in foreign affairs. As we have seen previously, the relationship between president and prime minister was always an issue in the Fifth Republic; with Sarkozy the president was clearly the dominant figure and the prime minister was more a coordinating director of the cabinet. Sarkozy quickly brought a lighter style to the Élysée Palace, showing himself, for example, in jogging outfit, which would have been impossible to imagine with all his very formal predecessors. As promised in the election campaign, Sarkozy wanted in many fields a rupture with the past, which he did.

The successful start of Sarkozy's presidency brought the Left very much in disarray. Even before the presidential elections, there were severe splits in the Left between those who wished to move more to the center and those who wanted to keep a very leftist position. These splits became more severe after the presidential elections, with much blame going around for the election defeat. For the parliamentary elections a few weeks later, the party of Sarkozy, Union for a

Popular Movement (UMP), could increase its voter strength from 33.3 percent to 39.5 percent in the first ballot.

Thus, Sarkozy could use his increased popularity to help his party. Also importantly, Sarkozy did profit from a split of the party of Bayrou, the UDF. Some members of the UDF founded a new party to the right of Bayrou, called New Center, who received 2.4 percent of the votes in the first ballot and allied itself with the UMP of Sarkozy. Bayrou created his own new party more to the left, called Democratic Movement; it received 7.6 percent of the votes. Thus, the UDF no longer exists. The Socialists did not do as badly as expected despite their internal fights; with 24.7 percent of the votes they stayed at about the same level as five years before. On the other hand, the parties at both extremes of the party spectrum lost. The National Front of Le Pen went down from 11.3 percent in 2002 to 4.3 percent. This was even worse than the showing of its leader in the presidential elections. In 2011, Le Pen left the leadership of the National Front to his daughter Marine who brought new energy to the party and will be a candidate for the presidential election in 2012. The Communists were down from 4.8 percent to 4.3 percent. The Greens lost, too, going from 4.5 percent to 3.3 percent in the first round of elections.

As we have learned in Chapter 3, the French parliamentary election system greatly helps the largest party, and this happened again in 2007. As we recall, to be elected in the first ballot a candidate needs 50 percent + 1 in his or her district. As Table 4.3 shows, only a single Socialist reached this threshold compared with ninety-eight UMP candidates, including the prime minister, Fillon.[27] All together, 110 candidates were elected in the first ballot with the remaining 467 seats filled in the second ballot one week later. For the reasons explained in Chapter 3, in the second ballot in almost all districts only two candidates remained, mostly a candidate of the left and one of the right. With this winner-takes-all system, the largest party has the advantage, and, indeed, the UMP received 216 additional seats for a total of 314 seats from both ballots. The Socialists could add 184 seats to the one they won in the first ballot. Compared with the previous elections, for both ballots together, the Socialists could take away quite a few seats from the UMP. What had happened between the two ballots so that the UMP, which had improved its voter percentage in the first ballot, did not do as well in the second ballot? The French election system allows voters to have second thoughts between the two ballots. With the presidency in the hands of the UMP and the prospect that the UMP would get an overwhelming majority in parliament, many voters came to the conclusion that it would be a good idea to strengthen the Socialists in the second ballot. This shows that the French election system allows for quite sophisticated voting.

Despite such strategic voting in favor of the Socialists, the fact remains that Sarkozy's party continued to control parliament, although with a reduced majority. The basic result of the 2007 presidential and parliamentary elections was that France remains divided between the Right and the Left, or as the French say, "entre la droite et la gauche." Bayrou failed in his effort to establish a strong centrist party. French people since the French revolution in 1789 have stayed either to the left or to the right.

TABLE 4.3

Voter support and parliamentary seats for the 2007 elections to the French National Assembly. First round (June 10) and second round (June 17) results

Party	First Round Results (June 10) Voter Support (%)	Seats	Second Round Results (June 17) Voter Support (%)	Seats
UMP	39.5	98	46.4	314
PS	24.7	1	42.3	185
PCF	4.3	—	2.3	15
NC	2.4	7	2.1	22
PRG	1.3	—	1.6	7
MoDem	7.6	—	5	3
Verts	3.4	—	5	4
MPF	1.2	2	—	2
Others	11.4	2	4.3	25
Total		110		577

Notes: UMP = Union for a Popular Movement; PS = Socialist Party; PCF = French Communist Party; NC = New Centre; PRG = Radical Party of the Left; MoDem = Democratic Movement; Verts = The Greens; MPF = Movement for France. The Election Politique Web site classifies the "others" as "diverse left" (15 seats), "diverse right" (8 seats), and "diverse" (2 seats).

Source: Election Politique.

Sarkozy's honeymoon was quite short, and later in 2007, he had already begun to lose popularity. He was criticized for being hyperactive and behaving like a celebrity. Politically, he had to deal with protests and strikes against his economic and social reform program, especially after the outbreak of the global economic and financial crisis. In poor neighborhoods on the outskirts of Paris, where most inhabitants are Muslim immigrants from North Africa, there were violent riots. As might have been expected, the many enduring problems of France could not be quickly solved, even by a new president full of energy. As his tenure in office continued, Sarkozy lost more and more popularity. He became increasingly authoritarian in his leadership style losing contact with ordinary French people.

CABINETS AND LEGISLATURES

What is the interplay between cabinets and legislatures? Legislators in Washington DC take a very active role in drafting legislation. In Europe, legislation is usually proposed by the cabinet, and if the cabinet enjoys a majority in parliament, few changes are normally made by the legislature. Does this mean that European parliaments are weak? Not necessarily. To be sure, cabinets tend to draft legislation, but cabinets depend on the confidence of parliament. The key power of parliament is indeed to appoint and possibly to throw out cabinets.

In Washington DC it is striking how, most of the time, members of the Senate and the House are not in the chambers for plenary sessions. They are busy in the lobbies and their offices and rush only to the chambers for votes. In European parliaments, attendance at plenary sessions is usually much higher, for example, at the question-and-answer sessions of the British House of Commons. Debates are sometimes quite lively, occasionally even rowdy. In the Italian or Ukrainian parliaments, for example, there may even be brawls and scuffles. Why this difference across the Atlantic Ocean? One reason is that U.S. legislators have much more staff than their European colleagues, and because these staff members need time-consuming supervision, legislators have less time available to attend plenary sessions. More importantly, political parties are more salient in Europe than in the United States. This has to do with the election systems used in Europe. As we discussed in Chapter 3, candidates depend in Europe much more on their parties to be elected to parliament than candidates in the United States. Also of great importance is the role played by European parties for cabinet formation, as discussed earlier in this chapter. Given this importance of political parties in Europe, it is easy to understand that members wish to vigorously present their positions in plenary sessions of parliament. For each debate, parties have their speakers who are supported by applause by their party colleagues, while they may be hassled by opposing parties. Thus, plenary sessions may be quite a spectacle. In Washington DC by contrast, political parties are much less important; members of Congress have to make sure that they remain popular in their districts and states. Therefore, they have less motivation to sit in the chamber if the issue that is being debated is not immediately relevant to their districts and states.

In Washington DC committees most often meet in public, and their hearings get great public visibility. In Europe it is very different. Parliamentary committees most often meet behind closed doors, which is a further explanation of why plenary sessions are more attended. Members of parliament wish to present in public the position they took in the committee meetings.

ADVANTAGES AND DISADVANTAGES OF PARLIAMENTARY AND PRESIDENTIAL SYSTEMS

In Chapter 13 on power sharing, we will argue that in deeply divided societies particular constitutional features may have a higher chance of achieving social peace than others. With the breakdown of the Soviet Union and the formation of many new and independent Central and Eastern European countries in the 1990s, questions of "constitutional engineering" have emerged. In other words, what advantages and disadvantages do various forms of political institutions have? Is it possible that some institutions can make a tense political situation even worse by systematically excluding particular groups, while others allow for the inclusion of a variety of such groups into government and thus alleviate potential problems?

One can think of constitutions very much like architectural structures. Architects and urban studies specialists have uncovered that it is possible to literally build aggression into some structures. High-density buildings with little green space, few trees, and no area for children and adolescents to play tend to generate aggression among the inhabitants of such structures. The same logic can be applied to constitutions: If they systematically disadvantage particular groups, limit their opportunities to voice their opinions, either underrepresent them or not represent them at all, and provide privileged access to some and not to others, it is possible to build political upheaval into particular constitutions. In this chapter we have highlighted cabinet formation, which speaks directly to the relations between the executive and legislative powers. What are the advantages and disadvantages of presidential systems and parliamentary systems?[28]

The main advantages of presidential systems are threefold. First, legislative terms are fixed. Americans are used to very "regular" election intervals. Every four years, like clockwork, there is a presidential election. This regularity provides executive stability that allows for predictable policy planning. The president cannot be removed, save via the impeachment clause.

Second, the chief executive is popularly elected. This enables the American president to claim to speak for the majority of the people. In parliamentary systems the chief executive, the prime minister, cannot claim to have the same kind of popular mandate as an American president, although in systems with two major parties it is very clear to voters who will be their prime minister, depending on which party they vote for. This is not always so clear, however, in multiparty systems, from which the prime minister emerges as a result of protracted negotiations after the legislative elections.

Third, presidential government is "limited government" as a result of the separation of powers. This stands in stark contrast to the "fusion" of powers in parliamentary systems, where in the case of Great Britain, the executive and legislative authorities almost always are made up of the same party. This puts enormous power into the hands of the prime minister. However, in the American case, the founding fathers ensured that presidential powers are checked and balanced by separate institutions in order to make it as difficult as possible for any one particular institution to dominate the political agenda.

Through examining the disadvantages of presidentialism, it becomes clear that in most cases they are simply the obverse of the very advantages just highlighted. For instance, the fixed legislative terms can easily be interpreted as leading to "temporal rigidity," meaning incapacity of the legislature to impose changes on executive authority. Once a president has won an election, there is no mechanism, save for impeachment, to remove him or her from power. This incapacity for changing the commander in chief can prove detrimental when cataclysmic circumstances such as wars necessitate a quick adjustment of leadership to a changing environment or when a president is involved in questionable affairs. An example is Richard Nixon, who continued to stay in power for over one-and-a-half years after it became public knowledge that he was involved in the Watergate scandal.

Another disadvantage of presidentialism derives directly from the separation of powers argument: Precisely because there is separation of powers, there is gridlock. One could describe the American constitution as "gridlock by design." This was most clearly shown during the Clinton administration when Bill Clinton waved his "veto pen" and blocked budget bills coming from the Republican Congress, leading to shutdowns of governmental services on two occasions. This is particularly relevant if there are incoherent majorities between the president and the two houses of the legislature, which means that either one or even both houses are of a different party from the president's. It is of course less of an issue if there are coherent majorities.

The third disadvantage is closely connected to the second: If there are incoherent majorities, who is accountable for policymaking? If one or both of the two houses are of a different party than the president's, inevitable finger-pointing arises as to whose fault it is if policymaking comes to a screeching halt.

Finally, a fourth disadvantage of presidentialism is that it tends to operate in an environment with low party loyalty. Being a loyal member of a party does not guarantee success at the ballot box. Oftentimes, "running against Washington" is precisely what proved successful for some politicians in America, even when the president was from their own party. In a presidential system, success of a representative depends on what he or she did for the district or state that is going to elect her or not. As a result, the tendency to engage in inefficient pork-barrel policies is much higher in a presidential system than in a parliamentary system.

Proponents of parliamentary systems highlight the advantages that come with "fusion" between the executive and legislative powers. As we have noted, after parliamentary elections have taken place, the majority party usually also installs the prime minister, leading to a fusion of executive and legislative power. This means no gridlock, clear accountability, and high efficiency of policymaking. In parliamentary systems, particularly with two parties, it is very clear who is responsible for political outcomes, whether they are good or bad. There is no finger-pointing from one branch of government to the next.

Another advantage is that parliamentary systems operate in an environment of strong party loyalty. Intense party loyalty tends to encourage political debates that center on national, encompassing issues rather than district-based issues. It is for this reason that pork-barrel policies are much less of a problem in parliamentary systems than in presidential ones.

Alas, just as we have seen in presidential systems, it is possible to see disadvantages in the very advantages of parliamentarism as well. Precisely because parliamentarism is built on the principle of fusion, it could be argued that it gives too much power to the executive. Those who favor more limited government would be very much concerned with the enormous powers of a prime minister and his or her cabinet.

Finally, because in parliamentary systems executive authority not only emerges from the legislature but is also responsible to it, the legislature can bring down the government by a vote of no-confidence. As we have seen in the case of Italy, this device may make for rather unstable governments. While some decry this ability of the legislature to bring down cabinets as "instability," others call it "flexibility."

What becomes obvious is that the choice between presidential and parliamentary systems is driven by negative trade-offs. If effectiveness of policymaking is more important than lengthy debates, a parliamentary system is preferable. If democratic debate, direct election of the president, and separation of powers are more important than effectiveness of policymaking, a presidential system is preferable. Another trade-off refers to stability or flexibility of government: If stability is desired, a presidential system will deliver that, while a parliamentary system will always allow, in the words of Walter Bagehot, a certain "revolutionary reserve"[29] that might come in handy if a change in executive authority becomes necessary.

There are many reasons for preferring either—a presidential or a parliamentary system. One consideration is which system tends to lead to better policy outcomes. A recent worldwide study gives the advantage to parliamentary systems:

> The evidence presented here suggests that to the extent that the nature of the executive makes a difference, parliamentary systems offer significant advantages over presidential systems. In no case examined here does parliamentary rule seem to detract from good governance. In most policy areas, particularly in the areas of economic and human development, parliamentary systems are associated with superior governance.[30]

The authors of the study argue that what makes parliamentarism "a more reliable vehicle for good public policy is its capacity to function as a coordinating device. . . . Parliamentarism should be more successful than presidentialism in coordinating diverse views and interests, all other things being equal."[31] This finding, of course, does not mean that the United States should change to a parliamentary system. Yet, it still is worthwhile to consider such findings in thinking about the future of the United States.

HEADS OF STATE

In semipresidential systems like in France, the president has important executive functions but is also head of state. This is similar to the United States, where the president is both chief executive and head of state. In Europe, however, the more common pattern is that the roles of head of state and chief executive are played by two different individuals. The head of state is either a monarch or an elected president and has mainly representative functions.

Monarchial Head of State

Great Britain probably best illustrates the functions of a monarch in a modern European democracy. The reigning monarch is Queen Elizabeth II. She appoints the prime minister, but this appointment is a pure formality. It makes for a colorful ceremony with a symbolic value when the queen invites the leader of the winning party to come to Buckingham Palace and asks him or her to form Her Majesty's next government. The losing party is called Her Majesty's opposition. An even grander ceremony takes place when the queen opens the first session of parliament with a speech. The speech is written not by the queen but by the prime minister, who uses it to announce the new government's program.

In former centuries the symbolic trappings of the monarch also had substance. The king or queen was an important political actor who, for example, had a great say in the appointment and dismissal of the prime minister. Together with other institutions, such as the House of Commons and the House of Lords, the monarch ruled the country. But in a long and slow process, the monarchy lost its substantive power. Today, the saying is that the queen *reigns,* and the prime minister *rules.* Only the trappings of the queen's power remain, but these trappings have great symbolic value.

The monarchy is quite popular in Great Britain. In our bureaucratic and anonymous world, the public seems to have a great need for colorful images. This need is not well fulfilled by modern-day politicians who, at best, give the impression of being efficient managers of huge government programs. At worst, they appear power-hungry, inefficient, and sometimes even corrupt. In contrast, the royal family does not have to run for office, and its members cannot be held accountable for what goes wrong in the government. Thus, in an ironic way, for a long time the absence of political power contributed to the popularity of the monarchy. The queen was a symbol holding the British nation together.

In recent times, however, the British monarchy has lost some of its popularity. Family quarrels, separations, and divorces are the main reasons. All of a sudden, the royals appeared to be an ordinary family with ordinary problems. It became more difficult to look up to them and to admire them as role models. There were additional problems, such as the fact that the queen agreed only reluctantly to pay taxes. Sensationalism in the media contributed greatly to the problems of the royal family. Prince Charles, next in line for succession, has had particular difficulties. In addition to his divorce problems, he is somewhat unsure about how to define his public role. In addition to undertaking the usual ceremonial duties, he sometimes speaks up on controversial issues such as modern architecture and education. It remains to be seen whether he will retain this frankness if, one day, he becomes king. This could cause problems, because the monarchy is supposed to stay above politics.

Although Americans may be most familiar with the British monarchy, several other European democracies also have monarchs. These countries include Belgium, Denmark, Luxembourg, the Netherlands, Norway, Spain, and Sweden, as well as the tiny countries of Liechtenstein and Monaco. In some of these countries, the monarchical trappings are not quite as splendid as in Great Britain. An extreme case of a stripped-down monarchy is found in Sweden. According to a 1974 constitutional amendment, the king is not even symbolically allowed to appoint the prime minister or open parliament. The Swedish king has become more of a citizen like everyone else. He does not even get special parking permits. The main task of the Swedish king is to cut ribbons, open museums, and make state visits.

A bizarre episode in Belgium in 1990 shows how politically weak the position of European monarchs has become. The Belgian king declared that in good conscience as a Roman Catholic, he could not sign a new law permitting abortion.

To circumvent the unexpected difficulty, the cabinet temporarily suspended the king and promulgated the law on its own power. Afterward, parliament was called into a special session to reinstate the king.

Spain illustrates how even in modern times there may be situations where a monarch exercises political power. Spain was a dictatorship until the death of Francisco Franco in 1975. Afterward, the monarchy was reestablished with Juan Carlos I as king. Instead of trying to have dictatorial powers for himself, he helped to lead his country to a democratic form of government. But for some time, the Spanish democracy was still frail because Franco supporters remained influential in the armed forces and the police. At one point, these groups attempted a coup to overthrow the democratic government. Some officers holding weapons in their hands entered parliament and began shooting in the air. They hoped to get the support of the king, but Juan Carlos acted forcefully in the defense of democracy and had the coup participants imprisoned. In normal times, he prefers to act as the symbolic figurehead of his country, but if new threats to the Spanish democracy should occur, he can be counted on to step in and exercise a political role.

Civilian Heads of State

Germany serves as a good illustration for a civilian head of state. In the long history of Germany, emperors and kings have played significant roles. After Germany's defeat in World War I, however, the country sent its emperor into exile. When the Federal Republic of Germany was established in 1949, its constitution provided for the office of federal president as head of state. How is the president elected, and what are his functions? Is he as politically powerless as the European monarchs? The German president is elected by a special assembly that consists of all members of the lower house of the federal parliament (the Bundestag) and an equal number of deputies from the state parliaments. Successful candidates must have a reputation that transcends party lines.

The role of president has been interpreted very differently by the people who have filled the office up to now. The first president, Theodor Heuss, played the role of political philosopher, often speaking out forcefully on fundamental questions of the democratic order. He instructed the German people on the value of democracy in a critical period of their history. Gustav Heinemann tried to be a "citizen president," seeking contact with ordinary men and women and visiting them in their homes. Walter Scheel brought great elegance to the presidency and sponsored many splendid performances by artists at the presidential palace. Richard von Weizsäcker was a rather political president, often speaking out on the great questions confronting the country.

Compared to the European monarchs, the German president exercises more political power and leadership, but also runs the risk of crossing the fine line where he or she might suddenly become too political. Walter Scheel had such an experience at the beginning of his term, when he was rebuked by the chancellor, Helmut Schmidt, who told him, in no uncertain terms, that it was not the business of the president to run the foreign policy of the country. This episode shows the delicate nature of the role played by the German president. Unlike a monarch, whose prestige is assured by a royal background, the German president must earn his or her prestige through public statements that must be neither trivial nor too overtly political. On rare occasions the president has to take over important functions. A recent example, discussed earlier in the chapter, was in 2005, when President Horst Köhler had to decide whether to follow the recommendation of Chancellor Gerhard Schröder to dissolve parliament and to call for early elections (which he did). In May 2009 Köhler was reappointed for another term, but resigned in 2010 over remarks made concerning German military interventions abroad. He argued that sometimes economic interests may demand military interventions; this remark was interpreted in the media to refer to Afghanistan although later Köhler tried to clarify that it was meant in a general sense. But the damage was done for him. This episode reinforces the point of how delicate the position of a German president is; he should speak up on public affairs but not too specifically.

Whereas the German president has more a ceremonial role like a monarch, there are other countries where the president is powerful. As we have seen earlier in the chapter, this is the case in France and some countries in Central and Eastern Europe. In these cases, the president is elected by the people, and we speak of a semipresidential system.

The main message of this chapter is that a parliamentary system is not necessarily unstable. It depends very much on the number and kind of political parties elected to parliament, and this in turn depends to a large extent on the parliamentary election systems discussed in the previous chapter. In order to understand how political parties are constrained by the institutional setting, one has to grasp the complex interactions between rules for parliamentary elections and rules for cabinet formation. To add to this complexity, we introduce in the next chapter the court systems of European democracies.

KEY TERMS

administration   93
cabinet   92
confidence of
   parliament   93
collective responsibility   96
constituency   97
grand coalition   103

minimal-winning
   coalition   106
minority cabinets   110
oversized coalitions   106
party discipline   94
parliamentary system   91
prime minister   91

semipresidential
   systems   91
shadow cabinet   94
vote of no-confidence   93
Weimar Republic   104
whip   97

DISCUSSION QUESTIONS

1. The Italian examples raise a most intriguing question: When do governments come to an end in parliamentary systems? When there is a new prime minister? When there is a new election? When there are new parties in government?
2. Who is more powerful: a president or prime minister?
3. Which system, parliamentarism or presidentialism, enjoys more "checks and balances"?

4. How important is "stability" for a political system? Can a system be "too stable"?
5. In parliamentary systems, legislators can depose a government with a vote of no-confidence. Is this an expression of "democracy" or does it invite dysfunctional political behavior?
6. In which system, parliamentary or presidential, do parties play a bigger role? Why?
7. In which system, parliamentary or presidential, does money play a bigger role? Why?

NOTES

1. Craig R. Whitney. A Talk with Helmut Schmidt. *New York Times Magazine,* September 16, 1984, p. 118.
2. *BBC News.* Cook Quits over Iraq Crisis, March 17, 2003.
3. Anthony King and Nicholas Allen, 'Off with Their Heads': British Prime Ministers and the Power to Dismiss. *British Journal of Political Science* 40 (2010): 249–278.
4. Giacomo Benedetto and Simon Hix. The Rejected, the Ejected, and the Dejected: Explaining Government Rebels in the 2001–2005 British House of Commons. *Comparative Political Studies* 40, no. 7 (2007): 755–781.
5. www.labour.org.uk, May 2007.
6. www.labour.org.uk, June 24, 2007.
7. Patrick Gordon Walker. *The Cabinet* (London: Jonathan Cape, 1970, 151).
8. Mark Wickham-Jones. Anticipating Social Democracy, Preempting Anticipations: Economic Policy-Making in the British Labour Party, 1987–1992. *Politics & Society* 23 (December 1995): 486–487.
9. *The Sunday Times,* April 30, 1995.
10. For the classical formulation of why minimal-winning coalitions should form, see William Riker, *The Theory of Political Coalitions* (New Haven, CT: Yale University Press, 1962).
11. As we have seen in Chapter 2, the Christian Democrats in Bavaria are called the Christian Social Union (CSU).
12. In Germany the prime minister is called *chancellor.*
13. Three Cantons split in the past, resulting in six half-cantons. Each of these half-cantons has only one representative in the Council of States. There are 20 full Cantons, hence a total of 46 seats in the Council of States.
14. *Neue Zürcher Zeitung,* April 10, 1996.
15. Nicholas Aylott and Torbjörn Bergmann. Almost in Government, But Not Quite: The Swedish Greens, Bargaining Constraints and the Rise of Contract Parliamentarism. Paper presented at the European Consortium of Political Research, Uppsala, April 2004.
16. Joaquín Artés and Antonio Bustos. Electoral Promises and Minority Governments: An Empirical Study. *European Journal of Political Research* 47 (May 2008): 329.
17. Torbjörn Bergman. Formation Rules and Minority Governments. *European Journal of Political Research* 23 (1993): 55–66.
18. Sona Golder. Bargaining Delays in the Government Formation Process. *Comparative Political Studies* 43 (2010): 3–32.
19. Carol Mershon. The Costs of Coalition: Coalition Theories and Italian Governments. *American Political Science Review* 90 (September 1996): 534.
20. *New York Times,* March 31, 1994.
21. For example, Le Monde, *The Guardian, Neue Zürcher Zeitung,* and Süddeutsche Zeitung.
22. *New York Times,* March 29, 1994.

23. Ibid.
24. BBC News. David Wiley. "Berlusconi Says: 'I Am Like Jesus,' " February 13, 2006.
25. Paolo Bellucci. Why Berlusconi's Landslide Return? *Politische Vierteljahresschrift* 49 (December 2008): 616.
26. Theodore J. Lowi and Martin A. Schain. Conditional Surrender: Charles de Gaulle and American Opinion. *PS. Political Science and Politics* 25 (September 1992): 498–506.
27. Sarkozy, of course, was not a candidate for parliament although he took a very active part in the parliamentary election campaign.
28. This debate follows loosely the chapter called "Introduction." In Arend Lijphart, ed., *Parliamentary vs. Presidential Government* (New York: Oxford University Press, 1992, 118–127).
29. Walter Bagehot. [1867] The English Constitution. The Cabinet. In Arend Lijphart, ed., *Parliamentary vs. Presidential Government* (New York: Oxford University Press, 1992, 66–71).
30. John Gerring, Strom C. Thacker, and Carola Moreno. Are Parliamentary Systems Better? *Comparative Political Studies* 42 (March 2009): 353.
31. Ibid., 355.

Courts

I n order to understand the court system in Europe, one has to consider also the European Union (EU) with its very powerful European Court of Justice (ECJ), with which we will deal at the end of the chapter.

The countries of *continental* Europe are all influenced by the legal tradition of ancient Rome, where **code law** prevailed. Great Britain deviates from this pattern in having a tradition of **common law**, where judges continually reinterpret old precedents in the light of new circumstances. Code law, by contrast, is characterized by complex bodies of categories and subcategories that give the courts limited discretion in handling particular cases. The classical code law is the Napoléonic code system, which Napoléon introduced in France after the Revolution and which under French revolutionary influence spread to the other countries of the continent. The Napoléonic codes were conceived as positive legal commands that judges were strictly obligated to obey, to avoid a government of judges. As Alec Stone puts it:

> The judge's role was a subservient and bureaucratic one; he was required to verify the existence and applicability of statutory norms to a case at hand, but he could investigate the work of the legislature no further. . . . Judicial review was all but unthinkable.[1]

In the United States, on the other hand, judges have always enjoyed great political influence. They have, in particular, the authority to overturn as unconstitutional decisions of the other branches of government. As Shapiro and Stone explain:

> In the American model of review, any judge of any court, in any case, at the behest of any litigating party, has the power to declare a law unconstitutional. This power is what Americans always think of when they see **judicial review**.[2]

At first, Europeans took the United States as a negative example of a nation practicing a government of judges. But in the latter half of the nineteenth century, European legal scholars increasingly began to argue for the merits of constitutional judicial review. Thanks to the influence of one of these scholars, law professor Hans Kelsen, Austria was the first European country to introduce constitutional judicial review after World War I. Constitutional review as practiced in Europe means that only separate, specialized courts, the so-called constitutional courts, exercise review powers. After 1945, an increasing number of European countries introduced such constitutional courts. When, in the 1970s, authoritarian regimes fell in Greece, Spain, and Portugal, these countries, too, introduced constitutional courts.

In the United States, judicial review is of a concrete nature in the sense that a real case or controversy is a precondition for judicial review to take place. Judicial review in this concrete sense is also known in Europe. In addition, Europe embraces the concept of **abstract judicial review**, which means that a legislative text is reviewed by the constitutional court before the text becomes law. Various combinations of the two review forms occur in different countries. Germany, for example, has both a concrete and an abstract form of judicial review; France has only an abstract one. Abstract review is initiated by politicians, who refer legislation directly to the court. As Stone puts it, the court undertakes, so to speak, a "final reading" of a bill. In doing so, the decision making of the judges is closer to legislative decision making than when they apply the constitution to concrete litigation.[3]

We now look at five countries that handle judicial review in very different ways: Great Britain, Switzerland, Germany, France, and Hungary.

GREAT BRITAIN

American readers may be surprised to learn that the British have no written constitution in the sense of a single document. British political institutions, practices, and civil liberties have evolved over many centuries. Some of the resulting rules are codified; others exist only as unwritten customs and conventions. Even the most fundamental laws have no special status and can be changed by parliament, just like any other laws. Great Britain is said, therefore, to have an unwritten constitution.

In their daily work, the courts apply the law to specific cases, but they have no right to say whether a law is constitutional. Questions of constitutionality rest in the hands of parliament. Does this lack of constitutional judicial review by the courts lead to an arbitrary regime? Is there a danger that the majority in parliament will abuse its power to rewrite and reinterpret the constitutional rules according to selfish interests? Where are the checks and balances in this system? These are troublesome questions for someone accustomed to the American system.

The British system is based on a very different philosophy of government. In Great Britain, the main task of the voters is to elect parliament, which alone has the legitimate right to express the will of the people. Because the people give full power to parliament, it would be illogical—according to British tradition— for a high court to check the actions of parliament. These checks are made by the people in the next election. If the majority in parliament interprets the constitution against the wishes of the people, the voters can replace the governing party at the next election with the party in opposition (see Chapter 4).

Does this system run the risk that one day a governing party might restrict democratic freedoms or even cancel future elections? In other words, what prevents a governing party from establishing a dictatorship? The answer is a commonly accepted democratic political culture. The British system is based on the assumption that everyone accepts certain basic rules of the game. One such rule is that free elections take place at regular intervals. There are also many commonly accepted rules concerning the protection of individual freedoms, some of which go back to medieval times. The British assume that no governing party will ever dare touch these fundamental rules. Thus, the stability of the system is ultimately based on an element of fair play.

Within the framework of commonly accepted basic rules, parliament can take whatever actions it sees fit. Thus, parliament can nationalize key industries, and no court can intervene with the argument that such a measure violates the constitution. Parliament can also decide abortion matters in whatever manner it sees fit. Parliament is sovereign, and it alone can say what is constitutional. For many American observers, this lack of judicial review is appalling. Which is the better system—the British or the American? One could argue that the voters have greater influence in Great Britain, because they can replace the governing party with the opposition, thereby hoping to reverse earlier decisions of parliament. One example of such a reversal is when Labour nationalized key industries, only to have them again denationalized by Conservatives when voters sent that party back into power. With this system, the will of the people can be quickly translated into political action. As Richard Bellamy of University College London argues, the British system "is more legitimate than the judicial process at resolving disagreements."[4]

In the United States, voters can influence Supreme Court decisions only in an indirect and tenuous way. They can vote for a particular presidential candidate in the hope that, if elected, he or she will have the chance to nominate new judges. In the confirmation process, senators often listen to the views expressed by voters. All this is true, but it must be remembered that often the composition of the Supreme Court does not change much over many years because there are no term limits for Supreme Court judges—not even a mandatory retirement age. One also has to take account of the fact that judges often develop in directions not anticipated by the president nominating them or the senators confirming them. Under all these circumstances, the Court may be unresponsive to the immediate wishes of the people. The decisions of the Court may not correspond to the prevailing public opinion of the time. Although this system appears less democratic than the British system, it has the advantage of giving more continuity to the law of the land. Who should be the watchdog for the constitution: parliament, which is directly accountable to the people, or judges, who are more detached from popular pressures? There are good arguments on both sides.

Although Great Britain has no constitutional judicial review, it has so-called **statutory judicial review**, which means that judges have the right and the obligation to review what in the country is lawful and what is not. This includes reviews of administrative regulations, which may be struck down by the courts. Thus, the role of British courts should not be downplayed too much because, after all, they can interpret the meaning of a law when they apply it to concrete cases. This gives a certain amount of power to the courts.

It should also be mentioned that for more than 600 years, the House of Lords had certain judicial functions. It served as the supreme court of appeal. This function was not exercised by the House of Lords as a whole but by 12 so-called law lords. They are highly qualified judges appointed by the queen on the recommendation of the prime minister. Law lords had a seat in the House of Lords but did not usually take part in controversial political discussions. This quite archaic arrangement reveals the influence of tradition in Great Britain. Recently, however, it was recognized that it is strange if members of a legislative branch also have judicial functions, and in 2005 both the House of Commons and the House of Lords decided that the law lords should be separated from the House of Lords and form a special supreme court of appeal. This special court of appeal, the Supreme Court of the United Kingdom, began to operate in August 2009.

SWITZERLAND

In contrast to Great Britain, Switzerland does have a single document that serves as its constitution, but, like Britain, Swiss courts do not have the right to determine whether a particular law is constitutional. In the Swiss case, this decision is ultimately made by the people in a **referendum**. Thus, the Swiss go a step further than the British in giving final authority over constitutional questions—they give it not merely to the representatives of the people but to the people themselves. Most Swiss believe that in a true democracy the most vital decisions must be made not by judges or members of parliament but by the citizens. Are the citizens mature and legally educated enough to decide complex constitutional issues? Switzerland is a good case for examining this question (see also Chapter 6).

How is it organized so the voters can decide questions of constitutionality? First, voters have the right to call for a popular referendum on every bill decided by parliament. The only requirement is that 50,000 signatures be obtained, which is relatively easy in a country of 7.5 million inhabitants. There are many motives for calling a referendum on a particular bill, but one possible reason is that some voters may feel that the bill violates the constitution. It is then up to the voters to decide whether this is so. A bill is enacted into law only if no referendum is called or if the bill is accepted in the popular vote.

The voters also have the final say on constitutional amendments. All constitutional amendments decided by parliament must be submitted to the voters. A minimum of 100,000 voters can also submit a constitutional amendment of their own, which will first be debated by parliament but finally decided in a popular referendum. This instrument of the popular constitutional initiative is widely used and can be applied to whatever question the people wish to decide. If the voters wish to amend the constitution in a particular way, neither parliament nor the courts have the power to intervene. Recently, a constitutional initiative was launched to establish a system of hiking trails throughout the country. Constitutional lawyers might argue that this issue is not important enough to be included in the constitution. The people decided otherwise, so the Swiss constitution now contains an article about hiking trails.

From the perspective of a clear and systematic distinction between the levels of constitution on the one hand and laws on the other, it is bothersome that sometimes the voters approve constitutional amendments that really belong in a law or even an administrative regulation. A far greater problem arises, however, if the voters add an article to the constitution that contradicts other parts of the constitution. Such an extreme case occurred early in the twentieth century, when a constitutional initiative was accepted prohibiting the killing of animals according to Jewish kosher rites. On the surface, the proposal was presented as an animal protection measure, but its real intent was clearly anti-Semitic. As Beatrix Messmer correctly states, democratic rights were manipulated "to discriminate against a minority group."[5] The referendum allowed anti-Semitic feelings to be expressed in the secrecy of the voting booth. Did such an amendment contradict the religious freedom guaranteed by the constitution? One would assume so. However, if the people themselves decide that the two parts of the constitution are compatible, so be it. The people interpret what is constitutional, and no court can overrule their decision, because the people are the highest authority in the land—the sovereign, as the Swiss like to say. A very recent example of the Swiss voters showing their ultimate authority against the will of parliament was the referendum decision November 29, 2009, to ban the further construction of minarets in Switzerland. This decision made very negative internationl headlines, but the Swiss sovereign had spoken and nothing could be done about it.

The examples of the kosher rites and the banning of minarets show the dangers of giving ultimate power over the most basic constitutional questions to the people. Unlike judges, voters may be less concerned with the logical consistency of their decisions. Because most voters have little, if any, legal training, there is a risk that they follow their emotions and prejudices rather than logic. Thus, the people may act like a whimsical dictator. On the other hand, participation in referenda may help to educate voters, making them more responsible and consistent in their judgments. Thus, fortunately, the referendum on kosher rites a hundred years ago remains an isolated extreme case, and the article was in the meantime eliminated from the constitution.

What about constitutional initiatives that violate international law? In this respect, the Swiss parliament in 1996 for the first time set limits on constitutional initiatives. The Swiss Democrats, a party of the New Radical Right, had collected enough signatures for a constitutional initiative, the acceptance of which would have allowed asylum seekers to be expelled from Switzerland even if war continued in their country of origin. Such an amendment to the constitution would have violated an important principle of international law, the principle of *non-refoulement,* according to which refugees have the right not to be sent back to a country at war. Recognizing the obligation of Switzerland to uphold this principle, the Swiss parliament declared the initiative of the Swiss Democrats as invalid so that it was not submitted to the voters. It is interesting to note that this decision of invalidation was made by parliament and not by the courts.

GERMANY

Germany is a good illustration of a country with a strong **constitutional court.** After World War II, it tried to learn from the manner in which Hitler overthrew the Weimar Republic. Hitler based his power, in many respects, on newly written laws. The courts at that time possessed only a very weak tradition of constitutional judicial review and, therefore, were hesitant to strike down these laws as unconstitutional. As a consequence, Hitler was able to argue that he had acted within legal limits. When the constitution of the Federal Republic of Germany was written, great care was given to avoid the possibility of a dictatorship being established by seemingly legal means. The key responsibility for this endeavor was given to the Federal Constitutional Court, which is located in the city of Karlsruhe (thus the saying that Karlsruhe has decided).

The structure of the court was heavily influenced by the American occupation authorities, who used the U.S. Supreme Court as a model. The German court, however, consists of two units called senates, which have equal power but exercise mutually exclusive jurisdiction. The First Senate decides issues arising out of ordinary litigation; the Second Senate handles disputes among branches and levels of government. The members of the Constitutional Court are selected by parliament based on a rule of party apportionment. The court is administratively independent; it has its own budget and the right to hire and fire its employees. In the relatively brief history of the Federal Republic, the court has established its moral and political authority as watchdog of the constitution. Like the Supreme Court in the United States, the Constitutional Court in the Federal Republic has played an important role in the abortion issue. When the government coalition of Social Democrats and Free Democrats liberalized the abortion law in 1974, Christian Democrats brought the issue to the court, which declared the new law unconstitutional. The judges argued that the right to life guaranteed by the constitution also applied in principle to the unborn child. Following this decision, parliament enacted a less liberal law. It is noteworthy that the right to life was included in the constitution in order to prevent atrocities such as those committed under Hitler. The hope was that the Constitutional Court would remain strong enough to strike down any act violating the constitutionally guaranteed right to life.

After German unification, the court once again had to deal with the abortion issue. East Germany had a much more liberal abortion law than West Germany. The newly elected parliament of the united Germany tried to find a middle ground between the two practices. But the new law, passed in June 1992, was challenged in court. On May 28, 1993, the Second Senate of the Constitutional

Court ruled in a differentiated way, accepting many parts of the law and rejecting others. The basic ruling was that in the first three months abortion was legal only in the case of rape, when the life of the mother was in danger, or when the child had a hereditary defect. In all other cases, abortion would be illegal—but not punishable. At first, this seemed a paradoxical ruling, and there was great confusion in the initial commentaries by politicians and journalists. The ruling ran to 183 pages. When the details emerged, it became clear that the court was saying that the implications of an illegal abortion were that it could not be done in a state hospital and that state-funded health insurance was not available. Poor mothers, however, could receive welfare payments. This ruling shows to what extent the German Constitutional Court is willing to get immersed in minute legislative details.

Another interesting court decision was made in 1992 concerning public subsidies to political parties. Such subsidies began in 1959. They were increased significantly by a law in 1989, which was pushed through parliament by all major parties except the Greens. The latter took the law to the Constitutional Court, which decided that the law was indeed, in large part, unconstitutional. The court did not deny that the political parties had a certain right to be reimbursed by the state for part of their costs, but it objected to the fact that, according to the new law, parties were financed to about 60 percent by the state.[6] The principle established by the court was that the parties had to draw the major part of their financial resources from private hands. This case is a good illustration of how the German Constitutional Court is able and willing to stand up against the interests of the major political parties.

A last example to illustrate the importance of the German Constitutional Court stems from the decision in 2005 to have early elections for the Bundestag, the lower house of the German parliament. As seen in Chapter 4, the coalition of Social Democrats and Greens under the leadership of chancellor Gerhard Schröder had difficulties implementing its economic reform program because of resistance at the left wing of the coalition. According to the German constitution, Schröder and his coalition did not have the power to call for early elections. Such a decision was up to the president of the country (for this office, see Chapter 4), to whom Schröder recommended that early elections be held. The president followed this recommendation, but some members of the Bundestag brought the matter to the Constitutional Court with the argument that the coalition of Schröder still had a working majority in parliament, thus calling early elections violated the constitution. Here again, the Constitutional Court had the ultimate say, and as we have seen in Chapter 4, the outcome was that the court allowed early elections.

FRANCE

The constitution of the Fifth Republic in 1958 created a **Constitutional Council,** which was a new development for France. The council has nine regular members who are appointed for a nonrenewable term of nine years by the president of the republic and the presidents of the two chambers of parliament, the National Assembly and the Senate. As a somewhat strange feature for an American reader, former presidents of the republic are de jure life members of the Constitutional Council, adding to the nine regular members.

It is also somewhat strange to an American reader that the French Constitutional Council is not at the summit of a hierarchy of lower courts. In this sense, the Constitutional Council cannot properly be called a supreme court. As Alec Stone puts it, the Constitutional Council "does function as a kind of legislative chamber within parliamentary space, and an umpire in the political game." In what sense is the Constitutional Council an umpire? It supervises parliamentary work, stepping in at the point after which a law has been voted upon but before it is promulgated. The Constitutional Council has the authority to censure an entire law or part of it. For changes in political institutions of France it is mandatory for the Constitutional Council to step in. For ordinary laws and international agreements, the court only steps in when asked by either the president of the republic, the prime minister, the president of the National Assembly, the president of the Senate, 60 members of the National Assembly, or 60 members of the Senate. Alex Stone concludes that "one simply cannot understand the French legislative process without an understanding of the role, direct or indirect, of the Council." The Constitutional Council also rules on the lawfulness of presidential and parliamentary elections.

There is another judicial body in France, the **Council of State** (*Conseil d'Etat*). It has about 300 members who are recruited from the top ranks of the prestigious school of public administration, the ENA (École nationale d'administration). The Council of State steps in earlier in the political decision process than the Constitutional Council, namely, before a bill is submitted to the cabinet. The highly professional members of the Council of State examine the judicial soundness of the draft bills. The Council of State is also the highest administrative court in France, ruling on conflicts between different administrative units and complaints against the administration.

HUNGARY

When the countries of Central and Eastern Europe went through a transition to democracy after 1989 (Chapter 11), by and large they adapted a system of judicial review following in particular the examples of Germany and the United States. Hungary is a good example of this trend toward judicial review in Central and Eastern Europe, which we will illustrate by discussing a decision made by the Hungarian Constitutional Court on February 23, 2009. It concerns an amendment to the Hungarian Competitive Act. The issue was a two-year occupational ban for top executives in companies involved in illegal cartels. The court had no objection that such executives should be punished by not being allowed to have top executive offices in any company for two years. The court objected, however, to the procedures leading to such occupational bans, because the burden of proof was with the executives, which violates the principle of innocence until proven guilty. According to the controversial amendment, it was up to the executives to exculpate themselves in proving that they did not directly take part in the decision making about illegal cartels or that they had raised objections. On this ground, the court declared the amendment as partly unconstitutional. In this way, the court got involved in minute details of legislation holding up the important constitutional principle that nobody should be forced to prove his or her innocence.

THE EUROPEAN COURT OF JUSTICE

The European Court of Justice (ECJ), not to be confused with the European Court of Human Rights which we will discuss in Chapter 14, is located in Luxembourg, and has 27 judges, who are appointed by "common accord" of the national governments of the member countries.

The judges of the ECJ take an oath to decide cases independently of national loyalties. They are able to follow this oath to a large extent. Two aspects of the court's decision-making process help them to do so: first, the secrecy of their deliberations, and second, the absence of the recording of dissenting opinions in the court. As a consequence, to a large extent the judges can free themselves from accountability to their home governments.

A first landmark decision came in 1963 in *Van Gend & Loos v. Nederlandse Administratie der Belastingen*. A private Dutch importer invoked the common market provisions of the Treaty of Rome against the Dutch government, which attempted to impose customs duties on specified imports. The court proclaimed:

> The Community constitutes a new legal order . . . for the benefit of which the states have limited their sovereign rights, albeit within limited fields, and the subjects of which comprise not only Member States but also nationals. Independently of the legislation of the Member States, Community law therefore not only imposes obligations on individuals but it is also intended to confer upon them rights which become part of their legal heritage.[7]

With this ruling, the court established that individuals in the EC have rights that they can enforce against their own national governments. The Dutch government had argued that the application of the Treaty of Rome over Dutch law was solely a question for the Dutch national courts. The ECJ ruled otherwise, stating that "henceforth importers around the community who objected to paying customs duties on their imports could invoke the Treaty of Rome to force their governments to live up to their commitments to create a common market."[8]

A second landmark "constitutional" decision of the ECJ was *Costa v. ENEL*, which established that where a term of the Treaty of Rome conflicts with a national statute, the treaty must prevail. In a later publication, Judge Federico

Mancini justified the decision with the argument that the supremacy clause "was not only an indispensable development, it was also a logical development."[9] His logic was that in a supranational organization, community law must prevail over member state law in cases of conflict. With the ratification of the Maastricht treaty, the ECJ even received the right to impose a penalty payment on a member country that fails to comply with its judgment.

A case decided by the ECJ on March 6, 2007, illustrates nicely how the court can overrule national legislation.[10] The case concerns Italian legislation on which betting operators need a license. Excluded from getting licenses are operators who have shares traded on the stock market so that speculation is not possible by betting on stocks. Italian authorities limited the number of awarded licenses to 1,000 for sports betting and 1,000 for horse betting. Stanley International Betting, Ltd., an operator incorporated under English law with a license of the City of Liverpool, became active on the Italian betting market with three Italian operators with contractual links to Stanley. These three operators had no Italian license and were threatened with criminal penalties of up to three years' imprisonment. They appealed to the ECJ with the argument that they were excluded from receiving an Italian license because the shares of Stanley are traded on the stock market. In this way, the EU principle of freedom to provide services was said to have been violated.

The court acknowledged that the Italian legislation on betting places restrictions on the freedom to provide services. However, according to the court, such restrictions may be justified for moral, religious, or cultural reasons, and also in light of the financially harmful consequences of betting for individuals and society. The court also accepts that there are reasons why the Italian authorities limit the number of licenses they issue. But the court does not accept the blanket exclusion of specific categories of operators, in this case of operators whose shares are traded on the stock market. The court acknowledges that, in principle, criminal legislation is a matter for which the member states are responsible. However, criminal legislation may not restrict the fundamental freedoms guaranteed by the EU, and this is said to be the case for Italian legislation on betting with the clause to exclude all operators whose shares are traded on the stock market. Therefore, Italy cannot apply criminal penalties to the three contractual operators of Stanley. This is a good case to show how the ECJ can overrule national legislation and also how the court can go into detail on which clauses of a particular legislation violate EU law and which do not.

The ECJ has become very important in the legal system of the EU. Individuals, national governments, and the institutions of the union must respect the rulings of the court. Mary L. Volcansek makes this general point for Italy in writing that "in the space of three decades, the Italian Constitutional Court accorded supremacy to EC law in the Italian legal system."[11] What holds for Italy also holds for all other EU countries.

Do national governments bring each other to court in Luxembourg? On the basis of Article 170 of the Treaty of Rome they can do so, but this article is rarely applied. The reason is that confrontations between member countries are potentially dangerous for the stability of the EU. To prevent such inflammatory disputes, the court has actively and successfully encouraged the increased use of Article 169 procedures, whereby it is the European Commission that initiates court action against a particular member country for not following community legal obligations. This device has a more objective character and allows a member country to more easily accept a ruling of the court than if it is directly confronted by another member country. To depoliticize its rulings even further, the ECJ often tries to settle an issue on the basis of Article 177, which allows it to define an issue not in terms of a dispute between national governments but between private parties of the respective countries. All this shows once again the great influence of the court on the internal life of the EU. Lawyers in the member countries increasingly pay attention to the rulings in Luxembourg, and the ECJ has become an important subject in the teaching of European law schools. If Americans wish to do business in Europe, it is to their advantage to become familiar with the ECJ.

Even in areas such as criminal law, where national law has always been understood to reign supreme, European law is taking precedence over national law. In a far-reaching decision in September 2005, the ECJ ruled that the EU has the power to introduce harmonized criminal law for its member states, creating for the first time a body of European criminal law that all members must adopt.[12] The reason why this is so crucial is that one of the last vestiges— namely, control over how to punish criminals and on what grounds—has largely moved from the national level to the supranational level. National authorities will continue to police particular offenses, and national judges will still adjudicate whether a crime has been committed, but with this ruling, the European Commission gained the right to request member states to enforce various EU laws by using civil and criminal penalties.

This ruling was occasioned by a conflict between the Council of Ministers and the European Commission, which challenged the former about its interpretation of the "Framework Decision on the Protection of the Environment Through Criminal Law." The Council of Ministers, representing national interests, argued that, as EU law currently stands, member states cannot be forced to impose criminal penalties established by the EU. The European Commission, the most supranational institution in the EU, disputed this view and asked the ECJ to adjudicate this dispute, with the ECJ ultimately supporting the Commission's stance.

There is no European national guard, such as the National Guard in the United States, to enforce EU law, but the ECJ can rely quite well on the member countries to enforce its rulings. To be sure, the national governments may sometimes protest over a particular ruling of the court, as seen with the ECJ decision about criminal law, but ultimately they will accept the legitimacy of the ruling. One of the most celebrated instances of a member country defying the court was the *Sheepmeat* case in 1979, in which the court ruled against the French government for imposing restrictions on the import of sheep meat from Great Britain. At first, France defied the ruling, but after losing in the first two instances, it accepted a third ruling of the court and asked merely for a delay in implementing its obligations.

INCREASED IMPORTANCE OF COURTS

There is a trend in many European countries, and in particular at the level of the European Union, to give more weight to courts in the political decision process. Courts, however, have by far not the same importance in Europe than in the United States. The major difference is that European courts are much less confronted with big emotional moral issues. The death penalty is a case in point. In the United States, courts have to deal with the question whether the death penalty and what forms of the death penalty violate the constitutional principle against cruel and unusual punishment. By contrast, in Europe the death penalty is politically no issue at all since there is consensus that it is against the basic human right of bodily integrity. The European Union indeed does not accept any member country practicing the death penalty. Turkey, in order to prepare membership in the European Union, has abolished the death penalty. Other emotional, moral issues such as abortion, homosexuality, school prayers, and flag burning are of little importance in the public debate in Europe compared with the United States. When these issues still come up in Europe, they are often handled by parliaments or popular referenda and not by courts. Further differences between Europe and the United States are that the American judicial system is more adversarial and operates more with juries. Having pointed out differences in the court systems between Europe and the United States, it is also noteworthy that these differences become smaller with European courts gaining importance.

KEY TERMS

abstract judicial
 review   136
code law   135
common law   135

Constitutional
 Council   141
constitutional court   140
Council of State   142

judicial review   135
referendum   138
statutory judicial
 review   138

DISCUSSION QUESTIONS

1. Since Great Britain does not have a written constitution, which body determines, in effect, whether a law is constitutional or not?
2. What explains the presence of judicial review in the United States, and its absence in Great Britain?
3. Who decides in Switzerland whether a law is constitutional or not?
4. The function of supreme courts is generally described as interpreting the constitution. However, does judicial review not give courts great influence in shaping, that is, in making, laws? Does this power not interfere with the authority of parliaments, whose job it is to make laws?[13]

NOTES

1. Alec Stone. The Birth and Development of Abstract Review: Constitutional Courts and Policymaking in Western Europe. *Policy Studies Journal* 19 (Fall 1990): 81.
2. Martin Shapiro and Alec Stone. The New Constitutional Politics in Europe. *Comparative Political Studies* 26 (January 1994): 400.

3. Stone, The Birth and Development of Abstract Review, 82.
4. Richard Bellamy. The Democratic Constitution: Why Europeans Should Avoid American Style Constitutional Judicial Review. *European Political* Science 7 (March 2008): 11.
5. Beatrix Messmer. The Banning of Jewish Ritual Slaughter in Switzerland. *Leo Baeck Institute Year Book LII* (2007): 185–194.
6. *Neue Zürcher Zeitung,* April 10, 1992.
7. Anne-Marie Burley and Walter Mattli. Europe Before the Court: A Political Theory of Legal Integration. *International Organization* 47 (Winter 1993): 62–63.
8. Ibid., 61.
9. Ibid., 66.
10. www.curia.europa.eu, March 6, 2007.
11. Mary L. Volcansek. Impact of Judicial Policies in the European Community: The Italian Constitutional Court and the European Community Law. *Western Political Quarterly* 42 (December 1989): 580.
12. Europe Wins the Power to Jail British Citizens. *TimesOnline,* September 14, 2005.
13. Stone, The Birth and Development of Abstract Review, 81.

Referenda

We have to be aware of the distinction between a **representative** and a **direct form of democracy**. If a democracy is representative, the citizens elect their representatives, who then make the substantive decisions. In a direct democracy, substantive matters are decided by the citizens themselves in referenda. Switzerland practices the referendum the most of all European countries. The notion of direct citizen involvement in actual decision making has deep roots in Swiss history. In medieval times, the pastures high in the mountains were communal property; thus, decisions about these pastures were made communally—for example, when exactly in early summer to bring the cows up to the alpine pastures. When modern Switzerland was established with the constitution of 1848, its founders drew on these ancient traditions. The Swiss spoke in a mystical way of reviving the old democratic freedoms. They remembered Old Switzerland too nostalgically, however. For example, they forgot that there were many serfs who did not share in the communal property of the pastures. However imperfect reference to the historical reality of medieval times was, it was crucially important that the nineteenth-century founders of modern Switzerland could cite direct democratic traditions that they were trying to restore. Combined with the revolutionary ideas of the Enlightenment, these old democratic traditions led the Swiss to incorporate the popular referendum in the constitution of 1848. In the beginning, the referendum was limited to constitutional amendments proposed by parliament. Later in the nineteenth century, the people themselves received the right to propose constitutional amendments. The voters were also given the right to call for a referendum on legislative bills. In Chapter 5, we described the rules with regard to the number of signatures necessary for a referendum to be held.

When the referendum was introduced, it was expected to have an innovative effect. The founders of modern Switzerland wished to overcome the inaction of the old regime and its dominance by a few ruling families. They anticipated that voters would be open to change, but in fact, the opposite was true, and the referendum has often had a delaying effect. The best example is the introduction of female suffrage. Parliament was prepared much earlier than ordinary male voters to grant women the right to vote. Several amendments to the constitution that would have established female suffrage were defeated in referenda. The margin of defeat, however, was smaller each time until finally, in 1971, women were given the right to vote. This example is typical in the sense that it shows how it often takes a long time to convince the Swiss voters to accept a new idea. Once an idea is accepted by the voters, however, it sticks much better. Thus, male voters now accept women in politics quite easily, and since 2010 four of the seven seats in the Federal Council, the Swiss cabinet, have been occupied by women. The slow pace of Switzerland is also seen with regard to the EU. Switzerland is still not a full member of the EU, but in several referenda Swiss voters agreed to intensify the relationship with the EU with a set of bilateral treaties. An important such step was taken in February 2009, when Swiss voters accepted that the free labor market with the EU be extended to the new EU members, Romania and Bulgaria (see Chapter 14).

Of course, it is not always undesirable to delay a decision. Delay can prevent precipitous decisions that are regretted in retrospect. There have been quite a few cases in which the Swiss voters were wise not to move as quickly as their leaders desired. For example, some negative referenda prevented Switzerland from expanding its system of higher education as quickly as countries such as the Federal Republic of Germany had done. Today, it is generally agreed that these referenda had the positive result of less crowding in Swiss universities, as compared to overcrowded German universities.

Although the referendum generally has had a delaying effect, on some occasions new ideas have been brought into public debate as a result of a referendum. Some students had the original idea of making one Sunday every month traffic-free on Swiss roads. This not only would have saved energy but also would have brought some calm to everyday life. Once a month, the highways would have been opened to strollers and bicyclists. The students collected enough signatures to allow the proposal to be submitted to a referendum. All major political parties and interest groups found the idea well intentioned but impractical. The students received broad support in the popular vote, but their proposal was still narrowly defeated. Despite this ultimate defeat, this is a good illustration of how the referendum can help to bring unorthodox ideas to public attention.

There are also cases where fresh ideas pass in the referendum. An example is the so-called Alp Initiative, where environmental groups collected enough signatures for the demand that within 10 years all heavy trucks passing through Switzerland be put on railroad flatbeds. Although the federal parliament shared the view that more trucks should be put on rails, it rejected the initiative as too extreme. Yet, 52 percent of the voters accepted the initiative.

How responsible are Swiss voters when they participate in a referendum? Is there a danger that they simply vote for their own narrow interests? Is there a threat that the **interests of minorities** are neglected? There is always the possibility of a **tyranny of the majority**. And, yes, there are cases in Swiss history when minorities suffered from the results of a referendum. In Chapter 5, we described how an anti-Semitic constitutional amendment prohibiting the slaughter of animals according to kosher rites was approved. Another conflict over minority rights concerns conscientious objectors. For a long time, parliament was willing to allow them to serve the country outside the army, but attempts to change the constitution in this direction failed in several referenda, until finally the voters, too, accepted the idea that conscientious objectors need protection.

Such examples show the worst side of the referendum, but in other cases the referendum has revealed consideration for minority rights. Illustrative are several referenda on the issue of foreign workers in the 1970s. During the economic boom of the 1960s, Switzerland admitted so many foreign workers that they came to number more than 1 million in a total population that was then 6 million. This foreign presence was felt in many segments of Swiss society: In some school classes foreign children outnumbered Swiss children. Many Swiss no longer felt at home in their own country and began to refer to the "foreignization" of Switzerland. Politically, an anti-aliens movement developed, with its adherents demanding a severe reduction in the number of foreigners allowed in Switzerland. This movement launched several constitutional initiatives that would have forced hundreds of thousands of foreigners to leave the country almost immediately. Swiss voters were greatly tempted to accept these constitutional initiatives. Not only was the economic boom over, but Switzerland also gave the impression of being overcrowded, with too much traffic on the highways and a severe housing shortage. To be sure, all major political parties and interest groups recommended rejection of the constitutional amendments as morally wrong. But there was the obvious danger that frustrated voters would vent their antiforeigner prejudices. No rational justification was necessary, only a mark on a secret ballot. The constitutional amendments received broad popular support but were defeated each time, although sometimes quite narrowly. In recent years, however, the anti-immigration movement became better organized with the right-wing Swiss People's Party taking the lead. It launched a constitutional initiative requiring stricter and faster measures to expel immigrants with a criminal record. Against the will of the Federal Council and the Federal Parliament, Swiss voters accepted the initiative although it violated some international law.

How does the Swiss voter make his or her decision in a referendum? Is the Swiss citizen a wise sovereign who is well informed and carefully weighs all arguments for and against a proposal? The referendum has certainly had an **educating effect** and has raised the level of political knowledge, but the Swiss citizen should not be viewed too idealistically. Propaganda is an important feature in referenda campaigns. Even more than in elections, the views of citizens can be molded in referenda. In elections, most voters have some long-standing party loyalty that is difficult to change. But in a referendum, voters may be very unfamiliar with the issue and consequently much more open to propaganda effects. Money and organization are, therefore, important weapons in referenda. However, a costly campaign can sometimes also backfire by creating sympathy for the financially weaker side.

Voter turnout in referenda is often shamefully low, sometimes only between 30 and 40 percent. At other times, however, the interest of the voters is great; in 1992, an unusually high 78 percent participated in a referendum on the membership of Switzerland in the European Economic Area. For the expansion of the free labor market to Romania and Bulgaria in February 2009, turnout was also relatively high at 51 percent. Many explanations for the generally low turnout have been offered by scholars and other commentators. Might four times a year (on average) be too often to call on voters to cast their ballot? Have the issues become too complicated? Are the causes deeper? Do they lie, for example, in a selfish retreat into private lives or a general distrust of politics? In fact, the explanation of the generally low voter turnout probably lies in a combination of these and possibly other factors.

The greatest weakness of the referendum as practiced in Switzerland is that **unconventional minorities** are not sufficiently protected. The greatest strength of the referendum is the **legitimacy** it gives to political decisions. An increasing problem in modern democracies is the lack of legitimacy of many political decisions. Thus, transferring more political responsibility from politicians and bureaucrats to the people means the voters share the blame and cannot complain too much about the democratic legitimacy of the decisions.

For a long time, Switzerland was the only European country practicing the referendum at a significant level. In recent years, however, there is a trend all over Europe to refer political decisions more often to referenda. Voters increasingly feel that they are qualified enough to speak for themselves. They reject the idea that all decisions should be made by professional politicians, whom they tend to view with decreasing respect. Many recent corruption scandals have eroded public respect for politicians. Today, many European citizens have begun to ask why politicians know what the people need better than the people themselves. A push for referenda also comes from a development described in Chapter 2—namely, that the traditional party labels have lost meaning when it comes to new issues such as drugs and the environment. Voters often have little knowledge of which party to vote for in order to do something about such issues. Would it not be better in such cases to let the voters speak for themselves in a referendum? Even when party labels still do have meaning, many European voters feel that important decisions are made not by the parties but by powerful interest groups and state bureaucracies. A vote for a particular party may not have any great impact in certain cases, and interest groups and bureaucracies are almost immune to election results. Here again, voters may wish to exercise their influence not only in elections but also in referenda.

David Butler and Austin Ranney argued some time ago that referenda "are almost certain to increase in number and importance in the years ahead."[1] This has indeed happened in many European countries. Illustrations are Sweden and Austria, which settled the tricky issue of nuclear power in referenda. In Italy and Ireland, the divorce issue was controversial for many years and was finally submitted to a referendum. For matters at the level of the European Union, the referendum has gained particular importance, as we will see in Chapter 14.

In May of 2007, Romania used the referendum to settle a severe conflict between the president and the prime minister. As we have seen in Chapter 4, many European countries have both a president and a prime minister, and sometimes it is not clear how the functions of the two roles are differentiated. Such a conflict emerged in Romania and went so far that the prime minister used his majority in parliament to depose the president. This decision was submitted to the voters for approval, and three-quarters of the voters decided that the president should stay in office. Generally speaking, European voters get more and more say through the increased use of referenda on issues ranging from deciding on the European constitution to whether a president should be deposed.

Although there is a trend toward referenda in Europe, one should not overlook the arguments that are made against this trend. The eighteenth-century philosopher and constitutional lawyer Montesquieu formulated in a classical way the basic objection to the popular referendum. He was willing to give to the people, except the lowest class, the right to elect their representatives. With regard to the referendum, however, Montesquieu argued that the people were not capable and enlightened enough to make substantive political decisions.[2] Great Britain is the country where today one most often hears fundamental objections to the referendum. Whereas supporters of the referendum stress that democracy is, above all else, government *by* the people, the British see the ideal of democracy best fulfilled in government *of* and *for* the people. At the core of this notion is the belief that parliament can better speak for the people than the people themselves. Parliament is *of the people* in the sense that its members are elected by the citizenry; but once elected, parliament is sovereign and has not only the right but the duty to make decisions for the people. According to British political thinking, parliament cannot delegate this duty to anyone else— not even to the people.

How do the British justify the idea that decisions are best made in parliament? There is a certain sacred mystique about the British House of Commons, located in Westminster Palace on the Thames River in the heart of London. Westminster is considered the birthplace of modern parliament, and there, generation after generation, the people have spoken out through their representatives. In the British view, the crucial point is that the **voice of the people** is not only heard but debated. In this process of debate, the people's true needs are expected to be clarified and to emerge in a "purified" form. Thus, the "sum" of the people's will as expressed in the decisions of the House of Commons is more than the mere addition of what each individual citizen desires. Arguments are judged not simply according to the frequency with which they are expressed but also according to their logic and plausibility. Parliamentary debate also takes account of the intensity with which a position is held. The British doctrine is that in a referendum the voice of the people is expressed in raw form, whereas in parliamentary debate these manifold voices are integrated through negotiation into a more coherent overall will. The members of parliament are able to exercise a strong leadership role with this doctrine. They are not simply messengers for the demands of the voters; their task is, rather, to put those demands into the larger context of the common good. This approach is supposed to lead to the best possible legislation.

As might be expected, the reality of the House of Commons does not correspond to this idealistic doctrine. Debates are often partisan and rancorous, and they sometimes deteriorate into shouting matches. Despite such behavior, the doctrine that parliamentary debate helps to transform the will of individual voters into the general will of the people still helps to justify the belief that a true democracy should be of a representative, not a direct, nature. The British have held, however, a national referendum: in 1975, over Britain's continued membership in the European Community, now known as the European Union (Chapter 14). Two years earlier, when the Conservatives were in power, Britain had joined the European Community. Labour was badly split on the issue, and they saw no other way to resolve their internal conflict when they came to power than to organize a national referendum. The notion that parliament is sovereign was not formally overthrown with the referendum, however, because it was explicitly stated that the referendum was to be advisory only. The governing Labour Party followed the advice of the people, who, according to the referendum, wished to remain in the European Community.

The 1975 referendum may have set an important precedent. It can be argued that if a British government ever wishes to withdraw from the EU, it will first have to obtain the assent of the voters in a referendum. The possibility of a referendum was discussed for the ratification of the 1991 Maastricht treaty, formally known as the Treaty on European Union. But the Conservative government of John Major prevailed with its argument that the instrument of the referendum was alien to the parliamentary tradition of the country. Major stressed the advantages of parliamentary scrutiny against a decision in a referendum "where many votes may be cast on matters wholly unrelated to the treaty." By contrast, the House of Commons "will scrutinise the bill line by line, clause by clause and vote on it in the same way."[3] Major presented here in a classical manner the British argument against the use of the referendum. In 2011, however, Great Britain organized for a second time a national referendum, this time over a change in the parliamentary election system, as we have already seen in Chapter 3.

In the United States in the 1970s, there was some movement in Congress to introduce the referendum at the federal level, but this movement never got off the ground, and the issue has disappeared from the political agenda. Based on the European experience with the referendum, should the issue be brought up again in Washington DC? Would it be beneficial for the United States to have referenda not only in some states like California but also at the national level?

KEY TERMS

educating effect   150

interests of
  minorities   150

legitimacy   151

representative/direct form
  of democracy   148

tyranny of the
  majority   150

unconventional
  minorities   151

voice of the people   152

DISCUSSION QUESTIONS

1. Does the result of a referendum in general reflect the "will of the people"?
2. Who is most likely to turn out for a referendum?
3. The constitution of the United States is based on "We, the people . . . . ," and yet, there are no national referendums in the United States. Should there be?
4. Are referenda in general more applicable to small or large states?
5. Is it correct to say that policies based on referenda are more democratic than policies enacted by legislators in parliament?
6. Are referenda equally useful for any political issue? For instance, are referenda equally useful for deciding whether immigrants should have access to public benefits or whether to engage in a mix of fiscal policies and austerity programs in order to create higher economic growth?

NOTES

1. David Butler and Austin Ranney. *Referendums: A Comparative Study of Practice and Theory* (Washington, DC: American Enterprise Institute, 1978, 226).
2. Montesquieu. De l'Esprit des Lois. In Roger Callois, ed., *Œuvres Complètes,* vol. 7 (Paris: Gallimard, 1951, 400).
3. *Financial Times,* September 8, 1992.

Federalism

Federalism brings political decision making closer to the people. The opposite of a federalist form of government is a **unitary government** in which all important decisions are made in the capital of the country. We will use France as an example of a unitary form of government. In a federalist country, many important political decisions are made not at the national level but at lower levels of governments, such as states and **cantons**. For federalism to exist, **subnational units** must have some autonomy, especially in financial matters. Federalism is most secured if subnational units can raise their own taxes. When we add in the level of the European Union (EU), governmental structures become more complex since many political issues are decided at the European level. For unitary countries, this means that we have to deal with both the EU and the national levels of government. For federalist countries, we have three levels: the EU, the national, and the regional levels. In this context, political scientists often use the concept of **multilevel government**, which is further explained in Chapter 14.

The Latin root word of federalism, *foedus,* means "tie" or "bond." A federalist system of government consists of autonomous units that are tied together within one country. In a federalist government, the individual units are not simply bureaucratic districts of the central government; instead, they have their own independent power, which is constitutionally guaranteed. In other words, under federalism, government activities are divided and sometimes shared between one central and several regional governments. In unitary governments, the regional units are merely bureaucratic in nature.

Most European countries have a long history of centralization where no autonomy was given to regional units. Switzerland, by contrast, was for centuries merely a loose military alliance of sovereign cantons like Zurich, Bern, and Lucerne. This was a good basis for federalism when modern Switzerland with its own constitution was created in 1848. Among European countries Switzerland is the prototype of a federalist country. With a population of only 8 million, it is divided into 26 cantons and about 3,000 local communes. Taxes are raised at all three levels with only about one-third going to the federal level.

Switzerland has great linguistic and religious diversity. It has four official languages, all of which are explicitly mentioned in the constitution: According to the 2000 census, 63.7 percent of the Swiss population speak German, 20.4 percent French, 6.5 percent Italian, and 0.5 percent Romansh, which belongs to the family of Romance languages and is spoken only in Switzerland. The remaining 8.9 percent of the population, mainly foreigners, speak a large variety of languages, none of which have an official status. With regard to religion, 41.8 percent of Swiss said that they are Roman Catholic, 35.3 percent Protestant, 7.5 percent another denomination, mainly Muslim immigrants, and the remaining 15.5 percent did not give any religious denomination. Switzerland's regional differences range from remote mountain valleys to cosmopolitan cities such as Zürich and Geneva. Despite this diversity, Switzerland enjoys high political stability.

A major reason for this stability is indeed its federalist structure. Switzerland's cantons are highly autonomous, and some of them proudly call themselves republics. The official name for the canton of Geneva, for example, is Republic of Geneva. Swiss federalism developed from the bottom up, in the sense that the cantons existed before the Swiss Confederation. The cantons built a *foedus*, to use the Latin expression, or bond, holding them together within a single political system. Thus, federalism in Switzerland can be compared to federalism in the United States, where the original 13 states also existed before the Union.

To understand Swiss federalism, it is important to emphasize that the cantons, not the linguistic communities, are the building blocks. All but four of the cantons are linguistically homogeneous. In the canton of Geneva, for example, public school students are taught only in French. Leaving educational and cultural matters to the cantons alleviates a thorny problem for a multilingual country; for instance, the Swiss do not have to fight at the national level over which textbooks should be used in the schools. Such issues are handled at the cantonal level.

However, other important issues must be dealt with at the national level. And here, there is always the possibility that blocs of cantons may form along linguistic lines, so that the language differential might still have political importance. Divisions among the country's linguistic groups occur, for example, in foreign policy, in particular with regard to the relationship of Switzerland to the EU, in that the French speakers are more willing to join than the German and Italian speakers.

Overall, such head-on confrontations between French- and German-speaking cantons are not too frequent. One reason is that the border between French- and German-speaking Switzerland is located in three bilingual cantons, blurring the distinction between linguistically based blocs of cantons. More important, neither the German-speaking nor the French-speaking parts of Switzerland are internally homogeneous. Important differences cut across the linguistic borders, and on certain issues some German speakers may have more in common with French speakers than with other German speakers. This is often true from an economic perspective: The tourist and banking industries, for example, are located in all three major linguistic areas. It would be very different if they were concentrated in only one language area. In that case, economic and linguistic interests would reinforce each other.

It is also significant that the Catholic–Protestant division cuts across the border between German and French speakers. Some German-speaking cantons are predominantly Catholic and others are Protestant, and the same internal division can be found among the French-speaking cantons. If the religious and linguistic areas were the same, it would be much more likely that coherent blocs of cantons would confront one another. With linguistic, economic, and religious lines cutting across one another in a complex way, Swiss politics is character-ized by constantly shifting coalitions. A German-speaking mountain farmer of the Catholic faith may have interests in common with other German speakers on one issue, with other Catholics—irrespective of language—on a second issue, and with other mountain farmers—irrespective of language and religion—on a third issue. Due to these shifting coalitions, no single group is a permanent majority; each group risks being in the minority on at least some issues.

Switzerland has no dominant capital, another factor that has helped make federalism work. If a country has a strong center, such as Paris in France, it is difficult to decentralize power, not only in form but also in fact. The Swiss parliament and the executive Federal Council are located in the capital, Bern, but the Swiss supreme court is located in French-speaking Lausanne. Bern is only the fourth-largest city in Switzerland: Zürich, Basel, and Geneva each have more inhabitants. Bern is also not Switzerland's business or cultural center. Swiss federalism gives some powerful instruments for the exercise of power to the economically weaker cantons. As in the U.S. Congress, the parliament in Switzerland has a second chamber in which each canton holds two seats, regardless of population.[1] Furthermore, when a constitutional amendment is submitted to a referendum, acceptance requires not only a majority of the voters but also a majority of the cantons. Another important aspect of Swiss federalism is that the cantons are regularly consulted about the drafting of federal legislation. Although this involvement seems to give a strong voice to the small cantons, a growing weakness of Swiss federalism becomes appar-ent in this process of **cantonal consultation**. As a country with a highly devel-oped economy, Switzerland is increasingly confronted with complex issues that require specialized expertise. This development puts the smaller cantons at a disadvantage, because they often lack the necessary professional staff to prepare well-researched answers for the federal authorities. This raises the question of how far decentralization can be taken without endangering the problem-solving capacity of a country.

How about federalism in other European countries? The most dramatic change from a unitary to a federalist government occurred in Germany after the defeat of the Nazis. Under Hitler, Germany was a unitary state, with all political power concentrated at the center in Berlin. This government structure was seen as a major factor in Hitler's ability to take total control of his country. After his defeat in 1945, the occupying powers were eager to dismantle Germany's centralized government structure. The French even suggested breaking up Germany into several independent countries so that the military might of the German people would be broken forever. The division of Germany into eastern and western parts after World War II should be seen in this same context. Although the Western powers were not happy that the Soviet Union had established a Communist state in East Germany, they were not too unhappy that Germany was divided into two parts.

The effort to decentralize power in Germany was also apparent in 1949, when a democratic government was established in the three Western zones. The structure of that government—in accordance with the wishes of the three occupying powers, the United States, Great Britain, and France—was federalist in nature. The importance of this was reflected in the new country's name, the Federal Republic of Germany. Like the United States, the Federal Republic was divided into states (*Länder*). There were 11 Länder within the Federal Republic.[2] Some, such as Bavaria, had a long tradition of autonomy, and even independence, in German history. With German unification in 1990, five more Länder were added, so that today Germany consists of 16 Länder. Like the American states, the German Länder have areas for which they are solely or mostly responsible, such as education. The federal parliament has a second chamber, the **Bundesrat**, in addition to the Bundestag. The government of each German state sends representatives to the Bundesrat, where all federal bills that impact Länder affairs must be passed. Federalism has helped to decentralize power in Germany. Important decisions are made not only at the federal level, but also in the state capitals. The negative side to this system is that government responsibilities are sometimes blurred. Despite this drawback, federalism has become firmly established in the German political culture.

Like Hitler in Germany, Mussolini established a strongly centralized structure of government in Italy. When democracy was restored after World War II, Italy remained a unitary state. To be sure, the 1948 constitution provided for autonomous regions, but this part of the constitution was only implemented for five so-called special regions at the periphery, such as the island of Sardinia. It was only in 1970 that regionalization was extended to the entire country, and Italy is now divided into 20 regions, each of which has a regional parliament and a regional cabinet. Why did this regionalist development occur in Italy? The main reason is not that the central government in Rome had too much power but, on the contrary, that it had too little. For many centuries, Italy had cultural and geographic but not political unity. Only during the second half of the nineteenth century was the country united politically, and its historically rooted political diversity is still felt today. The people of Naples, for example, have not forgotten that they had their own kingdom for centuries. Given the different historical traditions of the various regions of Italy, it is often difficult for the central government to exercise its authority today. Add bureaucratic sloppiness and corruption, and it is easy to see why the central government in Rome is often inefficient. The impetus behind regionalization is the hope that by bringing government closer to the people, its efficiency will increase. This is the same argument made in the United States for transferring more power from Washington DC to the states.

Can Italy's government now be classified as federalist? Compared with the American states and the German Länder, the Italian regions are weak. The fact that most of their revenues come from taxes collected by the central government and not by the regions is especially detrimental to their autonomy. On the other hand, regional authorities are elected by regional voters, not appointed by the central government. Thus, whether Italy today is classified as a unitary or a federalist government depends on the criteria used. Arend Lijphart is probably correct in his classification of Italy as still unitary because the autonomy of the regions is not yet sufficiently guaranteed by the constitution.[3] Yet, things are in flux, and, as we have seen in Chapter 2, Italian regional parties have recently gained momentum, especially the Northern League under its charismatic leader, Umberto Bossi.

Spain is another country with a strong regionalist trend. Francisco Franco, like his Fascist friends Hitler and Mussolini, established a strongly centralized government. When democracy was restored after Franco's death in 1975, the central authorities were immediately confronted with demands for regional autonomy. These demands, which were suppressed under Franco, could now be articulated under a democratic form of government. The demand for more autonomy is particularly intense and sometimes even violent in the Basque province, which has a cultural tradition distinct from that of the rest of Spain. The Basque problem is further complicated by the fact that Basques also live across the French border (see more on the Basque problem in Chapter 12). Other Spanish provinces, such as Catalonia and Andalusia, also seek more autonomy.

In Great Britain, too, the central government in London is confronted today with vigorous demands from regional movements. These demands come mainly from the Scots, the Welsh, and the Irish Catholics in Northern Ireland. Although Great Britain's official name is the United Kingdom of Great Britain and Northern Ireland, it remains to be seen how united the country can remain. The Irish Catholics were fighting for a long time and to some extent still today for independence from Great Britain and unification with the Republic of Ireland (see Chapter 12). In Scotland and Wales, although the main demand is for more autonomy, some people seek independence. The cases of Spain and Great Britain show that a federalist trend can, in fact, become so strong that separation becomes an option. This issue was raised in the United States in the Civil War.

Traditionally, the most unitary state in Europe has been France, the "one and indivisible nation." The basis for its unitary government structure was established in the time of **absolutism** of the Bourbon kings and was later reinforced by the regimes of Napoléon I and Napoléon III. As a result of these historical developments, Paris dominates the country like no other capital in Europe. Paris is not only the political but also the artistic, intellectual, and economic center of France. Nearly every fourth French person lives in metropolitan Paris. From a Parisian view, the rest of France is often considered, in a condescending way, as provincial. The departments into which France is divided are established as bureaucratic districts of the central government, not as means for local self-expression. Government buildings throughout France display no regional flags, only the national blue-, white-, and red-striped flag. But even in France, regional movements have begun to demand more local power—in Brittany, Alsace, and on the island of Corsica, for example. Some concessions to these movements have already been made. Thus, it was a gesture of symbolic value when the prestigious École nationale d' administration was transferred from Paris to Strasbourg, the main city in Alsace. As a correspondent for the *New York Times* wrote, "It is one of the more extraordinary sights in France: the future elite of the country, the exquisitely articulate men and women who will rule ministries and state industries, gathered…hundreds of miles from the corridors of power in Paris."[4] But it was equally of symbolic value when the highest administrative court of France decided that the elite school had to be moved back to Paris.[5] This episode shows how strong the unitary tradition in France still is.

Among the smaller European democracies, the federalist trend is most apparent in Belgium, which was formerly a strictly unitary country and is now federalist in its institutional structure. The delicate language situation is behind this change in structure. In addition to a small German-speaking group, the two major linguistic groups are French-speaking Walloons and Dutch-speaking Flemish. Relations between Walloons and Flemish are especially tense in the capital, Brussels, and its suburbs, where the language border is often contested. There are endless debates, for example, about the language to be spoken at particular post offices. To the outside world such incidents may seem trivial, but they are indicative of underlying tensions between the linguistic groups. Belgium has now been transformed from a unitary to a federalist government structure. The details of the new structure are complex: Belgium is divided into three regions—French-speaking Wallonia, Dutch-speaking Flanders, and bilingual Brussels. In addition to these three regions, its governmental structure contains three so-called cultural communities: French, Dutch, and German speakers. To make things even more complicated, the Dutch-speaking community has been united with the Dutch-speaking region, so that there are altogether five governmental units.[6]

Although there is trend toward more federalism in Europe, one should not overlook the arguments against this trend. One hears warning that public monies may be wasted if each sub-national unit tries to solve problems on its own, because unnecessary **duplications** may occur. It is also argued that fairness in the treatment of all citizens can only be guaranteed if national standards for areas such as education and health care are set and implemented.

KEY TERMS

absolutism 159
Bundesrat 158
cantonal
  consultation 157

cantons 155
duplications 160
multilevel government 155

subnational units 155
unitary government 155

DISCUSSION QUESTIONS

1. Is federalism always preferable to a unitary form of government, or are there also major advantages to a unitary form of government?
2. Federalism appears to be a more democratic form of government, but is it a more "effective" form of government, that is, a government that can "get things done" at a national level?
3. In contrast to "effectiveness," do you think federalism is a more "efficient" (getting the most out of given amount of resources) form of democracy?
4. Do you think that federalism works better in smaller countries than in larger ones?
5. Some people argue that federalism is more democratic because it narrows the space between people's votes and political outcomes. However, can you think of a disadvantage of federalism as far as the quality of Democracy is concerned?
6. Do you think that federalism is preferable in a homogenous society (similar in language, religion, ethnicity, race, etc.), as opposed to a heterogeneous society?

NOTES

1. For the half-cantons, see Chapter 3 and note 12 in Chapter 4.
2. Berlin (West) was also a Land but had special status.
3. Arend Lijphart. *Democracies: Patterns of Majoritarian and Consensus Government in Twenty-one Countries* (New Haven, CT: Yale University Press, 1984, 169–186).
4. *New York Times,* February 13, 1993.
5. *Neue Zürcher Zeitung,* June 5–6, 1993.
6. *Neue Zürcher Zeitung,* April 24–25, 1993.

Social Movements

As political scientist Hanspeter Kriesi correctly states, social movements "are highly elusive phenomena which are inherently difficult to grasp."[1] What do these movements have in common? Kriesi considers a social movement "to be an organized, sustained, self-conscious challenge to existing authorities on behalf of constituencies whose goals are not effectively taken into account by these authorities."[2] The key element of this definition is that social movements attract **dissatisfied outsiders** who challenge the policies of the authorities. And, in contrast to political parties and economic interest groups, social movements are only loosely organized. As Kriesi puts it, "Except for a small group of core movement activists who staff the social movement organization, individual citizens are solicited for active participation in movement campaigns only for limited periods of time."[3] Such campaigns try to catch the public eye using actions such as street demonstrations, hunger strikes, occupations of buildings, and petitions. Kriesi says about action campaigns:

> Each action campaign is spatially and temporally limited. The totality of the action campaigns concerned with a particular challenge makes up the movement. To the extent that there is a degree of coherence and continuity to the challenge, it is secured by the organizational infrastructure of the movement.[4]

To explain the activities of social movements, Figures 2.2 and 2.3 are helpful. Figure 2.2 shows on a two-dimensional space the New Radical Right as authoritarian economically somewhat to the right. In Figure 2.3 the Greens are located on the leftist postmaterial position. The point in the present chapter is that at these two locations there are not only two political parties but also many social movements as defined above. There are many people at these two locations who are dissatisfied with the traditional political parties and interest groups. At the leftist postmaterial position we find in particular the environmental movement; the peace movement; Third World and antiglobalization movement; the women's movement; and the lesbian, gay, bisexual, and transgender movements. We begin the chapter with the presentation of these leftist postmaterial movements. Social movements of the New Radical Right are mainly antiimmigration movements.

ENVIRONMENTAL MOVEMENT

In Europe, as in the United States, there is an increasing concern about the environment. In Europe the concern may be even more immediate, because Europeans live in much more crowded conditions than Americans. Most European countries have a much higher population density than the United States. The Netherlands, the most densely populated European country, has 13 times more people living per square kilometer than the United States. For the European Union at large, population density is four times higher than in the United States.

Concern about the environment in Europe began in the 1960s, primarily with regard to water pollution. At that time, the problem was basically seen in technical terms. It was thought that sufficient know-how and financial resources could remedy the situation. This expectation was justified with regard to water pollution, and today some European rivers and lakes are cleaner than they were 40 years ago. Swimming is even allowed at a few places where it was prohibited only a short while ago, and salmon can be found today in London's Thames River.

In the 1970s, worries began to develop about the environmental impact of **nuclear power,** and the discussion took a more fundamental turn. People questioned whether there should be limits to economic growth in order to eliminate the need for provision of more and more energy. For many environmentalists, disposal of radioactive waste material became a symbol for technological development over which the experts had lost control. Fears were expressed about genetic damage to future generations.

During the 1980s, the environmental question assumed greater urgency when it began to be publicly reported that many of Europe's forests would be dead by the end of the century because of air pollution. This brought home the problem to many who had not been particularly concerned before. Today **global warming** has very much moved to the forefront of public consciousness. Suddenly, warnings about catastrophic consequences to nature are relevant not merely to the indefinite future but also to the present.

The fight against air pollution became a prime political issue, but the task was much more difficult than the fight against water pollution: Dirty air cannot simply be cleaned mechanically like dirty water. The fight for clean air must begin at the sources of pollution, and many environmentalists believe that the fight cannot be won without basic changes in people's lifestyles. (Concerning the question of a simpler lifestyle, see also the discussion on the Green Party in Chapter 2.) Some steps have already been taken to change the lifestyles of

Europeans in environmentally sound directions. Strong efforts have been made, for example, to curtail private transportation and to bring about a shift toward using more public transportation. Many European inner cities now ban private cars and allow only public transportation, taxis, and bicycles. Particularly advanced in this respect is Groningen, the Netherlands' sixth-largest city.[5] It has a large car-free center, and today 57 percent of the population use a bicycle to travel in the city. There is ample parking space for bicycles. Economically, the city has staged a remarkable recovery. In the inner city rents are rising, and businesses like it. Indeed, shopkeepers on streets in which cars are still permitted have demanded that cars be banned from their streets, too.

European business leaders are also increasingly receptive to environmental concerns, accepting the principle that environmental costs of production be added to the selling price of products. Expressed in technical economic terms, this means that external environmental costs are internalized into the selling price. When you buy, for example, a battery for your flashlight, the cost for the recycling of the battery is already included in the price. When you have used up the battery, you can bring it back to any store selling batteries. With this system, a very high number of batteries are recycled in a professional manner, which is excellent for companies in the recycling business and for the environment. Thus, the principle that external costs are internalized into the selling price is ultimately good for innovative businesses in this area and in some countries has resulted in high recycling rates. In Switzerland, for example, 67 percent of all batteries are recycled. This is good but not good enough for the Swiss Environmental Agency, which wants to bring this figure at least to 80 percent.[6]

How is the environmental movement in European countries organized? Because of its multilayered historical development, it has anything but a unified structure. Associations for the beautification of nature as a first layer existed long before the general public became concerned about the environment. Traditionally, these associations promoted such causes as the protection of rare plants and animals and the building of foot trails. Mostly organized in an old-fashioned way, they reacted rather slowly when environmental questions became politically explosive issues. Most of these older associations eventually adapted their organizational structures to the new political situation, and today many of them play an important role in the environmental movement.

A second layer of environmental groups arose more or less spontaneously from specific local issues. These groups became known under the term **citizen initiatives.** When a town or a neighborhood was threatened with some environmental danger, such as toxic waste or a nuclear power plant, and no political parties or other organizations were willing to help, ordinary citizens often took the initiative and organized to defend their interests. Because their fights sometimes continued for years, after a while these groups tended to take on a more sustained organization, often directing their attention to other issues and staying together even when the original issue had been settled.

A third layer appeared when environmentalists began to organize their own political party. In Chapter 2 the development of the Greens as an environmental party was described. However, the **Green Party** does not speak for the entire environmental movement. Many environmentalists prefer to stay outside a party framework, whereas others try to work within the older parties—a fourth layer of the environmental movement. Most of the political parties in Europe have recently turned their attention to environmental concerns. This is particularly true not only of the Socialists but also of the Conservatives. The latter play with the word *conservation* and argue that conservation of nature has always been a key point in Conservative thinking.

When asked in surveys about their most immediate concerns, citizens in Europe rank the environment much lower than 10 or 20 years ago. The global financial and economic crisis has brought issues such as unemployment, the cost of health care, and immigration very much to the forefront. The environment is also less of a hot political issue because the environmental movement was so successful that its demands have now almost been universally accepted by all political parties, at least in their programmatic statements. This does not mean that there is no longer work to be done with regard to the environment in Europe. For example, despite excellent public transportation, there are still too many private cars on European roads, contributing to air and noise pollution. Such external costs of private cars are more internalized in the price of gas than in the United States, making gas much more expensive in Europe than in the United States. Nevertheless, the price of gas in Europe would have to be raised still much higher for all external costs of private driving to be internalized.

PEACE, THIRD WORLD, AND ANTIGLOBALIZATION MOVEMENTS

The movement against war goes in cycles in European history. Beginning in the 1920s, after the atrocities of World War I, pacifists sought complete disarmament so that no other war would ever occur, but these early pacifists could not prevent the coming to power of Adolf Hitler and the outbreak of World War II, with its even greater atrocities. The 1950s brought mass protests against **nuclear armaments**, especially in Great Britain and the Federal Republic of Germany. During the late 1960s, students all over Western Europe organized massive demonstrations against the military involvement of the United States in Vietnam. At this time, the European peace movement began to be closely linked with Third World issues. The war in Vietnam was seen as an **imperialist enterprise** of the foremost power of the Western world against a poor, Third World country. In recent times, the concern for world peace and the well-being of poor Third World countries is increasingly also expressed in the antiglobalization movement. Its main targets are the big international companies that are criticized for exploiting the third world and in this way contributing to local wars over scarce resources such as food, as people struggled not to starve to death. (See more on the antiglobalization movement in Chapter 15 in the context of globalization.)

With the beginning of the Reagan era in the early 1980s, the European peace movement got a new push. The deployment of American nuclear missiles in Europe—decided by NATO in 1979—became the prime target of peace activists, many of whom wished to abolish the entire American military presence in Europe. The professed goal of the **peace movement** was to distance Europe from the tensions between the Soviets and the Americans. A policy of neutralism or nonalignment was advocated for Europe. Even more than in earlier periods, peace and Third World issues were closely linked. The military help of the United States for the Contras in Nicaragua came under particular criticism by the European peace movement. Another prominent target was the support of Western countries and multinational corporations for the white apartheid regime in South Africa. In both Nicaragua and South Africa, the European peace movement saw the rich West use military force and other forms of oppression against poor, Third World groups.

The end of the Cold War plunged the European peace movement into a deep crisis that began in December 1987, when Mikhail Gorbachev, for the Soviet Union, and Ronald Reagan, for the United States, signed the Intermediate Range Nuclear Forces (INF) Treaty, which mandated from both sides the withdrawal of all medium- and short-range missiles in Europe. The first reaction of the peace movement to the INF Treaty was celebration. As political scientist Diarmuid Maguire describes it for Britain:

> On the day the INF Treaty was signed local peace groups lit beacons all over Britain as a mark of celebration. Greater Manchester Campaign for Nuclear Disarmament organized a victory march at which slices of sponge cake were distributed . . . thousands of women surrounded Greenham Common (a missile site) to celebrate the future departure of Cruise missiles.[7]

Was the signing of the INF Treaty and the ensuing end of the Cold War indeed the result of the actions of the peace movement? Did its mass demonstrations in the early and mid-1980s pay off? Although this is what the peace movement claims, another plausible interpretation is that it was the initial deployment of American missiles in Europe that ultimately helped the cause of peace. Only when the Soviets saw that the Americans were willing to continue to defend Europe did they agree to negotiate about the missiles. According to this interpretation, the peace movement was not a help but rather an obstacle to peace. If the movement's mass demonstrations had been successful in preventing the deployment of the American missiles, the danger of aggressive actions by the Soviet Union would have increased greatly. Which interpretation is correct? An objective answer is difficult to give, perhaps even impossible. Both sides will continue for years to insist on their own interpretation.

Despite all their celebrations, the peace activists were also worried. As Maguire has found for Britain:

> Campaign for Nuclear Disarmament organisers were worried that the beginning of change at the top of international politics would lead to the end of the movement from below . . . the dilemma for Campaign organisers was how to raise movement morale by claiming a success without exacerbating the process of demobilisation.[8]

Unfortunately, the INF Treaty and the end of the Cold War did not mean peace in Europe. As we see in Chapter 12, ethnic and national conflicts dramatically increased, in particular in former Yugoslavia. Did this increase in violence lead to new activities of the peace movement? Not at all. To be sure, there were some individual actions in support of peace in Yugoslavia, but no mass movement by any count. In contrast to the time of the Cold War, it was much more difficult to identify the villains against whom one could organize mass rallies. Atrocities were committed by all sides—Serbs, Croats, and Muslims. As Alice Holmes Cooper demonstrates, the peace movement was severely split over the war, especially in Germany.[9] When the issue of whether Germany should participate in the peacekeeping action of NATO in Bosnia came up, a part of the German peace movement was supportive, accepting that sometimes weapons have to be used for the sake of peace. But another part of the German peace movement took a fundamental pacifist position, arguing that the use of weapons is always wrong.

A new lift for the European peace movement came with the war in Iraq. There were again large street demonstrations. In Italy, for example, rainbow flags with the peace sign (*pace*) could be seen at many houses. Generally speaking, Europe has a much more pacifist tradition than the United States. In Europe there is much more of a political left that can be mobilized in the name of peace. Churches are also more willing in Europe than in the United States to become politically active in the name of world peace.

WOMEN'S MOVEMENT

For an American reader, the women's movement in Europe is relatively easy to understand because it raises, although with some delay, many of the same issues that the women's movement in the United States has raised. In many ways, the women's movement has had a more difficult time in Europe, because individualism is less emphasized than in the United States. (For the lesser role of individualism in Europe, see also Chapter 1.) In Europe, the notion that not only individuals but also **groups** have basic rights is much more common than in the United States. In Europe, the family as a group is treated as a crucial economic unit; the argument has been made for a long time that the important consideration is that each family has a decent income. From this premise it follows that in the case of a lack of jobs, families with two breadwinners should give up one job to families with no breadwinner at all. This has meant for a long time—and still does to some extent—that a woman has to give up her job in favor of a man. It is precisely against this situation that the growing women's movement protests and argues that women, as individuals, should have their own inalienable rights.

The belief that women are not the equal of men has deep roots in European history. Popular culture has had a profound effect on how women should behave. Under the influence of the women's movement, studies have been done about eighteenth- and nineteenth-century books on marriage for young women, which were widely read at the time. The basic message of these books was that wives should be subservient to their husbands. Fulfillment in their lives would come from providing their husbands with a pleasant home where they could find peace and tranquility far from the struggles of the outside world. According to these books, it was a wife's duty to discover the wishes of her husband and to make every attempt to fulfill those wishes. If the husband was in a bad mood and complained loudly, it was recommended that the wife keep calm. There were no such guidebooks to how men should behave toward their wives. Men's task was simply to earn a living. In return, they had the right to be spoiled by their wives.

It was not only in popular but also in high culture that women were put in a subservient role. The women's movement points to many sexist remarks in the long history of European philosophers, poets, and writers. An extreme example is the often-quoted statement by the nineteenth-century German philosopher Friedrich Nietzsche, in which he said that men should take the whip when they go to a woman. Such writings in both popular and high culture had a strong influence on the behavior of women. Women themselves were eager to follow the set standards because they were socialized to accept them as desirable behavior. As in Marxism (Chapter 2), here too, we can speak of the existence of a false consciousness. Just as many proletarians did not rebel against their exploited status, many women gladly accepted their inferior position. In this context, it is noteworthy that in Europe many women fought against the introduction of women's suffrage. Politics was considered by them to be something dirty and from which women should be kept, in their own best interests.

In legal terms, the situation for European women has dramatically improved. Women's suffrage has been introduced everywhere. Switzerland was the last country to enfranchise women, by means of an all-male popular referendum in 1971 (Chapter 6). Although legal discrimination against women has largely been remedied and women participate more in the labor force, there is still much discrimination. In European universities, for example, there are presently very few women who have attained the rank of professor. As in the United States, the argument is made that female students need female teachers as role models. Special women's days are organized at many universities to draw attention to these demands, and student newspapers have special issues devoted to women's issues. Research projects are launched to study discrimination against women. The push for more opportunities for women may be strongest and most visible in the universities, but there are also efforts to increase leadership positions for women in political parties, churches, unions, and other areas.

For the women's movement, this push has not only a quantitative but also a qualitative aspect. The goal is not merely to increase the number of women in leadership positions, but also to redefine the role expectations for women leaders. Women should not simply try to imitate the role patterns of men in leadership positions. What, then, should be the proper behavior of women in leadership positions? This issue is hotly debated among feminists, and many different opinions are articulated. The necessity of a special women's culture is stressed, but it is not altogether clear what the key characteristics of this culture should be. A common theme is that female leaders should think in less compartmentalized terms than male leaders. Some feminists say that female leaders would tend to see political issues in more global terms. Thus, they would, for example, be more sensitive to how too-rapid economic growth may negatively influence the quality of life of ordinary people. With such a broader view, women would apply a more general principle of rationality, whereas male leaders would tend to be rational in a narrower sense, concentrating on how a particular decision would influence profit levels but forgetting the impact it would have on the environment. Thus, the argument is not that male leaders would be more rational and female leaders more emotional; rather, the difference would be that women would include broader elements in their decision making than men.

That leaders can be both men and women, and that this should be expressed more clearly in everyday language is an issue about which the women's movement is very concerned. The specific words we use in both public and private domains determine how we see the world. If language refers to leadership positions only in masculine form, we tend to think of leaders only as men. In languages such as German and French, this problem is even more acute than in English, because in these languages the article has both a masculine and a feminine form. Whereas in English the article *the* can refer either to a man or a woman, in German the article *der* refers to a man and the article *die* to a woman. The same difference exists in French with the articles *le* and *la*. Nouns, too, may have masculine and feminine forms. The English term *director* is, respectively, *Direktor* in German and *directeur* in French in the case of a man, and *Direktorin* and *directrice* in the case of a woman. The women's movement insists that in such cases the feminine form should be used as often as the masculine form so that the language properly expresses that directors may be both men and women. Some professions have traditionally been so dominated by men that a feminine form does not even exist. Thus, in French there is only a masculine form for professor, namely *professeur*. Should the feminine form *professeuse* be introduced, or should a female professor be called *madame le professeur?* Some critics consider such issues to be trivial, but many people in the women's movement argue that equal status for women will never be achieved if our languages are not changed properly.

The women's movement also has many specific projects, in particular rape crisis centers, houses for battered women, hotels for women, taxis for women, bookstores for women, discos for women, self-defense courses for women, music for women, theater for women, and self-actualization groups for women. There is a strong element of **group solidarity** in the women's movement. In today's anonymous world, sisterhood gives many women an emotional and natural bond. To be with other women gives them a feeling of satisfaction. There was occasionally an alliance between the women's and the Marxist movements, both of which fight for exploited groups in society. However, many women found among Marxists the same male chauvinism that appears in society at large and decided to stay among themselves. The hope is that in the women's movement, a feeling of togetherness will develop and that every woman will have the same status and the same say. The women's movement has the ambition to practice internally a lifestyle of fundamental democratization and thus to serve as an example for society at large.

Several studies have shown that Europeans are beginning to develop a more positive attitude toward a stronger role of women in politics and society; thus one may conclude that the women's movement has been quite successful in Europe. European women are also more protected by an extensive welfare state that provides for generous child care, day care, job protection, health care for both mother and child, and many other such programs. As a result, the reason why the women's movement in Europe is not as vocal as the American one is because many women's concerns have already been addressed via the welfare state. Women also have gained more access to important political positions than in the United States. In the Scandinavian countries, for instance, women are quite numerous in important political positions. In Sweden's 2006 parliamentary elections, for example, 164 of the 349 MPs (47 percent) were women compared to 38.4 percent in 1990. In May 2009, the percentage of women in the U.S. House of Representatives was 16.8 and in the Senate it was 15.3.

Women have also held the most important political position in a country: Margaret Thatcher led the way as British prime minister from 1979 to 1990. In another large European country, Germany, Angela Merkel became chancellor in 2005. In the 2007 French presidential elections, Ségolène Royal was a serious contender, gaining 47 percent of the votes even though she ultimately lost to Nicolas Sarkozy. (For further discussion of these three prominent women in European politics, see Chapter 4.)

Political measures are also being taken to expand the role of women in the business sector. An unusually far-reaching measure was put in effect in Norway in 2006, requiring that in the next two years 40 percent of the board members of the nation's large, publicly traded private companies be women. Karita Bekkemellem, the minister of children and equality, said of the measure: "The government's decision is to see that women will have a place where the power is, where leadership takes place in this society. This is a very forceful affirmative action, but it will set an example for other centers of society."[10] That this Norwegian law could go into effect does not mean that all men were supportive of it. As a male business leader formulated his criticism: "It is contrary to the principles of a free society to tell private businessmen whom they must put on their corporate boards."[11] He did add that businessmen will comply with the law.

THE LESBIAN, GAY, BISEXUAL, AND TRANSGENDER (LGBT) MOVEMENT

Just like the environmental movement and the women's movement, today's LGBT (lesbian, gay, bisexual, and transgender people) movement started in the 1960s, a period characterized by the turning of established morals on their head and the questioning of traditions and authority. The early gay and lesbian movements used similar rhetoric as the civil rights movement, which is that gays and lesbians have a "right" to openly live their life and not to suffer discrimination as a result of their lifestyle. Traditionally, countries have meted out serious punishments for people engaging in homosexual acts.

In 1978, the International Lesbian and Gay Association was founded. This organization lobbied and continues to lobby the United Nations and national governments for gay and lesbian human rights. The gay and lesbian movement was seriously challenged in the early 1980s by more conservative political forces when the first AIDS (acquired immunodeficiency syndrome) cases appeared as a result of infections with HIV (human immunodeficiency virus). At first, AIDS was described as a "gay disease," and many conservatives argued that homosexuals were finally reaping God's wrath for their behavior. The conservative political climate in the United States at the time made it very difficult for the disease to overcome the "gay" stigma. It took President Reagan four years from the appearance of the disease in 1981 to finally utter the word *AIDS* in public for the first time in 1985.

European countries took a more pragmatic approach to AIDS. Once it became clear that this was a disease of potentially epidemic proportions, the well-oiled public health systems were pressed into service. Already by 1987, Dutch authorities decided that all Dutch people should receive the highest-quality care and treatment of this disease as part and parcel of the general, **universal access** for every Dutch citizen to their health-care system on the basis of "distributive justice." Every hospital, and all hospital staff including nursing homes would treat and care for AIDS patients.[12]

Today, much more is known about the social determinants of the spread of AIDS and how best to combat it. AIDS is transmitted not only through homosexual contact, but also through heterosexual contact and through intravenous drug use. A small percentage of infections have also occurred as a result of tainted blood supplies. The Dutch have instituted a needle exchange program, which has proven to significantly reduce HIV and hepatitis C infections. This "harm reduction" approach is practiced in other European countries such as Spain, Portugal, Switzerland, and the United Kingdom. There are also needle exchange programs in some American cities such as San Francisco, California; Portland, Oregon; and Seattle, Washington. Even though the Centers for Disease Control and Prevention and the National Institutes of Health favor needle exchange programs, the United States does not provide federal funding for this policy.

It is estimated that the majority of HIV infections (58 percent) in Western Europe are spread by heterosexual contact as a result of commercial sex work conducted mostly by illegal immigrants from Eastern Europe. In Eastern Europe the country with by far the highest infections rates is Ukraine where the number of newly diagnosed HIV infections per year more than tripled between 2000 and 2009 from 5,485 to 16,241. The main mode of transmission appears to be injection drug use combined with needle sharing.[13] In Western Europe, the number of newly diagnosed HIV infections per year more than doubled between 2000 and 2009 and increased almost 350 percent between the same period in Eastern Europe per 100,000 population.[14] One of the challenges in treating HIV infections is gaining the **trust** of communities that are affected. Many HIV-infected persons are illegal immigrants, belong to ethnic minorities, had bad experiences with authorities in the past, or all three. Affording care to

HIV-positive people in these groups will go a long way to stave off the spread of HIV in the general public. This will require an end to the stigmas and **discrimination** against migrants and other ethnic minorities and their full incorporation into the public health-care system. At the European Lisbon Conference on HIV and Migration, Mary Haour Knipe came to the conclusion that migrants must be included in HIV/AIDS surveillance, treatment, and care as a matter of social justice and human rights and that the effectiveness of interventions is greatly increased when there is universal access to the health-care system.[15]

The purpose of the LGBT movement was originally to point out the daily discrimination such persons had to endure and to fight for public acceptance of their lifestyle on the basis of civil and human rights. Since then, the movement has spawned a multitude of organizations that are involved in community organization, pushing for same-sex marriage, organizing illegal immigrants with AIDS, supporting infected members of ethnic minorities, and other such activities. Oftentimes, such organizations are crucial in the effectiveness of official public health policies as these organizations enjoy the trust of the infected communities.

BOX 8.1 EUROPE'S HIV INFECTION RATE HAS DOUBLED SINCE 2000

On World AIDS Day, the European Center for Disease Prevention and Control (ECDPC) and the World Health Organization issued a report indicating that the rate of HIV infection in Europe nearly doubled between 2000 and 2007.

"One challenge faced by all countries is that many of the people living with HIV are unaware that they are infected," said ECDPC Director Zsuzsanna Jakab. A further challenge is that the groups most affected vary from country to country, meaning prevention must be approached differently in different settings.

According to the report, Europe's annual rate of new HIV diagnoses rose to 75 per 1 million people in 2007 from 39 per 1 million people in 2000. Forty-nine European nations logged a total of 48,892 new HIV cases in 2007. Among the report's findings:

- In all of Eastern Europe, injection drug use was the chief route of HIV transmission.
- The highest rates of new infections were found in Estonia, Ukraine, Portugal, and the Republic of Moldova.
- High rates were also noted in Latvia, Kazakhstan, Uzbekistan, the United Kingdom, Belarus, and Switzerland.
- Sex between heterosexuals was the main route of transmission in Central and Western Europe, though infections among men who have sex with men were rising as well.
- Of heterosexually transmitted cases, about 40 percent were found among people originating from nations with generalized HIV epidemics. ■

Source: The Body, The Complete HIV/AIDS Resource. December 2, 2008. http://www.thebody.com/content/world/art49636.html

Particularly in Europe, the LGBT movement has gained broad acceptance. In big cities such as Berlin, London, and Rome, this movement manifests itself in frequent lively and colorful parades of **gay and lesbian pride.** An example is a huge parade held in Rome on June 16, 2007. It had an official character because it was sponsored by the city of Rome, the region of Lazio, and the national Ministry for Equal Opportunity. Cabinet members of the Center-Left government coalition also participated in the parade. Similarly, the Swedish prime minister Fredrik Reinfeldt participated in the Stockholm Gay Parade, while the Church of Sweden announced that it would also officially participate in the parade (see Box 8.2).

The fact that these officials are participating in such parades is witness to the success and broad acceptance of such identity politics issues. For instance, while the U.S. federal government does not recognize same-sex marriage (although some states, such as Massachusetts, Connecticut, Iowa, New Hampshire, Vermont, and Maine, recognize same-sex marriage), there are currently five countries in Europe where same-sex marriage is allowed with all the attendant privileges such as adopting children, rights of inheritance, taxation, and power of attorney: the Netherlands, Belgium, Spain, Sweden, and Norway. Across Europe there is a remarkable variation in public opinion about same-sex marriage. Figure 8.1 shows the results of a Eurobarometer public opinion poll in 2006. The question was: "Do you agree with homosexual marriages being allowed across Europe?"

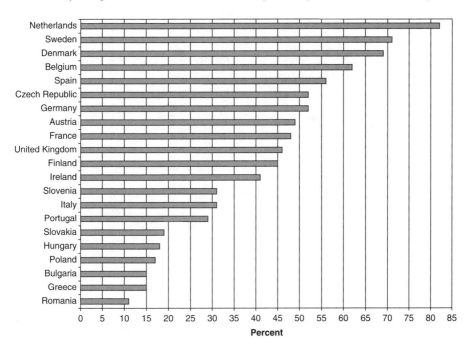

FIGURE 8.1

Eurobarometer public opinion poll 2006: "Do you agree with homosexual marriages being allowed across Europe?"

Source: Eurobarometer, 2006.

BOX 8.2 SWEDISH CHURCH TO JOIN STOCKHOLM GAY PRIDE

August 2, 2007

The Swedish Lutheran Church will march for the first time in the Gay Pride parade in Stockholm under the slogan "Love is stronger than everything," the Church announced on Thursday.

"For the first time ever, the parade at the Pride festival will have a delegation from the Swedish Church," it said in a statement.

The parade will go through the streets of the Swedish capital on Saturday.

The Church said the delegation would include about 30 people including two deans from the Stockholm and Uppsala cathedrals.

It said it also wanted to "break the masses' big silence" regarding gays, bisexuals and transexuals.

"The Swedish Church is a Church open to everyone," Uppsala priest Ann-KatrinBosbach explained.

Sweden, already a pioneer in giving same-sex couples the right to adopt children, looks set to allow gays to marry in the Lutheran Church by introducing a new marriage law in January 2008.

If the so-called "gender neutral" marriage legislation is adopted, the Scandinavian country would become the first in the world to allow gays to marry within a major Church.

Stockholm Pride is Scandinavia's largest Gay Pride celebration and last year 45,000 persons participated, according to its organizers.

Homosexuality was not legalized in Sweden until 1944. ■

Source: www.thelocal.se/8081/

The Netherlands tops this list with over 80 percent of Dutch agreeing with homosexual marriage across Europe, followed by Sweden, Denmark, and Belgium. There is no majority support for such a policy in France and the United Kingdom and, generally, Eastern European publics show the least agreement for homosexual marriage in Europe. Like in the United States, some European countries are attempting to find ways to legalize some sort of same-sex partnership, short of calling it "marriage." In 2005 a same-sex marriage referendum in Switzerland took place, with the result that 58 percent of the Swiss supported a form of homosexual partnership, although it is not called "marriage" but rather "registered partnership."

Despite such official recognition, there is still much hostility and discrimination toward gays and lesbians emerging from right-wing political parties, particularly in Eastern Europe, where homosexuality is still very much taboo. Nevertheless, the LGBT movement has come a long way and has developed from a movement into an important part of the vibrant civil society in Europe.

ANTIIMMIGRATION MOVEMENT

The New Radical Right constantly and intensively mobilizes against too many immigrants, especially unskilled people coming from Africa, the Middle East, and Eastern Europe. Many of these protest actions result in violence because it often happens that people of leftist postmaterial movements organize counter-protests at the same public spaces. Authorities are greatly concerned about such violent events, and many policemen and policewomen suffer injuries in attempting to restore order. From the point of view of the authorities, it is particularly difficult to enter in contact with antiimmigration movements because they do not have clearly identified leaders, are hardly organized, and appear spontaneously at unexpected places.

One event which received worldwide attention occurred in 2009 when the Federal People's Initiative (Eidgenössische Volksinitiative) of Switzerland, backed by the right-wing Swiss People's Party, called for a referendum (see Chapter 6) on banning minarets, which are the slender towers that often surround mosques with balconies from which Muslim *muezzins* (Priests) call for prayer. The result was that 57 percent of the Swiss citizens combined with a majority of cantons supported this initiative with a voter turnout of 53 percent. This vote required an amendment to the Swiss constitution to expressly forbid the construction of minarets. The four existing minarets in Switzerland were unaffected by the vote.

This vote came as a surprise as most of the Swiss established parties and party **elites** believed that this referendum would fail. The positive result, however, indicates a large number of Swiss citizens are becoming uncomfortable with the increasing visibility of Islamic symbols such as mosques and various forms of headscarf. Opponents of the result believed that this law would be overturned by the European Court of Human Rights. However, very recently, on July 8, 2011, this very court upheld the ban on the building of minarets on the basis that prohibition of constructing minarets does not undermine the freedom of religion for Muslims.[16]

While this referendum was supported by the Swiss People's Party, it originated and was driven by a group of like-minded people who believed such minarets endanger the Swiss culture. The point is to show that this is an example of how movements, short of actually being political parties, can have significant effects on political outcomes, particularly in countries that allow for referenda.

Immigration is also an important issue in the United States, but in our judgment not to the same extent as in Europe. After all, the United States is an immigration country, which historically is not the case for European countries. Therefore, it is not surprising that many Europeans worry about too many immigrants from far away countries. Many other Europeans, however, want to have as much as possible open borders to the world. These are two positions opening a deep divide in European societies.

This chapter has shown us that in order to understand European politics, we have to look beyond political parties and also consider the role of the various social movements. The complexity of European politics is further increased when we add, in the next chapter, economic interest groups and the state to the picture.

BOX 8.3   COURT UPHOLDS SWISS BAN ON MINARETS

Twenty months have passed since the citizens of Switzerland voted to amend their constitution and ban the future construction of Muslim minarets, but only in recent days has it become clear that the will of the Swiss people may be allowed to stand.[. . .]

Silvia Bär, deputy secretary-general of the right-wing People's Party, which supported the minaret ban, told swissinfo.ch that the party had expected that the Strasbourg ruling would go the way it did.

> "As we have always said, the minaret initiative does not affect either the freedom of religion nor the right to practise a religion," she said. The party expects to see the same ruling in the cases that are still pending.
>
> Walter Wobmann, the chairman of the committee that launched the anti-minaret initiative, told the Swiss News Agency that he was "naturally pleased" at the ruling— but added that the court could hardly have decided otherwise. "We are a sovereign state, the people voted clearly in favour of the minaret initiative and the initiative had been declared valid," he said.

Wobmann's point regarding the rights of sovereign states would once have seemed obvious; the notion that foreign populations could simply impose their culture or religion on their hosts would have been absurd. The bureaucrats of the European Union seem driven to obliterate any semblance of national sovereign from continent, but the Swiss have a degree of resistance to such efforts because the Swiss people rejected the European Economic Area (EEA) in December 1992—and therefore the Swiss government indefinitely suspended negotiations for EU membership. However, the European Court of Human Rights is not directly connected to the EU's legal system; as a member state of the Council of Europe, Switzerland is a part to the European Court of Human Rights—and thus subject to the court's potential meddling in something as fundamental as an amendment to the Swiss constitution.[. . .]

Opponents to the constitutional amendment have even weighed whether or not Switzerland might withdraw from the Human Rights Convention in order to reassert their national sovereignty—a prospect which they find unlikely. As Walter Kälin, an international human rights lawyer, told SwissInfo: "There have always been certain circles that have called for Switzerland to withdraw from the Human Rights Convention. Thought is free, and politicians can demand this kind of thing if they want to. But withdrawal would not be a matter for a nationwide vote; it would need a majority in parliament. And I really can't imagine such a thing."

In 1998, Recep Tayyip Erdogan, the man who would one day become Prime Minister of Turkey, declared, "The mosques are our barracks, the domes our helmets, the minarets our bayonets and the faithful our soldiers . . ." Four years later, his party was swept to power, and now Erdogan urges Turks living in Europe to actively resist assimilation into Western civilization. Given the history of a series of brutal Turkish invasions which reached the heart of Europe (most famously, the Battle of Vienna in 1683), is it any wonder that the Swiss would want to ban "Turkish bayonets" from being raised within their borders? ■

Source: James Heiser, *New American*, July 14, 2011

KEY TERMS

DISCUSSION QUESTIONS

1. Social movements tend to wax and wane over time. What do you think could explain this variation?
2. In what way is it plausible to think of social movements as being inimical to democracy, and in what way is it plausible to think of them as being the embodiment of democracy itself?
3. What would you describe as the functions of social movements?
4. How are social movements different from political parties?
5. In a country that subscribes to "freedom of religion" such as Switzerland, how democratic is it if a majority of Swiss ban the construction of minarets?

NOTES

1. Hanspeter Kriesi. Support and Mobilization Potential for New Social Movements: Concepts, Operationalizations and Illustrations from the Netherlands. In Mario Diani and Ron Eyerman, eds., *Studying Collective Action* (London: Sage, 1992, 22). See also Hanspeter Kriesi, Ruud Koopmans, Jan Willem Dyvendak, and Marco G. Giugni. *New Social Movements in Western Europe. A Comparative Analysis* (Minneapolis, MN: University of Minnesota Press, 1995).
2. Kriesi, Support and Mobilization Potential for New Social Movements, 22.
3. Ibid., 23.
4. Ibid., 22.
5. www.groningen.nl, June 2007.
6. www.bafu.admin.ch.
7. Diarmuid Maguire. When the Streets Begin to Empty: The Demobilisation of the British Peace Movement After 1983. *West European Politics* 15 (October 1992): 79.
8. Ibid., 79–80.
9. Alice Holmes Cooper. Public-Good Movements and the Dimensions of Political Process. Postwar German Peace Movements. *Comparative Political Studies* 29 (June 1996): 267–289.
10. *New York Times*, January 12, 2006.
11. Ibid.
12. Frans van den Boom and Paul Schnabel. The Impact of AIDS on the Dutch Health Care System. In Theo Sandfort, ed., *The Dutch Response to HIV: Pragmatism and Consensus* (London: Routledge, 1998, 135–153).
13. HIV/AIDS Surveillance Report in Europe 2009, World Health Organization, 2001.
14. Ibid.
15. http://www.eatg.org/.
16. Julia Slater and Alexander Künzle. Strasbourg Minaret Ruling Causes No Surprise. *Swissinfo.ch*, July 8, 2011.

The State, Corporatism, the Great Meltdown of 2008, and the Greek Debt Crisis of 2011

Europian politics is characterized by close cooperation between the state and economic interest groups. Such cooperation is often referred to as corporatism, "tripartism," or "social partnership." Whatever the term used, this cooperation between the state and economic interest groups represents one of the most distinctive differences between European and American politics. Before discussing how this is so, we first have to explain that in Europe the state may often operate as a political actor in its own right. Representatives of the **state bureaucracy** meet with representatives of major economic interest groups, and in these meetings attempts are made to find common solutions to the economic problems of the country.

THE STATE AS A POLITICAL ACTOR

The concept of the **state** has a different meaning in Europe than it does in the United States. For Americans, the term refers primarily to the 50 states of the Union. It is also used to refer to important political figures with the term *statesmen*. In Europe, the distinction is made between the *state* and *politics*—in German, for example, between *Staat* and *Politik*, and in French between *état* and *politique*. One of the difficulties of comparative politics is translating certain key concepts from one language into another. The concept of the state is a good illustration of such difficulties of translation.

In Europe, the concept of the state grew out of a very different historical context than it did in America. No American leader has ever declared, "I am the state" (*L'état, c'est moi*), as did King Louis XIV of France. In France, prior to the revolution of 1789, the term *state* referred to the governmental institutions built by the kings of the Bourbon dynasty over several centuries. This royal family considered it a personal accomplishment to have given France a governmental structure; the French state was, in a way, its private possession. The Bourbon kings used "their" state to rule the territory of France. To give **legitimacy** to this rule, the kings claimed to act in the name of God. Thus, they were supposed to have a higher mission to fulfill. The instrument of their rule was the state, which took on a sacred character. The doctrine evolved that the state had its own interests. The bureaucrats working for the state were socialized to believe that they were obligated to serve these interests. This was particularly true during the period of French absolutism in the seventeenth and eighteenth centuries. Absolutist regimes prevailed during this time in many other European countries, such as Prussia, where the same doctrine of a higher state interest developed.

In contemporary Europe, the notion of a higher **state interest** is perhaps most pronounced in France. The past 200 years of French history have been characterized by many upheavals, and today the French are already living under their Fifth Republic (see Chapter 4). Through all the crises, the state bureaucracy has continued to work and has looked after the interests of the state. Top bureaucrats enjoy very high social status in France. Future state bureaucrats are rigorously trained at special postgraduate schools. Admission to these schools is extremely competitive, and the students who are accepted are immediately treated as the elite of their country. They form a special, distinguished class, with its own norms and values, whose goal is to excel in the service of the French state. A lifelong career with the state is considered to be more attractive and prestigious than a career in the private sector. High political offices are often filled by top bureaucrats.

Knowledge of the high social status of French bureaucrats sheds light on the important role of the state in the French economy. Because they feel that they are the elite of the country, state bureaucrats have, for centuries, been empowered to make important economic decisions. To be sure, governments of the Left tend to give more power to the state than governments of the Right; however, the political Right also has a positive view of the state.

The French bureaucracy exemplifies in a particularly pronounced form the general characteristics of the state bureaucracies in Europe. But the British **civil service**, for example, is also well known for its high professional standards and independence. And to understand the Italian government, it is important to know that the state bureaucracies continue to function whenever one of Italy's cabinet crises occurs.

Given the important role of state bureaucrats in European countries, we must ask exactly what these bureaucrats mean when they claim to represent the interests of the state. How do they know what is in the interest of the state? As we will see in Chapter 2, Marxist sociologists argue that state bureaucrats simply help to maintain the capitalist system, and when bureaucrats speak of the interests of the state, they really mean the interests of the **capitalist** class. According to this Marxist analysis, the main function of the state is to preserve order and thus prevent any uprisings of the working class. Another critical view of the role of state bureaucrats is that they mainly defend their own career interests. When they refer to the interests of the state, they primarily mean the interests of the state bureaucracy itself. Thus, they try to get larger and plusher buildings, larger staffs, higher salaries, more travel money, and so on.

Political appointees are much rarer in Europe than in the United States. With a new American administration, the top echelons of the bureaucracy in Washington DC are replaced with supporters of the new president. In Europe, the normal pattern is that most high-ranking civil servants stay on the job. In this way, there is much more continuity, which contributes to the perception of the state as an independent actor in the political game. Profiting from analyses of European democracies, many political scientists have taken a second look at the usefulness of the input/output framework for the study of the political dynamics of the United States. Despite more frequent replacements in the top bureaucratic positions, there is much evidence that Washington bureaucrats, too, have become important political actors in their own right. Often, they do not simply implement decisions made by the president and Congress but are themselves decision makers. Thus, the concept of the state is also useful for the analysis of the United States.[1]

ECONOMIC INTEREST GROUPS

In the United States many **economic interest groups** are active in the political process. Farmers, teachers, bankers, truckers, miners, and others are politically organized. For Americans, to represent special interests has mostly a negative connotation. The impression evoked is that a special interest group seeks privileges detrimental to the common good of the country. In American political thinking, the influence of such groups should ideally be as limited as possible. Many people believe, for example, that members of Congress should be unencumbered by such special interests and instead should strive to make decisions for the higher common good. In this view, special interest groups should be kept to the lobbies of the Capitol, and it is from this perspective that interest groups are called lobbies in the United States.

The term **lobby** makes less sense in a European context. An official of an economic interest group often may also sit in the national parliament, where he or she usually does not hesitate to speak for his or her interest group. Thus, interest groups are heard not only at hearings and in the lobbies, but also in parliament itself. To understand the situation of economic interest groups in Europe, one must consider the long European tradition of economic interest group participation in political decision making. This tradition goes back to the medieval **guild** system in which bakers, butchers, and similar occupational groups were tightly organized in European towns. These guilds not only regulated their internal affairs, but also played an important role in the political life of the community. Although the guild system has since been dissolved, the doctrine that occupational groups should have a central place in politics persists. It is a sign of this continuity that guilds still flourish in many European cities,

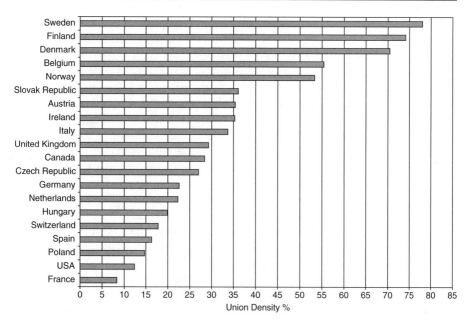

FIGURE 9.1

Union density rates in 20 countries in 2003.

Source: Visser [2006]. Data for Belgium and Austria refer to 2002. Data for Switzerland refer to 2001. Data for Hungary, the Czech and Slovak Republics, and Poland refer to 2001.

although in a new form—as prestigious private clubs with important social functions. In Zürich, for example, the guilds organize a popular parade through the streets of the city every spring. Most members of these modern-day guilds no longer belong to their respective occupational groups but come from high-status professions such as law, medicine, and business. Memories of the guilds are also kept alive in the names of streets and fashionable restaurants. With this historical background, it is understandable that in European politics economic interest groups are not relegated to the lobbies of parliament but are allowed entry to parliament itself. This raises the question of the relationship between political parties and economic interest groups.

Many more Europeans join an economic interest group than a political party (for membership in political parties, see Chapter 2). It is seen as a more immediate personal advantage to belong to an economic interest group than to a political party. Figure 9.1 shows union density (the percentage of workers who are unionized) data. By far the strongest union density is observable in the Scandinavian countries.

It is also important to note that membership fees in economic interest groups are usually higher than in political parties. The combination of larger membership and higher membership fees means that economic interest groups tend to be much more affluent than political parties. The trade unions, for example, are more affluent than the Socialist parties and the business associations more affluent than the Conservative parties. These differences in financial resources are vividly seen in the headquarters, where it is not uncommon to find economic interest groups located in luxurious office buildings with huge staffs, whereas political parties have modest rooms and small staffs. In a few countries, notably Germany, the financial condition of the parties is somewhat better than elsewhere as a result of government contributions.

The overlap between membership in political parties and economic interest groups varies greatly from country to country. Such variation is evident in the **trade union** movement. In Germany, Great Britain, and Sweden, for example, the trade unions have a single national organization, and most trade union leaders also belong to the Socialist Party. In other countries, such as France, Italy, and Switzerland, the trade union movement is split into several separate national organizations, each having a special affiliation with a different party. Switzerland, for example, has three major trade union organizations; the largest is close to the Socialists and the second largest is aligned with the Christian Democrats.

Business associations, as might be expected, have a close affiliation with Conservative and Free Democratic parties. In some countries, farmers have developed their own agrarian parties: In Sweden, the Center Party was originally an agrarian party and still represents farmers' interests to some extent. In countries without a special agrarian party, farmers mostly support parties of the political Right, but some small farmers, mainly in Italy and France, are Socialists or even Communists. White-collar employees and their interest groups are usually not close to particular parties but pursue the strategy of having good relations with all the major parties.

Whether leaders of economic interest groups run for a parliamentary seat varies greatly from country to country and from one interest group to another. German trade union officials, for example, are more likely than their French counterparts to run for parliament. From the perspective of democratic theory, is it desirable that leaders of economic interest groups sit in parliament? A negative response might arise from the fear that giving voice to special economic interests in parliament could decrease the chances that decisions will be made for the common good. But one could also argue that it is better to hear the representatives of economic interests in the open forum of parliamentary debates. In this way, positions are made clearer to the general public than if interest groups remain in the lobbies. Moreover, the responsibility of a parliamentary seat might lead to more moderation in the positions of interest-group representatives than if they stay outside parliament.

What about the policy programs of the various interest groups? We do not cover them as we did the programs of the political parties. There are a few reasons for this: First, the programs of the interest groups are to a large extent self-explanatory and can be deduced from the groups' names. Thus, it is easy to guess that teachers' associations fight for higher wages for their members. At a more specific level, we come immediately to minute details. Do teachers' associations support merit pay, and, if so, how should a teacher's performance be measured? At this specific level, there is wide variation from country to country and even within countries. Entire monographs have been published on the policy programs of teachers' associations in Europe. The same is true for medical associations, bankers' associations, trade unions, trade associations, and so on. More interesting than such detailed program descriptions is the question of how the demands of the various economic interest groups influence the political decision-making process and its outcomes. This question takes us to the next section, which looks at the interactions between economic interest groups and the state.

PLURALISM AND CORPORATISM

Pluralism means that there is a plurality of interest groups, all of which try to influence the decisions of the state. The state itself is relatively "weak" vis-à-vis interest groups. The term *weak* refers to the reduced capacity of the state to push its preferences through as compared to the preferences of the various interest groups. In pluralist systems, the autonomy of the state is limited by its inability to keep interest groups at arm's length. The United States is a prime example of a country where interest groups wield significant influence in the policymaking process. *Corporatism* is a formal cooperation between the state and interest groups with the goal of finding mutually acceptable solutions. Pluralism and corporatism have to be seen as the poles of a continuum with many variations in between. American readers are familiar with interest-group pluralism; corporatism, on the other hand, needs explanation.

The notion of corporatism as a form of government has deep roots in European history, dating from the Middle Ages. In our present era of individualism, it is difficult to imagine how in medieval times the lives of individuals were embedded in and subordinated to the groups to which they belonged. Membership in these groups was not voluntary but compulsory. A baker in a medieval town had no choice as to whether to join the professional bakers' organization; all bakers had to belong to their guild. These guilds were hierarchical. At the bottom were apprentices, who trained to become journeymen and later, perhaps, masters of their craft. The guild established rules specifying how many journeymen and apprentices a master could employ. Standards were also set as to how much could be produced—for example, how many loaves of bread a baker could bake. In addition to guilds, there were other "corporations," such as universities, whose internal differentiation was primarily between professors and students. The word *university* comes from the Latin term *universitas magistrorum studentiumque*, meaning "corporation of professors and students."

Corporations played a crucial role in the government of a medieval town. Together with town officials, they managed public affairs. Decision making was characterized by mutual accommodation and bargaining; the ideological basis was a harmonious model of society. Each corporation was seen as a part of a living body, and the parts had to cooperate for the entire body to stay healthy. The main function of the individual in this organic view of society was his or her contribution to the whole. In fact, the word *corporatism* finds its roots in the Latin term *corpore*, which means "body." When all the different parts of society work together, the "whole is more than the sum of its parts," as so powerfully stated by one of the most important sociologists, Emile Durkheim.

It was only during the Enlightenment that philosophers began to place the individual at center stage. They proclaimed that individuals had natural rights independent of the groups to which they belonged, a notion alien to medieval thinkers. The French philosopher René Descartes (1596–1650) made the influential statement, *"Cogito, ergo sum"* (I think, therefore I am), indicating that the potential to think is the crucial element in human existence. The capacity of thought makes the individual free and gives him or her inalienable rights— among others, the right of free association. Individuals should be able to choose freely the groups to which they belong. Based on this right, political parties were founded, bringing together people of similar ideological orientations. This was the beginning of modern democracy, first put in practice in the United States and, shortly thereafter, in France. The old harmonious model was replaced with the notion of **competition**. The emerging political parties competed for members and votes. Decisions increasingly were made with the device of the majority principle. The building blocks of society were no longer organic groups, but individuals free to choose for themselves.

Notions of democracy based on individualism and competition in nineteenth-century Europe led to much turmoil, unrest, and bloody revolutions. As a result, there was a backlash, accompanied by nostalgic longing for the old order of cooperation and harmony and a view of modern democracy as divisive and contrary to the laws of nature. Motivated by such views, in 1922 Benito Mussolini overthrew the frail Italian democracy and established Fascism based on a corporate form of government. Although similar forms of government were established in other countries, Mussolini was most explicit in the implementation of corporatist ideas: The will of the people should be represented not by political parties but by the natural economic forces of society. A national assembly should bring together the interests of farmers, businesses, workers, and so forth. Because everyone belongs to an economic sector of society, everyone would be represented. Interests would not be antagonistic but would **complement** each other for the good of the entire country. It would only be necessary for the *Duce* (leader)—Mussolini himself—to give clear directions as to which way the country should go. The result would be the reestablishment of order and strength for the Italian state. As a symbol for this strength, Mussolini used the Roman term *fasces*, which led to the concept of Fascism (Chapter 2). In Roman times, *fasces* meant a bundle of birch rods tightly held together.

Because of its association with Fascism and its atrocities, the concept of corporatism was discredited for many years after World War II. It has only been since the 1970s that some political scientists have once again begun to use the term *corporatism*. To distinguish their idea of corporatism from Mussolini's, these political scientists speak often of *neocorporatism, liberal corporatism, societal corporatism,* or *democratic corporatism*. Whatever term they use, they claim that some European democracies have a corporatist form of government. The example cited most often is Austria, where laws have established chambers of business, labor, and agriculture. Membership in these chambers is compulsory. Representatives of the chambers meet regularly under the chairmanship of the federal chancellor to hammer out crucial economic decisions. Other countries frequently characterized as corporatist are Norway, Sweden, and the Netherlands. By contrast, the United States, Canada, New Zealand, and Australia are considered to be classical cases of interest-group pluralism.

At its core, corporatism in a modern democracy deals with the interactions among organized business, organized labor, and the state bureaucracy. These three actors cooperate at the national level in the pursuit of what they see as the public good. It is important for this definition that negotiations are not merely bilateral between business and labor, but **trilateral**—that is, inclusive of the state bureaucracy as well. The participation of the state bureaucracy as an independent actor in its own right is a crucial element of corporatism. The state bureaucracy's representatives meet around the same table with the representatives of the major business and labor organizations. These economic interest groups are not merely consulted but are themselves active decision makers. The style of decision making is characterized by bargaining. The interests of the three actors in corporatist decision making are usually quite divergent in the initial phases, but the three share a common belief in the existence of an optimal solution for the public good.

The representatives from all three sides are usually professional economists who are proficient in the same economic language; consequently, problems are usually addressed in a highly technical and professional way. To determine an optimal wage settlement, for example, a huge amount of data is brought into play concerning inflation, unemployment, balance of payments, money supplies, budgets, and so on. The negotiators generally expect that a careful analysis of all the data will allow them to determine the optimal wage level for the long-term interests of the country. In these negotiations, state bureaucrats are not only **mediators** between business and labor but also defenders of the interests of the state as a special entity. If corporatist decision making is successful, the final outcome is acceptable to all three sides, although it will most likely not correspond precisely to the initial demands of any one of the partners.

Besides wage settlements, other economic issues may be dealt with in a corporatist way, such as public works programs or measures to help exporters. The range of issues may be even broader, including questions of old-age pensions, taxes, and budgets. Through such an extension of corporatist decision making, political parties and parliament may lose many of their essential functions. To be sure, decisions reached in a corporatist way must still pass the parliamentary procedure, but this can amount to pure formality if the proposals submitted to parliament have already been accepted by the corporatist actors. As a qualifier to the argument that corporatism weakens political parties, one must add that party leaders may play an important role in labor and business organizations.

Although classical corporatism is trilateral—that is, between business, labor, and the state bureaucracy—other actors, such as farmers, bankers, and consumers, can be added. The concept of corporatism becomes increasingly fuzzy as one moves away from its core definition. Is it still useful to use the term *corporatism* when the state bureaucracy calls in, for example, medical professionals and social workers for a decision about the implementation of a disability program? As we see later in this chapter, such conceptual fuzziness plagues empirical research about corporatism.

As was said at the beginning of this section, corporatism can be seen as the polar opposite of pluralism. In a pluralist system of government, economic interest groups stand outside the institutional framework of government. Their representatives are not appointed to official governmental commissions; they, therefore, do not act as decision makers, as they do in corporatism. Their role is, rather, to influence government actions from the outside, mainly through lobbying elected officials and state bureaucrats. In these lobbying efforts, business, labor, and other economic interest groups are in competition with one another, and each group exercises as much pressure as possible. Therefore, pluralism may also be called *pressure-group politics*. Whether economic interest groups exercise more influence in a corporatist or a pluralist system cannot be answered a priori but is an open question for empirical investigation.

THE THEORY OF CORPORATISM

If countries differ in the degree to which their decision making is corporatist or pluralistic, these differences must be explained in their causes and consequences. The literature offers several explanatory factors. The **vulnerability** of a country to international market forces is said to be of prime importance for the emergence of corporatist decision making. This factor would explain why corporatism is particularly prominent in smaller countries that depend heavily on imports and exports. The name of the game in such countries is not so much internal competition between business and labor as it is survival of the country in the world market. Political scientist Klaus Armingeon compares the situation of such countries in the world market to a nutshell on the high seas. Just as such a nutshell has no control over the waves of the sea, a small country has no control over the waves of the world market.[2] Under these circumstances, labor is very much aware that the country's products must remain competitive in international markets to prevent high domestic unemployment. Business, on the other hand, knows that it needs a satisfied and productive labor force in order to stay internationally competitive. Because both labor and business realize how much they depend on each other, they are more willing to engage in corporatist decision making. In a small country, this would be all the more likely to happen because there tend to be many close personal contacts among the national elites and because a small country may more easily develop a sense of community among the entire population.

A second factor identified by theorists of corporatism as contributing to corporatist decision making is a **strong labor movement**. For a labor movement to be strong, membership must be high, and a single, centralized organization must exist. Under these conditions, business is confronted with an adversary that it cannot easily ignore, and one that has the advantage of being able to negotiate settlements that will be upheld by the entire labor force. In contrast, if the unions have few members and are split and decentralized, business has little assurance that a settlement negotiated with union leaders will also be accepted by the rank and file. Thus, it is hypothesized that strong unions facilitate corporatist decision making. Some corporatist authors argue, however, that this hypothesis is valid only if still another factor comes into play: a Socialist government.[3] Under this additional condition, the unions are interested in helping their "friends" in government to stabilize the economy. The Socialists, in turn, use their governmental power to guarantee that the settlements reached in corporatist decision making are actually implemented. Consequently, the unions will not fear being left in the cold by a hostile government. If, on the other hand, strong unions face a Conservative government, chances for corporatist decision making decrease. The unions may be reluctant to help the government and thereby to increase its electoral chances. The unions may also be afraid of being ultimately betrayed by a Conservative government.

Is corporatism more likely when the economy booms or when it is in crisis? In the former case, it is labor that is more likely to withdraw from corporatist arrangements, and in the latter case, business. When the economy booms, the workforce is in short supply, which gives labor a strong position with regard to wage demands. It may hope to get these demands better fulfilled by strikes or threats of strikes than by corporatist negotiations. When the economy is in crisis, on the other hand, business may no longer be interested in corporatist negotiations but prefer to obtain lower wages through threats of layoffs or actual layoffs. These arguments show that corporatism has as a precondition that both labor and business take a long-term perspective, at least over an entire business cycle and possibly over several cycles. The state bureaucrats, as the third actors in corporatism, are likely to encourage such a long-term perspective because the interests of the state are, by nature, long range.

What are the consequences of corporatist decision making? Here, too, the literature presents interesting hypotheses. The effects of corporatism on the economy of a country are seen by some theorists as positive. They hypothesize that corporatist decision making allows for a more flexible response to changes in the international market because internal domestic compensation is possible. If a sector of the economy is threatened by changing international factors, corporatist decision making allows the system to come to its aid. On the other hand, free-market purists argue that in the long run a country will be haunted by such rescue operations because they are undertaken against the verdict of market forces. Economist Manfred E. Streit speaks in this context of the danger of "institutional sclerosis." He warns that the participants in corporatist decision making are less able to solve the problem of obtaining reliable knowledge to steer the economy than the free market already does.[4] But supporters of corporatism reply that human and material costs are sometimes too high if market forces alone are allowed to dominate, so joint steering by the state and the major economic interest groups may be needed in certain cases.

In another respect, corporatism is seen in a still more negative light. It is argued that successful corporatist negotiations presuppose a subservient trade union membership, so labor leaders have sufficient leeway for making deals. If rank-and-file members criticize such deals, their criticism must be repressed in order for corporatist decision making to continue. In other words, corporatism is not compatible with true **internal democracy** in the trade unions. As a consequence of the lack of internal democracy, labor leaders may begin to look out more for their personal interests than for the interests of their members. They may also be tempted to accommodate business leaders and even to adopt their lifestyle. Streit speaks in this context of "the feudal barons of our time,"[5] and argues that, eventually, ordinary members of the unions will realize that their needs have been forgotten, and they will revolt against the decisions reached in a corporatist way. This argument leads to the conclusion that corporatist decision making is ultimately unstable because of its elitism, which eventually causes dissatisfaction and disruption at the rank-and-file level of the working class.

A necessary first step for an empirical test of the corporatist theory is a classification of a sufficiently large number of countries on a continuum from corporatist to pluralist. To arrive at such a classification with the necessary reliability and validity is a formidable task. Although there is general agreement among scholars on the approximate location of most countries on the corporatist–pluralist continuum, there is much disagreement on their specific locations. There are even some countries for which wide disagreements exist on the approximate classification.

The **classification** of the degree of corporatism in a country is usually based, in a first approximation, on the presence or absence of particular institutions. One particular indicator of corporatism is the existence of a permanent institution such as an economic and social council, where the representatives of the state bureaucracy and the major economic interest groups meet on a regular basis. However, such institutions are sometimes merely shells without much substance. In such cases, the original classification must then be modified. France, for example, has the Economic and Social Council, the existence of which seems to indicate a high degree of corporatism; in fact, this council has little political importance.

For Switzerland, the problem is, in a way, reversed. Switzerland has no economic and social council and no similar permanent institution, so corporatism seems weak; yet, some authors classify Switzerland as strongly corporatist. For the Netherlands, some classifications have shifted over time. On the one hand, the Dutch have their Social and Economic Council, but, on the other hand, this council seems to have lost much of its importance since its heyday in the 1950s.

Great Britain offers still another example of why it is not sufficient to look at institutions in order to classify a country on the corporatist–pluralist continuum. In 1962, the National Economic Development Council was created, which brought together representatives of government, business, and labor. When Margaret Thatcher became prime minister in 1979, this institution lost all practical importance but continued to exist on paper until it was formally dissolved in 1992.

Despite all the difficulties with the corporatist–pluralist continuum, one of the authors (Markus Crepaz), working together with Arend Lijphart, arrived at a classification of a large number of countries on this continuum.[6] The idea was to establish a composite measure of corporatism based on the judgments of 12 corporatist experts published in the literature. Included were those countries for which at least six scholarly judgments were available, which resulted in a total of 18 countries, ranked in the following way, from the most to the least corporatist:

Austria, Norway, Sweden, the Netherlands, Denmark, Switzerland, Germany, Finland, Belgium, Japan, Ireland, France, Italy, Great Britain, Australia, New Zealand, Canada, and the United States

For the interpretation of this ranking, it is important to note that there was relatively little disagreement among the experts on the classification of the countries at the extremes of the continuum. Austria, Norway, and Sweden were classified by all experts as strongly corporatist; the United States and Canada were classified as strongly pluralist. The greatest disagreements emerged for the classifications of Japan and Switzerland, for which the judgments of the experts varied widely.

With the six most corporatist countries being small in size, the ranking supports the hypothesis that small size increases the likelihood of corporatism. A closer look at the ranking also confirms that the more corporatist countries tend to have strong trade unions and, frequently, Socialist governments.

Many empirical studies have demonstrated that corporatism matters. Corporatist countries tend to have lower strike rates, lower inflation, lower unemployment, and higher economic growth.[7] Compared with pluralist countries, corporatist countries also tend to have lower income inequality, spend more on the welfare of their people, have fewer citizens in poverty, have lower crime rates, and have even lower environmental pollution levels.[8]

THE FUTURE OF CORPORATISM

Despite these impressive results, many observers have noticed three developments that may ring the death knell of corporatism: postmaterialism, postindustrialism, and globalization.

Postmaterialism (see Chapter 2) refers to the rise of new political issues such as the environment, women's rights, pacifism, and a general orientation toward a more grassroots democracy. Postmaterialism is incompatible with corporatism on two grounds: substantive and procedural. The **substantive** one is self-explanatory: Corporatism centers on materialist issues, such as economic growth, unemployment, inflation, and working conditions. "Post"-materialism is about exactly the opposite issues, such as the environment. Increasingly, "productive interests" (i.e., corporatist interests) clash with the so-called protective interests, such as environmental concerns. Why do they clash? Because the "secret of corporatism" has always been to establish social harmony on the basis of economic growth. Unfortunately, economic growth is often incompatible with environmental concerns. Postmaterialism also clashes with corporatism on **procedural** grounds. For corporatism to work, as mentioned, it has to be organized in centralized, hierarchical structures. Postmaterialism is the opposite—it believes in decentralization and grassroots democracy. Many of the central organizational features of corporatism, such as organization of interests in peak association, compulsory membership, and the principle of unanimity—are incompatible with notions of grassroots democracy and decentralization of power.

The second reason corporatism may decline in importance is the rise of a **postindustrial society.** We have already highlighted the fact that the power of labor organizations is directly connected to their unionization rates—the more workers are organized, the more power they have vis-à-vis the employer's organizations. Corporatism is built on the traditional nineteenth-century industrial class conflict between the captains of industry and the mass labor unions that organize against them. However, at the beginning of the third millennium, these images do not apply anymore. The secondary sector (the industrial sector) of most of the modern European economies contributes less than 25 percent to the gross domestic product (GDP), with the **service sector** typically contributing between 65 and 70 percent and agriculture the remaining 5 percent. People who work in the service sector (lawyers, bankers, professors, insurance agents, real estate agents, teachers, etc.), so-called white-collar workers, are much more difficult to organize than blue-collar workers in the industrial sector. The reason is that many of these white-collar workers are very much removed from the strongly hierarchical nature of the nineteenth-century factory production process. The relationship between a "boss" and a "worker" in a modern law office or bank is much more collegial than the strictly class-based, hierarchical relationship in the old days of unfettered capitalism. In addition, among the qualifications of white-collar workers are their abilities to think for themselves, to be creative and innovative, and to think "out of the box." All of this conspires to a reduced willingness of many white-collar workers to be led by an organization that emphasizes hierarchy. As a result, not only are unionization rates dropping in industrial unions, but they have fallen particularly sharply in service sector unions, again unsettling the balance of power between capital and labor.

The third contender for the "end of corporatism" thesis is **globalization** (Chapter 15). Corporatism is a "national" concept; that is, it is a nation-specific approach to deal with economic and political challenges. As mentioned, the central actors of corporatism are the state, the labor unions, and the employers' organizations. Over the past decade, however, some observers have raised the issue of globalization, meaning that as a result of advances in information, transportation, and communication technologies, capital can move to whichever location best maximizes profits. This allows capital an "exit" option: If labor unions do not agree to the demands of capital, the latter can pack up and move their production facilities outside of the country to a location with lower wages and fewer or no regulations. Capital can move; domestic labor in industrialized democracies usually cannot. In order to avoid such "capital flight," labor has to give inducements to capital to stay at home, such as tax reductions, wage reductions, and fewer regulations in areas such as the environment. Sometimes, capital might even play off one country's offers to attract investment against another country's, leading to what is sometimes called the "race to the bottom"— that is, the company has an incentive to move to the location with the lowest wages, the lowest worker's protection, the least environmental regulation, and so on. Capital's exit option shifts significant bargaining power to its side, with labor having little to counter the exit threat, thus unsettling the "balance of power" between capital and labor.

Many scholars have noticed as a result of this shift in power a decline in corporatism, even in the most traditional corporatist countries such as Austria and Sweden. However, the financial and economic crisis of 2008 has given corporatism a new lease on life as the "laissez-faire" American model disintegrated, shattering the very assumptions of the free-market philosophy. For the foreseeable future, the relationships between states and markets will be re-calibrated in favor of the state. Capitalism will not disappear, but it will be reigned in, muzzled, and re-oriented towards a financial order that, in the words of Tony Blair, is "based on values other than the maximum short term profit."[9] The next section will examine in brief the origins of the market downturn of 2008 and explain the differences in responses to the crisis between continental European countries and the United States.

COMPARING EUROPEAN AND AMERICAN RESPONSES TO THE GREAT MELTDOWN OF 2008

The "state," or as American observers would call it, the "government," returned with a vengeance as a result of the bursting of the housing bubble, which led to what Peter Gourevitch called the "Great Meltdown of '08" (GM '08).[10] The belief in the magical workings of the invisible hand and what John Maynard Keynes termed "animal spirits" (casting aside a healthy pessimism in markets, in short: hubris), guiding the markets to everyone's best interest, has been torn asunder and is being replaced by the very "visible hand" of the state, even more so in the United States than in Europe. In order to understand the different responses to the GM '08, we need to briefly examine its origins.

Believing that home prices would never drop significantly, commercial banks in the United States began to offer mortgages under ever more competitive conditions, first reducing the down payments potential homebuyers had to make up front; then offering adjustable rate mortgages (often starting out with very low "teaser rates" that then would "re-set" after a few years, often to rates so high that people could not afford the mortgage any longer); then offering "interest-only" mortgages where homebuyers only had to pay the interest, not the principal, of the loan for a given period. Finally banks began to approve mortgages for people without even asking them to show proof of income. Such mortgages made it increasingly possible for less well-to-do people to buy homes, often beyond their capacity to pay for the mortgage. In other words, mortgages were increasingly extended to people with low incomes or poor credit histories—so-called sub-prime loans. In addition, government-sponsored corporations such as Freddie Mac and Fannie Mae began easing restrictions in order to increase the viability of loans to low-income homebuyers. These loans were then bought by Wall Street investment banks such as Lehman Brothers and Bear Stearns, which "securitized" them by slashing them into different tranches and selling the rights to the income generated by these loans as "mortgage-backed securities." These securities were often combined with government, corporate, and consumer debts to create so-called collateralized debt obligations (CDOs). Finally, these CDOs were traded on international capital markets and bought mostly by institutional investors such as pension funds, insurance companies, university endowments, and hedge funds located in the United States, Asia, and Europe.

The problem was that these "securities" were not really "mortgage-backed." When more and more people could not afford to pay back their mortgages, and home prices collapsed, the financial house of cards collapsed, too. Suddenly, credit froze up (because the CDOs were bundled, it was not possible to distinguish "good" from "bad" debt, and so no bank was willing to lend any longer); trust was shattered; businesses closed because of the credit squeeze; the stock market plummeted; widespread foreclosures occurred; people became unemployed; demand faltered; and economic growth slumped.

The responses to the crisis on both sides of the Atlantic were quite different, and these differences became most visible during the G-20 meeting in London in April 2009 that brought together the leaders of the world's 20 most powerful nations. Even though Barack Obama admitted that his country was at fault for perpetrating the economic crisis ("It is true [...] that the crisis began in the United States. I take responsibility even if I wasn't even President at the time"), his proposal for a global stimulus package fell on deaf ears as far as most Europeans were concerned, particularly Nicolas Sarkozy, the French president, and Angela Merkel, the chancellor of Germany. Obama's only ally was the British prime minister, Gordon Brown, who hoped to achieve a "global new deal" by persuading the continental Europeans to put up a massive stimulus package. Two visions of how to organize the relationship between market and state collided: the "Anglo-Saxon" model—that is, the laissez-faire, unregulated market model—against the state-interventionist, corporatist, and redistributive model of continental Europe.

Merkel and Sarkozy strenuously argued against a massive, global, stimulus package. They claimed that their states are already pumping millions of euros into an ailing economy via the social safety nets these countries have (compare the social expenditures as a percentage of GDP in Figure 1.1). When the economy falters, all kinds of "automatic stabilizers" come into place: job protections, unemployment insurance, active labor market policies, and others. These are monies that go directly into the pockets of people, increasing demand and stabilizing the economy. While such policies have been derided by the followers of the Anglo-Saxon model as sclerotic, requiring too high taxes, undermining competitiveness, and slowing economic growth, it turns out that the automatic stabilizers are crucial for an economy in a downturn because they bolster demand by keeping people in their jobs. While unemployment was generally lower in the United States than in Germany during good economic times, in this economic crisis, unemployment grew much faster in the United States than in Germany with a rate of 9.5 percent for the former and 8.3 percent for the latter in June 2009.

Instead of an additional stimulus package, Sarkozy and Merkel suggested a global framework to regulate international markets. Both argued that the

BOX 9.1 "FAILURE IS NOT AN OPTION—HISTORY WOULD NOT FORGIVE US"—NICOLAS SARKOZY

The world expects that we speed up the reform of the international financial system. The world expects that we rebuild, together, a new form of capitalism, better regulated, with a greater sense of morality and solidarity. This is a precondition for mobilizing the economy and achieving sustainable growth. This crisis is not the crisis of capitalism. On the contrary, it is the crisis of a system that has drifted away from the most fundamental values of capitalism. It is the crisis of a system that drove financial operators to be increasingly reckless in the risks they took, that allowed banks to speculate instead of doing their proper business of funding growth in the economy; a system, lastly, that tolerated a complete lack of control over the activities of so many financial players and markets. [. . .] This week, however, we must also attach the same level of priority and sense of urgency to making progress on the issue of regulation of financial markets. World growth will be all the stronger for being sustained by a stable, efficient financial system and by the kind of renewed confidence in the markets that will enable resources to be better allocated, encourage lending to pick up again and allow the return of the flow of private investment capital toward developing countries. ■

Source: Der Spiegel, April 1, 2009.

Great Meltdown of '08 was enabled by lax financial regulation, tax heavens, hedge funds, and suspect rating agencies. In their perception, global financial capitalism has run amok and needs tighter regulation (see Box 9.1).

This emphasis on regulation, and the much stronger medicine of "nationalizing" ailing industries if need be, is consistent with the European understanding of the role of the state, which is to guide markets to achieve more equitable outcomes. This stands in stark contrast with the United States, where the term "nationalization" is anathema, although in effect, by bailing out AIG, a large insurance company, the American public is now part owner of that company. As far as U.S. banks are concerned, widespread nationalization has not occurred, even though some economists believe that this would have been the right path (see Box 9.2). The idea to let equity holders take a loss, in effect, to disown them of their share in their bank, is incompatible with the individualistic American understanding of property. The various bailouts in the United States (of banks, car companies, and insurance agencies) favored shareholders and the managers who were left in place to remedy the same mistakes that many of them were responsible for in the first place.[11] Nationalization would have meant severing the shareholders and managers from their property and putting the government in charge—an action that would have been difficult for most Americans to swallow. Pumping public money into private banks did not do much to unfreeze the credit markets, precisely because control over the banks and their business strategies remained in private control. In fact, huge scandals

BOX 9.2 NATIONALIZE THE BANKS. WE ARE ALL SWEDES NOW!

The U.S. banking system is close to being insolvent, and unless we want to become like Japan in the 1990s—or the United States in the 1930s—the only way to save it is to nationalize it. As free-market economists teaching at a business school in the heart of the world's financial capital, we feel downright blasphemous proposing an all-out government takeover of the banking system. But the U.S. financial system has reached such a dangerous tipping point that little choice remains. [...] Last year we predicted that losses by U.S. financial institutions would hit $1 trillion and possibly go as high as $2 trillion. We were accused of exaggerating. But since then, write-downs by U.S. banks have passed the $1 trillion mark, and now institutions such as the International Monetary Fund and Goldman Sachs predict losses of more than $2 trillion. [...] Nationalization is the only option that would permit us to solve the problem of toxic assets in an orderly fashion and finally allow lending to resume. [...] Nationalizing banks is not without precedent. In 1992, the Swedish government took over its insolvent banks, cleaned them up and reprivatized them. Obviously, the Swedish system was much smaller than the U.S. system. Moreover, some of the current U.S. financial institutions are significantly larger and more complex, making analysis difficult. And today's global capital markets make gaming the system easier than in 1992. But we believe that, if applied correctly, the Swedish solution will work here. Sweden's restructuring agency was not an out-of-control bureaucracy; it delegated all the details of the cleanup to private bankers and managers hired by the government. The process was remarkably smooth. Basically, we're all Swedes now. We have used all our bullets, and the boogeyman is still coming. Let's pull out the bazooka and be done with it. ∎

Source: Matthew Richardson and Nouriel Roubini, the *Washington Post,* February 15, 2009.

erupted when it became known that some of the banks used the public monies to buy other banks, or to pay for lavish parties and junkets, and to excessively remunerate the very CEOs who created the disasters in the first place.

Nationalization is much less of a controversial issue in Europe. In the past, many European banks used to be public to begin with. Today, it is not unusual that the state controls a large percentage of the banks' shares. There are of course also private banks in Europe, but if they become insolvent, nationalization is a process that does not raise that many eyebrows in Europe. In the fall of 2008, authorities partially nationalized the Benelux bank Fortis, and a similar part-nationalization took place with the British bank Bradford & Bingley.[12] As early as 2007, the Bank of England acted as a "lender of last resort" for Northern Rock, one of the United Kingdom's largest mortgage lenders. States can provide that crucial ingredient of "trust" that no private entity can—trust that people will not lose their deposits and thereby prevent a "run on the banks" which proved so devastating during the Great Depression.

Clearly, the reactions of the continental Europeans and the Americans to the GM of '08 were quite different. How can we explain those differences? Here we come full circle to our discussion in the first chapter: The differences have to do with the paternalist role of the state, attitudes toward risk, class consciousness, the presence or absence of a professional civil service, and history.

The Paternalist Role of the State

The European feudal experience looms large in understanding the differences between the European and American approach to dealing with the GM '08. Feudalism in Europe was initially replaced with absolutist regimes in which the state still had tremendous power. This can best be seen in Louis XIV's finance minister, Jean-Baptiste Colbert (1619–1683), who heavily regulated, or "directed" the French economy via the state (*dirigisme*). Even in the wake of the death of absolutist regimes and in the ascent of popular sovereignty, European states remained powerful, as demonstrated in corporatist traditions and in the easy embracing of nationalizing of industries or of pushing for tougher global regulation of financial markets in the current economic downturn.

Attitudes Toward Risk

The European social model is designed to protect the people from the "vagaries of the market" and to equalize "life chances." This is why France and Germany were not in favor of a global stimulus package—they already had one in the form of generous unemployment benefits, job protections laws, active labor market policies, and so on. It is true that these policies are themselves a function of the strong influence of Socialist parties and unions in Europe for more than a century; at the same time, such policies, despite some griping now and then, enjoy widespread popularity. With the absence of strong unions and Socialist parties in the United States, Obama had to call for such an extraordinary "bailout of Main Street" via extending unemployment insurance for Americans on a one-time basis, while for Europeans, this is perceived to be a right as a result of being a citizen.

Class Consciousness

Europeans view capitalism as a zero-sum game, which means that when one gains, another loses. This is why, appeals by Chancellor Merkel to create a capitalism with "a human face," or President Sarkozy's representation of financial capitalism as "immoral," have such resonance in Europe. In June 2009, a fascinating debate erupted in Switzerland about the so-called **Abzocker**, meaning CEOs and top managers who made exorbitant amounts of money while regular employees hardly saw any salary increases. These extremely high wages were seen as an indication of the greed that is at least partially responsible for the GM '08. A Swiss businessman created a public initiative calling for more transparency in salaries, bonuses, "golden parachutes," and other forms of remuneration. According to various polls, 75 percent would support such an initiative while only 9 percent would vote against it.[13] It is hard to imagine a discussion about the "humanity" or "morality" of capitalism in the United States, or even serious attempts at curbing the salaries of successful American CEOs.

Civil Service in Europe

The relative autonomy of the European state is manifested in the cadre of highly trained, professional, nonpolitical (i.e., even when governments change, these "bureaucrats" remain in their positions) public servants with the authority to implement policies such as partially nationalizing industries. In the United States, there is no concept of an autonomous state that could take on such tasks, nor is there trust in public officials. What is more, there is not a highly trained civil service sector (such as in France, Germany, or Japan) that would be capable of taking on such a task.

Finally, History Matters

This is visible particularly in Germany's refusal to support a global stimulus plan. The reason can be traced to the terrible inflation that Germany experienced in the early 1920s, paving the way for the rise of National Socialist Party. Inflation (price increases) was so rampant that money became worthless very quickly, leading German homemakers to use paper money as kindling to start a fire in their stoves. Fear of inflation has become part of the German political culture, so any proposals that might have inflation as a consequence are rather shunned in Germany.

We have thus far emphasized the differences between European and American reactions to the GM '08. However, there is one similarity: despite the differences in degrees between European and American politics, the logic of capitalism is prevalent on both sides of the Atlantic. What the GM '08 in fact demonstrated is the structural dependence of "governments" (in America), or the "state" (in Europe) on private capital in a capitalist economy. Societies and governments are so dependent on the functioning of large companies, particularly when they become "too big to fail" (meaning that if they failed, this failure would create widespread social dislocation, riots, and upheavals), that even conservatives in the United States support bailouts with taxpayers' monies, even though this action contravenes the very logic of competitive capitalism, wherein the market mechanism supposedly separates winners from losers. On both sides of the Atlantic, the state is ultimately dependent on an accumulation of capital that is as frictionless as possible, for without it, states and perhaps even democracy would collapse. In that sense, workers will always get the short end of the stick, because the state will not come to their aid in the same way as it is bound to come to the aid of capital when the economy turns sour.[14]

The Greek Debt Crisis, 2011

As we noted above, when a business is large enough to generate widespread social dislocation as a result of impending economic collapse, the state has an inherent interest in bailing it out. What about when a country suffers a serious economic crisis? Who would bail out a country? If that country happens to be lucky enough to be part of the European Union, there are similar reasons at work as to why the European Union would bail out a country. This is actually what happened in 2010 and 2011 when the European Union, particularly France and Germany, extended massive financial assistance to Greece which would have otherwise defaulted. How did Greece get into such dire straits?

In 2001 Greece joined the euro zone, meaning it traded in its previous currency (the drachma) for the euro. In order for a country to join, it had to fulfill the so-called **convergence criteria:**

1. The total sovereign debt outstanding had to be less than 60 percent of GDP.
2. The annual budge deficit could not be higher than 3 percent of GDP.
3. The national inflation rate had to be within 2 percent of the best-performing member states.

In 2004 it became clear that Greece fudged many of these criteria. It turned out that both the national debt as well as the annual budget deficit were in fact much higher than their official numbers. The investment bank Goldman Sachs advised Greece to come up with a scheme of complicated cross-currency swaps where public debt in dollars and yen was traded with Euros on the basis of fictional exchange rates. The effect was that it made it look like Greece's debt was lower than it actually was since this additional debt did not show up in the official debt statistics. After Greece joined the euro zone, eventually it had to account for the additional debt. As Greece suddenly became much poorer, Goldman Sachs, a crucial accomplice in this fudging of the official debt statistics, suddenly became much richer, to the tune of $300 million.[15]

In October of 2009, leaders in the EU were shocked to learn that Greece's budget deficit was 12.5 percent of GDP, double the amount that most analysts assumed. Not only did Greek lawmakers lower taxes, but they also engaged in unrestrained spending, much of it to groups with special access to political power such as the unions, and other entities who had established patron–client relationships with the state such as public employees, as well as people receiving public pensions. Greece has a large number of public employees whose salaries and pensions make up one-third of its budget. In addition, Greece spent significant amounts on defense in order to keep up with its nemesis, Turkey, across the Aegean Sea. While the average European NATO member spends 1.7 percent of its GPD on military expenditures, Greece spent about 4 percent in 2010.

During the summer of 2011, as the crisis reached a boiling point, it became known that public employees who had to carry files as part of their job received an additional boost to their salaries of about $400, bus drivers would receive over $430 in addition for simply showing up on time for work, and people employed on the state railways would receive more than $550 in addition to their regular salary for washing their hands at the job. This, in turn, particularly enraged French and German citizens who were asked with their tax money to bail out Greece. While these forms of **patronage** are certainly not the sole cause of the budget crisis, they highlight the problems of corruption, bribery, and tax evasion that are rampant in Greece. The "black economy," that is, economic transactions for which no taxes are paid to the state, is estimated to be in the neighborhood of $20 billion a year. Transparency International estimates that about one-third of all economic transactions are done in the "black economy."[16]

In April 2010, the statistical authority for Europe, Eurostat, reported that the true budget deficit of Greece is 14 percent—much higher than originally thought. Shortly thereafter, the EU together with the International Monetary Fund extended their first emergency bailout package to Greece in the amount of $154 billion. In another round of budget "adjustments" in October 2010 Greece was forced to admit that its budget deficit is even higher than originally indicated, namely 15.4 percent of GDP. In response, international credit rating agencies, such as Moody's and Standard and Poor, reduced Greece's status to "CCC," meaning that Greece is highly vulnerable with a low capacity to meet its financial obligations. Greece's CCC rating is currently the lowest in the world.

To the chagrin of many European governments and citizens, the bailout package of 2010 had no discernible impact on the budget situation, requiring a second, massive emergency injection of funds from the EU and the International Monetary Fund, in the amount of 110 billion euros in June 2011. This time, the heads of the state in the EU, particularly Angela Merkel and Nicolas Sarkozy, made an extension of additional credits dependent on Greece's agreement to drastically cut spending, increase taxes, sell public assets, and use other measures. In a close vote, on June 29, 2011, a slight majority of members of the Greek Parliament (155 out of 300) agreed to accept draconian austerity measures, such as increases in property taxes and value-added tax in addition to a "solidarity tax"; tax increases on tobacco, gas, and alcohol; salary cuts for federal employees; reduction in pension payments across the board; rescinding existing tax breaks; making the tax structure more progressive (i.e., those with higher incomes will pay higher taxes); reducing government spending significantly; increasing the retirement age; and privatizing public property such as the two largest ports in Greece, Thessaloniki and Piraeus.[17]

Predictably, this led to massive riots and protests in Syntagma Square, outside the Greek Parliament in Athens, which was besieged by protesters who camped out in front of the parliament. In July of 2011, the Greek unions called for general strikes which paralyzed the city of Athens and led to regular clashes in the evenings between police forces in riot gear and protestants armed with rocks. The weapon of choice seemed to have been high-powered, green laser pointers, made in China, which they aimed at the eyes of the police. In the summer of 2011, Greece's national debt stood at 160 percent of its GDP.

In October 2011 a report from the "Troika" (the European Union, the International Monetary Fund, and the European Central Bank) revealed that Greece will very likely default on its debt raising doubts as to whether the euro and, with it, the European Union project might survive this Greek tragedy. On October 26, 17 European countries, under the leadership of Angela Merkel and Nicolas Sarkozy, hammered out a deal which included a 50 percent write-off of Greece's debts (meaning that states and individuals who held this debt immediately lost 50 percent of their claims), about 1 trillion euros ($1.4 trillion) in bailout funds, and, among other things, a commitment from Italy to take measures to reduce its debt. It is instructive to recognize that this agreement contained measures not only designed to save Greece from default, but to save the euro as the common currency of Europe.

To the consternation of Merkel and Sarkozy, and many other European leaders, the Greek prime minister George Papandreou blindsided the rest of the world by arguing that this rescue package should be put before a referendum in Greece, leading to an immediate drop in the international stock markets. Whether Papandreou might not have felt strong enough to agree to this deal or whether he believed he could not proceed without public support, what is clear is that such a referendum could have spelled doom not only for the euro in Greece but also for Greece's continued membership in the EU. During the G-20 meeting in Cannes, Merkel and Sarkozy took Papandreou aside and after some tough words had been exchanged he was persuaded to scrap the idea of a referendum. His wavering on this issue led to a vote of confidence in the Greek parliament which he barely survived but which also signaled that the parliament supported the rescue deal suggested by the EU leaders to help Greece avoid default and to save the euro. On November 10, Lucas Papademos became the new prime minister of Greece heading a unity government, in which all major parties share power, tasked with administering the tough austerity package attached to the EU leaders' bailout plan, and once these measures are implemented, early elections will be held, most likely in the spring of 2012.

Some economists have argued that Greece's troubles stem from its joining the euro zone in 2001.[18] It is true that without having its own currency, one option remains closed for Greece which is to devalue its currency, making its exports cheaper and its imports more expensive. However, this is a useful strategy only for countries whose exports are a large percentage of GDP, which is not the case for Greece. For the member countries in the euro zone, the exchange rates vis-à-vis other currencies are set by the European Central Bank in Frankfurt. Besides, the trouble in Greece also highlight the larger challenges of an incomplete integration of the EU. There is a disconnect between the monetary union that has been achieved via the euro and the fiscal and political disunion that characterizes much of the relationships between countries. This crisis might paradoxically lead to a "deepening of the EU" insofar as it clearly demonstrates that stronger fiscal and political institutions, such as a European-level finance ministry, or the establishment of euro bonds (similar to the American treasury bonds) are necessary to complement the monetary union.[19] "On December 9, 2011 the EU, with the exception of the United Kingdom, did agree to a "fiscal compact" in which the countries of the Euro zone would enshrine the debt and deficit ceilings into their constitutions and, failing to meet these criteria, would be held responsible via harsher sanctions than before." At the same time it is also true that Greece's economic troubles are largely self-inflicted.

It is clear that these are trying times for the EU and its currency. It would have terrible consequences if Greece were to default as a member of the EU. There would be contagion effects, that is, a Greek default would infect other weak European economies such as Portugal, Italy, and Spain, the other members of the "PIGS" group (Portugal, Italy, Greece, Spain). While the Greek drama is still unfolding, it appears that the next candidate in trouble is Italy which is a much bigger economy. Italy defaulting on its sovereign debt obligations would have catastrophic effects on the euro as well as on the whole EU project and the world economy since Italy, the third largest European economy, is "too big to bail." Already the interest rates on its government bonds are at an almost unsustainable level of 6.6 percent, meaning that it is increasingly expensive for Italy to borrow money to pay its debt. The first casualty of these gathering dark clouds has been their prime minister Silvio Berlusconi who had lost so much support in his coalition and even in his own party that he was forced to submit his resignation as prime minister.

Ultimately, these issues are a function of different development levels across EU countries. Being in the EU means sharing in a community of fate under the motto "one for all, all for one," where the bigger brothers, such as Germany and France, have to come to the aid of their smaller ones when they fall on their nose (see Chapter 14).

KEY TERMS

Abzocker   195
business associations   182
capitalist   179
civil service   179
classification   188
competition   184
complement   184
convergence criteria   197
corporations   183
corporatism   178
economic interest
   groups   180

euro zone   179
globalization   190
guild   180
internal democracy   187
legitimacy   179
lobby   180
mediators   185
patronage   198
pluralism   183
postindustrial
   society   190
procedural   189

service sector   190
state   178
state
   bureaucracy   178
state interest   179
strong labor
   movement   186
substantive   189
trade
   unions   182
trilateral   185
vulnerability   186

DISCUSSION QUESTIONS

1. Corporatism is often described as "elitist." The United States does not have levels of corporatism comparable to Europe. Does that mean that crucial decisions about politics and economics are made by "the people," or are there other kinds of elites in the United States? If yes, who are they?
2. Why is a European type of corporatism unthinkable in the United States?
3. Corporatism is closely connected to the "state." Why is this so?
4. Many observers have argued that corporatism is no longer sustainable in an age of globalization. Why?

5. The ideology of postmaterialist, or "green," parties is often described as being incompatible with corporatism. Why is this so?
6. What is the difference between pluralism and corporatism?
7. Corporatism sometimes goes under the label "expertocracy," meaning that it is government by experts. Should corporatism wane, as many observers have argued that it will, who would take the experts' place?
8. Figure 9.1 shows that the Scandinavian countries have the highest union density rates. What do you think could be the political and social consequences of such high union density rates? In Chapter 1 we have seen that the same countries also have the highest social expenditures as well as the highest redistributive capacity. Do you think that these are linked, and, if yes, how?

NOTES

1. Timothy Mitchell. The Limits of the State: Beyond Statist Approaches and Their Critics. *American Political Science Review* 85 (March 1991): 81, 94.
2. Klaus Armingeon. Korporatismus in Wandel: Ein Internationaler Vergleich. In Emmerich Tálos (Hg), *Soziale Partnerschaft: Kontinuität und Wandel eines Modells* (Vienna, Austria: Verlag für Gesellschaftskritik, 1993, 299).
3. R. Michael Alvarez, Geoffrey Garrett, and Peter Lange. Government Partisanship, Labor Organizations, and Macroeconomic Performance. *American Political Science Review* 85 (June 1991): 539–556, and Nathaniel Beck, Jonathan N. Katz, R. Michael Alvarez, Geoffrey Garrett, and Peter Lange. Government Partisanship, Labor Organization, and Macroeconomic Performance: A Corrigendum. *American Political Science Review* 87 (December 1993): 945–948.
4. Manfred E. Streit. Market Order and Welfare Politics: The Mirage of Neo-Corporatism. Research Unit for Societal Developments, University of Mannheim, Working Papers, no. 3, 1987.
5. Ibid.
6. Arend Lijphart and Markus M. L. Crepaz. Corporatism and Consensus Democracy in Eighteen Countries: Conceptual and Empirical Linkages. *British Journal of Political Science* 21 (1990): 235–256.
7. Markus M. L. Crepaz. Corporatism in Decline? An Empirical Analysis of the Impact of Corporatism on Macroeconomic Performance and Industrial Disputes in 18 Industrialized Democracies. *Comparative Political Studies* 25 (July 1992): 139–168.
8. Markus M. L. Crepaz. Explaining National Variations of Air Pollution Levels: Political Institutions and Their Impact on Environmental Policy-Making. *Environmental Politics* 4 (1995): 391–414.
9. Merkel Sarkozy. Blair Call for New Capitalism. *CNBC*, January 8, 2009. http://www.cnbc.com/id/28557738
10. Peter Gourevitch. The Great Meltdown of '08: Six Variables in Search of an Outcome. *APSA-CP Newsletter* 20, no. 1 (Winter 2009).
11. One exception was Obama's "firing" of Rick Wagoner, the CEO of General Motors, as a condition for the company's receiving further public funds. In July 2009, a much smaller General Motors emerged from bankruptcy, with the American government 60 percent owner of the car company.
12. Europe's Plan: Nationalize Banks, rather than Sustain Them. *Christian Science Monitor*, September 30, 2008. http://thestockmasters.com/europe-banks-nationalize-093008.html.
13. Abzocker Initiative spaltet die Parteien. *Thurgauer Zeitung*, June 27, 2009.

14. Markus M. L. Crepaz. From Semisovereignty to Sovereignty: The Decline of Corporatism and Rise of Parliament in Austria. *Comparative Politics* 27 (1995): 45–65.
15. Der Spiegel, "How Goldman Sachs Helped Greece to Mask its True Debt," by Beat Balzli, February 8, 2010.
16. Die Presse, Gegen Griechenlands Systemfehler braucht es mehr als nur sparen, June 29, 2011.
17. Heute.at. Das Griechische Sparprogram im Detail.
18. Mark Weisbrot. Why Greece Should Reject the Euro. *The New York Times*, May 9, 2011.
19. Iain Begg, A Deepening European Union. Council on Foreign Relations, June 14, 2011. http://www.cfr.org/eu/deepening-european-union/p25272.

Policy Outcomes

In this chapter, we are moving from theory to the real world of political outcomes. Some of you may have asked yourself whether all those issues that were covered in this book up to this chapter actually matter in terms of explaining variations in policy outcomes. Why would different historical experiences of nation building matter? Does it really matter what kind of parties a country has or what kind of electoral system there is, how the interest group system is structured, or how active social movements are in a country?

The answer is that policy outcomes are a direct result of all the things we have covered in the first nine chapters of this book. Some students may not be that interested in the arcane details of how electoral systems work, but they want to know how much taxes they will need to pay once they join the workforce, what kind of health care they will get, whether their economy is globally competitive, what happens to them should they become unemployed, what kind of education their children will receive, will there be social security in their old age, will they be riding in high-speed rail systems or on four-lane interstates, the degree of poverty and inequality in their country, the air and water quality, and even how long they are going to live, or even the likelihood of civil war in their own country. Obviously, these are things that everybody wants to know and most of the answers can be found in the first nine chapters of this book.

In this chapter, we try to bring students into our discussion of European politics in a more active way by challenging them to explain variations in **policy outcomes** among European democracies and also in comparison with the United States. We will define what is meant in political science by a policy outcome, and then we will give **comparative data** on a wide range of policy outcomes in Europe and the United States. The task then is to explain, for example, why taxes are higher in Sweden than in Switzerland, or why poverty is higher in the United States than in the Netherlands. There is a wealth of **explanations** for such questions in the political science literature, and there is a lively and vigorous debate about the merits of the various explanations.[1] As we wrote at the end of Chapter 9, such debates are both expected and healthy when it comes to establishing **causal connections** among political variables. For possible explanatory variables, students should look at all previous chapters. Do features of parliamentary election systems, for example, have a causal impact on the level of governmental health expenditures? Do political systems that allow for referenda have lower or higher tax levels?

Even with the casual view of a tourist, it is easy to see differences in policy outcomes from one European country to another. Trains, for example, are more punctual in Switzerland than in Italy. And, because trains are mostly government-run, their punctuality can be considered a governmental policy outcome. One might ask why the Italian government is less able than the Swiss government to make its trains run on time. If tourists become ill on a European vacation, they can compare the quality of health care in the various European countries. Parents moving from one country to another can see where their children get the best education. There are literally thousands of criteria according to which one can evaluate the policy outcomes of a country. A specialist in education may wish to know on a cross-national basis how well students learn to read, whether there is sex discrimination in the educational system, what the social status of teachers is, and so on. An expert in criminology will have a similar multitude of questions regarding crime.

How can we systematically explain **variations** in policy outcomes? In the first eight chapters, we encountered many factors that may help us with such explanations. Does the economic performance of a country, for example, depend on the strength of the various political parties, on the pattern of cabinet formation, or on the level of government centralization? Does it have something to do with the influence of interest groups on the policymaking process? Or, can the differences in policy outcomes even be linked to the different processes of modernization in Europe and the United States?

Whatever the answer, the very assumption is that politics makes a difference. The operative term of almost every political campaign is change, meaning that if enough voters vote for a particular party, some kind of change will occur. This means that the candidates and the voters must believe that politicians actually have the **capacity** to effect change. After all, if things could not be changed, why bother to vote in the first place? Unfortunately, it is not that easy. As we have already learned in Chapter 9 and will revisit in Chapter 15, the degree to which politics can affect particular outcomes has been seriously challenged by globalization, calling into question the sovereignty of states to achieve particular outcomes. Still, the basic proposition of democratic politics is that people have choices, and depending on what is chosen, they will get different outcomes.

In this chapter we will compare various European democracies together with the United States across a range of outcomes. In analyzing differences it is important to realize that "change" can occur along two dimensions: across **time** and across **space**. It is important to keep in mind that changes over time *within* one country are qualitatively different as compared to differences *between* countries. Making comparisons across countries requires an understanding of "systemic effects." For instance, it may be difficult for an American voter to imagine that political parties in Sweden run, and win, on the basis of tax *increases*. Carl Bildt, Conservative challenger to the Social Democrats, campaigned for tax cuts in the 1998 general election campaign. He lost to the Social Democrats, who were running on the basis of tax *increases*. Referring to the 1998 general election campaign, "Talking about tax cuts in this campaign is like swearing in church," said Toivo Sjoren, the research director of the Sifo opinion-surveying firm.[2] A similar scenario was present during the 2002 campaign. In the period leading up to the election, the Swedish prime minister, Göran Persson, declared that "Welfare is not free. You have to pay for it, and that is why we say no to the tax cuts."[3] And again the Social Democrats won. In the 2006 elections, however, a coalition of four parties of the Right won with a program of tax cuts (see Chapter 4). The Social Democrats warned that tax cuts would reduce benefits for the needy, but this time they lost. This Swedish example shows that it is not only interesting to make cross-country comparisons but also to compare a country over time. Why did the Social Democrats with a program of no tax cuts win in 1998 and 2002 but lose in 2006? This is perhaps a topic for a term paper.

Comparing outcomes across systems, it is important to know something about the "systemic" differences between countries. By **systemic** we mean things such as different political institutions, different forms of interest representation, different "cultures," and many of the elements that we have highlighted in this book so far in Chapters 1 through 9. What follows are country rankings across many different policy fields. The task for students in this chapter is to draw upon the insights gained from the previous chapters and attempt to analyze and understand why countries occupy particular positions compared to other countries. The comparative position of countries compared to others is not accidental—policy outcomes represent the combined interactions of modernization, political parties, interest groups, the electoral system, social movements, and all the other elements we covered in the earlier chapters. Most graphs include three ex-Communist Eastern European countries, the Czech Republic, Poland, and Hungary. In interpreting their position, it is useful to keep their different history in mind.

At this point, it is useful to discuss the difference between policy **output** and policy **outcome**. Policy output might mean, for example, a political program, or taxes, or particular regulation to achieve a particular outcome. In other words, policy output is not the "result" itself; rather, it is a way to achieve, via political programs, taxes, regulation, and so on, a particular result. Say, for example, that a country wants to reduce air pollution and in doing so produces legislation that forces factories to install so-called scrubbers in their chimneys to clean the air. If after a particular period of time, all factories have such scrubbers installed, that is an example of policy output. It does not represent the actual result yet. The actual outcome of that policy, it is hoped, would be reduced air pollution.

There are many instances in which a particular policy output fails to achieve the expected policy outcome. One example is immigration policy in

Germany. After the first oil shock in 1973–1974, Germany stopped labor immigration. Yet, the number of immigrants continued to increase as a result of family unification and later as a result of asylum seekers. This incapacity to control the borders led to horrific attacks on immigrants in Germany and is at least partly responsible for the electoral success of radical right-wing parties in the eastern parts of the country. Another example is health policy in the United States. America has by far the most expensive health-care system in the world, yet its health outcomes, measured in terms of life expectancy and infant mortality, are below par given that its health-care system encompasses one-sixth of the American economy. Other countries achieve much better results with much lower costs.

This chapter is an exercise in "applied political science." In other words, it is an attempt to demonstrate that history, institutions, political structures, and so on matter. They have **systematic**, and sometimes even **predictable**, outcomes. However, connecting outcomes and outputs is sometimes quite difficult because, surprisingly, relatively little research has investigated the determinants of policy outcomes. Not all outcomes are driven only by the factors that we have highlighted in the previous nine chapters. Some outcomes can be explained by individual behavior, others by the natural resource endowment of countries, and still others simply by the geographic location of countries. However, even in the arena of seemingly individual choices, such as whether to smoke, whether to buy guns, or what foods to purchase and eat, the impact of politics is ubiquitous. Thus, public policy affects what appear to be individual choices as well as the provision of public goods, such as the environment. Think of the government's antismoking campaigns, for example, or the obligation to wear seat belts in cars, or the fashion in which governments manage public lands and attempt to protect natural resources. Politics enters into all the policy outcomes and outputs presented in the next section, even though it sometimes seems that the outcomes are a matter of individual behavior. Some outcomes, such as obesity, which is fast becoming a major public health crisis in many developed democracies, at first appears to be simply a matter of individual choice. But is it really? Or is it a matter of "class"? Are obese people generally well-to-do, or are they generally poor? If it is the latter, political explanations are highly relevant in explaining variations in obesity rates across countries. In the next section, let us pretend to be policy analysts and go on a creative, and perhaps somewhat speculative, journey to find out whether there is a systematic way of understanding the bewildering variety of policy outcomes. The United States is included in all the following statistics as a comparison case. However, the United States is a very large and diverse country with tremendous regional and local differences. A comparison between Alabama and France on many of the following indicators would most likely yield different results than between Vermont and France. The federalist character of the United States adds to this diversity.[4] This section is particularly useful as a starting point for more extensive research to delve deeper into the determinants of policy outcomes and outputs and lends itself ideally to term paper assignments.

EXPLAINING VARIATION IN POVERTY RATES

The degree of poverty among a country's residents is a highly relevant policy outcome. Poor people tend to be less educated, encourage education less among their children, live in unhealthy conditions, vote less, and, in general, have fewer "life chances" than the middle class.

Poverty is measured as a percentage of people who earn less than 50 percent of the median income. We do not pretend to offer all possible explanations for variations in poverty of populations. However, students still should get a good sense of how such explanations are derived and are encouraged to apply similar approaches to the other figures that we show later in the chapter in order to answer the quintessential comparative politics question: How can differences and similarities in policy outcomes be explained?

Figure 10.1 shows two policy outcomes: the percentage of households living in poverty (defined as the living below 50 percent of the median income) and total taxes on income and profits as a percentage of GDP. This is an example

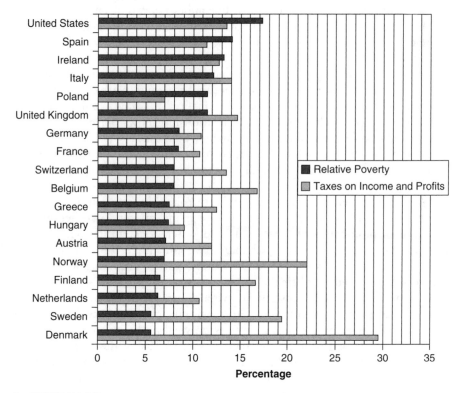

FIGURE 10.1

Relative poverty for total population in 2004–2005 (percentage of households below 50 percent of the median income) ordered from highest to lowest poverty and Taxes on Income and Profits in 2006 (as percentage of GDP).

Source: For relative poverty: Luxembourg Income Study, LIS Key Figures; for Taxes on Income and Profits: OECD Factbook, 2010.

of the difference between policy output and policy outcomes. Taxes represent an example of policy output, whereas poverty is an example of policy outcome. Taxes are a "steering instrument" to achieve a particular outcome. The taxes dimension indicates the degree of "state interventionism" and highlights to what extent people are willing to tolerate the state extracting funds from them for redistribution toward specific outcomes such as equalizing life chances or increasing military security.

Figure 10.1 is ordered from highest to lowest poverty, indicating that the United States is at the top of the poverty scale while two Scandinavian countries, Sweden and Denmark, have the lowest poverty levels. Although the United States shows the highest poverty its taxes on income and profits are significantly higher than in so-called welfare states such as Germany, France, Norway, Austria, and the Netherlands.[5] This is intriguing because many observers admit that while European welfare states provide security to its people, it must come at the expense of higher taxes. At first glance, it appears that in a number of European countries people enjoy excellent public transportation systems, national healthcare plans, free-to-almost-free public education, subsidized housing, and other publicly provided supports without exorbitant tax rates. What might account for the varying rates in poverty and total taxes across these modern democracies?

Figure 10.1 also shows taxes on income and profits in tandem with relative poverty rates. Could there be a connection; that is, could relative poverty have something to do with tax? If you glance at Figure 10.1 how would you guess the two are related? A closer look at the relationship shows that the higher the tax level, the lower relative poverty—but why would that be? Political scientists have provided many theories as to what could explain different rates of poverty across a range of countries. We will divide these theories into two groups: institutional and historical.

Let us start with an **institutional approach** in explaining poverty. "Institutional" means that the rules of the game matter; in other words, that different political institutions will yield systematically different political outcomes. (See Chapters 2–4). In Chapter 2 we introduced the various parties and learned that Socialist or Social Democratic parties are first and foremost concerned with equality. Their major claim is that in order for democracy to function properly, people must first have a minimum of economic security. Such political parties are committed to narrowing the gap between the rich and poor via redistributive means (by taxing wealthy households and redistributing these funds to the poorer segments of society in the form of social assistance, health care, and welfare nets). The effects of subsidized education, public transportation, universal health care, and other government entitlements are that people of lesser means gain access to jobs that they would otherwise not have, enabling them to more fully participate in political life—in short, Socialist or Social Democratic parties strive to equalize the "life chances" of citizens. The cumulative effect of the existence of such left-wing party programs is that poverty is reduced and the playing field is somewhat leveled. Political scientists call this the "parties do matter" hypothesis.

In Chapter 3 we examined electoral systems and discovered that when a country has proportional representation (PR), it also tends to have more parties and the level of "electoral distortion" is smaller. More parties means that more voices are heard (i.e., wider segments of the population, organized in political parties, want a piece of the economic pie). Oftentimes, coalition governments are necessary to secure majorities in the respective national parliaments. This, in turn, leads to a tendency of the government parties to engage in policies that satisfy the desires of their constituencies, culminating in higher spending for public goods such as social security, education, income replacement programs, retraining programs, and so on. Such "consensual" political institutions give access to more political players, resulting in more equality. Ultimately, the effects of such programs are such that that fewer people live in poverty. John Huber and G. Bingham Powell have shown that what they called the "proportionate influence systems" (of which proportional representation is a major part) produces policies that are closer to the desires of the electorate than what they termed "majority control systems," which has majoritarian electoral systems as a major part.[6]

In Chapter 4 we introduced parliamentarism and contrasted it with presidentialism. We learned that parliamentarism is characterized by fusion of executive and legislative powers while presidentialism separates these two powers. How could these different types of executive/legislative relations explain differing poverty levels? One approach might be what in political science is called the "veto point" hypothesis. Institutions can be thought of as "check valves" that control the flow of power. The more valves need to be turned, the more difficult it is to get water flowing. So it is with policies. The more power is institutionally diffused, the more difficult it is to change the status quo, as is the case for presidential systems. However, the fusion principle allows for quicker policy creation and implementation than separation of powers. A parliamentary system can institute reform rather quickly, precisely because the legislative and executive powers are fused. After World War II, when many left-wing parties came to power under a parliamentary system, they instituted generous welfare programs, which ultimately brought about a reduction in poverty levels.

Socialists would argue that such programs do not simply redistribute incomes, but that they level the playing field for poorer people by allowing them to attain education, skills, protecting them from the accidents and sickness, and providing for them in old age. More education and skills will increase opportunities for people who otherwise would not have had a chance to compete in a capitalist society. More education and skills means a lesser chance of becoming poor.

So far we have used what might be called "formal" institutional structures to explain the variation in poverty across different countries. However, in Chapter 9 we discussed in detail the logic of corporatism. One of the most intriguing aspects of corporatism is that the relationships between capital and labor are not specifically anchored in the respective constitutions of most corporatist countries. Thus, we may call corporatist or pluralist forms of interest group representation "informal" political institutions.

Why would more corporatist countries have lower levels of poverty? As we noted in Chapter 9, corporatist bodies, that is, representatives of labor and capital, have come to the conclusion that it is better to accommodate their differences than to compete against one another. Trade unions play a central role in corporatism policymaking and since they represent workers, their policies are aimed at increasing the wages and working conditions of that segment of society. As a result of highly organized unions, wages tend to be higher, or, if they are lower, workers at least enjoy relative job security, which results in lower poverty rates. Proponents of a more free-market persuasion might argue that corporatist countries are becoming less competitive and will eventually lose in the face of globalization. It is interesting to note that this need not be the case. Figure 10.6 shows the "global competitiveness index" and reveals that among the top five most highly competitive economies, four are among the most corporatist countries in the world. Leading the list is Switzerland, followed by Finland, Sweden, Denmark, and in fifth place, the United States. It appears that capitalist economies can be organized in very different ways from the American model and still be successful.

It is tempting to go back one link in the causal chain and ask, Why are there strong trade unions, Socialist parties, and proportional representation systems in most European countries, but not in the United States? To answer such large **macrostructural** questions it is necessary to delve deeper into the history of nation building, our second major theoretical approach in explaining variations in poverty. We want to caution the reader that the historical explanations offered are meant to be rough sketches, solely designed to demonstrate how large-scale, historical forces are affecting contemporary politics.

In Chapter 1 we laid out some of the fundamental differences between American and European politics: the lack of a feudal past and the fact that America was "born modern." This instilled a strong bourgeois impulse among the country's settlers, who rejected state intervention and helped to establish a strong sense of independence. These sentiments were buttressed by a Puritan religion that placed the individual in a prominent role.

In addition, the very history of American nation building made it very difficult for Socialist parties to gain a foothold among the working population. The constant arrival of waves of immigrants who spoke different languages and followed different religions made it extremely difficult to organize such disparate groups. The sectarian nature of Protestant Socialist organizers prevented the signing up of Catholics among their ranks, thereby excluding large numbers of potential party members who could have given much more thrust to the Socialist movement in America. Finally, Frederick Jackson Turner's frontier thesis (Chapter 1) is also plausible as an explanation of why Socialist parties failed: The abundance of free land that was there for the taking tempted many to move west and become capitalists themselves instead of working to organize Socialist parties in cities on the Eastern seaboard. Thus the "social question" that so plagued many European countries in the late nineteenth century never became an equally divisive issue in the United States. In fact, one might argue that "Without this [European] welfare adaptation it is doubtful that capitalism would have survived, or rather, its survival, 'unwelfarized,' would have required a substantial repressive apparatus."[7]

Thus, Americans are not used to looking to the state for help or assistance, something Europeans have no trouble with. Centuries of feudal rule have made Europeans more accepting of such a paternal force. It is of course true that throwing off the yoke of feudalism culminated in some of the bloodiest revolutions in Europe, but with the establishment of popular sovereignty and democracy, Europeans come to expect that the state looks out for the welfare of all (*Gemeinwohl*). Class conflict thus led to the establishment of strong trade unions, Socialist parties, and a proactive, paternalist state that ensures that citizens are educated and protected in times of unemployment, accident, sickness, and old age. Such programs culminate ultimately in lower poverty rates but higher taxes than in America.

So, different institutions, cultures, and the fashion in which countries became modern matter a lot. They directly affect where your tax money goes and which type of society you have—whether it is an individualist society centered on freedom with a "weak" state and religion as a strong influence or a communal society centered on equality with a "strong" state and religion as having relatively little influence.

These different "values" are manifested in countries' budgets. For instance, Figure 1.1 shows social expenditures across many modern societies, with Denmark, Sweden, and France spending almost 29 percent of their GDP on social welfare programs such as old-age benefits, health benefits, and family benefits, while the United States is second to last on that list, spending only about 16 percent of its GDP on such programs but grappling with the highest percentage of poverty and income inequality, as shown in Figures 10.1 and 10.3.

EXPLAINING FURTHER POLICY OUTCOMES

Now it's your turn: What follows are a number of tables showing policy outputs as well as policy outcomes. What explains the relative position of some of the countries? Pretend to be a policy analyst—how would you explain, for instance, the position of the United States vis-a-vis many other European countries in the following figures?

Policy outcomes that affect all members of society include the "big three": economic growth, unemployment, and inflation. The state of the economy is traditionally one of the hottest topics during an election campaign. In some regions of eastern Germany, unemployment reaches 20 percent, giving rise to regional radical right-wing parties. Similarly, inflation—which measures the changes in the consumer price index—is a crucial measure of government performance. Inflation appears in the form of rising prices, which can directly affect people's disposable income if their wages do not rise concomitantly with prices. Finally, economic growth, which is generally measured as the annual increase in the value of all goods and services produced (GDP), is the most important measure of the economic well-being of a society. Figure 10.2 shows these three measures across a range of European democracies and also the United States.

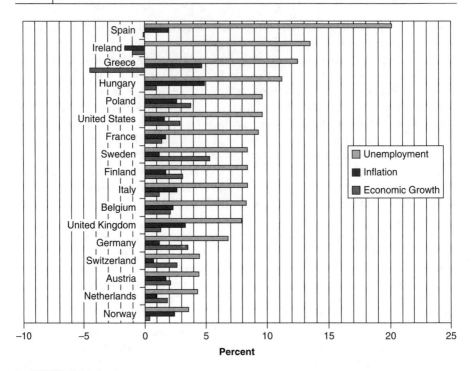

FIGURE 10.2

Economic growth, inflation, and unemployment ordered from highest to lowest unemployment in 2010.

Source: OECD Economic Outlook, 2011.

What could explain the variation of these three measures across the set of industrial societies? Are there particular reasons to believe that some political parties may favor more or less unemployment, inflation, or both? Would leftist parties favor policies that produce lower unemployment than inflation or vice versa? Would rightist parties favor economic policies that would create lower inflation than unemployment or vice versa? What about economic growth? Are there reasons to believe that some parties on the political spectrum would not favor economic growth? Or would all political parties favor economic growth? What are the potential "costs" of economic growth, and which political parties' fortunes might be positively affected by highlighting these "costs"? The data in Figure 10.2 are from 2010 which is more than a year after the Great Meltdown of 2008. How would you explain the dire economic difficulties that Spain, Ireland, and Greece find themselves in that year? On the other hand, a modern welfare state like Germany has weathered the economic crisis quite well, particularly compared to a laissez-faire-oriented United States. How is that possible? Finally, how would you explain that countries like Austria, the Netherlands, and Norway not only have had relatively small economic growth rates but they also have low unemployment rates?

One of the often-cited definitions of politics is Harold Lasswell's: Who gets what, when, and how? Who gets which pieces of the economic pie? A central

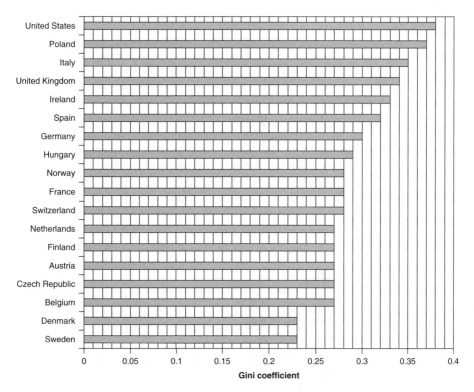

FIGURE 10.3

Gini coefficient for 18 democracies in the mid-2000s.

Source: OECD Factbook 2010.

principle of democracy is equality, where each vote counts the same. But what about the economic system—Is there equality there? How egalitarian are modern societies? Is economic inequality among groups consistent with the idea of democracy? The Greek philosopher Plutarch was very much aware of the corrosive forces of inequality. He declared that "The most fatal ailment of all republics [is] the imbalance between rich and poor."

The *Gini coefficient* is the most useful of all measures of income inequality, because it captures inequality across the whole range of incomes. The Gini coefficient was developed by the Italian statistician Corrado Gini in 1912. The range of the coefficient is between 0 and 1. Zero means perfect equality with everybody having the same income, and 1 means perfect inequality; in other words, one person has all the income and nobody else has anything.

In Figure 10.3 countries are ordered from highest to lowest income inequality, with countries like the United States and the United Kingdom leading the list and those like Finland, the Netherlands, and Denmark indicating the lowest income inequality. How can this be explained? Is equality of income important?

It may be possible that some of the outcomes we are trying to explain are a result of political participation of voters. Ultimately, voting is the essence of democracy. In a democracy, people get the government and policies they deserve, or so one would think. It's voters who at least partially determine what kind of policies are enacted. How do the various countries stack up in political participation vis-à-vis each other? One measure of political participation is voter turnout. People vote for very different reasons: They vote because they feel very strongly about a particular issue, because they are socialized into a particular political milieu that emphasizes voting as a duty of citizens, or because of habit. Figure 10.4 shows that there is quite some variation across modern democracies in terms of voter turnout. The figure shows the percentage of registered voters who actually voted. Since in most European countries registration is automatic, the numbers would have been similar had they been expressed as percentages of the voting age population (VAP). The United States' registration requirements, however, are more onerous. Thus, if the voter turnout for the presidential election in 2008 were expressed as a percentage of the voting age population, the turnout would have dropped to slightly over 57 percent as opposed to the 70 percent indicated in Figure 10.4. There are remarkable differences in voter

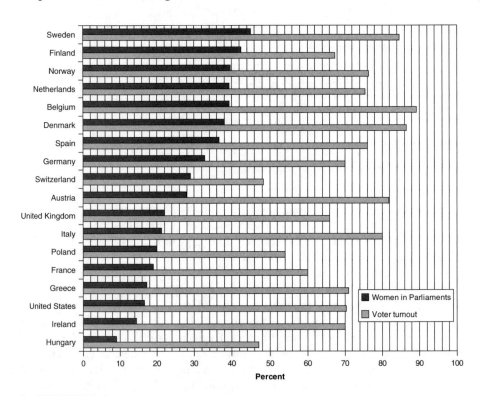

FIGURE 10.4

Women in parliaments (percentage of women representatives in the Lower House, latest elections) ranked from highest to lowest and voter turnout to most recent parliamentary elections (with the exception of the United States) defined as percentage of registered voters who actually voted.

Source: For Women in Parliaments: Interparliamentary Union, Women in Parliament 2011; for voter turnout: International Institute for Democracy and Electoral Assistance, Voter Turnout Database, 2011.

turnout observable: while almost 90 percent of Belgians and almost 85 percent of Swedes go to the polls, not even 50 percent of the Swiss and Hungarians cast their ballots. What might explain this variation?

Another measure that some observers argue is important is participation of women in parliaments. Even though both of these measures are included in the same graph, this does not suggest that there is necessarily a connection, although there might be. Women, it is argued, have different political interests than men, and if women were more equally represented in parliaments, policy production would reflect women's interests, such as parental leave, day care, and social welfare issues, to a greater degree. Three Scandinavian countries are at the top, having the highest percentage of women in parliaments (lower house), and the United States, Ireland, and Hungary bring up the rear. What can explain the distribution of women in parliaments across these modern democracies?

Staying with the theme of gender, the World Economic Forum has recently established an index called the Gender Gap Index. It is designed to measure the size of the gender gap in four critical areas of inequality between men and women. The first is economic participation and opportunity. This element examines outcomes on salaries, participation levels, and access to highly skilled employment. Second, the index examines differences in educational attainment, particularly outcomes with regard to basic and higher-level education. Third, the index also includes political empowerment and compares outcomes on representation and decision-making structures. Finally, the index also includes health and survival issues, particularly with regard to differential outcomes on life expectancy and sex ratio.

A pattern begins to emerge. The Scandinavian countries have the smallest gender gap. Might this have something to do with the fact that Scandinavian countries also have the highest percentages of women in their national parliaments? Or does it have to do with the high union density rates, or perhaps with the low poverty rates? If yes, how would these mechanisms work? As shown in Figure 10.5 the United States is in the middle of the field and, remarkably, countries such as France and Italy show very high inequality in outcomes between the genders: They are even more unequal than Eastern European countries such as Bulgaria and Poland.

Some might say that a highly interventionist state may produce less poverty and help level the playing field among social strata, but that it would ultimately undermine economic dynamism and competitiveness. The World Economic Forum also has collected data on the competitiveness of nations and presented it in an index called the Global Competitiveness Index.

The Global Competitiveness Index is composed of twelve elements that are critical to economic growth: *Institutions, Infrastructure, Macroeconomic Stability, Health and Primary Education, Higher Education and Training, Goods Market Efficiency, Labor Market Efficiency, Financial Market Sophistication, Technological Readiness, Market Size, Business Sophistication, and Innovation.* The index ranges from 0, meaning low-growth competitiveness, to 7, meaning maximum-growth competitiveness. Figure 10.6 is ordered from high to low global competitiveness index.

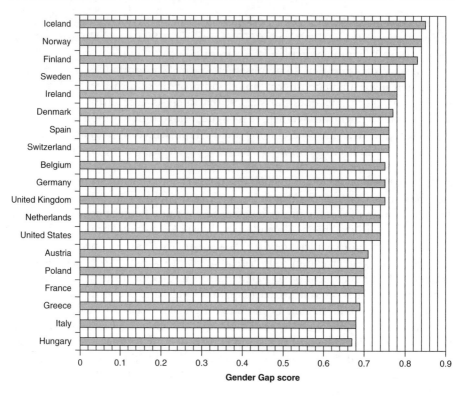

FIGURE 10.5
Gender Gap 2010 index.

Source: World Economic Forum, Gender Gap Index.

Even a cursory glance at Figure 10.6 shows an intriguing result: counting European countries only and the United States for comparison purposes, the leader of the pack is Switzerland, closely followed by Sweden, a highly interventionist state with strong Socialist party influence for decades, strong unions, high female participation in their national parliaments, and high public expenditures. In third place is the United States with no Socialist parties in Congress and a highly individualistic, antiwelfare political culture. Basically on par with the United States in terms of global competitiveness is Germany: a cushy welfare state with much lower relative poverty than the United States and even lower taxes on incomes and profits. This is intriguing insofar as many observers argue that it is not possible to have both: a wealth-creating, dynamic economy and a protective welfare state as the taxes used to finance the "nanny state" would lead to an inefficient allocation of resources and undermine the capitalist spirit. Poor people in a capitalist society are just the collateral damage to the frictionless unfolding of capitalist accumulation. Figure 10.6 shows that it does not have to be that way: countries like Germany and Sweden seem to have it both ways: it appears that generous social safety nets with all their attendant advantages (better education, greater life expectancy, less crime,

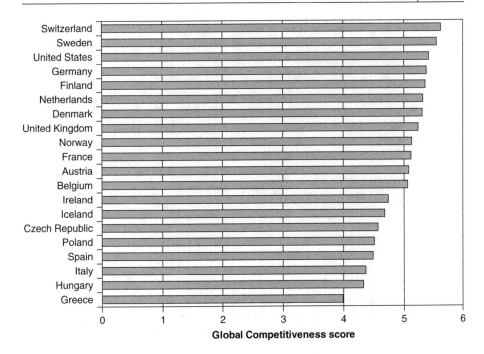

FIGURE 10.6

Global competitiveness index 2010 ranked from highest to lowest (consisting only of European countries and the United States for comparison purposes including all countries; the top five are: Switzerland, Sweden, Singapore, the United States, and Germany).

Source: World Economic Forum, Global Competitiveness Index, 2010.

less infant mortality, less poverty, more equal "life chances") do not undermine the economic global competitiveness of these societies. If that is in fact true, what are the implications of these observations for American politics?

One of the most important policy outcomes is health. For a society to be productive, it has to be healthy. Countries lose billions of dollars per year as a result of workers who are absent from work due to illness. In addition, treating sick people from preventable diseases such as AIDS, lung cancer caused by smoking, or obesity absorbs huge resources that could be employed in other areas. For example, the Centers for Disease Control and Prevention in the United States estimate that obesity alone created economic costs to the tune of over $148 billion in 2008.[8] In the United Kingdom, obesity has tripled over the past 20 years. Obesity in the United Kingdom is responsible for an estimated 18 million sick days a year; it shortens people's lives by nine years on average, and its economic costs are an estimated 2 billion pounds a year.[9]

Figure 10.7 shows three measures: health spending as a percentage of GDP (an output measure), and two outcome measures—male life expectancy at age 65, and infant mortality (deaths per 1,000 live births). The graph is ordered from the highest to lowest level of infant mortality. Figure 10.7 shows that the United States has the highest infant mortality, and a middling life expectancy for

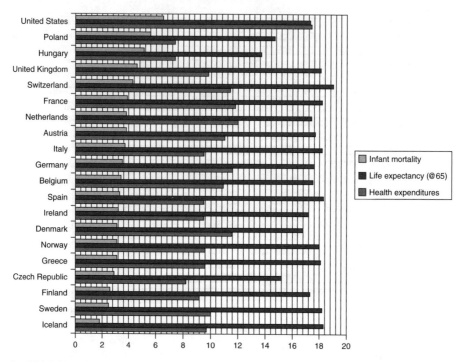

FIGURE 10.7

Total health expenditures (private and public) as a percentage of GDP, Life expectancy of males at age 65 (in years), and infant mortality (deaths per 1,000 live births). Data refer to the year 2009.

Source: OECD Health Data, June 2011.

males age 65. What is most surprising is that this less-than-stellar performance is achieved with by far the highest total health expenditures across all countries. More than half the countries in the sample have higher male life expectancies at age 65, significantly lower infant mortality rates at much lower costs. Finland, Sweden, and Iceland show the lowest levels of infant mortality achieved with much lower health expenditures than in the United States.

Why is it that most European countries achieve better health outcomes at a much lower cost than the United States? It is widely believed that the United States has the most advanced medical technology and the most educated physicians. Why is it that health care is so expensive in the United States, yet achieves such comparatively poor results?

Figure 10.8 examines, what the OECD calls, quality of life indicators such as murder rates, "youth inactivity," obesity, and the number of inmates per 10,000 population. Figure 10.8 is ranked from highest to lowest for murder rates. What becomes immediately obvious in this comparison is the very large difference between murder rates and even larger differences between the prison population in the United States compared to the rest of Europe. Switzerland is ranked second in murder rates per 1 million population with less than half the murder rate of the

United States. As far as prison population is concerned, the United States' figure is almost four times bigger than the second-ranked country, Poland, prompting Peter Baldwin to claim that "The murder rate and the number of prisoners in America is both off the European scale."[10] What might explain this huge difference?

Similarly, when it comes to obesity, the United States is leading the pack followed by the United Kingdom and Iceland. Is obesity simply the result of individual food choices people make? Does it have a social, or perhaps even a class basis? If yes, what would explain that poorer people tend to be obese? Form a policy advisor's perspective, what would you recommend in term of policies combating obesity?

The fourth graph in Figure 10.8 concerns "youth inactivity," defined by the OECD as "youths who are not in education nor training, or in employment."

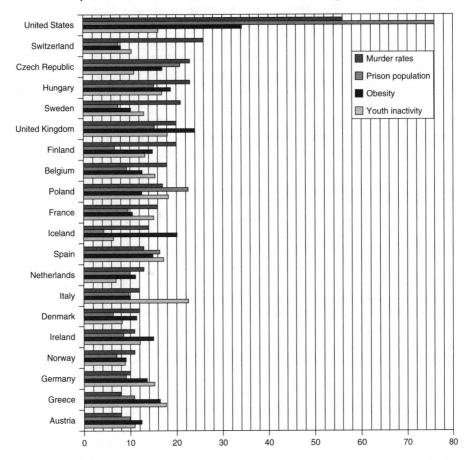

FIGURE 10.8

Murder rates (per 1 million population) ranked from highest to lowest, prison population per 10,000 inhabitants, total obesity (males and females with a body mass index of more than 30) as a percentage of population, and youth inactivity of 20–24-year-olds as a percentage of that age group.

Source: OECD Factbook 2010, Quality of Life Indicators and for Murder rates: OECD crime statistics, verifiable.com.

According to the OECD such individuals are "at risk of becoming socially excluded persons with incomes below the poverty-line and lacking the skills to improve their economic situation."[11] In this category, Italy is the leader, followed by Poland, the United Kingdom, and Greece. According to this statistic, about 23 percent of Italian youths age 20 to 24 are neither in school or training, nor in employment. Can you think of any reasons as to why this might be the case and why youth inactivity in the United States is significantly lower than Italy's?

There is hardly a government that does not realize how crucial it is to have an educated citizenry. At a very basic level, democracy itself is not possible without an educated citizenry. But even at more mundane levels, education is crucial in a globalized world in which skills are absolutely essential to succeed, not only for individual companies but also for countries as a whole. In the international competition for foreign direct investments (i.e., private companies that are investing significant resources in a country other than the one in which they are headquartered), a highly educated workforce combined with an excellent infrastructure and political stability can be considered to be the most important reasons why such companies invest their resources. Today, it is understood that "human capital" (i.e., knowledge and education) is as important as investment capital (i.e., land and machinery). In the explanations we offered about the determinants of poverty, we already highlighted the crucial nature of education.

Figure 10.9 shows one "output" measures and one "outcome" measure. The outcome measure is the so-called PISA measure, which stands for the Organization for Economic Cooperation and Development's (OECD) "Program for International Student Assessment," whose purpose it is to "assess how effective school systems are in providing young people with a solid foundation of knowledge and skills that will equip them for life and learning beyond school."[12] The figure shows the mathematics skills of 15-year-olds. The output measure is the educational expenditures per student ranging from primary, secondary, postsecondary to tertiary education, expressed in 000's of dollars in 2006 measured in constant prices and purchasing power parities.

The graph is ordered from the highest to the lowest per student education expenditures in the United States, Switzerland, Norway, and Sweden at the top and Italy, the Czech Republic, Hungary, and Poland at the bottom of the scale. Again, an interesting picture develops: A number of European countries achieve high outcomes, as measured in the PISA mathematics scores, with relatively low expenditures, while the United States is a big spender on education but is significantly below the OECD average as far as the mathematics skills of 15-year-olds are concerned. This mirrors the results in the health-care area (Figure 10.7) where high spending (output) does not yield a particularly healthy society in the United States (outcome). What do you think could explain this counterintuitive outcome? In fact, Figure 10.9 shows that there is nary a relationship between spending and educational achievement. Poland, which spends about one-third per student compared to the United States, achieves a slightly better outcome than the United States and Sweden achieves an almost identical outcome with more than twice the expenditures of Poland. Can we use what we have learned in this chapter so far to explain these interesting results?

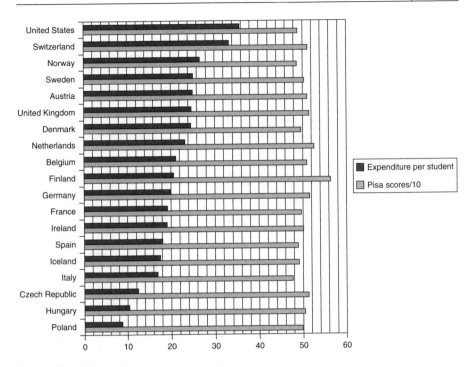

FIGURE 10.9

PISA student achievement scores in 2006 (mathematics scale, average of males and females),and expenditures on educational institutions per student (in thousands of US dollars at 2006 ppp's) across all educational categories (primary, secondary, post secondary, and tertiary).

Source: OECD Factbook 2010.

The state of the environment has become a critical political issue over the past two decades. Figure 10.10 shows carbon dioxide emissions per capita in metric tons. Carbon dioxide is one of the main contributors to global warming and stems mostly from the burning of fossil fuels, such as gasoline and oil, but also from gas flaring and the production of cement. One of the biggest contributors to the production of carbon dioxide is vehicular pollution: Burning 1 gallon of gasoline produces 22 pounds of carbon dioxide.[13] Environmental issues have become so pressing that in many European countries during the 1980s, Green parties gained representation in their parliaments, and they have increased their strength in recent years (see Chapter 2).

The United States indicates the highest per capita carbon dioxide emissions in 2007, with over 19 metric tons per person. The next biggest emitters following with some distance are Finland, the Czech Republic, and the Netherlands. Hungary and Sweden produce less than 6 metric tons of carbon dioxide per capita, and Switzerland, the lowest emitter, is just below 5 metric tons per capita. These are intriguing results. Some of these outcomes are a function of the size of the country, its geographic location, and its specific resource endowment,

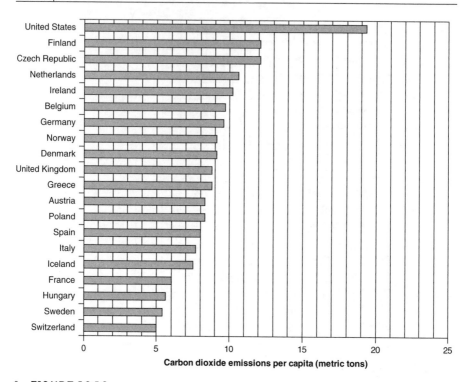

FIGURE 10.10

Carbon dioxide emissions per capita in 2007 measured in metric tons

Source: World Bank, World Bank Development Indicators.

although these outcomes are all mediated by politics. How would you explain such outcomes? Does a country's climate play a role? In our explanations offered previously, we highlighted the role of the system of interest group representation, called *corporatism*, and its opposite, *pluralism*. Is it possible that the pluralist form of interest group representation in the United States has something to do with the results in Figure 10.10? For example, in the United States until very recently, sport utility vehicles (SUVs) were exempt from the federal CAFE (corporate average fuel economy) standards, allowing such cars to become bigger and heavier without having to conform to fuel efficiency guidelines. How would you construct an explanation as to why SUVs were exempt from such guidelines (and very recently, however, made to conform to rather modest fuel efficiency standards) using the pluralism/corporatism dimension? Does it have something to do with energy production in various countries? How is France's energy production different from that of the United States? Why are the small Nordic countries such as Norway and Finland such heavy emitters of carbon dioxide?

Perhaps we should also examine a more encompassing measure—one that captures the capacity for "environmental sustainability," that is, the capacity of a country to produce goods and services without unduly damaging the environment. Fortunately, such an index, called the Environmental Performance

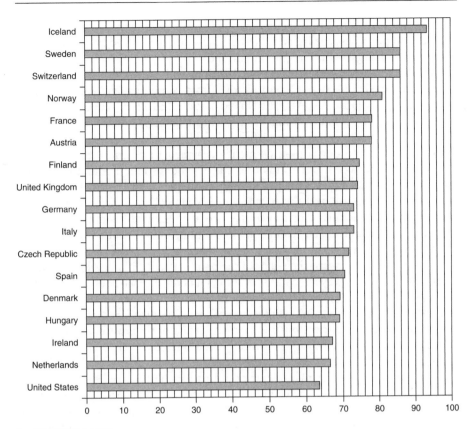

FIGURE 10.11

Environmental Performance Index 2010.

Source: Yale Center for Environmental Law and Policy, Yale University.

Indicator, is available for the year 2010. The index is published by the Yale Center for Environmental Law & Policy together with the Center for International Earth Science Information Network at Columbia University in cooperation with the World Economic Forum and the Joint Research Center of the European Commission. It is shown in Figure 10.11.

The index consists of 10 components of different weighting: environmental health (measured, among others, by the quality of drinking water and indoor air pollution), air quality (measured by the levels of regional ozone as well as urban particulates), water resources (measured by what is called "nitrogen loading," among others), biodiversity and habitat (the space of wilderness protection and ecoregion protection), productive natural resources (measured, among others, by the degree of overfishing and agricultural subsidies), climate change (measured, among others, by energy efficiency and the amount of renewable energy), the state of agriculture, fisheries, and forests.[14]

According to this index, which ranges from 0 to 100, the countries that rank the highest are Iceland, Sweden, and Switzerland, , and those that rank the lowest (within the group of European countries and also including the United States for comparison purposes) are Ireland, Netherlands, and the United States. These are intriguing rankings—what might explain them?

Finally, to what extent are developed nations willing to support development in less developed countries? One measure of that commitment is called "official development assistance (ODA)." The United Nations has a long-standing goal that developed nations should commit 0.7 percent of their gross national income to official development assistance. Official development assistance is defined as "government aid to developing countries designed to promote the economic development and welfare of recipient countries. Loans and credits for military purposes are excluded."[15] Aid includes grants, "soft loans" (where the grant element is at least 25 percent), and the provision of technical assistance. A significant proportion of development assistance is aimed at promoting sustainable development in poorer countries, environmental protection, and population programs.

Official development assistance is often taken as a measure of "compassion" of the rich countries toward the plight of the poor countries. No developed country wants to appear "stingy," yet the statistics speak louder than politicians' talk. This was highlighted when a UN official, in the wake of the horrific tsunami in Southeast Asia on Boxing Day (December 26) in 2004, complained about the fact that "The foreign assistance of many countries now is 0.1 or 0.2 percent of the gross national income. I think that is stingy, really."[16] It was mostly the United States that felt offended by this statement, although, as measured in terms of a percentage of GNI, the United States is not alone among rich countries in missing the UN goal of 0.7 percent. In terms of GNI per capita, the United States contributes only around 0.16 percent of its GNI toward official development assistance, while countries such as Norway, Sweden, and Denmark voluntarily exceed the 0.7 percent mark by contributing 0.95 percent, 0.93 percent, and 0.81 percent of their GNI, respectively, in 2007. Then at the bottom of the ranking are Italy (0.18), and the United States and Greece, each contributing 0.16 percent of their GNI to official development aid.

It is important to realize, though, that in terms of actual money, 0.16 percent of American GNI (roughly $2.2 billion) is significantly higher than 0.95 percent of Norway's GNI (around $3.8 billion) in 2007 (see Figure 10.12) Yet, it is true also that most American development assistance goes to Israel and Egypt, two major allies of the United States in the Middle East. Perhaps another measure might capture the concept of "generosity" even better. How much do people give **per capita** toward official development assistance? Using that measure as shown in Figure 10.12 the most generous donors are the Norwegians, the Swedes, and the Danes, with the stingiest being the Italians, the Americans, and the Greeks. The United States is ranked 15th out of 16 countries in terms of ODA as measured as a percentage of GNI. The United States is widely considered to be a very generous country ready to help with significant contributions when natural disasters strike. On the other hand, its official development assistance is rather modest. How would you explain why the Nordic countries are leading this pack while countries like Greece and the United States appear rather stingy with foreign aid?

There are many more policy outcomes that could be analyzed—for instance, the percentage of people imprisoned, gun ownership, government deficits, subsidies,

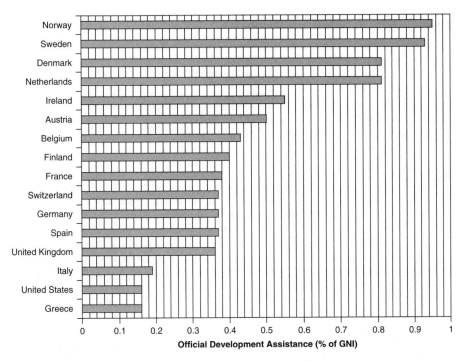

FIGURE 10.12

Official Development Assistance in 2007 (ODA) in percent of GNI (Gross National Income).

Source: OECD, Official Development Aid Statistics, 2011.

production of crucial strategic goods such as coal and steel, migration levels, hours worked, labor productivity, trade, savings rates, and foreign direct investment. The important lesson of this chapter is that most, if not all, of these policy outcomes and outputs are a direct result of many of the factors we discussed in the first nine chapters of this book. The questions posed in this chapter should make for some exciting term papers, since they highlight the connection between political parties, electoral systems, social movements, different histories in terms of modernization, and the actual political outcomes that affect us all. Perhaps the most important lesson of this chapter is that politics matters. This is worth remembering when the next election comes around and we citizens are asked to vote. After all, is it not true that in democratic systems people get the policy outcomes they deserve?

KEY TERMS

capacity   204
causal connections   204
comparative data   203
explanations   203
institutional
   approach   208

macrostructural   210
outcome   205
output   205
per capita   224
policy
   outcomes   203

predictable   206
space   204
systematic   206
systemic   205
time   204
variations   204

DISCUSSION QUESTIONS

1. Previously, we cautioned students to distinguish between "policy outcomes" and "policy outputs." What is the difference between the two?
2. What could turn the most well-intentioned policy output into a failure (i.e., an unintended policy outcome)?
3. In Chapter 9, we learned that globalization affects the political economics of all nations. How is this so? Would globalization make it easier or harder for governments to achieve the intended policy outcomes? Why?

NOTES

1. A classic in this regard is Douglas Rae and Michael Taylor. Decision Rules and Policy Outcomes. *British Journal of Political Science*, 1 (1971): 1, 70–90. See also, Kent Weaver and Bert Rockman. *Do Institutions Matter? Government Capabilities in the US and Abroad* (Washington, DC: Brookings Institution Press, 1993). Also recommended is, *Democracy and Institutions: The Life Work of Arend Lijphart*, by Markus M. L. Crepaz, Thomas A. Koelble, and David Wilsford (Ann Arbor, MI: The University of Michigan Press, 2000).
2. Warren Hoge. Swedish Party Pledging Expanded Welfare Gains Slim Victory. *New York Times*, September 21, 1998.
3. *BBC News*, September 14, 2002.
4. Peter Baldwin, *The Narcissism of Minor Differences. How America and Europe Are Alike* (New York: Oxford University Press, 2009).
5. It is important to note however, that the US has the lowest taxes on goods and services. (OECD Factbook, 2010).
6. John Huber and G. Bingham Powell, Congruence Between Citizens and Policymakers in Two Visions of Democracy. *World Politics* 46 (April 1994): 291–326.
7. Gabriel Almond. Capitalism and Democracy. *PS: Political Science and Politics* 24, no. 3 (1991): 473.
8. Eric A. Finkelstein, Justin G. Trogdon, Joel W. Cohen, and William Dietz. Annual Medical Spending Attributable to Obesity: Payer- and Service-specific Estimates. *Health Affairs* 28, no. 5 (2009): w822–w831.
9. House of Commons. *Ninth Report. Tackling Obesity in England.* 2001, http://www. publications.parliament.uk/pa/cm200102/cmselect/cmpubacc/421/42103.htm
10. Baldwin, *The Narcissism of Minor Differences*, p. 78
11. OECD, OECD Factbook 2010: Economic, Environmental and Social Statistics, Quality of Life Indicators, Youth Inactivity, June 2010.
12. OECD, OECD Factbook 2005: Economic, Environmental and Social Statistics, s.v. International Student Assessment—definition, 2005.
13. The National Energy Foundation. CO2 Calculator. Available online at http://www. nef.org.uk/energyadvice/co2calculator.htm.
14. For a detailed operationalization of the concept, http://epi.yale.edu/
15. OECD, OECD Factbook 2005: Economic, Environmental and Social Statistics. Paris, 2005.
16. Ashish Kumar Sen. "Relief Efforts Stingy, Says U.N. Official," *The (Chandigarh) Tribune*, Online Edition, December 29, 2004.

The Legacy of Communism in Central and Eastern Europe

Until 1989, the countries of Central and Eastern Europe belonged as satellite countries to the Soviet bloc. They were imprisoned and separated by the **Iron Curtain** from the Western European countries. This was the time of the **Cold War**. Although Communism crumbled in Central and Eastern European countries, its long years still has an influence on these countries today.

In order to make this argument, we can refer to the term *path dependency*. This is an important concept in political science that means that the historical path of a country always has some influence on the present. The past constrains to some extent the viable options for the present. Renowned political scientist Stein Rokkan has demonstrated in his seminal research that current party systems are dependent on the path that a country took centuries back, for example in the Reformation and the French Revolution.[1]

If such long-ago events still have a contemporary influence, this is all the more so for such a recent event as the Cold War, especially because the Cold War was such a crucial episode in European history. People in Central and Eastern Europe were trapped and could not escape; they risked being shot if they tried. When visiting Berlin today, one is still reminded of the **Wall** dividing the city during the Cold War and the people who were killed attempting to cross over it. In the Communist countries in Central and Eastern Europe, people who dared to speak out against the regime were severely punished: They lost their jobs, were sent to prison and labor camps, and even may have lost their lives in mysterious car accidents with probable involvement of the secret state police. Visiting Warsaw and Budapest, for example, one can see many monuments, plaques, and exhibits reminding us that in these countries the memories of the Cold War are still fresh and painful.

The continuing impact of the Cold War can also be demonstrated with the statistical data presented in Chapter 10. To the extent that data were available, we included three former Communist countries: the Czech Republic, Hungary, and Poland. Figure 10.7 reveals that these three countries are at the very bottom in terms of life expectancy. The Communist legacy is also manifested in low global competitiveness scores; Hungary is second to last in global competitivenessas shown in Figure 10.6. Only Greece, burdened with enormous debts (see Chapter 9), displays a lower global competitiveness. These data make clear that the Cold War still has an influence on how well European countries are currently doing, with Western European countries generally faring better than Central and Eastern European countries.

The fact that Central and Eastern Europe came under Communism is to a large extent due to the imperialistic power of the Soviet Union. However, Communism also held some intellectual attraction, so that it had some support in Western Europe as well, in particular in Italy and France. The intellectual base of Communism was Marxism, which was developed in the nineteenth century. We have discussed Marxism in Chapter 2 when presenting the roots of Communism as a political ideology.

After World War II, the Soviet Union established brutal rule over the countries of Central and Eastern Europe. As Winston Churchill expressed it eloquently, the Iron Curtain went down, and behind this curtain, the Soviets enforced State Communism. This meant that the economies of the Central and Eastern European countries were to a large extent **nationalized**, and state bureaucrats planned economic activities in a centralized way. There were no free elections and no freedoms of speech and religion. Political dissidents were sent to prison and to concentration camps in Siberia. This was clearly a **dictatorial** regime. From a Marxist view, one could argue that this was a historical necessity, because after the revolution the proletariat had to establish a dictatorship in order to erase all traces of capitalist thinking (see Chapter 2). There were many Marxists in the West who, for a long time, accepted this interpretation; for example, the famous French philosopher and writer Jean-Paul Sartre. But there were many other Western Marxists who early on began to recognize that what was happening in the Soviet Union and its satellite countries had nothing to do with Marxism but was a continuation of Russian absolutism and imperialism from the time of the Czars. The proletarian revolution, after all, would first have to occur in the most industrialized countries, such as England and Germany, but certainly not in mostly rural Russia. How much can Karl Marx be held accountable for what happened in his name under Soviet rule? Are philosophers ever responsible for what politicians do with their writings?

The year 1989 was a memorable one—for this was when State Communism crumbled in Central and Eastern Europe. This was an important turning point, not only for the countries involved, but also for world politics. The Cold War, which had raged for more than 40 years, came to an end. The dramatic events of 1989 came as a surprise to nearly everyone. There was always much speculation about the future of the Communist countries in Central and Eastern Europe, but none of the predictions turned out to be correct. As Ronald A. Francisco puts it in retrospect:

> The ossified regimes of Eastern Europe toppled like so many dominoes in the autumn of 1989....Taken as a whole, this was arguably the most significant event since 1945. Yet no one foresaw it....There was widespread recognition of serious problems, but no one predicted the sequential collapse of successive regimes in revolutions largely devoid of violence.[2]

Prior to 1989, there were two prominent predictions about what would happen in the future in Central and Eastern Europe. One was that no real internal changes would ever occur in Communist totalitarian regimes. The other prominent prediction about the future of Communism was that increased contact with the West would cause slow, gradual changes in Central and Eastern European countries.

What exactly happened in Central and Eastern Europe in the historic year of 1989? To understand the events of that year, one must be aware that these countries were satellites of the Soviet Union and not masters of their own destiny. It is impossible to say what would have happened if the Central and Eastern European countries could have chosen their own Communist path. In this context, it is interesting to mention the **Spring Movement** of 1968 in Czechoslovakia, when the Communist Party of that country, under the leadership of Alexander Dubcek, launched reforms that were meant to lead to Communism "with a human face." That spring was a time of great hope and excitement. The reform-minded Communist leaders in Czechoslovakia saw the possibility that the ideas of Marx could finally be implemented in a true sense and not perverted as in the Soviet Union. Social justice and democracy seemed possible in a Communist-run country. For a few months, Czechoslovakia was in a fever. Freedom of speech existed, the arts blossomed, and there was lively discussion about the exact direction of the reforms. But the experiment was stopped in August of the same year, when Soviet tanks rolled into Prague. The people in the streets tried to hold discussions with the Soviet soldiers, putting flowers into their guns, but in vain. The reformers were ousted and stripped of their influence; some of them were arrested, some sent to labor camps. Thus, it is impossible to say where the reforms would have led. It remains speculation whether Communist Czechoslovakia without the Soviet interference could have turned democratic with all the basic liberties such a system entails.

What we have, then, is a test of Soviet-style Communism. This type of Communism failed dismally with regard to the economy, the environment, and, most important, basic freedoms. The secret state police had a devastating influence on the life of ordinary people, who lived in constant fear. Even the Communist Party members became more and more disillusioned with the failed system, but State Communism in Central and Eastern Europe would not have dissolved itself so easily without the momentous events that took place in the Soviet Union itself. The real trigger for what happened in 1989 was the decision of Soviet leader Mikhail Gorbachev to let the Central and Eastern European countries go their own way. At first, there were merely vague hints that a basic policy change might take place. Thus, early in 1989, the Soviet foreign ministry spokesman began to speak in a lighthearted way of the new "Sinatra doctrine," referring to a song by Frank Sinatra with the lyrics "I did it my way." The implication seemed to be that the countries in Central and Eastern Europe should do it their ways, too. On July 7, 1989, the Warsaw Pact repealed the doctrine, according to which it had the right to intervene in "brother" countries in order to protect Communism. It was this doctrine that justified the Soviet tanks rolling into Czechoslovakia in 1968. But by the summer of 1989, the real intentions of the Soviet Union still remained ambivalent. It was only in mid-October of 1989, during the crisis in East Germany, that it became fully clear that the Soviet Union had withdrawn its threat of military intervention.

What happened in Central and Eastern Europe once the threat of Soviet military intervention vanished? Each country took a somewhat different path. To be sure, 1989 can be seen as a year of one big revolution, but there were interesting national differences in the way revolution took place. As illustrations, we compare Poland, Hungary, East Germany, Ukraine, and Russia.

POLAND

In 1981, developments in Poland seemed to support the claim that Communist regimes would never truly change. When **Solidarity**, the trade union led by the charismatic Lech Walesa, became too active and too popular among the Polish people, the Communist Party cracked down hard. Solidarity was banned, many of its leaders were arrested, and a state of emergency was declared. Once again—as in 1968 in Czechoslovakia, 1956 in Hungary and Poland, and 1953 in East Germany—Communism had shown its iron fist. Despair and frustration spread among the Polish people. The stiff and grim-looking General Wojciech Jaruzelski, who headed the government, became the symbol for the apparent unchangeability of Communism. In the Soviet Union, Leonid Brezhnev was still in power and Soviet troops were at hand, threatening intervention if the Polish Communists were not tough enough.

When Gorbachev came to power in Moscow in 1985, the situation began slowly to change for the better in Poland. In 1986 political prisoners were released. In 1988 the Communist government made some timid steps to liberalize the economy, and travel to the West was made easier. In 1989, Solidarity, which had continued to be active underground, was legalized again, and the Communists began roundtable discussions with Lech Walesa and his Solidarity colleagues. Why the softening of the Communist rulers? Of crucial importance was the deteriorating economic situation, in particular the staggering foreign debt. Interest on this debt could no longer be paid, and Poland seemed at the brink of collapse. The Communist leaders could not think of any other way out than to begin a dialogue with the banned opposition.

The round table between the Communists and Solidarity led to a complicated deal about a formula for elections to the Sejm, the Polish parliament. Solidarity was allowed to run candidates, but only one-third of the parliamentary seats were open for competition. The Communist Party, still insisting on keeping its leading role in the state, claimed the other two-thirds for itself. Therefore, it was guaranteed from the beginning that the Communists would keep their parliamentary majority. The elections took place on June 4, 1989, and brought a triumph for Solidarity, which swept all seats that were contested. There was great surprise around the world about these results. Formal power was still in the hands of the Communists. They recognized, however, that they had to share power with Solidarity. Complicated negotiations began again. The result was a complex scheme of power sharing. Parliament elected Jaruzelski president and, in this capacity, head of state. In return, the Communists were willing to select someone from Solidarity as prime minister. Lech Walesa declined the offer for himself, and one of his close associates, Tadeusz Mazowiecki, became prime minister on August 24, 1989.

A further twist in the arrangement was that, within the cabinet, the military and the state security apparatus remained in the hands of the Communists. Overall, the arrangement did not reflect the fact that Solidarity had won all parliamentary seats that were open for competition. The Polish people clearly supported Solidarity, but the Communists were dragging their feet. Despite the verdict of the people, they were unwilling to yield the crucial power over the military and the security forces. Poland shows how difficult it was, even in 1989, to unsettle the Communists. But the momentum against the Communists became so strong that they were unable to cling to their remaining power. There was much push for free elections.

The first completely free Polish election, with all seats open for competition, took place on May 27, 1990, at the local level. The results were a big victory for Solidarity and a total defeat for the Communists. The latter had tried to save themselves by confessing to all their mistakes in the past. Mieczyslaw Rakowski, the first secretary of the Communist Party, acknowledged at the party congress in January 1990 "the abandonment of political democracy" as the main failing. The party went so far as to dissolve itself and create a new party with the label "Social Democratic." The Communists avidly tried to distance themselves from their past. But all these efforts were in vain, and even as a new party with a new name, the Communists received only 0.2 percent of the votes in the local elections of May 27, 1990; indeed a catastrophic result!

Solidarity won the overwhelming number of seats in the councils of Poland's biggest cities: in Warsaw 301 of 345, in Gdansk 56 of 60, and in Cracow 72 of 75. For the entire country, Solidarity received 41 percent of the votes. Where did all the other votes go? They went to independent candidates and to a great variety of tiny parties. The most striking result was that none of the newly created parties could really catch on. With these local elections, Poland had not yet crossed the threshold to a true multiparty system. Instead of dominance by the Communists, Solidarity dominated. This does not mean that basic changes in the direction of democracy had not taken place. The local elections were indeed completely free, and Poland now enjoyed all the basic civil liberties, such as freedom of speech and freedom of religion. But a country needs more than one strong party for a functioning democracy.

National parliamentary elections were held in October 1991. They still did not lead to a clear party system. The largest party received only 12.3 percent of the votes in the **Sejm**, the lower house of parliament. Altogether, 29 parties were represented in the Sejm. As soon as parliament gathered, the situation became even more confusing, because some of the parties split or united and individual deputies changed parties or became independents.

Was the fragmentation in the Polish parliament mainly a consequence of the electoral system? At first it may appear so, but a second look reveals that other factors must have played a more important role. A system of party list proportional representation (PR) was used for the election of the Sejm, and no minimal threshold had to be reached for a party to enter parliament. The only advantage for the larger parties was that they received a **bonus** in the sense that 15 percent of the seats were set aside for parties that received at least 5 percent of the total vote. This put the small parties at a small disadvantage but still allowed them to enter parliament. Thus, it appears that it was indeed the election system that allowed so many small parties to receive parliamentary representation. This was the interpretation of a *Newsweek* correspondent who wrote of "proportional representation gone wild."[3]

There are, however, two arguments against such an interpretation of the election results. First, there was no single national electoral district, which would have favored small parties, as in the Netherlands (Chapter 3). Rather, Poland had relatively small districts, with an average of only 10.6 deputies per district. Therefore, 10 percent of the votes were needed to get representation in the average district. However, the outcome was that from district to district different parties got representation, so that the overall number of parties in the Sejm reached the high number of 29.

Second, and more important, the elections to the Senate, the upper house, were held by the winner-take-all system, which, as in Great Britain, should work against small parties. But in the Senate, the number of parties gaining representation was even higher than in the Sejm. In the Senate races, only winning counted, but candidates from very different parties won from district to district. The conclusion is that, to some extent, the electoral system may have contributed to the **fragmentation** of the Polish legislature, but there were other factors involved. The main factor being that, with its heroic history, the Solidarity movement was such a strong umbrella that its various factions found it difficult to emerge as well-structured independent parties. In contrast to Hungary, the "founding" Polish parliamentary elections led to a diffuse party system.

The Democratic Union grew directly out of Solidarity. It corresponds roughly to the Free Democrats in Hungary. Another party that grew directly out of Solidarity was the Center Citizens' Alliance. It was somewhat more for state economic interventions, somewhat more authoritarian than the Democratic Union, and somewhere more at the center of the party system—as its name implies. The former Communists ran now under the label Democratic Left Alliance and did quite well, much better than in the local elections of the previous year. Several parties ran with a Catholic platform; others claimed to represent peasants or particular regions. There were also several nationalistic parties—for example, the

Confederation for an Independent Poland. Two parties used the label Solidarity, although most Solidarity members had organized in other parties. There were also some frivolous aspects in the emerging party system, in particular with regard to the Beer Lovers' party. In a democracy citizens may certainly organize however they wish, and beer drinkers may have common interests that they want to represent in parliament.

To understand Poland's transition to democratic elections, it is necessary to cover also the second national elections that took place in September 1993. For these elections, an important modification in the electoral law was in force. With the goal of reducing the number of parties in parliament, the Polish legislature had introduced a 5 percent threshold for a party to enter parliament. The example of the 5 percent threshold in Germany had a great influence on this decision (see Chapter 3). The former Communists, now called the Democratic Left Alliance, reinforced their comeback.[4] After receiving merely 0.2 percent of the votes in the May 1991 local elections, and having increased their support to 12.0 percent in the October 1991 national elections, they were now up to 20.4 percent. The Polish Peasant Party increased its voters' share also, from 8.7 percent to 15.4 percent. The Democratic Union declined slightly, from 12.3 percent to 10.6 percent. Three other smaller parties reached the 5 percent threshold: the Union of Labor, the Confederation for an Independent Poland, and the Non-Party Bloc to Support Reform.

The 5 percent clause had fulfilled its purpose: The number of parties represented in the Sejm was dramatically reduced from 29 to 6. An important unplanned consequence also occurred: The Democratic Left Alliance with 20.4 percent of the votes received 37.2 percent of the seats (171) and the Peasant Party with 15.4 percent of the votes arrived at 28.7 percent of the seats (132). Thus, the two leading parties, although together they had a mere 35.8 percent of the votes, got 65.9 percent of the seats. And yet the electoral system was meant to be proportional, with the exception of excluding tiny parties with less than 5 percent. Why the discrepancy between votes and seats? What had happened? Apparently something very different from the pattern in Germany, where the proportion of voter support tends to correspond closely to the proportion of parliamentary seats.

The big difference between these first Polish elections with a 5 percent threshold and the German situation was that many more Poles "wasted" their votes as compared to Germans. Indeed, about 35 percent of Polish voters supported parties that stayed below the 5 percent threshold. Why the difference? The German voters had adapted their behavior to the 5 percent threshold and were careful not to vote for a party with no chance of making the threshold. In later elections, as Poles learned how the system works and gathered more information about the chances of success of the various parties, they, too, became more careful not to waste their votes.

After the Polish elections of 1993, the *New York Times* wrote of a "victory of the former Communists."[5] Was it actually a victory? Yes and no. The former Communists were certainly winning in the sense that they received the most votes of all the parties. It was also a victory for them that the other successful party, the

Peasant Party, had been a close ally during the Communist regime. The Peasant Party had been one of the so-called bloc parties, which were allowed to run their own candidates but factually belonged to the Communist bloc. The Peasant Party could be considered the rural branch of the Communists. Now, in the 1993 elections, which were absolutely free, these two former Communist parties together received two-thirds of the parliamentary seats! As the *Times* reporter writes, this was indeed a victory. But it must also be stressed that the two parties received only about one-third of the votes, and that it was only thanks to the change in the electoral system that they got two-thirds of the seats in parliament.

Having made this argument, it must also be recognized that the 1993 elections brought a spectacular comeback for the former Communists. Why? One reason was that the change to a market economy brought, for many voters, hardship and insecurity:

> Forty years of Communism had ingrained expectations of social security that the new parties failed to provide. The architects of Poland's "shock therapy" knew that there would be victims in their game plan—pensioners, unskilled young people, middle-aged workers made redundant by privatization—but gambled that those losers would not stall the march to a full market economy.[6]

A second reason for the good showing of the former Communists was that many educated young people, especially women, resented the newly gained strong political influence of the Catholic Church. Of particular concern to these voters was the strict antiabortion legislation rammed through parliament by the parties close to the Church. The parties supported by the Catholic Church suffered a severe defeat; the Church had overestimated its political influence. Although very religious, Poles did not wish the Catholic Church to dominate the political life of the country. Under Communism, the church could play an important political role as protector of the democratic opposition. With democracy now established, Poles wanted the Church to concentrate on its religious duties.

A third reason for the good election result of the former Communists was that they had changed greatly. The leader of the Democratic Left Alliance, Aleksander Kwasniewski, had played only a minor role in the old regime. At the time of the 1993 election, he was only 39 years old. As a student of economics at Gdansk University, he had been chairman of the Communist student organization of Poland. He then became editor of two youth newspapers, and in 1985, junior minister in the Communist government. In the election campaign, Kwasniewski tried to make a clear break with the old-line Communist past, declaring:

> There shouldn't be a shadow of a doubt to the party's position on Stalinism and other Communist crimes. Does it make me sad that a lot of these people who were Communists, committed these crimes? Yes, it does....We are ready to take part in a pragmatic coalition which looks toward the future, not the past. We are about resolving problems in domestic and foreign policies. We need competent people in office....Our program has not a single thing that would remind you of Communism. If someone in our party proposed a return to a central command economy, he would have to be expelled, not for being a Communist but for being an idiot.[7]

The Democratic Left Alliance is comparable to the Social Democrats in Western Europe (see Chapter 2). It supports democracy and, to a large extent, the free market also. So it was somewhat misleading when the Western media wrote of an election victory of the former Communists. To be sure, most leaders of the Democratic Left Alliance belonged to the old Communist Party, but they were in its reformist wing. By 1993, the old hard-line Communists had completely vanished from the political scene of Poland.

The description of the Polish transition to democratic elections should have shown us in a forceful way how election results may be shaped by election rules. These rules are never neutral but always favor some parties over others. We have already made this argument in Chapter 3, and the Polish situations described here should help to reinforce it.

We have to look not only at the transition to democracy but also at the maintenance of a democratic system. It was a good democratic sign when elections in 2005 brought a peaceful change of power from a coalition of the Left to a coalition of the Right. It was a little odd, however, that the two most powerful positions were held by the twin brothers Kaczynski, with Lech as president and Jaroslaw as prime minster. They both belonged to the Conservative party Law and Justice. More worrisome, they entered into a coalition with two very nationalistic and even racist parties of the far right, Self Defense and the League of Polish Families. In Chapter 2, we described the latter party as a typical representative of the New Radical Right, opposing membership in the European Union, opposing selling land to foreigners, advocating the death penalty, and holding anti-Jewish, anti-Roma, anti-German, and antigay and antilesbian positions. After much bickering in this coalition of the Right and the extreme Right, the Kaczynski brothers expelled the two extremist parties from the cabinet, which, therefore, became a minority cabinet. The Polish people became increasingly frustrated with some of the radical policies of the twin brothers. Thus, it was, for example, not understood why they launched a vetting process of as many as 700,000 officials, including university professors, for their Communist past. This seemed like a witch hunt. Public frustration about such events became so great that early elections had to be called for 2007, which brought a severe defeat for the two extremist parties of the Right, Self Defense and the League of Polish Families. A coalition of the center formed of Civic Forum and the Polish Peasant Party. With the weakening of the extremist parties of the right, the democratic system of Poland seems to have found a firm ground.

HUNGARY

The events in Poland had great influence in Hungary. There, a slow and tentative reform process had already begun in the early 1970s. Step by step, some free-market elements were introduced into the planned economy. Politically, reforms were much slower to come. It was only in 1988, when Gorbachev was already in office, that some political liberalization began to occur. The great surprise was how quickly this liberalization swept the country in 1989. During a visit to

Hungary in July 1989, one of us (Steiner) witnessed this liberalization firsthand. His account of this visit is as follows:

> As I sat in sidewalk cafés in Budapest, most of my Hungarian hosts spoke freely to me about the situation in the country, not sparing their critiques of the Communist Party. When I asked whether such frankness in a public place was not dangerous, the reply was "no more." Traveling through the countryside, I found the same frankness among much of the rural population. A railroad worker told me that recently he had spoken openly with his superior, a Communist Party member, and that only a year ago such frankness would have put him in prison. By the summer of 1989, the fear of the Communists had gone, although there was still some apprehension.

In Hungary, like in Poland, there was strong pressure from democratic forces for reforms. However, in contrast to Poland, the Hungarian Communist Party had a rather strong reformist wing that also pushed for these reforms. Its leader was Imre Pozsgay who, like Alexander Dubcek in 1968 in Czechoslovakia, claimed to fight for Communism "with a human face." The Hungarian Communists conceded publicly that in the past they had made grave mistakes, in particular by participating in the bloody repression by the Soviets of the democratic Hungarian revolution in October 1956. This mistake was prominently acknowledged in June 1989 when Imre Nagy, the leader of the 1956 revolution, was allowed a hero's reburial in Budapest. The entire Communist leadership was present, together with a huge crowd. During my visit, the bookstores were full of critical and touching accounts of how the Communists had crushed the 1956 revolution.

In the spring of 1989, the Communist rulers tore down the barbed wire at the western border of the country, and Hungarians were free to travel to the West. Indeed, a farm family, whom I had met during my trip, did visit us in Switzerland a few weeks later, receiving the travel visa without any difficulties. Further signs of a fundamental change occurred when the Communists were willing to take their symbol, the Red Star, from public buildings, and when freedom of religion was adopted. The most important element of political liberalization was free elections. As early as the summer of 1989 there were two by-elections for parliament that were free; in both cases the Communist candidate lost. General elections for parliament took place in March of 1990.

Each voter had two votes: one for a candidate in a single district and one for a party list. Overall, there were 386 parliamentary seats to be filled. From this total number, 176 seats were filled in single districts according to the winner-take-all system. In addition to the 176 single districts, Hungary was also divided into 20 larger districts, which corresponded to its 20 counties. At the county level, the remaining 210 seats were filled according to party list proportionality.[8] Thus, each voter could vote for a candidate in a small district and for a party list in a large district. Why exactly 176 seats by winner-take-all and 210 seats by proportional representation? Nothing magic about it; this was simply the outcome of the bargaining about the electoral law.

For the first free elections, debates took place not only about the election rules, but also about the timing of the elections. Parliament, which was still controlled by the Communists, decided that election of the president should come first, before the parliamentary elections. The date set for the presidential election was January 7, 1990; the date for parliamentary elections was set for later in the year. Four opposition parties—the Free Democrats, the Young Democrats, the Independent Smallholders' Party, and the Social Democrats—objected to this plan. They argued that parliamentary elections should be held first. The four opposition parties feared that an early presidential election would give an undue advantage to the Communist candidate. They considered it to be undemocratic to choose so important an official while the Communists still controlled all essential offices and such vital political advantages as access to state-run television and most of the press.

The four parties collected signatures in order to challenge parliament's decision on the date of presidential elections. For a decision of parliament to be submitted to a referendum, 100,000 signatures were required. The four opposition parties had no difficulties in meeting this requirement; they obtained more than double the needed number of signatures. The referendum was set for November 26, 1989. In the referendum campaign, the fronts took a rather complicated shape, because another opposition party, the Democratic Forum, supported the Communists' desire for an early presidential election. The proposed Communist candidate, Imre Pozsgay, was a moderate, and the Democratic Forum expected that it could work with him.

Thus, it was not easy for the Hungarian voters to decide which way to vote. The choice was not simply to support or oppose the ruling Communist Party. It was feared that voter turnout would be low, which would have been a bad start for the process of **democratization**. Fortunately, nearly 60 percent of the voters turned up at the ballot boxes, despite a severe snowstorm that set in during the evening. A turnout of 50 percent was required for the referendum to be valid. If it had fallen below this threshold, the referendum would have failed, whatever the outcome. The four opposition parties could celebrate a double victory: Not only was the referendum valid, it was also decided, although by a narrow margin, to delay presidential elections until after parliamentary elections.

The Communists accepted the outcome, and Pozsgay wisely said: "While in Eastern and Central Europe hundreds of thousands of people are marching in the streets to express their opinions, Hungarians are going to the ballot box to express their political will."[9] The Associated Press quoted a voter as saying, "We wanted to take into our own hands the possibility to decide on the people's future."[10] Following the referendum, parliamentary elections indeed came first, on March 25, 1990. The campaign did not have the professional smoothness of those in established democracies. Many things went wrong: microphones did not work, computers broke down, and so on. But these were mere technical flaws. What really mattered was that the campaign and the election itself occurred with very few irregularities. There were no incidents of violence and no intimidation of voters. According to the general consensus of foreign observers, the election took place in an atmosphere of freedom.

The headlines in the Western media after the elections were about the big defeat of the Communists.[11] This result may seem surprising, because, as we saw in Chapter 10, Hungary was the only Central and Eastern European country in which reforms were pushed by the Communists themselves. However, they received little credit from the voters on election day. Only 10.9 percent voted for the party list of the Hungarian Socialist Party, the new name chosen by the Communists. Most Hungarians were tired of the Communists, however reform-oriented they were. To the credit of the Communists, it should be noted that they gave up power graciously. Their party chairman declared: "We will be an opposition party. This, to use a religious term, will be penance for the party." Along the same gracious lines, the outgoing Communist prime minister stated: "I will hand over the reins head high and with a clear conscience. I don't have bitterness in my heart but satisfaction."[12] Who would have thought that one day Communists would yield power in this way?

When in 1989 the Communists embarked on a course of reform, the more Marxist-oriented wing split from the party and founded its own Hungarian Socialist Workers' Party. It fared even worse than the Reform Communists, getting 3.7 percent of the vote for its party list, which was below the 4 percent threshold required to be seated in parliament. This minimum threshold was also not reached by the Social Democratic Party, which had the support of its sister parties in Western Europe. Thus, the parties of the Left did altogether poorly in Hungary.

Who were the winners? We look first at the results for the party lists and turn later to the winner-take-all part of the elections. The two top vote-getters for the party lists were the Hungarian Democratic Forum with 24.7 percent and the Alliance of Free Democrats with 21.4 percent. The Democratic Forum roughly corresponds to the Conservatives in Western Europe, as described in Chapter 2. It cultivates a Christian image, and its overall message has rather strong nationalist overtones. Economically, the Democratic Forum stood for the free market, although advocating a cautious transition. The Free Democrats more or less correspond to their sister parties in Western Europe. More than the Democratic Forum, they stressed a quick transition to a free-market economy. The Free Democrats are also strongly individualistic, not putting as much emphasis on church and nation as the Democratic Forum. With 11.7 percent of the party lists, the Independent Smallholders' party came in third. Before the Communist regime, it was the largest party in Hungary. Its major campaign plank was that all land should go back to those who owned it in 1947, before the Communists took over.

We turn now to the election results in the 176 single districts. The electoral rules specified that to be elected in the first round, a candidate had to receive more than 50 percent of the votes. If no candidate reached this threshold, a second round of elections would be organized two weeks later. The top three finishers, plus all candidates who acquired at least 15 percent of the first-round vote, were eligible to compete in the second round. Candidates were so numerous that only five districts were able to declare a candidate elected in the first round. Thus, 171 seats were left to be contested in the second round. For both rounds together, the Democratic Forum was the big winner, taking a total of 114 of the districts; the Free Democrats were far behind, winning in only 35 districts. The Smallholders' Party and the Socialist Party each won in one district. The remaining 15 districts went to several small parties and some independent candidates. Thus, as expected, the winner-take-all part of the election favored the largest party. As the British say of the winner-take-all system, what counts is who is first past the post (see Chapter 3). Having come out as the frontrunner in the first round, the Democratic Forum had the necessary momentum to capture many districts in the second round. In the winner-take-all system, nothing is as successful as anticipated success, because supporters of smaller parties do not like to waste their votes and, therefore, cast them for a candidate with a real winning chance.

The election was able to weed out the minor parties and limit the political game to relatively few viable parties. Thus, as a *founding election*—to borrow a term from Guillermo O'Donnell and Philippe Schmitter[13]—it fulfilled its purpose in establishing a manageable party system. The Hungarian election system shares with the German system the characteristic that some members of parliament are elected by winner-take-all in single districts and others by party list proportionality in larger, regional districts. We should also note, however, an important difference between the two systems. As we remember from Chapter 3, in Germany only the votes for the party lists determine the total number of seats a party gets in parliament. In Hungary, by contrast, the two parts of the elections are independent of each other, so that the Hungarian system is more truly a **mixed system**.

In the fall of 2006, there was a bizarre episode in Hungary that raised worries of how successful the country's democratic transition was. The outgoing Socialist government under prime minister Ferenc Gyurcsany had just won reelection. In the election campaign, the Socialists had promised that they would bring the huge fiscal deficit under control. To implement this promise, Socialist members of parliament (MPs) met behind close doors. To the great frustration and anger of the prime minister, most MPs supported fiscal discipline only in principle but not with regard to their special interests. The prime minister then scolded his colleagues with the following words:[14]

> Evidently, we lied throughout the last year-and-a-half, two years. It was totally clear that what we are saying is not true. We lied in the morning, we lied in the evening.

A tape with these remarks was leaked, and under the heading " 'We lied to win,' says Hungarian prime minister," the prime minister's words spread quickly, not only in Hungary but around the world. The prime minister tried to clarify his remarks, saying that he wished to scold his colleagues who wanted to protect their special interests from budget cuts. He continued by saying that "We have to stop the deluge of lies which have covered the country for many years." These clarifications could not calm down the situation; the damage was done, and violent protests began in front of Parliament Building. An old tank was set in motion by a protester; tear gas, rubber bullets, and water cannons were used by the police. For a few days Hungarian democracy looked unstable to the outside world. It was troubling how this episode could lead to such ugly street battles. Whose mistake was it? Was the prime minister's statement about lying a real scandal, or did he act like a good coach, scolding his team for not fulfilling its election promises? Were the media irresponsible for taking a few sentences out of context, or did they fulfill their duty in informing the public about a scandal in the Socialist Party?

In the aftermath of this strange event, Gyurcsany continued as prime minister but was left by his coalition partner and as a consequence could rule only with a minority cabinet (for this concept see Chapter 4). He could not recover his reputation, and he finally resigned in the spring of 2009. His successor continued with the same shaky minority cabinet. These events show that after the smooth transition to democracy after 1989, Hungary recently has traveled quite a bumpy road, and there is much frustration in the population with the country's political leaders.

This frustration was expressed in the 2010 parliamentary election with a sounding defeat of the ruling Socialists. The big winners were the Free Democrats (Fidesz) who won 263 of the 386 seats. This gave them a two-thirds majority, which allows them to change the constitution on their own. This is a dangerous situation because under the leadership of Victor Orbán the party has moved from a centrist position very much to the right. Orbán developed into a very authoritarian leader, so much so that the European Union expressed concern about the functioning of Hungarian democracy. As a member of the European Union, Hungary has to adhere to basic democratic principles as any other member country. The concern of the European Union was in particular about a new law on the media, which unduly limited freedom of the press. Hungary made some changes but not enough to fully satisfy all the concerns of the European Union. The situation of Hungary is all the more problematic from a democratic perspective because at the right of the Free Democrats there is a truly extreme rightist party, Jobbik, that gained 16 percent of the votes in the 2010 elections. From a leader in the Central and Eastern European democratization process Hungary has become a laggard.

EAST GERMANY

Under Communist rule, East Germany called itself the German Democratic Republic (GDR). In West Germany, many people hoped that the "Democratic" in the name of the East German state would gradually become more meaningful as contact between the two German states became more frequent. This was, in particular, the position of the West German Social Democrats, but their hopes were greatly disappointed. The East German Communists were unwilling to liberalize. In the summer of 1989, when the Chinese Communists crushed the student movement in a very brutal and bloody way, East German high officials supported the Chinese authorities' actions, the only high-ranking Communist officials in Central and Eastern Europe to do so.

Yet 1989 brought dramatic changes to East Germany, too. The crucial element was the demonstration effect of events in Hungary and Poland. East Germans had easy access to West German television and were thus well informed about the reforms in the two countries. Watching how others moved forward made their own situation all the more unbearable. It was particularly important for the East Germans to see that the Soviets did tolerate the developments in Hungary and Poland, making no threats to intervene militarily. Thus, it became increasingly credible that the Soviets were indeed willing to let the Central and Eastern European countries go their own ways.

In September 1989, Hungary influenced the changes in East Germany not only indirectly, but also in a very direct way by allowing vacationing East Germans in Hungary to emigrate to the West. Travel within the Communist countries was always relatively free, and many East Germans spent their summer vacations in Hungary, which was known for its tourist attractions. When, in the spring of 1989, the Hungarians began to tear down the barbed wire at the western border to Austria, many vacationing East Germans exploited the situation to escape to the West. Austria put up tent cities at its borders to accommodate all the refugees, who were mostly teachers, doctors, engineers, and other skilled professionals. The conditions soon became so chaotic, with hundreds of East Germans attempting the flight every night, that the Hungarian government finally and officially allowed East Germans to travel to the West. This action was a breach of a treaty with East Germany, which greatly infuriated the East German government. It was unheard of in the Eastern bloc for one country to let the citizens of another country travel freely to the West.

When the East German government made it increasingly difficult for its citizens to go to Hungary, many went to neighboring Czechoslovakia, at the time still a hard-line Communist country. These East Germans sought refuge at the West German embassy in Prague. In front of the embassy, dramatic scenes occurred, with the Czech police trying to prevent East Germans from climbing over the embassy fence. These scenes were shown on TV all over the world and could also be seen in East Germany on West German TV. Symbols are always important in politics, and here was a very powerful symbol of how eager and desperate thousands of East Germans were to leave their country. What made these scenes so damaging for the East German regime was that most refugees were young people who apparently saw no future in their country.

The West German embassy in Prague became so overcrowded that the situation became untenable with regard to hygiene. Finally, the East German government gave in and allowed the refugees to travel by special trains to West Germany, although insisting that the route be through East German territory. This turned out to be a serious mistake, because other East Germans tried to board the trains when they stopped in the East German city of Dresden. Again, pictures of great symbolic power flashed over the TV screens of the world, showing the refugees with tears of joy in their eyes, arriving at West German railway stations. These pictures could also be seen in East Germany, and there were emotional moments when young refugees waved, with the help of the TV cameras, to their aging parents left at home.

More and more East Germans went to the streets to demonstrate for reforms. Of particular importance were the marches every Monday evening in Leipzig. How did the Communist leaders react? With many of them having publicly supported the Chinese crackdown earlier in the year, would they apply the same method in their own country? Erich Honecker, the 77-year-old party boss, seemed unyielding. Although he later denied it, he is said to have given the order to the police to shoot at the demonstrators, but he was ousted and replaced by a younger man, Egon Krenz. The opening of the Berlin Wall on November 9, 1989, was not a carefully calculated decision but rather the result of much confusion and bumbling in the East German leadership. However, the decision was made and it was immediately greeted with great ecstasy, well captured in Box 11.1. The celebrations of East and West Berliners standing on the Wall were the most powerful of the pictures that symbolized the end of the Cold War. Many American presidents and other Western leaders had called for the Wall, the symbol of the division of the world, to be torn down, and now it was open!

After the opening of the Wall, it was discovered that the leaders in East Germany had lived in great luxury. They had maintained hunting lodges stuffed with Western goods. In Wandlitz, north of Berlin, they had an exclusive housing enclave protected day and night by the state's secret police. These revelations brought an outcry from the population, in particular from Communist rank-and-file members, who felt betrayed by their leaders. Some of the top leaders,

BOX 11.1 THE OPENING OF THE BERLIN WALL

East Germany on Thursday declared the end of restrictions on emigration or travel to the West, and within hours thousands of East Germans swarmed across the Berlin wall in a mass celebration of their newly won freedom....The East German leadership announced permission to travel or emigrate would be granted quickly and without conditions. The leadership said East Germans would be allowed to move through any crossing into West Germany or West Berlin, including through the wall..."We know this need of citizens to travel or leave the country," said Günter Schabowski, a member of the Politburo who made the announcement at a news conference on Thursday evening. "Today the decision was made that makes it possible for all citizens to leave the country through East German crossing points." A tentative trickle of East Germans testing the new regulations quickly turned into a swarm of ecstatic people, who were met in the middle of the crossings by crowds of flag-waving, cheering West Germans. Some West Berliners came in cars and offered to take those from the East on a tour, and others clambered on top of the wall, unbothered by border guards. By 1 A.M. today, celebrating Berliners, East and West, had filled the celebrated Kurfürstendamm, blowing on trumpets, dancing, laughing and absorbing a glittering scene they had only glimpsed before on television. ∎

Source: New York Times, November 10, 1989.

including Honecker himself, were expelled from the party. Later, Honecker and several other former high officials were arrested on charges of high treason. The indignation at Honecker and his regime increased still more when it was discovered that leftist terrorists of West Germany in the past had been offered refuge in Communist East Germany for many years. Honecker was brought to court, but for health reasons he was never tried, and finally he was allowed to move with his wife to join their daughter in Chile, where he died. A few other East German leaders were actually tried and convicted.

It is important to stress that Honecker did not give up power voluntarily. It was an unusual set of circumstances that forced him out. It was also good luck that his orders to shoot were not obeyed, so that a bloodbath was prevented. He was a cruel dictator, exploiting his people, spying on them through the state secret police, giving orders to kill those who tried to escape to the West, all the while living in luxury and splendor.

By early 1990, there were 2,000 to 3,000 East Germans leaving every day for West Germany. There was increasing demand for unification of the two German states. At demonstrations the main slogan changed from "We are the people" to "We are one people." In March 1990, free elections took place in East Germany. In the aftermath of these elections, Germany was united on October 3, 1990.

UKRAINE

In Ukraine, it took a long time for the old Communists to yield power to an opposition party. The change came only in December 2004, and in a highly dramatic form. Ukraine had been part of the Soviet Union and, when the latter broke apart in 1991, Ukraine declared its independence in a popular referendum with the approval of over 90 percent of the voters. The same day as the referendum, the voters elected Leonid Kravchuk president. He had moved up the ranks of the old Soviet Communist Party, becoming finally member of the politburo in the Ukraine region. In the next presidential election in 1994, he was defeated by Leonid D. Kuchma, another important leader in the old Soviet Union, mainly as manager of its largest missile factory. Kuchma was reelected president in both 1994 and 1999. Although the first three presidential elections were competitive, there were many irregularities, and the entire political system was plagued by corruption. During these years, the nongovernmental organization Freedom House was rating Ukraine as only partially free.

When Kuchma's third term was up in 2004, he wanted his prime minister, Victor F. Yanukovich, to succeed him. This time, the opposition put up a popular candidate, Victor A. Yushchenko. He had made his career mainly as a banker, but at one time he had been prime minister for Kuchma, with whom, however, he later broke. The party of Kuchma tried to rig the election in its favor, and, as soon as the election results were in, it quickly declared Yanukovich the winner. But popular resistance was strong, and large numbers of citizens came out to protest the rigging of the elections. After many days and nights of protest, the Supreme Court declared the elections invalid and ordered new elections. Testimonies before the Supreme Court revealed widespread fraud and ballot stuffing. Adding to the overall crisis situation was that the candidate of the opposition, Victor Yushchenko, was poisoned with **dioxin**, which led to severe health problems, including disfiguration of his face. There were only speculations of who could have done the poisoning, and no one was charged. In the new elections, Yushchenko won. He had to concede, however, that his power was somewhat weakened in favor of parliament, where the old regime still enjoyed a great deal of power.

The main lesson of the Ukrainian transition to truly free elections is that ordinary citizens have power if they dare to go to the streets to protest a corrupt regime. The mass demonstrations in the capital of Kiev and elsewhere in the country led to a real revolution, called the **Orange Revolution**, named after the campaign color of Yushchenko. Hundreds of thousands of his supporters protested in bitter cold and did not give up until new elections with fairer rules were called. Because Yanukovich also had supporters, especially in the countryside, there were fears of **civil war** and a breakup of the country, but fortunately this did not happen. Mass demonstrations do not necessarily have to turn violent. Among the protesters, an uplifting feeling persisted that they had the power to direct the country in a democratic direction, and the old regime was wise enough not to use police force to break up the demonstrations. Unfortunately, corruption also was rampant in the new regime, which shows that erasing a pattern of corruption in a country is not an easy task.

The Orange Revolution also did not bring the desired **political stability** to the country, as much in-fighting broke out among the new rulers. There was, in particular, a severe conflict between the president and the prime minister, Yulia Tymoshenko, which led to the resignation of the latter. Through shrewd maneuvers, Yanukovich, the losing candidate in the presidential elections, became prime minister. We have seen, in Chapter 4, that there is always a delicate power relation between a president as head of state and a prime minister as head of the government. This relation turned out to be particularly fraught in Ukraine because the president was pro-Western, and the prime minister pro-Russian. A real crisis began to brew in the spring of 2007 when President Yushchenko dissolved parliament and called early parliamentary elections. Prime Minister Yanukovich opposed this decision fiercely, because with a new parliament there was a chance that he would no longer be prime minister. In May 2007, a military confrontation between the two camps seemed imminent. President Yushchenko put troops of the pro-Russian minister of the interior directly under his personal command and ordered them to march to Kiev to restore law and order. On their way, they were stopped by special police forces under the control of Prime Minister Yanukovich. No shot was fired, but the situation was extremely tense. In the meantime, the interior minister was urgently brought to the hospital, and rumors circulated that he had been poisoned by supporters of President Yushchenko. Under these circumstances, one can speak in a literal sense of a poisonous political atmosphere. Democratic stability in Ukraine in the spring of 2007 was in danger. There were real hostile feelings between the two camps, with mutual suspicions of lies and corruption. When in a country different military and police units take orders from opposite sides of the political spectrum, democracy is in real danger. At the brink of military confrontation and after much bickering from both sides, early elections were finally held on September 30, 2007. For these elections, Yulia Tymoshenko had created her own political party, which was quite successful. This gave her leverage to come back as prime minister. Her relationship with President Yushchenko, however, remained so tense that the country remained politically unstable.

A lesson of the Orange Revolution is that the **international community** can exercise a positive influence. The president of Poland and high-ranking representatives of the European Union (EU) and the Organization for Security and Cooperation in Europe arrived quickly on the scene of the crisis of 2007 as successful **mediators**. This mediation, however, was not easy, because Russian president Vladimir Putin supported the candidate of the old regime and considered Ukraine as being in the Russian sphere of influence. Ultimately, Putin accepted that Yushchenko became president, but relations between Russia and Ukraine remained tense, in particular about gas pipelines from Russia to Europe through Ukraine The Ukrainian example shows that the international community may not always speak with one voice when it comes to the transition of a country to democratic elections. Thus, a power game may go on not only internally in the respective country but also internationally. Ukraine is an example of a country in which the maintenance of the democratic regime did not get firmly established after a successful transition to democracy.

In the 2010 presidential elections, two well-known politicians of the past were the leading candidates, pro-Russian Yanukovich and pro-Western Tymoshenko. Again there were complaints about election irregularities and even court cases. Finally, Yanukovich was declared the winner. In 2011 Tymoshenko was brought to court for corruption charges, and when she did not accept the court and refused to stand up when told to so by the judge, she was jailed and later even sentenced to serve a prison term. This episode underlines that Ukraine has not yet become a stable democracy.

RUSSIA

An interesting case for a textbook about European politics is Russia. It is certainly important to the question of democratic transition. But does Russia belong to Europe? This question shows that it is unclear how far to the east Europe reaches. St. Petersburg in western Russia may very well be considered to be a European city; Moscow is already more doubtful in this respect; and even more to the east, Russia is certainly no longer European. There are no plans for Russia to enter the European Union, neither from the Russian nor the EU side. Therefore, a detailed description of the ups and downs of Russian democratization is outside the scope of this textbook. Recently, there have been many more downs than ups, and Vladimir Putin is more and more seen as an authoritarian leader, although the legalities of democracy are more or less kept up. In order to circumvent term limits for the presidency, Putin handpicked a close ally, Dmitry Medvedev, to run for president and made himself prime minister, an office where the key power now is.

In a recent development Putin announced that he wants to run again as president, which is possible since term limits apply only to consecutive terms. We hear in a credible way from professor colleagues in Moscow that on Russian television only commentators can speak up who are sympathetic to Putin. According to these colleagues the biggest problem in Russia is the judicial system. People can be arrested in an arbitrary way and being kept in prison without being charged in court. Corruption in politics is rampant. For the European democracies in Central and Eastern Europe, the increased display of **Russian power** is troubling. Putin has shown his strong hand toward former Communists countries in Central and Eastern Europe, for example, by forbidding under a pretext meat imports from Poland or playing the oil and gas card to have his will.

KEY TERMS

Bonus   232
Civil
   war   244
Cold War   227
Democratization   237
dictatorial   228
dioxin   244
Fragmentation   232

International
   community   245
Iron Curtain   227
mediators   245
Mixed system   239
nationalized   228
Orange revolution   244
path dependency   227

Political
   stability   244
Russian Power   246
Solidarity   230
Spring
   Movement   229
Sejm   232
Wall   227

DISCUSSION QUESTIONS

1. Why was it that some countries were better able to deal with the legacies of Communism than others? What are possible explanatory factors?
2. Can specific sets of institutional rules help or hinder in overcoming the legacies of Communism? If yes, what rules would that be and how would they affect a country's ability to leave Communism behind?
3. The more religious a country is, the easier it is to leave Communism behind and embrace liberalism and democracy. Would you agree or not? Why?
4. *Education:* Does a highly educated populace make the transition to democratic elections easier? Does it depend on the kind of education, for example, such as an emphasis on liberal arts?
5. *Old elites:* Should the old elites be put to trial? Is the death penalty an appropriate punishment in these circumstances? In South Africa after the overthrow of the apartheid regime, there were no criminal trials, but a truth commission. Does such a commission make the transition to democratic elections easier? Another possibility is simply to let the old elites participate in the transition to democratic elections, as in Spain and Hungary. Are there general rules regarding how the old elites should be treated, or does it very much depend on the specific cases, in particular on how brutal the old regime was?
7. *Institutions:* The founding democratic elections may be organized in very different ways. Do the election rules have an influence on how smooth the election process will be? Is the winner-take-all system preferred? Or is it better to go with rules of proportionality, and does it matter which specific rules of proportionality are chosen? Other institutional features may have an impact, too, for example, whether a country has a monarch, or whether it has a centralized or a federalist structure.

8. *International pressure:* In each of the cases we discussed the international community played a very different role. Here again many questions can be asked. Does a military occupation help or hurt the transition to democratic elections? Does it depend on who the occupiers are? Are international election observers useful? Who should these observers be?

NOTES

1. Stein Rokkan. *Citizens, Elections, Parties: Approaches to the Comparative Study of the Process of Development* (Oslo, Norway: Universitetsforlaget, 1970).
2. Ronald A. Francisco. Theories of Protest and the Revolutions of 1989. *American Journal of Political Science* 37 (August 1993): 663.
3. *Newsweek*, October 28, 1991.
4. John T. Ishiyama. Communist Parties in Transition: Structures, Leaders, and Processes of Democratization in Eastern Europe. *Comparative Politics* 27 (January 1995): 159–160.
5. *New York Times*, September 21, 1993.
6. Ibid.
7. *New York Times*, September 15 and 19, 1993.
8. Seats are distributed according to the Droop Largest Remainder formula. Unlike with the pure Droop formula, however, remainder seats are allocated only to parties with vote remainders greater than two-thirds of the vote quotas. Unawarded seats and unused votes are transferred to the national level for distribution.
9. *New York Times*, November 28, 1989.
10. Ibid.
11. For the electoral fate of the former Communist parties in the various Central and Eastern European countries, see Ishiyama. Communist Parties in Transition, 147–166.
12. *Raleigh (NC) News and Observer*, March 26, 1990.
13. Guillermo O'Donnell and Philippe C. Schmitter. *Transitions from Authoritarian Rule: Tentative Conclusions About Uncertain Democracies* (Baltimore, MD: Johns Hopkins University Press, 1986).
14. www.bbc.co.uk, September 18, 2006.

Nationalism and Ethnicity

In this chapter we address an important aspect of the culture of a country: nationalism and ethnicity. Culture has much to do with identity. Who are we? How do we define ourselves? **Identity** can be defined at an individual level. Readers of this book may ask themselves whether they see themselves primarily as boys or men, girls or women—a question of identity definition often not easily solved by American students in their transition from high school to adult life. Identity can also be defined at a collective level. With what group is my strongest identification? Here, the **nation** and **ethnic groups** as sources of identity come into play. In defining nation, we follow Walter Connor for whom the concept "connotes a group of people who believe they are ancestrally related. Nationalism connotes identification with and loyalty to one's nation."[1] If a nation corresponds to a country, we talk of a *nation-state*. A nation, however, does not necessarily have to correspond to a country. According to the definition of Connor, Scots are a nation within the United Kingdom, Catalans within Spain. A nation can also stretch across the borders of two countries like the Basques across the borders between Spain and France. When a nation is not a nation-state, one often speaks also of an *ethnic group*. Depending on the context, we will use both terms.

The ethnic group or nation with the most hapless plight in Europe are the Roma. The origin of the Roma seems to have been in India, and today they are spread out all over the world. In Europe, they are particularly numerous in Eastern European countries such as Romania and Poland. Together with the Jews, the Roma suffered most severely in the Holocaust. Still today, they are greatly discriminated against. Some people think wrongly that the Roma are nomads. To be sure, one may see Roma families begging at Western European railway stations, but Roma may very well be professionals such as doctors and lawyers.

Nevertheless, they face an uphill battle everywhere in Europe. France deported more than 10,000 Roma in 2009 and 8,500 in 2008. French President Nicolas Sarkozy is the most hostile of European statesmen toward the Roma. In the summer of 2010 he announced another wave of deportations and dozens of flights full with Roma left from Paris to Bucharest, Rumania, or Sofia, Bulgaria, on chartered airlines. Each of the Roma are given 300 Euros of "humanitarian repatriation aid" and shipped back to Eastern Europe after rounded up in their shacks by police in riot uniforms and dogs. Once the slums are cleared, they are bulldozed. Some observers suggest Sarkozy is pandering to the radical right in order to increase his re-election chances. While his polls saw a slight increase, many observers call these deportations "ethnic cleansing" and criticize Sarkozy for inhuman treatment of the Roma.[2] Strong national and ethnic identities may not be harmful and may even be considered a good thing, giving a feeling of belongingness to people. However, the negative consequences of such identities may lead to political instability and even violence. Unfortunately, Europe is not yet free of such negative consequences. The worst example is former Yugoslavia, which in the 1990s broke apart among tremendous atrocities. Europeans had hoped that after World War II such atrocities would no longer occur on its soil. We begin the chapter with this war in former Yugoslavia. We then continue with Northern Ireland and the Basque Country, both of which have seen ethnically based violence. With increased migration within Europe and also from outside Europe, the **ethnic composition** of European countries has become more complex, an issue that we address later. In Chapter 14, we will ask to what extent a European identity above all national and ethnic identities has developed with the creation of the European Union (EU).

WAR IN FORMER YUGOSLAVIA

Yugoslavia became Communist after World War II, but could keep its distance from the Soviet Union. After the fall of the Berlin Wall in 1989 and the disintegration of Communism in Central and Eastern Europe, the international community held no immediate worries about Yugoslavia. Attention was directed to other places such as Romania, East Germany, and the former Soviet republics. Thus, it was all the more unpleasant and surprising when violence broke out in Yugoslavia in 1991. Communist leaders such as the Serb Slobodan Milosĕvic and the Croat Franjo Tudjman had turned into fierce nationalists. Ordinary citizens who before did not seem to care too much about their ethnic and national identities began to shoot at each other. In the city of Sarajevo, where the various ethnic groups seemingly had lived peacefully together and where in 1984 a well-organized Winter Olympics had taken place, fierce fighting broke out. What happened to cause nationalism and ethnicity to suddenly reveal its ugly face?

To understand the situation one needs to delve deep into history. The term *Yugoslavs* means "South Slavs," which refers to the time of the great European

BOX 12.1 THE ROMA: WHY WE SHOULDN'T FEAR GYPSIES

I know too well its truth, from experience, that whenever any poor Gipsies are encamped anywhere and crimes and robberies, etc., occur, it is invariably laid to their account, which is shocking; and if they are always looked upon as vagabonds, how can they become good people? I trust in Heaven that the day may come when I may do something for these poor people.

These lines were written by Queen Victoria in 1836—wise words from a young girl. And just by writing them she had already done something for those "poor people." The loyalist thugs responsible for the hate campaign against the Romanian Gypsies in Northern Ireland might perhaps heed the words of the great-great-grandmother of their present Queen.

Queen Victoria drew attention to what is still the nub of the problem: that wherever Gypsies go they arouse suspicion. They look different, often with dark skin and wearing unusual clothes; they speak a different language, do not understand local customs and make little effort to integrate.

As soon as suspicion is aroused, local populations are inclined to jump to the wrong conclusion and innocent people may suffer. I too have been guilty of over-hasty judgments. While in Romania some years ago my passport disappeared and I assumed that it had been taken by Gypsies living in a slum that I had been visiting. I returned there and asked for my passport. They assured me they did not have it. I told them that I would have to go to the police. They begged me not to: local people and the police would be furious with them, they said, for having shamed them by stealing from a foreigner. I decided to go to the embassy in Bucharest and apply for a new passport. On the way I called in on friends with whom I had stayed earlier. They handed me my passport. I'd left it on a bedside table.

[...]The accepted view is that the Gypsies left areas in northwest India about 1,000 years ago and headed westwards, passing though Persia and Armenia and arriving in the Balkans in the fourteenth century. From there many continued farther west. There are account books from Holyrood House in 1529 that mention payments to Gypsies dancing for King James V of Scotland. In some places they were received favourably, in others not. Read any history of the Gypsies and you will find countless incidents similar to the one in Belfast. There is nothing new about Gypsies travelling around Europe, nor of them being made unwelcome.

What is new is the scale of the migration and the reasons for it. Nowadays tens, even hundreds, of thousands of East European Gypsies are travelling around the Continent. They have been leaving in droves since 2004 when visas were no longer required. Travelling long distances is now easy, and they have heard that good money can be made in Western Europe. There is one other important reason: the old way of life in Romania is breaking down. When I first went there most village communities were almost self-sufficient. They produced their own food and entertainment. Each village had its own sawmills and flour mills. Neighbours helped each other with farm work and young and old worked together in the fields. ■

Source: Times Online, July 1, 2009.

migration around A.D. 600. At that time, these Slavs moved from northeastern Europe southward to the Balkans and were therefore called South Slavs. Thus, initially all South Slavs belonged, broadly speaking, to the same ethnic group. This common origin explains why it is very difficult to distinguish members of the current ethnic groups by their physical appearance. Why did the various groups differentiate themselves from their common origin? The Croats and Slovenes lived mostly to the west and thus closest to Rome, the center of the Roman Catholic Church, which explains why these two groups became Roman Catholic. The Serbs and the Macedonians were mostly in the east, and under the influence of the Russian Christian Orthodox Church they became Christian Orthodox.

The Muslims living in Yugoslavia were originally Christians, too, living in the central region of Bosnia-Herzegovina. They practiced a controversial kind of Christianity that was considered heresy by the other Christian churches. They were inspired by the teachings of Mani, a prophet born in Babylon in A.D. 216, who stressed the human aspects of Jesus. Being without the backing of a powerful outside religious center, these so-called Manichaeans sought the protection of the Ottoman Empire when this empire expanded its influence on the Balkans, and most Manichaeans converted to Islam, voluntarily or by force. There is also the special case of the Albanians, who are ethnically not South Slavs. They are the dominant group in Kosovo. The minority in Kosovo are Serbs, and, as we will see shortly, the fact that Albanians and Serbs are different ethnic groups has greatly contributed to the problems in Kosovo.

According to the 1990 census, before war broke out, 36 percent of the people in the whole of Yugoslavia identified themselves as Serbs and 20 percent as Croats. The next largest group were the Muslims with 9 percent, living mostly in Bosnia-Herzegovina. As described earlier, these Muslims were also South Slavs, and in order to differentiate themselves from the other South Slavs, they identified themselves by their religious affiliation. Sometimes they are also called Bosniaks with reference to where most of them live. Another 8 percent were also Muslims, those living in Kosovo, but since they are of a very different ethnic group they like to be seen as Albanians. If this sounds complicated, it is. The ethnic and religious composition of former Yugoslavia was indeed of a perplexing complexity. Let us add that there were also 8 percent Slovenes, 6 percent Macedonians, while the remaining 13 percent were members of even smaller minorities such as Montenegrins, Turks, and Hungarians.

Looking back at history, over the centuries there was much fighting among the various groups. Nobel Prize–winner Ivo Andrić, in his book *The Bridge on the Drina,* gives a vivid literary description of how, over many generations, Muslims and Serbs lived together in a small town in eastern Bosnia at the Drina River.[3] He describes much cruelty between the two groups, but also warm friendships across ethnic lines. His novel was meant to give hope that despite all the differences, ethnic groups would learn to live peacefully together. Unfortunately, his hopes were not fulfilled. When the iron fist of Communism was lifted from Bosnia-Herzegovina, the old hatreds again emerged.

Over the centuries, the Balkans were very much under foreign domination, by the Ottoman Empire from the south and the Austro-Hungarian Empire from the north. In the nineteenth century the Ottoman Empire began to decay, which allowed the Serbs to form their own kingdom of Serbia and the Montenegrins their kingdom of Montenegro. In World War I the Ottoman Empire fell completely apart, as did the Austro-Hungarian Empire. What should happen with the Balkans? Without asking the people themselves, the **Versailles Peace Conference** created a very artificial entity first called the Kingdom of Serbs, Croats, and Slovenes. The king was a Serb; he established a very authoritarian regime. In 1929 he renamed the kingdom *Yugoslavia*. The other ethnic groups resented the dominance of the Serbs, and in 1934 a Croat assassinated the king.

In World War II, the power relations changed dramatically between Croats and Serbs. Croatia became a puppet regime of Hitler and committed many atrocities against Serbs, including concentration camps just for them. After World War II, Marshal Tito, who had fought the Nazis in the war, established a Communist regime. As noted, Tito was able to liberate himself from Soviet dominance, and there were no Soviet soldiers on Yugoslav soil. For Tito, ethnicity was not compatible with Communist ideas, and he organized the country in such a way that political lines did not follow ethnic lines. The republic of Croatia, for example, had a Serb minority of 11 percent.

Completing the ethnic picture of Yugoslavia in 1990, we should add that language did contribute to the ethnic divisions. Slovenes and Croats used the Roman alphabet; the other ethnic groups used the Cyrillic script. Thus, how people wrote gave a clear indication early on as to what ethnic groups they belonged to. There were also huge economic inequalities among the ethnic groups. Slovenia, on the Austrian border, had a per capita income that was about seven times higher than in Kosovo and about three times higher than in Macedonia and Montenegro.

After 1990, events in Yugoslavia took a dramatic turn. Slovenia and Croatia attempted to become independent countries. Should the international community accept such a move? Two fundamental international principles came into conflict with each other: **territorial integrity** and **self-determination**. Territorial integrity means that international borders can be changed only by peaceful means and by common agreement. Self-determination means that all people who so desire have the right to a sovereign and independent state.

Initially, the international community gave preference to the principle of territorial integrity. Thus, U.S. Secretary of State James Baker, during a visit to Yugoslavia in June 1991:

> ... told the presidents of the republics of Slovenia and Croatia, who are planning to announce some form of independence in the next few days, that the U.S. and its European allies would not recognize them if they wanted to unilaterally break away from Yugoslavia and that they should not expect any economic assistance.[4]

The Slovenian parliament had decided on September 27, 1990, that Yugoslav federal law would no longer apply within the borders of Slovenia. On December 23, 1990, 89 percent of Slovenian voters approved independence in a popular referendum. Croatian voters followed Slovenia's lead on May

19, 1991, when 93 percent approved independence for Croatia. The Yugoslav prime minister warned Slovenia and Croatia on June 24, 1991, that "the Federal Government will use all means to stop the republics' unilateral steps towards independence."[5] Despite this grave warning, Slovenia and Croatia formally declared independence the following day. On June 27, 1991, armed hostilities broke out between the Yugoslav Federal Army and the Slovenian Militia. By early August, the hostilities spread to Croatia.

Shortly after the beginning of hostilities, Germany began to push for international recognition of Slovenian and Croatian independence. As political scientist Beverly Crawford shows, there was strong domestic pressure in Germany for giving Slovenia and Croatia the right of self-determination. A link was made with the recent German unification, and, as the general secretary of the ruling Christian Democrats expressed it, Germany could not apply another yardstick to Yugoslavia "when we achieved the unity and freedom of our country through the right of self-determination." The two opposition parties, the Social Democrats and the Greens, also supported the principle of self-determination for the crisis in Yugoslavia.[6] The German foreign minister, Hans-Dietrich Genscher, presented the German view as follows: "To refuse recognition to those republics which desire their independence must lead to a further escalation of the use of force by the national [Yugoslav] Army."[7] For the Germans, the principle of territorial integrity of Yugoslavia was superseded by the principle of self-determination for Slovenia and Croatia. France, Great Britain, and the United States were at first reluctant to follow Germany's lead, but the newly united Germany used its strength to impose its will. Genscher flew to Slovenia and Croatia and received an enthusiastic welcome. The entire episode stirred troubling historical associations, because Nazi Germany dominated the two Yugoslav regions during World War II. On January 15, 1992, the EU recognized Slovenia and Croatia as sovereign, independent states. The United Nations followed suit on May 22, 1992.

In Slovenia, the hostilities were never severe and came to a quick end. Slovenia had the advantage of being the most homogeneous of the Yugoslav republics, with 90 percent of the population being Slovenes. In addition, it was the most Westernized and economically the most developed. Of all the parts of former Yugoslavia, Slovenia was the only one to reach some degree of political and economic stability relatively quickly. In 2004 it even joined the European Union as the first region of the former Yugoslavia, and in 2007 was allowed to join the euro currency.

Croatia had many more difficulties to overcome than Slovenia on the road to peace. As we have seen, Croatia had a substantial minority of Serbs, who were concentrated in a region called Krajina, located in the south-center of Croatia. In the old Yugoslavia, these Krajina Serbs had lived together with the Serbs of the Serbian Republic within the same national orders. Now, all of a sudden, they found themselves within the national borders of Croatia, and Serbia had become for them a foreign country. This situation was not accepted by the Krajina Serbs. They were supported in their resistance by the Serbian leaders in Belgrade, who still controlled the Yugoslav Federal Army. Heavy fighting erupted, and Yugoslav Federal Army planes even attacked the Croatian presidential palace in Zagreb.

In the international media, the Serbs appeared as the aggressors. Under the leadership of Milosevic in the late 1980s and early 1990s, they indeed displayed fierce nationalism and expansionism. Actions such as the attack on the Croatian presidential palace made the Serbs look like the guilty party. In fact, the situation was more complicated. We will present both sides of the arguments in this Croatian-Serbian war. It is then up to the reader to make a judgment. Let us begin the discussion with two American analogies, the War of Independence and the War of Secession. If we take the perspective of the American War of Independence, the Croats have all the rights on their side. Just as the American colonies liberated themselves from British domination, the Croats liberated themselves from Serb domination. But if we take the perspective of the American War of Secession, things look different. When the American South tried to secede from the Union, President Lincoln used all the federal forces to prevent this secession. In an analogous way, the Yugoslav federal authorities in Belgrade tried to prevent the secession of Croatia. Lincoln was successful; the Yugoslav federal authorities were not. Could it be that this is the reason that Lincoln is seen as hero, and the Yugoslav federal authorities as villains?

With regard to the specifics of Croatia, there is no question that with its unilateral declaration of independence it violated the territorial integrity of Yugoslavia. It was clearly an illegal act of the Croats to blockade the Yugoslav federal troops stationed in their garrisons in Croatia. But how else could the Croats have secured their right to self-determination? Was there any way to do so in a peaceful way and by mutual agreement?

How about the rights of the Krajina Serbs? Did they also have a right to self-determination? They thought so, and wished to either be independent or to join Serbia. Although the Krajina region had no common border with Serbia, it could have joined Serbia as a Croat **enclave**. This is not an uncommon solution in international law. Croatia severely restricted the rights of the Krajina Serbs, forcing them, for example, to replace Serbian road signs in their villages with Croatian signs. The EU was aware of the problem of the Krajina Serbs. It stated the following condition for diplomatic recognition of Croatian independence: "Guarantees for the rights of ethnic and national groups and minorities in accordance with the commitments subscribed to in the framework of the Conference on Security and Cooperation in Europe."[8] Personal assurances by the Croatian president, Franjo Tudjman, that the Krajina Serbs would be given a "special status" were sufficient for the EU to consider the required condition as fulfilled. Was this sufficient assurance, or should the EU have undertaken investigations on location to determine whether the rights of the Krajina Serbs were truly guaranteed? What were these rights anyhow? The EU distinguished conceptually between "minorities" and "territorially defined administrative units." The Krajina Serbs were considered only a minority, with the right of **autonomy** but not independence. Croatia, on the other hand, was considered a territorially defined administrative unit and was, therefore, entitled to independence. Did this conceptual distinction make sense?

Could not the Krajina Serbs also claim that they were territorially defined, since they lived in a relatively well-defined area? Should they not also have the right to self-determination? They made an effort to claim such a right and created the Serbian Republic of Krajina, but neither Croatia nor the international community recognized this entity. The Krajina region became more and more isolated and economically devastated. As a newspaper report put it, "The Krajina Serbs feel [they are] being pushed to the end of the world. The Croatian capital Zagreb is hostile territory, and the Serbian capital Belgrade only to be reached over insecure roads."[9] In June 1993, the Krajina Serbs organized a referendum in which they decided overwhelmingly to join Serbia and the Serbs in Bosnia-Herzegovina in a Greater Serbia. But, again, the international community did not recognize this referendum, which was called by a leading newspaper a "phantom referendum."[10]

Finally, there is the question of whether the international community played a proper role in the Croatian-Serbian conflict. The Secretary-General of the United Nations had initially stated that recognition of Croatia and any other Yugoslav entity "can only be envisioned in the framework of an overall settlement,"[11] meaning that issues such as the fate of the Krajina Serbs should be settled before diplomatic recognition of any new states could be considered. As we have seen, this position was at first supported by the United States, Great Britain, and France. Should this policy have been pursued even when Germany went ahead to recognize Croatia and Slovenia? The Secretary-General of the United Nations feared that premature recognition would lead to even greater violence. As we have seen, German foreign minister Genscher took the opposite view. In retrospect, who was right? With regard to the German policy, the question must be raised whether the Germans were sensitive enough to the historical aspect of Croatia having been a Nazi puppet regime in World War II. Could the hero's welcome of Genscher in Croatia not be interpreted by the Serbs as the beginning of a new German conquest? Was talk of a "Fourth German Reich" extending to Slovenia and Croatia only Serbian propaganda, or was such talk based on real fears? These are all difficult questions to ponder. In retrospect, political scientist Dusan Sidjanski argues that the early international recognition of Croatia "did not appease but, on the contrary, may have rekindled the nationalistic ambitions and the conflict between Croatia and Serbia."[12] Is he right? Because it is not possible to know what would have happened without early diplomatic recognition of Croatia, there is no definite answer to this question, which will be debated among historians for generations to come. In the current world, the proper behavior of the **international community** has great importance. As the war between Serbia and Croatia shows, it is not so easy for the international community to simply stay uninvolved. It was confronted with the question of whether or not to recognize Croatia as an independent country. Not to do anything and not to give recognition would have been an action, too. Thus, the international community was forced to act one way or the other. To stay out of the conflict was not an option.

If the situation in Croatia was complicated, it was even more complicated in Bosnia-Herzegovina, which had three major groups: 39 percent Muslims or Bosniaks, 32 percent Serbs, and 18 percent Croats. For the Muslims or Bosniaks, this was the only part of former Yugoslavia where they were the largest group. On March 1, 1992, 63 percent of the electorate voted for an independent Bosnia-Herzegovina. Compared with the referenda in Slovenia and Croatia, this support was not very high, indicating opposition by many Serbs and Croats living in Bosnia-Herzegovina. Quite a few Serbs and Croats did not even vote, boycotting the referendum altogether. Thus, from the very beginning, the Muslim-dominated government of Bosnia-Herzegovina was on shaky ground. The EU was aware of the dangers ahead and warned the government of Bosnia-Herzegovina "to grant to the members of the minorities and ethnic groups the totality of human rights and fundamental freedoms recognized by international law."[13] Based on the promise to do so, Bosnia-Herzegovina was recognized by the EU, and, on May 22, 1992, by the United Nations.

However, a horrendous war quickly broke out in Bosnia-Herzegovina. It seemed unbelievable that such brutalities could still occur in Europe. One had hoped that after the Nazi war crimes, life had become more civilized in Europe. Shamefully, the worst possible crimes happened: the rape of women, the killing of children, mass executions, concentration camps, and the expulsion of civilians from their homes. Serbs killed Muslims and Croats, Croats killed Muslims and Serbs, and Muslims killed Serbs and Croats. The worst offenders were the Serbs, particularly with the 1995 massacre in **Srebrenica**, where Serbs separated men from women and children and executed about 8,000 men. Estimates are that more than 100,000 people lost their lives in the Bosnian war.[14] About 40 percent of the dead were civilians, many of them children.[15] As a consequence of these atrocities, the Security Council of the United Nations decided that an international war tribunal should investigate these crimes and bring the guilty to court. This was the first time since the Nazi crimes that the international community established a war tribunal.

Macedonia was the fourth Yugoslav republic to be granted independence by the United Nations. This happened with much delay only in April 1993. The problem for Macedonia was that Greece was opposed to its independence, because immediately to the south of Macedonia is a Greek province with the same name. Greece feared that an independent Macedonia could put claims on the Greek province, trying to expand into a Greater Macedonia. During the Greek civil war in the late 1940s, the Yugoslav leader Tito had tried to piece together such a Greater Macedonia stretching to the Aegean Sea. Thus, the Greek fears were not unfounded. As the Greek prime minister said in an interview: "The generation that went through this war still remembers these things, and it's natural that the Greek people should be very sensitive concerning this issue."[16] Salonika, the capital of the Greek province Macedonia, is the birthplace of Alexander the Great. As one shopkeeper in Salonika said: "We are the true Macedonians. We've been here 3,000 years."[17] Given such emotions, it was not easy to find a solution. Finally, in the compromise that was worked out, the former Yugoslav republic received independence, but under the awkward name Former Yugoslav Republic of Macedonia. In 2004, the United States and other countries accepted that the name be abbreviated to Republic of

Macedonia. Other countries, however, Greece in particular, refuse to use the abbreviated name. With this dispute over the name, Greece has blocked the entry of Macedonia into the North Atlantic Treaty Organization (NATO) and the EU (see Chapter 14).

Then there is Kosovo, which did not get independence for a long time. It was not a proper republic in former Yugoslavia, but merely a province within Serbia. The rule adopted by the international community was that only republics of the former regime should get independence and not subunits of republics. This somewhat arbitrary rule played, as we have already seen, against the Krajina and also against Kosovo. For an understanding of the situation in Kosovo it is important to know that on its territory the Serbs fought their most important historical battle, the battle of Kosovo in 1389. They lost this battle against the Turks, but turned the defeat into a legend. As a *New York Times* journalist described the situation: "There is no holier place in the Serbian mind, and there are few Serbs who have not memorized parts of epic poems about the battle."[18] When former Yugoslavia fell apart, Kosovo's population was about 90 percent Albanian, most of whom were Muslims. As we have shown, the Kosovo Albanians are not South Slavs but a different ethnic group. They claim to have always lived in this region and wished for an independent Kosovo. The Serbs, on the other hand, wanted to keep this most holy place of their history in their own hands. In Chapter 13, we will show how in 2008 Kosovo declared its independence, which was recognized by some countries but not by others, most fiercely not by Serbia. In Chapter 13, we will also show how institutions of power sharing were used in former Yugoslavia in an attempt to bring stability to this region.

NORTHERN IRELAND

Northern Ireland is another trouble spot where nationalism and ethnicity have led to violence and more than 3,000 deaths since the 1960s. The conflict is easier to explain than the one in former Yugoslavia because in Northern Ireland there are basically only two groups confronting each other: British Protestants and Irish Catholics. On the surface, the problem appears to be a religious one, and the mass media usually speak of civil strife between Protestants and Catholics. But, below the surface, the battle is really between two ethnic groups: the British Unionists and the Irish Nationalists. The former happen to be Protestants and the latter, Catholics, but the conflict is not primarily about religious matters, although the religious dimension has some importance, too. Essentially, it is much more a struggle between two cultures unwilling to share the same **territory**. The Protestants want to remain part of the United Kingdom, therefore the term *British Unionists,* and the Catholics want to be part of the Irish nation, therefore *Irish Nationalists.*

John McGarry and Brendan O'Leary stress, too, that the conflict in Northern Ireland "is primarily ethno-national."[19] In medieval times, only the Irish lived on the island; ethnically they were Celtic. In the sixteenth and seventeenth centuries, Scottish settlers arrived in the northern part. They were the British Protestants just mentioned.

Politically, the entire island eventually came under British domination, which was harsh and never accepted by the Irish. The British rulers treated the Irish as inferior beings, and Irish literature is filled with angry descriptions of how the British prevented the Irish from being Irish on their own territory. Even during the time when Great Britain had an impressive colonial empire, the Irish issue occupied British leaders. The Irish wanted **independence**, which they called Home Rule. Finally, at the end of World War I, following a bloody uprising in Dublin in 1916, Ireland got its independence from Great Britain in 1921. Dublin became the capital of the Republic of Ireland, but Great Britain kept the island's Northern provinces. There the majority of the population was British by ethnic background and Protestant by religion. But a substantial minority of Irish Catholics also lived in Northern Ireland.

What we see in Northern Ireland are the difficulties British and Irish people have in trying to live together peacefully. The Irish want to make Northern Ireland part of the Republic of Ireland and consider the British foreign invaders. The British, on the other hand, argue that Northern Ireland is their home, where they have lived for centuries. As the majority in Northern Ireland, they want to remain a part of Great Britain and object to the notion that a minority could impose its preference on a majority. The important point is that the Catholics do not have a primarily religious grievance. Their complaint is, rather, that they are forced as Irish people to remain part of Great Britain. In this context, one may wish to discuss the question of when people can claim a right to live on a piece of land. After about 400 years, did the Protestant settlers have the right to stay in Northern Ireland? How about Serbs in Kosovo, who moved there more than 1,000 years ago, while Kosovo Albanians claim that they always lived in Kosovo? (See the previous section.)

When the Republic of Ireland obtained its independence in 1921 and Northern Ireland remained British, a parliament (Stormont) with extensive powers was established in Belfast, the capital of Northern Ireland. Protestants held a two-to-one majority in the country, and they practiced democracy in the traditional British way—by applying the majority principle both for parliamentary elections and cabinet formation. Given their numerical dominance, they easily won one parliamentary election after another and exercised all the governmental power. The local prime minister and all his cabinet members always belonged to the Protestant subculture, while the Catholics remained politically impotent. Over the years, this led to increasing dissatisfaction and frustration among the Irish Catholic population. In 1968 violence broke out, referred to by the British in a rather benign way as the "Troubles" in Northern Ireland. But these were more than mere troubles. The Irish Republican Army (IRA), which was active in the liberation struggle of Ireland in the nineteenth century and the beginning of the twentieth century, was reactivated and began to use terrorist methods. Ultimately, British troops intervened, and in 1972 the Belfast parliament was dissolved and direct rule by London was imposed.

The British tried to restore calm in Northern Ireland through a form of power sharing. A cabinet of moderate Protestants and Catholics was established in Northern Ireland, but within a few months a general strike of Protestant workers brought this experiment to a halt. The large majority of Protestants were not willing to change from a majoritarian to a power-sharing pattern of decision making. The Catholics, for their part, reacted with further civil strife. In Chapter 13 we will discuss, in the general context of the power-sharing literature, the specific obstacles to power sharing in Northern Ireland and how, finally, with the Good Friday Agreement of 1998, some important steps were made in the direction of power sharing (see Box 12.2).

BOX 12.2 LOYALIST WEAPONS PUT "BEYOND USE"

Two Northern Ireland loyalist paramilitary groups have said they have completed decommissioning.

The UVF and Red Hand Commando said their weapons and explosives were "totally and irreversibly beyond use." Another loyalist group, the Ulster Defence Association, confirmed it had started to decommission its arsenal. NI Secretary Shaun Woodward said it was "an historic day for Northern Ireland." Between them, the UDA and UVF killed almost 1,000 people in the Troubles. Four years ago, the IRA put its weapons beyond use in decommissioning witnessed by two churchmen. On Saturday, the UVF and the UDA said they had both engaged in "historic acts" of decommissioning. The leadership of the UVF/RHC said its disarmament process was overseen by the Independent International Commission on Decommissioning (IICD) and in front of international witnesses. It said the process had begun last Autumn but had been "suspended" following the dissident republican killings of a policeman and two soldiers in March. The process resumed after government assurances were given "that those responsible would be vigorously pursued." The leader of the UVF-linked Progressive Unionist Party, Dawn Purvis, said the "war is over," adding Saturday was a "momentous day." She said it showed that "peaceful, stable, inclusive democracy" was the way forward. She added: "Eventually loyalists and republicans must sit down for the good of our country, if we claim to be patriots." PUP representative Billy Hutchinson, who was a UVF prisoner, said the move "cements the peace process." In a separate statement, the UDA confirmed it had started a process that would lead to the destruction of all its arms. It said an act of decommissioning had been overseen by General John De Chastelain's decommissioning body. It said: "There is no place for guns and violence in the new society we are building. It is time to work for a better future." Frankie Gallagher, from the Ulster Political Research Group (UPRG), which has links with the UDA, denied they were negotiating a pay-off to complete decommissioning. "This is a process that we believe has to be done for the right reasons," he said. The decommissioning body later confirmed that it had witnessed a decommissioning event involving arms belonging to the UDA and the Ulster Freedom Fighters. "This is a significant move

(Continued)

> ### ▶ BOX 12.2 CONTINUED
>
> and we look forward to completing the process of putting all UDA/UFF arms beyond use at an early opportunity," a spokesperson said. The latest decommissioning comes ahead of Mr Woodward's August deadline for significant progress on loyalist arms. Speaking on Saturday, Mr Woodward said: "I have always kept faith with the peace and political process of which the decommissioning legislation has played a crucial part." The decommissioning moves by the loyalist paramilitary groups were broadly welcomed by the majority of Northern Ireland's political parties. First Minister Peter Robinson said: "I fully welcome this decision by each of the loyalist groups. I believe they have taken the right step, both for their own communities and for Northern Ireland as a whole." ■
>
> *Source: BBC News,* June 27, 2009.

BASQUE COUNTRY

The Basque country is yet another place in Europe where nationalism and ethnicity has caused widespread violence, with about 1,000 deaths since the 1960s. The Basque country, economically quite affluent, is located at the northeastern corner of Spain and reaches also into France. The Basques are an ethnic group with a very long tradition. They are united by a unique language, the historical origin of which is still unclear. It seems to be the oldest language in Europe, different from all the Indo-Germanic languages. For a long time, both Spain and France tried to suppress Basque language and culture on their respective territories. This suppression was particularly harsh under the dictatorship of Francisco Franco in Spain. It was during this dictatorial regime that in 1959 an organization was founded to fight for Basque independence. The name of this organization was *Basque Fatherland and Liberty Group,* in the Basque language, *Euskadi Ta Askatasuna* (ETA).

The ETA was willing to use **terrorist** methods to reach its goal. Its targets were mainly security forces, government officials, and politicians, but also tourist places to hurt the Spanish economy. Its most spectacular action occurred in 1973 with the assassination of Admiral Luis Carrero, the presumed successor of Franco. When, after the death of Franco in 1975, Spain made a successful transition to a democratic regime, the Basque country received considerable autonomy with its own local parliament. Although many Basque people were satisfied with this progress, the ETA insisted on Basque independence and continued its terrorist activities. The ETA operated with small, self-sufficient cells, so it was very difficult to penetrate the organization and break it up.

The ETA has a political wing, Sortu, until 2011 called Batasuna. The Spanish authorities have had great difficulties in handling this political wing of the ETA. On the one hand, attempts were made to separate the political leaders from the ETA and to negotiate with them. On the other hand, it also happened that the entire political leadership was arrested and sentenced to prison terms for collaborating with a terrorist group. The ambivalent position of the Spanish authorities was revealed even more when they entered secret but unsuccessful talks with ETA representatives. The Spanish population remains very upset with the terrorist activities of the ETA, and several times large numbers have taken to the streets to protest the activities of the ETA. As before Batasuna, Sortu, too, has been declared an illegal organization and thus cannot participate in elections.

An interesting twist in the Basque issue occurred in December 2004, when the Basque parliament approved, by a vote of 39 to 35, a proposal that says the Basque region has the right to **secede** from Spain. The Spanish prime minister reacted immediately, rejecting the Basque Declaration and arguing that it violated the Spanish constitution, the proposal having "no legal foundation."[20] The Basque parliament did not necessarily express a demand for independence; its point was rather that it was up to the Basques to determine their relationship with Spain. As was stated in the decision of the Basque parliament: "We express our will to form a new political pact that grows from a new model for relations with the Spanish state based on freedom of association." The president of the Basque region and main author of the plan elaborated on the meaning of the decision of the Basque parliament: "We are not proposing a project for breaking away from Spain, but we are formalizing a project for friendly coexistence between the Basque region and Spain....The Basque country is not a subordinate part of the Spanish state. The only way there will be a shared relationship with the state is if we decide there will be one."[21] This episode raises most interesting questions of democratic theory: Is it up to each region of a country to determine for itself what association it wishes to have with the other parts of the country? How important is it for the collective identity of a region to have this right of self-determination? Both questions were answered in the affirmative by the Basque parliament. According to its decision, the Basques are happy to remain part of Spain, but only if they can decide freely to do so.

How important is the question of independence in the current Europe anyhow? Both France and Spain belong to the EU and use the euro as common currency, and people can travel freely back and forth. As we will see in Chapter 14 on the EU, regions play an increasingly important role, with some of them crossing national borders. Is the Basque country not an ideal region within the EU? There are indeed many signs of the emergence of a cross-national Basque region. Basque is again taught in school, on both sides of the French–Spanish border. If it is geographically more convenient, schoolchildren are allowed to attend school on the other side of the border. In the town of Ainhoa, for example, located on the French side, about one-fifth of the children come from the Spanish side. Many people in the Basque region speak three languages: Basque, French, and Spanish. The traditional Basque ball game, pelota, which is comparable to squash, is played in the entire Basque region, regardless of the border between France and Spain. Farmers are allowed to graze their sheep on both sides of the border. Firefighting and recycling are organized across the border. In the daily life of the Basque country, the national border between France and Spain has lost much of its importance. Here, as a journalist notes, "Europe of the regions has become reality."[22] Given this situation, the notion of national independence has

BOX 12.3 BRITONS ARE THREAT TO BASQUE COUNTRY, ETA WARNS

Armed separatist group claims tourists "colonising" French Basque region.

Armed Basque separatist group ETA yesterday pointed to British holidaymakers and second-home buyers in the French Basque country as a threat to the region's future. In an interview published in the radical *Gara* newspaper yesterday, two leaders of the terrorist group named British visitors among those accused of destroying a Basque culture that ETA has vowed to defend with bombs and bullets. They said British visitors were part of a wave of "colonisation" of the Basque region in southwest France that was wiping out traditional farming culture and the ancient Basque language of Euskara. "If things do not change...these oppressed territories will become leisure areas for the English, for Parisians and people from Bordeaux," said an ETA member using the codename Gaueko. ETA has killed more than 800 people in a 40-year campaign of violence to try to create an independent Basque state. Although most of its attacks have been on Spanish soil, three of the seven Basque "provinces" that it wants to bring together are Labourd, Basse Navarre and Soule— all of which are in France. Historically ETA has used France mostly as a base from which to attack Spain. In recent years, however, it has also carried out a handful of attacks in France, killing two undercover Spanish police officers there in 2007. ∎

Source: The Guardian, May 25, 2009.

lost much of its importance, so that it seems antiquated that the ETA still continues its terrorist activities. The Basque country is well and alive as a vibrant European region with one part of the Basques also belonging to Spain, the other part also to France. The ETA thus fights an old battle that no longer fits the emerging political order of the EU. Yet, in June 2007, the ETA announced that it was calling off a 14-month-old cease-fire and taking up its armed fight again. This is indeed what ETA did, not only in the Basque country but also in the Spanish capital, Madrid, and the Spanish beaches. Sometimes nobody is hurt, but on other occasions, people are injured or even killed (see Box 12.3).

In Europe there is the risk that because of immigration, cleavages between natives and immigrants will become increasingly deeper, with the latter more and more stressing their ethnic and even national identities. (There is much more on immigration in Chapter 15.)

OTHER ASPECTS OF NATIONALISM AND ETHNICITY

Up to now, we have focused on negative aspects of nationalism and ethnicity, and indeed many disturbing negative aspects are evident. But more positive aspects also exist. Let us take the Scots as a positive example. Scotland has a long and rich history, during which it developed many traditions. Since the seventeenth century, Scotland has been part of Great Britain, and in recent years the Scots have once again become more conscious of their separate historical roots. There has been a rebirth in the popularity of old Scottish songs and poems. Increased attention to Scottish history and culture and an influx of tourists have made many Scots truly aware for the first time that they are different from the English. This heightened awareness is reinforced when Scots move to London, where their Scottish identity often increases rather than decreases. The rebirth of Scottish identity is not limited to the older generation but also occurs among young, highly educated people. Politically, the new Scottish nationalism has gained importance, and Scotland has gotten its own local parliament.

This increased importance of Scottish identity has not led to any particular animosities against the English, and certainly not to any violent incidents. For the Scots themselves, an increased sense of identity is mostly a good thing. The modern world has become more anonymous, with family and neighborhood ties breaking apart. In this situation, ethnic groups offer ties firmly rooted in the past. Nobody can take away the Scots' membership in the Scottish community; even if they move away from the region, they will always remain Scots. As long as one lives, one is united with the brothers and sisters of his or her ethnic affiliation. This belonging also links individuals with preceding generations and generations to follow, creating a historical perspective. What we have noted for Scotland is true for many other regions in Europe; for example, Catalonia in Spain, Sardinia in Italy, Brittany in France, Frisia in the Netherlands, and Bavaria in Germany.

The crucial point is that a strong ethnic identity does not necessarily lead to hostile feelings and even violent actions against other ethnic groups. It is important that an identity is not only **exclusive** but also allows the existence of other identities. In the modern world, multiple identities have positive consequences for political stability and cooperation. In its history, the great danger for Europe was fierce nationalism leading to many bloody wars. Fortunately, there are signs of a multilevel order emerging in Europe, with citizens still having a national identity but in addition also European and regional identities.

A historical perspective shows that the concept of the nation-state is not more than 400 years old (see also Chapter 1). It was created in Western Europe, with France as the prototypical example. In medieval times, there existed no French nation-state, nor any other nation-state, in Europe. Under the system of feudalism, no clear borders divided the sovereignty of one ruler from another. Rather, the various rulers—kings, dukes, barons, bishops, cities, monasteries, and so on—had overlapping rights. Within a particular village, both a duke and a monastery may have had the right to levy taxes. An individual peasant may have had obligations to both a bishop and a city.

It was only in the sixteenth century, with the beginning of absolutism, that the concept of **national sovereignty** became relevant. Within specific territorial borders a single ruler took over all the political power. To consolidate this power, the ruler tried to establish a common national identity among his or her subjects. Of particular importance was the imposition of a common language. This process of building the European nations took a long time.

In nineteenth-century France, for example, many people still did not speak French as a native language. Thus, it is historically quite a new phenomenon that Europeans feel part of nation-states.

European history of the nineteenth and twentieth centuries has shown how the concept of the nation-state, based on an exclusively defined national identity, can lead to catastrophic wars. The temptation is great for a nation-state to try to expand its borders and thus its national sovereignty. National interests risk clashing with one another at any time.

The idea for a more stable and cooperative European order is to redefine the concept of sovereignty in less national terms. Sovereignty would no longer belong exclusively to the nation-state but be divided among the European, the national, and the regional levels. The nation-states would certainly continue to exist and exercise important power, but some of their power would be transferred upward to the European level and some downward to the regional level. As we will see in Chapter 14, the EU makes efforts precisely in this direction. It is important to stress here that the EU is characterized both by a process of regionalization and a process of supranational integration.

For a new political order in Europe to be established, it is also important that regional political units are allowed to cut across national borders. As we have seen earlier in this chapter, the Basque region is a good example to illustrate this aspect. It stretches across the French–Spanish border at the North Atlantic Ocean. The Tyrol is another example of a region that was cut across by a national border but now flourishes again as an entity. The Tyrol belonged to the Austro-Hungarian Empire, within which it had developed its own cultural identity. After the demise of the Austro-Hungarian Empire in World War I, the southern part of the Tyrol was transferred to Italy, while the northern part remained with Austria. Italy tried to assimilate the South Tyrol into the Italian nation, in particular with regard to language, but there was fierce resistance among the South Tyrol people, who wanted to stay with their native German language and culture. Occasionally, resistance even took the form of armed attacks against the Italian authorities. Today, with both Austria and Italy being members of the EU, tensions have vanished in the South Tyrol. People there are once again allowed to be taught German in school. Contacts with the Austrian part of the Tyrol have been greatly facilitated. Although the Tyrol still belongs to two different nation-states, it again enjoys a life of its own with many common cultural and economic affairs. There is a strong Tyrol identity, but in the South it is coupled with an Italian identity and in the North with an Austrian identity, and both the South and the North have some **European identity**.

Cross-national regions may also grow out of functional economic circumstances. An example is the Regio Basiliensis in Greater Basel. The city of Basel is located in the northwestern corner of Switzerland, where Germany, France, and Switzerland come together at the Rhine River. Many German and French commuters work in nearby Basel. Many consumers from Basel shop for bargains in German and French stores. The airport of Basel is located on French territory, and a German railway station is based on Swiss soil. These and many other examples indicate how much the agglomeration of Basel forms an economic unity across national borders of three countries. At an organizational level, Regio Basiliensis has the task of coordinating economic activities in the entire region, regardless of national borders.

Cross-national economic regions emerge also in Central and Eastern Europe. An example is the Euroregion Pomerania, at the border between Germany and Poland; another example is the Euroregion Karpatian in the border area of Poland, Slovakia, Hungary, and Ukraine.[23] All these examples show how important regional thinking has become in Europe, even if the regions cut across national borders.

If Europe moves in the direction of a multilayered order with cross-cutting borders, one may ask whether such an order is not too complex. It does not seem too complex if we think of the problems confronting Europe. These problems are of a high complexity, and to solve complex problems, one needs a complex organization. The traditional organization based on nation-states is just too rigid. To be sure, there are still many problems for which the nation-state is the appropriate unit, but other problems need to be handled at the European level. And still other problems belong to the regional level, with some regions cutting across national borders.

The real issue is not whether Europe needs a complex political order. It is rather whether Europeans are able to adjust their thinking styles and their identities to such a complex order. Political thinking is, of course, easier if the national interest is the sole guiding post. Deciding whether something is good or bad for your nation is a simple question. In Europe of the future, thinking has to be more complex. Political issues need to be addressed at different levels. A particular solution may not seem in the immediate interest of your nation, but it may be beneficial for your region or for Europe at large. Because all levels ultimately depend on each other, in the long run the solution may be good for your nation, too. With such a thinking style, politics is transformed into a **positive-sum game**, which means that overall gains are higher than overall losses; in a positive-sum game, a gain for one side does not necessarily mean a loss for another side.

Symbolically, the new European order may best be expressed in the variety of flags that one would see in Europe. The national flags would still wave on the rooftops, but equally often one would see regional flags and the European flag. Because we are all also citizens of the world, the flag of the United Nations may also have its place in European towns and villages.

IMMIGRATION

Within the countries of the EU it has become very easy and unproblematic to move from one country to another (see Chapter 14). This, however, is not at all the case if someone comes from outside the EU, especially from former Yugoslavia,[24] Turkey, or Africa. Many people from these regions try to find work in Europe. Many **refugees** also try to come to Europe. Often, the line between immigrant workers and refugees is blurred, which puts the European authorities in severe dilemmas concerning whom to accept and whom to reject. If someone attempts to escape the economic misery, even starvation, in an African country, is this sufficient grounds to be considered a refugee? These are the hard cases to be decided by European authorities.[25] (See more on immigration problems also in Chapter 15 in the context of globalization.)

In former times, refugees were no problem when they came in small numbers from Communist countries. There were two main waves of refugees fleeing from Communism. In 1956, many Hungarians were able to escape before the Soviet tanks crushed the uprising in Budapest. In 1968, many were able to flee from Czechoslovakia before the Soviet tanks stopped the reform movement there. These refugees were most welcome in Western Europe. Most of them were highly educated, and during the economic boom of the time they were easily integrated in their host countries.

The welcome for such migrants soon wore out in Europe. In contrast to the refugees from Communist countries during the Cold War, the new asylum seekers integrated less easily into the European societies. First, their status was uncertain, and most knew that their request for asylum would ultimately be rejected. Second, they were too different to be able to integrate successfully. For both reasons, they most often preferred to stay among themselves and to give one another comfort. Some poor neighborhoods in the big European cities were thus transferred into ethnic enclaves of immigrants of all kinds, a mixture of refugees and immigrant workers.

In the German city of Mannheim, one of the authors (Steiner) has visited a neighborhood inhabited nearly exclusively by Turks. Turkish was spoken in the streets; the stores had Turkish signs and sold Turkish items, in particular Turkish food; women, according to Turkish tradition, wore black clothes and had their hair covered with white shawls. New Turkish immigrants naturally went to such a neighborhood, where they felt more at home. There they joined other Turks who had already lived in Germany for a long time. All over Europe, immigrants from less developed countries have established their own subcultures in the big cities. This new multiethnicity makes many Europeans ill at ease and hostile (see Chapter 2 on right-wing parties).

After September 11, 2001, and the war in Iraq, tensions with Muslims in Europe have further increased. Many Muslims feel vulnerable and even less welcome than before. On the other side, there are increasing complaints that many Muslims become fundamentalist and are unwilling to **integrate** into European societies. This conflict came most visibly to public attention when in 2004 the Dutch filmmaker Theo Van Gogh was assassinated by a Muslim extremist of dual Dutch-Moroccan nationality. Van Gogh, a descendant of the nineteenth-century painter, was an outspoken proponent of free expression. His short film *Submission*, shown on Dutch television, criticized the Muslim treatment of women. The film told the fictional story of a Muslim woman who was forced into a violent marriage, raped by a relative, and brutally punished for adultery. It featured actresses portraying abused Muslim women, naked under transparent Islamic-style shawls, their bodies marked with texts from the Koran that supposedly justify the repression of women.

The film provoked an angry outcry in the Muslim community. The killer of Van Gogh was most brutal, shooting the filmmaker on an open street in Amsterdam, slitting his throat, and stabbing his chest. Two knives were left in the torso, one pinning a five-page note threatening Western governments. In the aftermath of this assassination, mosques were set on fire, not only in the Netherlands, but, for example, also in Germany. All over Europe, this tragedy led to intense soul-searching. Did Van Gogh legitimately use his right for free expression? Are there limits to what one can do in a film? To what extent is it allowable for non-Muslims to criticize the teachings of Islam? Should Muslim immigrants make an effort to integrate into European societies? Should non-Muslims be encouraged to learn more about Islam and its history? How can Muslims and non-Muslims live peacefully together in Europe? These are all troubling questions showing that the immigration issue is a most difficult one for Europeans—more difficult than for Americans, who live in a country with a tradition of immigration.

In Europe there is the risk that because of immigration, cleavages between natives and immigrants will become increasingly deeper, with the latter more and more stressing their ethnic and even national identities (see Chapter 15).

KEY TERMS

autonomy 254
enclave 254
ethnic composition 249
ethnic groups 248
European identity 264
exclusive 263
identity 248
independence 258

integrate 266
international
   community 255
nation 248
national sovereignty 263
positive-sum game 265
refugees 265
secede 261

self-determination 252
Srebrenica 256
territorial integrity 252
territory 257
terrorist 260
"Troubles" 258
Versailles Peace
   Conference 252

DISCUSSION QUESTIONS

1. Does history side with winners?
2. To what extent does the American analogy of the Revolutionary and Civil War laid out above apply to the Yugoslav situation?
3. Why was Tito able to keep the peace for such a long time in Yugoslavia?
4. Was the war in former Yugoslavia a civil war? If yes, on what grounds would you justify the interference of the United States and NATO?
5. How would you describe the nature of the war in former Yugoslavia? Was it primarily fought over religious differences (Muslims against Christians) or ethnic differences (Croats against Serbs)?
6. Europe is fraught with pockets of local resistance to the centralized state, such as the Catalans in Spain, the Basques, or "Padania" (northern Italy). What explains such resistance?
7. Immigration, particularly Muslim immigration into Europe, has caused serious confrontations with the native population. Why is it particularly Muslim immigration that seems to create particularly serious tensions? Does the United States face a similar problem with its Muslim immigrants?

NOTES

1. Walter Connor, *Ethnonationalism. The Quest for Understanding* (Princeton, NJ: Princeton University Press, 1994), p. XI.
2. Ullrich Fichtner, Sarkozy's War against the Roma. *Der Spiegel Online*, September 15, 2010.
3. Ivo Andriç. *The Bridge on the Drina* (London: Allen & Unwin, 1959).
4. Thomas Friedman. Baker Urges End to Yugoslav Risk. *New York Times*, June 22, 1991.
5. *Financial Times of London*, June 25, 1991.
6. Beverly Crawford. Explaining Defection from International Cooperation: Germany's Unilateral Recognition of Croatia. *World Politics* 48 (July 1996): 505.
7. Marc Weller. The International Response to the Dissolution of the Socialist Federal Republic of Yugoslavia. *The American Journal of International Law* 86 (1992): 587.
8. European Press Consortium (EPC) press release. Doc. 128, 1991.
9. *Neue Zürcher Zeitung*, June 11, 1993 (translation Jürg Steiner).
10. *Neue Zürcher Zeitung*, June 21, 1993.
11. Report of the Secretary-General Pursuant to Security Resolution 721. Doc. S/23280, 1991.
12. Dusan Sidjanski. The Consequences of the Crisis of Ex-Yugoslavia on the European Union. *Newsletter of the IPSA Research Committee on European Unification* 6 (Spring 1993): 2.
13. Conference for Peace in Yugoslavia, Arbitration Commission, *Avis* No. 2, Para. 4.
14. *Neue Zürcher Zeitung*, May 27, 2005.
15. *Neue Zürcher Zeitung*, June 23, 2007.
16. *New York Times*, February 4, 1993.
17. Ibid.
18. *New York Times*, November 15, 1992.
19. John McGarry and Brendan O'Leary. Five Fallacies: Northern Ireland and the Liabilities of Liberalism. *Ethnic and Racial Studies* 18 (October 1995): 859.
20. *New York Times*, January 4, 2005.
21. *New York Times*, December 31, 2004.
22. *Neue Zürcher Zeitung*, July 31/August 1, 1993.
23. Personal communication, Professor Kazimierz Sowa of the University of Rzeszów, Poland.
24. With the exception of Slovenia, which is now a member of the EU.
25. For a full discussion of these issues, see: Niklaus Steiner. *International Migration and Citizenship Today* (London and New York: Routledge, 2009).

Power Sharing in Deeply Divided Societies

In Chapter 12 we explored how ethnicity can lead to deep **divisions** in a society. Deep societal divisions can also be caused by other factors, in particular language, religion, race, and social class. A society is deeply divided if its subgroups have strong identities and hostile feelings between them. Iraq is an example of such a deeply divided society. In the European context, Northern Ireland, Belgium, Bosnia-Herzegovina, and Kosovo are clear examples of deeply divided societies. How deeply is the United States divided, in particular along racial lines?

How can democratic stability be attained in such deeply divided societies? Political science theorists see the answer in the **sharing of power** among the deeply divided groups. This theory of power sharing is also called **consociational** theory.[1] The term *consociational* is rarely used in everyday language, but it has become prominent as a technical term in political science. Consociational democracies stand in contrast to competitive majoritarian democracies, the latter being characterized by a voting mechanism whereby a majority can impose its will on a minority.

DEVELOPMENT OF THE THEORY OF POWER SHARING

The distinction between consociational and competitive democracies was first made by Arend Lijphart and Gerhard Lehmbruch at the 1967 World Congress of the International Political Science Association in Brussels.[2] Their contributions opened an interesting discussion that continues to the present. Lijphart and Lehmbruch coined the term *consociational democracy* to draw attention to some smaller European democracies that were neglected in prior theorizing. In the 1950s and early 1960s, the thinking of political scientists about democratic regimes was influenced primarily by the experiences of the United States, Great Britain, France, Germany, and Italy. The first two countries seemed to have long traditions of democratic stability, whereas the latter three were plagued by periods of instability. This comparison raised the question of which factors might account for the level of democratic stability. A very influential hypothesis was formulated in 1956 by Gabriel A. Almond, who identified the political culture of a country as a crucial factor.[3] He postulated that a homogeneous political culture, like that of the two Anglo-American countries, is conducive to democratic stability, whereas a **fragmented** political culture, as in the large continental European countries, tends to lead to democratic instability.

However, Austria, Belgium, the Netherlands, and Switzerland seemed to contradict Almond's hypothesis because they appeared culturally fragmented yet democratically stable. Lijphart and Lehmbruch explained this deviation by observing that these countries practiced a consociational, rather than a competitive, mode of decision making. From this line of theoretical reasoning, a more optimistic view emerged than that contained in Almond's hypothesis: Culturally fragmented countries could hope to attain democratic stability if they used consociational, rather than competitive, decision making. In the meantime, attempts have been made to apply this consociational theory to divided countries such as Afghanistan, Iraq, Lebanon, South Africa, Northern Ireland, and Bosnia-Herzegovina. We will discuss such applications for some European countries later in the chapter.

Before doing so, however, we must clarify three crucial concepts of the theory. First, we must define what is meant by a culturally fragmented society and how it is different from a culturally homogeneous society. Second, consociational decision making must be clearly distinguished from competitive decision making. Third, we must establish what is meant by democratic stability and instability. Only with these clarifications will it become apparent what Lijphart and Lehmbruch had in mind with their theory.

For a country to be culturally fragmented or divided, the various groups must differ in such attributes as race, language, religion, and historical roots. Such attributes are known as **ascriptive** attributes, having been present from birth; they are virtually permanent. Ascriptive attributes may be contrasted with **achieved** attributes, such as occupation and education, which are the result of individual achievement and can be changed relatively easily during a lifetime. Differences in ascriptive attributes are a necessary, but not sufficient, condition for cultural fragmentation. For a country to be culturally fragmented, the people sharing the same ascriptive attribute must also develop a common identity and express it in a politically relevant way. If this additional condition is fulfilled, specific subcultures can be distinguished—for example, a Catholic and a Protestant subculture. People feel an identity as either Protestants or Catholics and are politically active in Protestant and Catholic organizations. Furthermore, relations among such subgroups are generally characterized by hostility.

What exactly do Lijphart and Lehmbruch mean when they say that the decision process among subcultures is consociational rather than competitive? A first characteristic is that executive cabinets contain representatives from all of the subcultures. If a country is divided between a Catholic and a Protestant subculture, for example, consociational cabinet formation means that both subcultures share power in the cabinet. Such encompassing coalitions are called **grand coalitions**. Besides the cabinet, grand coalitions may also form in other bodies, such as advisory commissions. A second feature of consociational decision making is a **veto power** for each subculture on matters involving its essential interests. If Catholics are a minority, parliamentary rules would require that changes in abortion laws, which are so important to Catholics, could not be enacted without the consent of the Catholic minority. A third characteristic is that parliamentary elections, the appointment of public officials, and the distribution of public funds among the subcultures are guided by the principle of **proportionality**. If Catholics make up 40 percent of the population, they should receive 40 percent of the top positions in the armed forces, for example. In other words, each subculture should receive its quota. Fourth, consociational decision making means that the individual subcultures have a great deal of **autonomy** in regulating their own affairs—having control over educational and cultural matters, in particular.

These consociational principles are very distinct from the principles of majoritarian decision making. If the majority principle is applied in resolving conflicts among subcultures in a fragmented society, minorities will always lose. If Protestants, for example, comprise two-thirds of the population and Catholics one-third, the former will always win. As we will see later in the chapter, this was exactly the situation in Northern Ireland, with Protestants as the larger group winning one election after another and controlling the executive branch of government. It is no wonder that Catholics were not satisfied with this form of government.

The crucial point in Lijphart and Lehmbruch's argument is that consociational decision making increases the probability of democratic stability in culturally fragmented societies. By democratic stability, they mean essentially that a country has a low level of civil violence and disorder, both actually and potentially. The application of consociational devices is necessary particularly when the cleavage structure of society is **reinforcing**, rather than **cross-cutting**. A reinforcing cleavage structure is one in which a society is not only divided along one dimension, say language, but that this division is overlaid by additional cleavages such as religion, region, and race. When cleavages are aligned in a reinforcing pattern, conflict is more likely because any member of society sees the "other" as not only being different in terms of language, but also in terms of region and race, and perhaps even additional differences. Thus, we say that such cleavages "reinforce" each other, leading to a very high potential for conflict. It is precisely in such societies that consociational devices are even more necessary than when cleavages are "cross-cutting" (Figure 13.1).

Cross-cutting cleavages are less problematic for social harmony because they slice up society into a microcosm of differences, and no single group is large enough to impose itself on others. In such a situation, power sharing is less necessary because cleavages cross-cut each other to such an extent that any group in power represents a microcosm of society and, as a result, will produce policies that will not systematically exclude other groups.

Society with re-enforcing cleavage structure	Society with cross-cutting cleavage structure

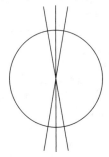
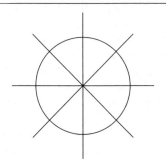

FIGURE 13.1
Two ideal typical societies with differing cleavage structures.

Why does one fragmented country make use of consociationalism and another does not? Much depends on the wisdom and foresight of the subcultures' leaders. If they are sufficiently aware of the centrifugal tendencies in their society, they may choose to attempt to counterbalance these tendencies via consociationalism. According to the term used by Lijphart, leaders need a spirit of accommodation.[4] This is not to say that leaders with such a spirit of accommodation are always free to adopt a consociational approach to decision making. Certain conditions may prevent consociational decision making, even if the leaders wish to use it. Consociational decision making is facilitated if at least some of the following conditions are present. Students may wish to discuss in their classes why these conditions are **favorable** for consociational decision making.

> None of the subcultures has a numerical majority.
> The subcultures have clear boundaries and can, therefore, easily be identified.
> There is relative economic equality among the subcultures.
> Each subculture has preeminent leaders who are internally respected and can speak for the interests of their subculture.
> There is some overarching loyalty across all subcultures to the country as a whole, the very existence of which is not questioned.
> The population of the country is relatively small.
> The country is under international pressure that is seen by all subcultures in the same light.
> The country has some tradition of accommodation and compromise.
> The overall load of unresolved problems on the country (unemployment, inflation, etc.) is not very great.

In Austria, Belgium, the Netherlands, and Switzerland, these conditions were mostly favorable, which allowed their leaders to practice consociational decision making. This practice was so successful that all four countries can now again afford to introduce more competitive elements into their decision making. This move away from consociational decision making is also part of the theory. If, as a result of consociational decision making, relations among subcultures remain peaceful for some time, cultural fragmentation begins to lose some of its importance, so that consociationalism is no longer necessary to preserve harmonious relations. You could say that successful consociationalism makes itself superfluous.

The Austrian case can be used to illustrate the dynamic workings of consociational theory. After its defeat in World War I and the demise of the Hapsburg Empire, Austria made an initial attempt at a democratic form of government in the 1920s and 1930s. At that time, Austria was a very fragmented society with two subcultures, the so-called red and black camps (Lager). That the military term *camp* was used to designate the two subcultures indicates just how deeply divided Austrian society was. The blacks were the middle-class bourgeois Conservative Catholics; the reds were the working-class anticlerical Socialists. The two camps were very segregated from each other, and Austrians spent most of their daily lives with members of their own camp. Politics was played according to the majority principle. The result was instability, civil strife, and even a brief civil war in the early 1930s. Austria then became easy prey for annexation by Hitler in 1938. After the atrocities of World War II and the concentration camps, surviving leaders of the two groups decided in 1945 to form a grand coalition of the two large parties. For about 20 years, blacks and reds ruled the country together according to the four consociational devices. Relations between the two subcultures became much more harmonious, and the subcultures themselves lost much of their importance. Marriage across subcultural lines, for example, was no longer uncommon.

The Netherlands was deeply divided among Catholics, Calvinists, and a secular group; the latter was further divided along class lines between Socialists and Liberals. As suggested by consociational theory, the politics of accommodation initiated in 1917 brought increasing stability, which in turn, particularly after the 1960s, decreased the importance of the subcultural rifts.

In Switzerland, consociationalism was used both for linguistic and religious cleavages (see also Chapter 7). Religiously, the cleavage was between Catholics and Protestants, and over the centuries there were five civil religious wars. Increasingly, consociationalism was practiced between the two religious groups, and today religious divisions have greatly decreased. Linguistically, Switzerland has four official languages—German, French, Italian, and Romansh—and here, too, consociationalism was practiced quite successfully, although the language issue is still quite sensitive.

In Belgium, the significance of consociationalism was strong for the language question and also for the relations between clerical and anticlerical Catholics. As in Switzerland, consociationalism has lost much of its importance for the religious issue, but not for the language issue at all. The division between Dutch-speaking Flemish and French-speaking Walloons has become so deep that Belgium has great difficulties to put together a functioning cabinet. There are no longer political parties encompassing both language groups. The traditional parties of Christian Democrats, Liberals, and Socialists have split along language lines, and language-oriented parties have emerged on both sides. The language issue is particularly acute in the capital, Brussels, where it is in many neighborhoods contested whether they should be Flemish or Walloon. Leaders of both sides in the Belgium conflict have more or less stopped to speak with each other in the old consociational spirit. There is even speculation that one day Belgium may fall apart into two separate countries. Things are being made worse by the fact that Belgium is one of the most indebted countries in Europe.

CRITIQUE OF THE THEORY OF POWER SHARING

How good is consociational theory? Has its "medicine" been tested sufficiently to ensure that it has the desired effect? Less metaphorically: Does consociationalism or power sharing really increase the probability of democratic stability? Do Austria, Belgium, the Netherlands, and Switzerland convincingly support the causality postulated by consociational theory? Here we encounter a difficult methodological problem common to all research in comparative politics: the small number of cases and their great complexity. Four countries obviously constitute a very narrow empirical basis. Even 10 or 20 countries would be too few cases to allow for the use of sophisticated statistical analyses. Contributing further to the methodological difficulty is the great complexity of the individual cases, which often prevents unambiguous identification of the causal effect of an individual factor. If a country changed from competitive to consociational decision making and all other variables remained constant, the independent effect of the change in decision mode could be determined. In reality, however, such experimental situations do not exist, because many other factors change as well.

We first use again the Austrian example to illustrate the difficulty of determining the direction of causality. As described earlier, the decision-making style in Austria's First Republic was majoritarian before civil war broke out in the early 1930s and an autocratic regime was established. By contrast, the Second Republic in the years after World War II practiced consociationalism, and democratic stability prevailed. If nothing save the decision mode had changed, we could safely conclude that this change caused an increase in democratic stability. However, because the Austrian situation changed in many other aspects as well, other plausible explanations for the increased democratic stability are available. One could argue, for example, that economic conditions after 1945 were much better than in the 1920s and early 1930s and that this improvement allowed democratic stability to blossom. Increased democratic stability in Austria could also be explained by changes in the religious life of the country. In the years after 1945, religious devotion declined rapidly, so that the old rift between clericalists and anticlericalists lost much of its importance. With the decreased prominence of religion, relations between blacks and reds became less divisive, thereby allowing a more stable democracy.

In addition, the **social stratification** of Austrian society changed noticeably during this period. The simple dichotomy between the bourgeois middle class and the working class, corresponding to an earlier phase of industrial development, was increasingly replaced with a more diversified social structure. Both the middle class and the working class became more heterogeneous, blurring class distinctions. Less class distinction meant less fragmentation between blacks and reds, providing yet another possible explanation for the higher level of democratic stability.

We can thus identify at least five variables that had different values in the First Republic and the beginning years of the Second Republic: decision-making mode, democratic stability, economic affluence, religious practice, and social stratification. How can we sort out possible causalities among these and perhaps still more variables? Truly convincing conclusions could only be reached if we could manipulate the variables in an experimental way. Because that is not possible, conclusions can only be more or less plausible.

The data for Belgium, the Netherlands, and Switzerland also allow for interpretations that conflict with the assumptions of consociational theory. Do these ambiguities mean that the theory should not be applied to countries such as Northern Ireland, Bosnia-Herzegovina, Afghanistan, Iraq, Lebanon, and South Africa? Certainly not. It is in the nature of comparative politics that the causal effect of a variable can never be tested in a laboratory. To require such tests would mean postponing practical applications forever and would make comparative politics irrelevant in crisis situations. Yet crisis situations exist in many parts of the world, and they cry out for solutions. Political scientists have the moral obligation to offer help. They must only be sure that their advice is given with the proper care and caution.

A precondition for testing a theory is the ability to **measure** its variables in a reliable and valid way. Here we encounter additional difficulties with consociational theory, as we would with any other theory. If consociational theory says that power sharing increases the probability of democratic stability in culturally fragmented societies, all three of the variables contained in this hypothesis should be measurable. What indicators can we use to tell how fragmented a society is, how much its political leaders use the consociational method of decision making, and how democratically stable a political system is? The Swiss case illustrates the problems inherent in answering these questions.

With regard to fragmentation, it is often stated that consociational theory is applicable to Switzerland because of its linguistic fragmentation into German, French, Italian, and Romansh. Other researchers argue, however, that despite the existence of four languages, Swiss society is quite homogeneous, so consociational theory is not applicable to the Swiss case. We must distinguish carefully between linguistic diversity and linguistic fragmentation. The former means that two or more languages are spoken in a country. Such linguistic diversity is a necessary, but not sufficient, condition for linguistic fragmentation. People speaking the same language may or may not develop a common and politically relevant identity. How is linguistic identity measured in Switzerland? One may use survey methods, asking people how strongly they identify with their language group. In one such survey, 14 percent of Swiss answered that they identified most strongly with their language group, compared with 33 percent who identified primarily with their local community, 24 percent with Switzerland at large, 19 percent with their Canton, 6 percent with the world, and 4 percent with Europe. One should also consider that 14 percent gave language as their second most important identity. Thus, 28 percent said that language was among their top two identities.[5]

How do we interpret these survey results? The task is not easy because the picture is mixed. Linguistic identity is of great importance for some Swiss but not for others. To make the interpretation of these data more complex, one also needs to consider that the relative importance of a person's identities may change from one life situation to another. In this context, the experiences of two students from the University of Geneva, who studied for a year at the University of North Carolina, are relevant. During their stay in the United States, they felt primarily Swiss. On arriving back at the airport in German-speaking Zürich, they felt that their primary identity was French. When they returned by train to the French-speaking region, still another change in identity took place; each now identified primarily with a Canton—Geneva for one student and the Jura for the other. This story illustrates the dynamic perspective of identities. A person's primary identity may change from one situation to another. It is difficult to capture such a fast-changing picture with survey techniques. Be aware, also, that surveys are conducted at the attitudinal level, and it is a well-known phenomenon that attitudes do not always translate easily into behavior.

Hence, we must also look at behavioral data. How does the behavior of the Swiss indicate their linguistic group identity? An often-used indicator is marriage across language lines. Do Swiss marry primarily within their language group? Take the example of French speakers: 77 percent marry other French speakers.[6] Again, the data are difficult to interpret. Because French speakers are concentrated in one region of the country, it is not surprising that most of them choose partners who live close by—other French speakers. Under these conditions, is it significant that 23 out of 100 marry someone with a different primary language? Some researchers think so and conclude that this figure indicates a low level of identity among French speakers.[7] Does a French speaker marrying outside his or her linguistic group necessarily have a low identity with other French speakers? Perhaps marriage to a spouse who speaks another language actually increases a person's linguistic identity, even if that person uses the spouse's language in daily life. Take the example of a man from Geneva who is married to a German-speaking wife and both are living in Zürich. Even if he speaks German with his wife, he may develop a stronger French-speaking identity than when he lived back home in Geneva. He may become more aware that as a French speaker, he has different values from German speakers. Of course, it is also possible that, in many cases, marriages between linguistic groups do, indeed, indicate a low level of linguistic identities. This discussion again shows the difficulty of interpreting data to measure cultural fragmentation.

Although surveys and intermarriage data may speak to the strength of subcultural identity, additional data are necessary to determine how a subcultural identity is expressed in a politically relevant way. To be politically relevant, a subcultural identity must find some form of organizational expression. Do French speakers in Switzerland have their own political party? This is not the case, and all attempts to establish such a party have failed. Does this mean that French speakers do not operate as an organized force in Swiss politics? Not quite. Looking at the Swiss party system in more detail, we see that French speakers often form a coherent subgroup in the national political parties. Thus, linguistic identities are expressed not among but within parties. Also, there are always some issues in the national parliament on which French speakers vote more or less as a bloc.

We should also determine to what extent the three other linguistic groups in Switzerland have identities that are expressed in a politically relevant way. Based on the data from all four groups, we could then make a judgment about Switzerland's linguistic fragmentation. Such a judgment is obviously much more difficult than measuring the annual snowfall in a country. Meteorologists have commonly accepted yardsticks, but no such measure exists for linguistic fragmentation; rather, constant debate continues in the literature about how best to measure the level of fragmentation. Because agreement has not been reached, it is not surprising that some authors classify Switzerland as linguistically quite homogeneous, whereas others see it as relatively fragmented. As a consequence, there is no agreement on exactly what the Swiss case tells us. For some researchers, Switzerland is a good test case for consociational theory because it is linguistically fragmented. For others, however, Switzerland is irrelevant for the theory because it has no potentially destabilizing fragmentation.

Such difficulties of classification also emerge for other countries. To be sure, it is generally agreed that Northern Ireland is highly fragmented and that Denmark is homogeneous, but what about the linguistic cleavage in Canada, or the racial cleavage in the United States? Are these rifts so deep that the two countries qualify as test cases for consociational theory? Is the racial cleavage in the United States deeper than the linguistic cleavage in Switzerland? How are cleavages compared if they are based on different attributes, such as language and race? Does a marriage across linguistic lines have the same meaning as one across racial lines? Such questions indicate once again the difficulty in measuring fragmentation.

Similar difficulties appear in trying to determine the prevailing political decision mode within a country. Again, the language situation in Switzerland serves as a good illustration. If we begin with the composition of the executive cabinet, the Federal Council, as an indicator, decision making among the language groups seems to be consociational. Although German speakers comprise 70 percent of the population with Swiss nationality, they never have more than five seats, and most often only four, in the seven-member Federal Council. Two or three seats always go to the linguistic minorities. This rule is not based on a constitutional article or a law but on custom and tradition, which guide the members of parliament when they elect members to the Federal Council. The principle that linguistic minorities get a proportionate share is applied to virtually all government positions. In the Swiss army, for example, there are seven 3-star generals; usually these positions are held by four German speakers, two

French speakers, and one Italian speaker, which even gives some overrepresentation to the minorities. Federalism, another consociational device, is also strongly developed in Switzerland (see Chapter 7).

Are these indicators sufficient for classifying decision making among Swiss language groups as consociational? Many researchers think so, but perhaps we should look more closely at how decisions are actually made. The linguistic minorities may have two or three representatives in the Federal Council, but they can still lose if the council makes its decisions in a majoritarian way. Decision making in the Federal Council is, in principle, treated as confidential, but occasionally there are leaks about how a particular decision was made. In the past, it seems that decisions were rarely made by majority vote, but rumors have it that it is now more common that a majority outvotes a minority in the Federal Council. This development shows that the pattern of decision making may change over time, so that one has to be careful to clarify the time period when making a definitive statement.

The picture is clearer for parliament, where deliberations are open to the public. In many cases, the Swiss parliament makes unanimous or near-unanimous decisions. Such cases have often been studied by consociational authors, who use them as illustrations to support their theory. However, in many other cases, Swiss parliament takes close votes, and such votes sometimes pit a German-speaking majority against the linguistic minorities. In Chapter 7, on federalism, we mention a few such cases. How frequent are they? Do they involve essential or only marginal issues for the linguistic minorities? If such votes occur, are some concessions nevertheless made to the minorities, or are they simply outvoted? These questions show that it is not a simple matter to measure the degree of consociational and majoritarian decision making.

Decision making among Swiss linguistic groups is certainly more consociational than is decision making among ethnic groups in Northern Ireland. But, if we compare the level of consociationalism in Switzerland and Austria, the judgment is much more difficult. And what about the United States? How consociational are relations between whites, African Americans and Hispanics? Is it significant that a tradition seems to have developed to have at least one African American or one Hispanic on the Supreme Court or perhaps even one from each side? Can this be seen as a consociational device?

Of all the variables contained in consociational theory, the degree of democratic stability is the most problematic to measure. Switzerland, for example, seems democratically very stable. Very little civil violence and disorder arises from the language question.[8] This seems to indicate that all language groups accept the democratic legitimacy of the political order. In the consociational literature, it is commonly accepted without much further inquiry that Switzerland is a stable democracy. Other literature, inspired by a Marxist view, ranks the democratic quality of Switzerland much lower. Its basic argument is that consociational arrangements are merely a ruse to cover up the real power structure. The most extreme formulation of this argument stems from sociologist and left-wing Socialist Jean Ziegler, who claims that essential power in Switzerland rests with the bankers in Zürich.[9] Ziegler speaks of structural violence against the working class and the linguistic minorities, by which he means that these groups are repressed in such a subtle way that they are not even aware of it. In this view, consociational devices help to make legitimate the existing repressive order in the eyes of the large masses of the people.

Without going as far as Ziegler, other critics complain that economic power is increasingly concentrated in German-speaking Zürich. Consequently, representation of the linguistic minorities in governmental bodies becomes somewhat symbolic if they lose their say in the corporate headquarters. Federalism could become an empty shell if most of the important economic decisions are made in Zürich. Do such critiques indicate an increasing dissatisfaction among the linguistic minorities, perhaps even a potential for future unrest? Is Swiss democracy not as stable, after all, as it appears to the consociational authors? Again, no agreement can be found in the literature.

Is the fact that they cannot agree on how to measure the key variables of their theory a bad sign for the consociational scholars? Physicists had little difficulty in agreeing on the definition of a meter or a kilogram. But in physics, the observer and the object of observation are separated, although measurements by the observer may have some influence on the phenomena being studied. This is all the more so in the social sciences, where both observer and observed are human beings. When social scientists publish their results, these results may be read by the objects of the study. Social scientists in this way become actors in the world they observe. To take the example of consociational theory, when Ziegler teaches and writes that Switzerland is characterized by subtle repression, his students and readers may begin to perceive Swiss reality in this light. Similarly, perceptions may be influenced by descriptions of Switzerland as a stable democracy.

How a researcher defines and measures a political variable is influenced by that researcher's political values. For all researchers to have the same values is not a desirable goal. With a pluralism of values, researchers will naturally arrive at different results. The application of consociational theory to Switzerland is a good example in this respect. For some researchers, Switzerland is linguistically fragmented and only remains a stable democracy, thanks to the practice of power sharing. For others, Switzerland is relatively homogeneous, and consociational arrangements serve only to legitimize the power of a small, elite cartel. Such different interpretations are not due merely to errors of measurement but also to fundamental differences in the value premises on which the research is based. It is healthy that such fundamental differences are aired in scholarly debates, and it speaks well for consociational theory that it has led to heated but interesting and enlightening discussion.

Among all theories recently developed in political science, consociational theory is perhaps the one most widely applied to trouble spots all over the world. Arend Lijphart has served on several occasions as an influential consultant to politicians in deeply divided countries. In the media, the term *power sharing* is often used to express the idea of consociational decision making. What are the chances of power sharing in such troubled countries as Northern Ireland, Bosnia-Herzegovina, Ukraine, Afghanistan, Iraq, and Lebanon?

None of the consociational theorists, of course, is naive enough to think that it would be a simple matter for such countries to adopt the consociational solution and that everything would then be fine. The theory explicitly recognizes that some countries are so deeply fragmented that there is no hope for power sharing to work. In such cases, the result is often civil war among the subcultures or the establishment of an authoritarian regime by one of them. If fragmentation is not extreme but still very high, power sharing may provide a glimmer of hope, and, as the consociational authors argue, probably the only hope. Considering this reasoning, the outlook for countries such as Afghanistan and Iraq is not very optimistic. But any hope must be based on the notion of power sharing. These countries are so deeply divided that a majoritarian form of democracy is not a realistic option. The hatred among the subcultures is so great that none would accept an electoral defeat based on majority voting, fearing that the victor would unduly exploit its victory so that the opposition would never have a chance to win a future election. Power sharing, on the other hand, would allow each subculture to maintain some control over the country's decision making. As Lijphart formulates it, the realistic choice for many fragmented societies "is not between the British normative model of democracy and the consociational model, but between consociational democracy and no democracy at all."

Lijphart becomes impatient with people who are unduly pessimistic about power sharing, and he warns them that if nobody tries power sharing, it will certainly not be adopted:

> If everyone is convinced that power sharing cannot be applied, nobody will even try to introduce it, and consequently it will certainly not be adopted. Or if it is introduced in a particular multiethnic society, the conviction that it is bound to fail will kill any effort to make it succeed—and that will surely cause it to fail. It is vastly preferable to think of success and failure in terms of probabilities rather than absolutes.[10]

In the next section, we will look more closely at the chances of power sharing in deeply divided Northern Ireland. Then we will turn to former Czechoslovakia and former Yugoslavia.

NORTHERN IRELAND

As we have seen in Chapter 12, Northern Ireland is deeply divided into Protestant British Unionists and Catholic Irish Nationalists. A first application of consociational theory can be made for the time after 1921, when the Republic of Ireland obtained its independence and Northern Ireland remained British.[11] As we remember, Northern Ireland got autonomy within the United Kingdom, and a parliament (Stormont) with extensive powers was established in Belfast, the capital of Northern Ireland. We also remember that Protestants held a two-to-one majority and practiced democracy in the traditional British way—by applying the majority principle for both parliamentary elections and cabinet formation. Given their numerical dominance, they easily won one parliamentary election after another and exercised all the governmental power. The local prime minister and all his cabinet members always belonged to the Protestant subculture, while the Catholics remained politically impotent. Although Protestants had enough numerical strength to win parliamentary elections, they rigged the system even more to their advantage.

Consociational theory expects that in deeply divided countries the majoritarian model of democracy endangers political stability, and this is precisely what happened when civil strife began in 1968. Northern Ireland is a good illustration of why the majoritarian model will not work in deeply divided societies. The country's experience is a negative lesson telling us what should not be done. Sometimes it serves as good advice to learn what should *not* be done.

If the majoritarian model does not work in a deeply divided society, this does not necessarily mean, of course, that the power-sharing model will work. Consociational theory expects that the power-sharing model has at least a chance to be successful, and Northern Ireland has indeed had some success with this model, although problems still linger to some extent.

Inspired by the successful Swiss experience with power sharing, in the 1970s the British government tried to restore calm in Northern Ireland through a form of consociational power sharing. A cabinet of moderate Protestants and moderate Catholics was established in Northern Ireland, but within a few months a general strike of Protestant workers brought this initial experiment to a halt. The large majority of Protestants were not willing to change from a majoritarian to a consociational pattern of decision making. The Catholics, for their part, reacted with further civil strife.

Why was it such a slow process with many setbacks to introduce power sharing in Northern Ireland? Let us apply the list of facilitating conditions for power sharing that we established in the first section of this chapter to the Northern Irish situation in the 1970s. We note first that there was no overarching loyalty of Catholics and Protestants to Northern Ireland as a political unit. The Protestants wished to remain British, whereas the Catholics wanted to join the Republic of Ireland. Thus, it is appropriate to refer to Protestants as *British Unionists* and to Catholics as *Irish Nationalists*. There was no loyalty to a common land. In this respect, the situation was different from that in Switzerland, where Catholics and Protestants, German, French, Italian, and Romansh speakers have always felt members of one political community despite all their differences.

Power sharing might still have worked if other factors would have been favorable, but they were not. It would have been easier if Protestants and Catholics each had a comparable numerical strength, as the blacks and reds in Austria did when forming their grand coalition in 1945. An even more favorable condition would have been three or four subcultures and none in a majority; this was the situation in the Netherlands when power sharing was introduced successfully. Northern Ireland had the most unfavorable condition with only two subcultures and one in a clearly dominant numerical position.

The fact that no clear territorial boundaries existed in Northern Ireland between Protestants and Catholics was a further unfavorable condition for power sharing. The two groups lived interspersed in the same cities, towns, and villages: One street was Protestant, another street Catholic. The lack of **spatial separation** made it impossible to apply the consociational device of subcultural territorial autonomy, in which the subcultures themselves could have regulated much of their own internal affairs. In this context a comparison can be made to Belgium, where relations between Flemish and Walloons are most problematic in Brussels, the city in which the two communities have no clear boundaries. The old saying that "good fences make good neighbors" seems to have some validity, although one must be careful not to overgeneralize in this respect. Good fences may also mean segregation with negative consequences.

A further negative factor in Northern Ireland in the 1970s was the internal rivalries and quarrels within both the Catholic and Protestant leadership. Neither group had uncontested leaders who could speak authoritatively for it. Therefore, neither subculture had representatives who could make deals that were also binding on their own members. An attempt by a political leader to negotiate a compromise with the other side was likely to be that leader's kiss of political death within his or her own group, because competing leaders would exploit such a step as weakness. The result was a tendency for the leaders of each side to outbid each other for the most extreme position.

Still another obstacle to power sharing in Northern Ireland was the region's many unresolved problems, especially a desperate economic situation characterized by a high rate of unemployment.

A seemingly easy way out would have been a territorial separation, with Protestants remaining in the United Kingdom and Catholics joining the Republic of Ireland. Unfortunately, this solution was not feasible because the communities of Catholics and Protestants were so highly interspersed. Massive resettlements, impossible from a practical perspective and morally repugnant, would have been required. In 1989, the political scientist Richard Rose expressed the view that a solution may be impossible:

> Northern Ireland is a challenge to the comforting belief that describing a situation as a problem guarantees the existence of a solution. In this strife-torn land where the United Kingdom meets the Republic of Ireland, there is no solution—if a solution is defined as a form of government that is consensual, legitimate, and stable.[12]

Since 1989, however, when Richard Rose expressed this pessimistic view, some positive developments happened in Northern Ireland. One first glimmer of hope was the rally for peace in Dublin in 1993 after a terrorist attack carried out by the Irish Republican Army (IRA) killed two children in England. A month after this peace rally, the IRA launched another attack in the very heart of London. Increasingly, violence has also been used by the Protestant side in Northern Ireland, in particular by the Ulster Freedom Fighters and the Ulster Defense Association. Both organizations have been outlawed by the British government, but they continued their terrorist activities.

A positive sign was the increasingly close collaboration between Great Britain and the Republic of Ireland with regard to Northern Ireland.

On December 15, 1993, the prime minister of Great Britain, John Major, and his counterpart in the Republic of Ireland, Albert Reynolds, signed a Joint Declaration on Northern Ireland. In this declaration, Great Britain concedes that it has no strategic or economic interests in Northern Ireland, which may join the Republic of Ireland if it wishes. The Republic of Ireland, on the other hand, concedes that any change in the status quo needs the support of a majority in Northern Ireland, thus giving to the Northern Irish Protestants a veto power. These were important principles articulated in a spirit of cooperation between London and Dublin.

Another positive sign in the Northern Irish conflict was the declaration of a cease-fire by the IRA on August 31, 1994. In its announcement, the IRA wrote:

> Recognizing the potential of the current situation and in order to enhance the democratic peace process and underline our definitive commitment to its success, the leadership of the I.R.A. have decided that as of midnight Wednesday, August 31, there will be a complete cessation of military operations. All our units have been instructed accordingly. At this historic crossroads, the leadership of the I.R.A. salutes and commends our volunteers, other activists, our supporters and the political prisoners who have sustained this struggle, against all odds, for the past 25 years. Your courage, determination and sacrifices have demonstrated that the spirit of freedom and the desire for peace based on a just and lasting settlement cannot be crushed. We remember all those who have died for Irish freedom and we reiterate our commitment to our republican objectives.[13]

The paramilitary organizations of the Protestants, the Ulster Freedom Fighters, and the Ulster Defense Association joined the cease-fire shortly afterward. On October 4, 1994, Gerry Adams, president of Sinn Féin, the political arm of the IRA, wrote on the op-ed page of the *New York Times*:

> It happened in the Middle East and South Africa, and now it is happening in Ireland. The momentous events of the past five weeks, starting with the Irish Republican Army's cease-fire on August 31, make it clear that people in power finally understand that the ability to live together—and to work out a political framework that accommodates different perspectives—is the greatest gift they can pass on to future generations....The Unionists have as much right to the land of Ireland as we have. I appeal to my Protestant brothers and sisters to join us in the search for a settlement acceptable to all Irish people—for a constitution that, like America's, includes checks and balances and a bill of rights with full protection for Ireland's minorities.[14]

Despite the conciliatory tone, neither the cease-fire announcement of the IRA nor Gerry Adams's article renounced the goal of a united Ireland. What the Protestants were offered was a constitution and a bill of rights protecting them as a minority in a united Ireland, but most Protestants still wanted to stay within Great Britain. Thus, in the fall of 1994, nothing was settled, but at least the killing had stopped. After several setbacks in the peace process, a great breakthrough came with the **Good Friday Agreement** in the spring of 1998.

Preceding this accord, intense international pressures acted on the warring parties. These pressures came from the governments of London and Dublin, which were working increasingly closely to bring about a solution to the troubles in Northern Ireland. Even more important, strong pressure came from the United States. President Bill Clinton invited the leaders of both sides several times to Washington, DC, where he did some heavy arm-twisting. Here is an issue for discussion: Was this intervention of President Clinton in the Northern Ireland conflict a good example of how the United States should exercise its influence in the world?

For the actual negotiations, former U.S. Senator George Mitchell was of crucial importance. At first, the leaders of the Catholic and Protestant groups were not even willing to talk with each other. Thus, Mitchell met separately with the two sides to find some common ground. An important step was when Catholic and Protestant leaders were willing to shake hands. Gerry Adams on the Catholic side and David Trimble on the Protestant side emerged as the key leaders who dared to make some steps toward each other. This was indeed a daring enterprise because both of these leaders had to fear for their lives—they were now considered as traitors by extremists within their groups. The Good Friday Agreement resulting from these negotiations contained the following stipulations:

Elections to the local parliament in Northern Ireland, the Stormont, shall be held according to principles of proportionality.

For the executive cabinet, all major political parties shall form a grand coalition.

The Republic of Ireland eliminates from its constitution the claim that Northern Ireland is part of the Republic of Ireland.

Although having a large amount of local autonomy, Northern Ireland remains a part of the United Kingdom. If one day, however, the people in Northern Ireland express their wish to join the Republic of Ireland, the United Kingdom shall honor this wish and let Northern Ireland go.

A Joint Irish–Northern Irish Council shall be established, which will have the power to deal with practical matters of importance to both sides of the border such as tourism, the environment, traffic, and agriculture.

The Good Friday Agreement was written in a spirit of accommodation and contained key power-sharing elements, in particular the principles of proportionality and grand coalitions. There was a "give and take" in the sense that the Republic of Ireland gave up its constitutional claim on Northern Ireland, and in return the United Kingdom accepted that Northern Ireland could one day join the Republic of Ireland if the people of Northern Ireland decided to do so. The Good Friday Agreement was put to a popular referendum for the citizens of Northern Ireland and was overwhelmingly accepted, with clear majorities among both Catholics and Protestants.

An important further step was made on November 17, 1999, when the two major political parties in Northern Ireland, the Ulster Unionists on the Protestant side and Sinn Féin on the Catholic side, made conciliatory public statements.[15] A key passage of the statement of the Ulster Unionists reads as follows:

> It is our belief that the establishment of the new political institutions and the disarmament of all paramilitary organisations will herald a new beginning for all sections of our people—a new, peaceful and democratic society, free from the use or threat of force.... Both of our traditions have suffered as a result of our conflict and division. This is a matter of deep regret and makes it all the more important that we now put the past behind us.

In similar accommodative terms, Sinn Féin states:

> Sinn Féin is totally committed to the implementation of the Good Friday agreement in all its aspects. We believe that the wholehearted implementation of the agreement has the capacity to transform the existing situation through constructive and dynamic political development. It is an unprecedented opportunity to start afresh. An opportunity to put behind us the failures, the tragedy, and the suffering of the past. There is no doubt that we are entering into the final stages of the resolution of the conflict.

Shortly after the publication of these two statements, in February 2000, the power-sharing cabinet began to operate with the Protestant David Trimble as first minister. But in Northern Ireland nothing is ever as simple as it sounds. There was still one sticking point not addressed in the Good Friday Agreement— namely, the disarmament of all paramilitary forces, called *decommissioning* in Northern Ireland. Decommissioning was so sensitive that no solution could be envisaged in the agreement.

Decommissioning was an issue for both Protestant and Catholic paramilitary forces. However, it had particular urgency for the Catholic IRA because Protestants were unwilling to cooperate as long as the IRA was not disarmed, and because Protestants were the majority in the country, they had more leverage than the Catholics on the issue of decommissioning. The IRA was in principle willing to decommission, but in a way that it should not be seen as a humiliating military defeat. Many Protestants, on the other hand, were precisely interested in humiliating the IRA. An attempt was made to proceed with the disarmament of the IRA under the supervision of international mediators under the chairmanship of Canadian General John de Chastelain. These mediators certified on September 27, 2005, that the IRA had destroyed its weapons. As de Chastelain put it, "We are satisfied that the arms decommissioned represent the totality of the IRA arsenal."[16] But this was not enough for Protestant extremists, who insisted that this turning in of weapons should occur in public, which the IRA rejected as an attempt to humiliate its members. The leader of these extremists, the Reverend Ian Paisley, exclaimed: "Instead of openness, there was the cunning tactics of cover-up and a complete failure by General de Chastelain to deal with the vital numerics of decommissioning."[17] By this Paisley meant that it was not in the public eye how many weapons the IRA had and how many of them were actually destroyed.

The cycle of violence had not yet completely come to an end. There was, for example, an incident in which Protestants rioted because a parade by the

Protestant Orange Order was banned from passing through Catholic neighborhoods. Such incidents reveal how deep-seated feelings of hostility still thrived in Northern Ireland. To have the right kind of power-sharing institutions is not enough. What is also needed is an improvement in the culture of mutual mistrust and hostile feelings. And such improvements take a long time, certainly in Northern Ireland.

Quite miraculously and unexpectedly, such an improvement happened in the spring of 2007. The key actor was the Protestant firebrand, the Reverend Ian Paisley, who all of a sudden became accommodative toward the Catholics. Many observers, including the authors of this book, had already feared that Paisley had to die before any progress was possible. After all, during his entire political life, Paisley had vehemently fought the Catholics, refusing even to talk with them. For Paisley, Catholics were of the devil, as he repeatedly said in public. What had brought about the dramatic change? Was it the wisdom of old age, with Paisley now 81? Nobody really knows; one may only speculate on what had changed in the internal world of Paisley. On May 8, 2007, Paisley became first minister of Northern Ireland. (This is the official title for Northern Ireland to differentiate it from the prime minister in London.) Deputy First Minister Martin McGuinness of the Catholic side was at one time one of the military leaders in the IRA. The speeches of the former deadly enemies were truly remarkable. Paisley exclaimed:[18]

> How true are the words of Holy Scripture, 'We know not what a day may bring forth.' If anyone had told me that I would be standing here today to take his office, I would have been totally unbelieving. I am here by the vote of the majority of the electorate of our beloved Province.... Today at long last we are starting upon the road—I emphasise starting—which I believe will take us to lasting peace in our Province.

McGuinness was not less positive:

> We strive towards a society moving from division and disharmony to one which celebrates our diversity and is determined to provide a better future for all our people.... As for Ian Paisley, I want to wish you all the best as we step forward towards the greatest yet most exciting challenges of our lives.

After he was sworn in, Paisley was even willing to travel to Catholic Ireland and to shake hands with its prime minister. But it must also be noted that despite the friendly words and actions, both leaders insisted that the ultimate goals for Northern Ireland had not changed deep in their minds. Paisley told his listeners on May 8, 2007: "I have not changed my unionism, the union of Northern Ireland with the United Kingdom, which I believe is today stronger than ever." McGuinness, for his part, just took the opposite position in stating that he believes "absolutely in a United Ireland." In June 2008 Paisley voluntarily withdrew from political life and was replaced as first minister by Peter Robinson, also a Protestant.

Although it took a very long time to reach this point, Northern Ireland is quite a success story for the implementation of the theory of power sharing.

Occasionally, however, there is still some remnant violence. Thus, in March 2009 an extremist splinter group of the IRA killed two British soldiers doing duty in front of their barracks (see Box 13.1). The charged political climate was revealed when all leadings politicians of the Catholic side immediately condemned this terrorist act with the strongest expressions. Despite all the progress, Northern Ireland remains a deeply divided society. In May 2009, one of us (Steiner) visited Belfast. He notes:

> Walking around in both Catholic and Protestant neighborhoods and talking with people, I heard that the mutual mistrust is still so high that almost everyone avoids going to the other side. In one particular neighborhood, only a highway separates Catholics and Protestants. An elderly Protestant man told me that in the past 40 years he had not set foot on the Catholic side of the highway.

FORMER CZECHOSLOVAKIA

A theory in political science can be used in a **postdictive** and a **predictive** way. *Postdiction* means that after an event has occurred, a theory is used to make sense of this event and to explain it in a post hoc way. With prediction, the theory is used to forecast an event. Political scientists oriented toward the natural science model of explanation claim that only successful predictions can say something about the validity of a theory. Political scientists oriented more toward the model of explanation used by historians work more with postdictions. Here is another issue for discussion: Which model is more appropriate for political science?

In the authors' view, both postdictions and predictions have a place in political science. Discussing the case of Northern Ireland, we used consociational theory in a postdictive way. The situation in former Czechoslovakia allows us to apply consociational theory in a predictive way. When consociational theory was formulated and developed in the 1960s and 1970s, Czechoslovakia was not considered because it was under Communist rule, so power sharing was not an option. When Communism was toppled in Central and Eastern Europe in 1989 (see Chapter 11), power sharing indeed became an option in Czechoslovakia because the country had two ethnic groups, Czechs and Slovaks. In an undergraduate honors seminar at the University of North Carolina at Chapel Hill, we used the list of favorable conditions for power sharing presented in the first section of the current chapter to make a prediction for Czechoslovakia. This prediction was published in the second edition of this textbook (1991, pp. 247–253) and stated that power sharing would be successful in Czechoslovakia.

At the time, we identified the numerical relationship between the Czechs and Slovaks as the only negative factor. Of the total population of the country, two-thirds were Czechs and one-third Slovaks. According to consociational theory, this is the worst possible situation, because the minority is at the mercy of the majority. Other factors, however, seemed more facilitating for power sharing in Czechoslovakia—for example, the nature of the boundaries between the two ethnic groups. The consociational theory is based on the old saying

BOX 13.1   ADAMS'S DISMAY AT ORANGE REJECTION

Sinn Fein leader Gerry Adams has described as "disappointing" the Orange Order's rejection of his call for direct talks between the organisations.

Grand Secretary of the Orange Order Drew Nelson, said there was "no prospect" of the leaderships meeting. Mr Nelson said if Sinn Fein was sincere Mr Adams should first apologise for the murders of Orangemen by the IRA. Mr Adams said Mr Nelson was "allowing his personal feelings to undermine his leadership responsibilities." "Republicans could put up exactly the same preconditions as Mr Nelson—we very consciously refrain from doing so," he said. Mr Adams had urged engagement with the Order's leadership in the wake of the violence in the Ardoyne area of north Belfast on Monday after a contentious Twelfth of July parade. He said it was time for the two sides to meet to work out a solution to six outstanding contentious parades. But Mr Nelson said: "There is no prospect of a meeting with Sinn Fein at any level in my opinion by the leadership of the Orange Order while they continue to justify and glorify the murders of our members," he said. "It would be entirely inappropriate to consider meeting with Sinn Fein until Gerry Adams or the leadership of Sinn Fein apologise for the IRA murders of the 275 Orangemen murdered during the Troubles by that terrorist group," he said. In response, Mr Adams said he had "never glorified IRA killings." "I have also stated my regrets at the deaths and injuries caused by republicans. This includes members of loyal institutions," he said. The West Belfast MP said Orange culture had a part to play in his vision of a united Ireland but that the six or seven parades which remain an annual source of tension could only be resolved through dialogue. "They (the Order) talk about being a Christian organisation, about neighbourliness, and I don't dissent from any of that and I don't say any of this to undermine the good decent people who were involved in the Orange, but why on earth can't they come forward and meet us?" he said. Mr Adams met Portadown Orangemen in 2008, a meeting which was criticised by the Orange leadership. ∎

Source: BBC News, July 17, 2009.

that "good fences make good neighbors." In 1990, Czechoslovakia had clear boundaries between Czechs and Slovaks; in the Czech Republic, there were only 3.8 percent Slovaks; in the Slovak Republic, only 1.1 percent were Czechs.[19] As a consequence—this is the argument of the theory—there should have been little potential for conflict in everyday life, which in turn should have facilitated power sharing at the elite level.

Another factor favorable for power sharing was the religious composition of Czechoslovakia. Of the people indicating a religious affiliation, 85 percent declared themselves Roman Catholic and 15 percent Protestant. This relative religious homogeneity should have helped to hold the country together across ethnic lines, and it should also have helped that the Protestant minority was not concentrated in one ethnic group but was about equally represented in both groups.

The relative economic equality between Czechs and Slovaks seemed still another factor favorable for power sharing. To be sure, as Jiří Musil points out, "The overall process of modernisation in Slovakia started later than in the Czech Lands."[20] But in recent times, the gap had narrowed; "from the macrostructural point of view, both societies became more and more alike."[21] By 1990, the per capita income in the Slovak Republic was 86 percent of the figure in the Czech Republic. For power sharing, it would certainly have been better if there were no economic gap at all. Czechoslovakia was clearly better off than many other multiethnic countries—for example, former Yugoslavia, to be discussed in the next section.

Another favorable condition for power sharing is an overarching loyalty to the country at large. As we will see in the next section, in this respect, too, Yugoslavia had very unfavorable preconditions. In Czechoslovakia, the situation was not ideal either, but it was much better than in Yugoslavia. Before 1918, both Czechs and Slovaks belonged to the Austro-Hungarian Empire, and thus already had a certain common history. After World War I and the demise of the Austro-Hungarian Empire, Czechoslovakia was created as an independent political unit, and in the interwar period practiced a quite successful democratic regime. During World War II the Nazis made Slovakia formally an independent country, but, in fact, they dominated both parts of Czechoslovakia. Under Communism, great efforts were made to downplay the ethnic differences between Czechs and Slovaks. In making our predictions in 1990, we assumed that the Czechs and Slovaks had developed a certain overarching loyalty to the country as a whole. This loyalty was bolstered by successful national sports teams, especially in ice hockey.

The consociational theory links the position of a country in the international system with the pattern of its domestic decision making. The specific hypothesis is that a common threat from abroad increases the likelihood of power sharing. An often-mentioned example is the presence of Soviet occupation troops in Austria from 1945 to 1955, which is said to have contributed to the Austrian power-sharing arrangement. In Czechoslovakia, even more common suffering stemmed from Soviet domination. Both Czechs and Slovaks were active in the dissident movement and often suffered together in the labor camps. This common fate is vividly described by Václav Havel in the letters to his wife, Olga, written from the labor camp in which he was imprisoned for subversion.[22] We assumed that this factor facilitated power sharing after the demise of Communism.

With 16 million people, Czechoslovakia was a relatively small country, which was yet another favorable factor for power sharing. Finally, the living standards in Czechoslovakia were relatively high compared with those of other former Communist countries. This, too, should have helped with power sharing. Our overall conclusion was that Czechs and Slovaks had quite good conditions to practice power sharing.

Initially, this prediction turned out to be true. The principle of proportionality was used for the first free elections that took place in June 1990, which was in accordance with consociational theory. Additionally, the Slovaks as the minority group got further protection. They had their own electoral district, and in the second chamber, the Chamber of Nationalities, they received the same number of seats as the Czechs. Cabinet formation also very much followed principles of power sharing, in the sense that each deputy minister had to be from the other ethnic group than the minister. If the minister of justice, for example, was a Slovak, the deputy minister of justice had to be a Czech, and vice versa. It was also of great symbolic value that when Havel as a Czech was made president of the country, great care was taken to ensure that the important position of president of parliament was filled by the Slovak Alexander Dubček. Havel also made many efforts to show that he was president of both Czechs and Slovaks—for example, opening a presidential office in the Slovak capital of Bratislava. With regard to the name of the country, sensitivities of the Slovaks were considered. As one Slovak deputy said in the deliberations on this issue, "When you are abroad, you always hear Czech, Czech, Czech. Slovakia is always left out."[23] To take care of such complaints, the cumbersome name Czech and Slovak Federative Republic was chosen, which expressed that the country had two distinct cultures.

In June 1992, the second free elections took place, and in the aftermath of these elections the country split into the Czech Republic and Slovakia. The key aspect of these elections was that the results were very different in the Czech and the Slovak parts of the country. Václav Klaus emerged as leader in the Czech Republic and Vladimir Mečiar[24] in Slovakia. Each could put together a winning party coalition in his part of the country, but these coalitions were of a very different nature.

Political scientist Herbert Kitschelt has located the two leaders in a two-dimensional space.[25] An economic dimension ranges from "spontaneous market allocation" to "political redistribution"; a cultural dimension from "libertarian-cosmopolitan" to "authoritarian-particularistic." *Libertarian* means to stress the importance of individual liberties; *cosmopolitan* means being open to the world. *Authoritarian* means obedience to authority rather than exercise of individual judgment; *particularistic* means to look after the interests of one's own group. Using Kitschelt's two dimensions, Klaus and Mečiar were exactly at opposite ends. Kitschelt characterizes Klaus as market-oriented and libertarian-cosmopolitan and Mečiar as economically redistributive and authoritarian-particularistic.

Separation was the outcome of the power struggle between these two leaders, neither of whom was willing to yield. Each recognized that the other could block him at the national level, but not within his own region. Thus, separation was ultimately in the political self-interest of both men. There were suggestions that the voters should decide the matter in a referendum. Opinion surveys indicated that the voters were for greater autonomy for both regions, but not for separation. Finally, the decisions were made by the politicians in very complex and sometimes obscure parliamentary maneuvers. Each side blamed the other for lack of flexibility, and separation was made against public opinion. To be sure, Czechs and Slovaks had expressed opposite political orientations in the June 1992 parliamentary elections, but they did not know at the time that these results would lead to separation.

What does this separation say about the validity of consociational theory? The theory always had a strong voluntaristic element in the importance it gives to the free will of leaders. The usual assumption is that the leaders of the various subcultures are more farsighted than the masses and that they use their free will to practice power sharing. In Czechoslovakia, the opposite happened. The leaders, against the wishes of the people, refused to share power, and they separated the country. Would the result have been different with leaders other than Mečiar and Klaus? Perhaps. There was perhaps a failure on the part of President Havel, who was personally committed to the unity of the country. He indeed tried to organize a popular referendum on the issue of separation. If the polls were correct, such a referendum would have gone against separation, but Havel lacked the necessary political skills to implement the idea of a referendum.

The factors identified in consociational theory allowed us to predict that at the mass level there would be a willingness to share power. To be sure, Czechs and Slovaks voted in the elections in opposite political directions, as mentioned above. The appropriate consociational reaction to these election results should have been to give more autonomy to each side. Federalism is, after all, a key element of consociationalism, but driven by Klaus and Mečiar, the development went all the way to separation. For a while, it seemed as though an economic and currency union would still be possible, but at the leadership level, the momentum for separation was simply too strong. It is important to note, however, that separation took place without any bloodshed and in an orderly, legal way. Political stability in the region was never really threatened. In this sense, the favorable conditions identified by consociational theory indeed had some positive effect. They could not prevent the "divorce," but at least they made it civilized. This is a good illustration of how sometimes it is difficult to judge whether a particular country fits or does not fit consociational theory.

FORMER YUGOSLAVIA

In Chapter 12 on nationalism and ethnicity, we described the intricacies of the situation in former Yugoslavia, how civil war broke out in 1991 and how the country fell apart. For Yugoslavia, too, in the fall of 1989, we made predictions about the chances of power sharing. In contrast to Czechoslovakia, for Yugoslavia we identified only one favorable factor for power sharing: the number and numerical strength of ethnic groups. With five to six major ethnic groups, none of which were in a majority position, Yugoslavia seemed at first sight well positioned to practice power sharing. One could expect a fluid multiple balance of power with changing coalitions. No group would be permanently left out, and none would always win. According to consociational theory, this seemed an ideal situation for power sharing.

All other factors, however, were unfavorable for power sharing. A first negative factor was that Yugoslavia lacked clear boundaries between the ethnic groups. There were six republics: Serbia, Croatia, Slovenia, Macedonia, Montenegro, and Bosnia-Herzegovina. The borders between these republics did not correspond to the ethnic boundaries. The most ethnically homogeneous republic was Slovenia, but even here only 90 percent of the people were Slovenes. In Croatia, 75 percent were Croats; in Montenegro, 69 percent Montenegrins; and in Macedonia, 67 percent Macedonians. The most heterogeneous republic was Bosnia-Herzegovina, with 39 percent Muslims (Bosniaks), 32 percent Serbs, 18 percent Croats, and the remaining 11 percent dispersed among other ethnic groups. Within Serbia, there were two autonomous provinces, Kosovo and Vojvodina. Kosovo was overwhelmingly Albanian; in Vojvodina there were many Hungarians. In Serbia proper, 85 percent were Serbs. Overall, Yugoslavia had very fluid boundaries among its ethnic groups, which, according to consociational theory, made power sharing difficult.

Another factor unfavorable for power sharing was the religious diversity of the country. As we have seen in Chapter 12, the three main groups were Christian Orthodox, Roman Catholic, and Muslim. What made the religious situation in Yugoslavia particularly difficult for power sharing was that Roman Catholics were concentrated in Slovenia and Croatia; Christian Orthodox in Serbia, Macedonia, and Montenegro; and Muslims in Bosnia-Herzegovina and Kosovo. Thus, religious cleavages were superimposed on ethnic cleavages, which is a much more explosive situation than if the two cleavage lines cut across each other. In Yugoslavia, religious conflicts could easily spill over into ethnic conflicts, and vice versa. To make matters worse, there was also a language cleavage superimposed on the two other cleavages: Slovenes and Croats used the Roman alphabet; the other ethnic groups used the Cyrillic script. Thus, how people wrote gave a clear indication early on as to which religious and ethnic groups they belonged.

There was a third factor unfavorable for power sharing in Yugoslavia—the huge economic inequality among the groups. Slovenia, on the Austrian border, had a per capita income that was about seven times higher than that in the autonomous province of Kosovo and about three times higher than that in Macedonia and Montenegro.

Yugoslavia also lacked an overarching loyalty among its people. As described in Chapter 12, after World War I it was put together out of disparate parts without any say of the local people. Slovenia, Croatia, and Bosnia-Herzegovina were remnants of the Austro-Hungarian Empire. The new country also included the Kingdom of Serbia and the Kingdom of Montenegro. This was a state with very little common history. It was therefore difficult for the people to develop overarching loyalties to the country as a whole.

With regard to the international situation of Yugoslavia, the key element was that under the leadership of Marshal Tito, the country liberated itself in 1948 from Soviet domination. Yugoslavia remained Communist, but it had no Soviet soldiers on its soil. Therefore, after World War II, there was no common suffering from foreign occupation, which could have brought the various ethnic groups closer together.

Another negative factor for power sharing was the poverty of the country. Measured by per capita income, Yugoslavia was twice as poor as Czechoslovakia. After 1985, a particularly severe financial and economic crisis hit Yugoslavia. The poor economic situation of the country was also expressed in such indicators as high infant mortality (25 deaths per 1,000 live births in Yugoslavia, compared with 13 in Czechoslovakia).

A final factor, the size of the population, could be considered as neutral in its influence on power sharing. With a population of 24 million, Yugoslavia was a midsized country in the European context.

Overall, in our undergraduate honors seminar at the University of North Carolina at Chapel Hill in the fall of 1989, we came to the prediction that Yugoslavia had little chance for power sharing. Even more darkly, we predicted that "(t)he country is now confronted with the danger of disintegration."[26] Although we did not expect the horrendous atrocities that occurred in the civil war (see Chapter 12), our analysis led us correctly to the prediction that the country would disintegrate. Here is a third issue for discussion: Could such a prediction have been made without the analytical help of consociational theory? Would other political science theories have been equally or even more accurate? It should be noted that the disintegration of Yugoslavia came as a great surprise to the international community, whose attention at the time was elsewhere, in particular on East Germany, the disintegration of the Soviet Union, and the treaty on European Union (informally known as the Maastricht treaty; for the latter, see Chapter 14).

Although power sharing was not even attempted for Yugoslavia at large, it may still work for some of the new nations emerging from the breakdown of the country. In this respect, there are great hopes for Bosnia-Herzegovina. After its extremely bloody civil war, attempts were made to establish a regime of power sharing. The international community still works hard in this direction. What are the chances for success? As we remember from Chapter 12, there are three major groups in Bosnia-Herzegovina—39 percent of the people are Muslims (Bosniaks) who identify themselves by their religion, 32 percent Serbs (who are Christian Orthodox), and 18 percent Croats (who are Roman Catholic).

The United Nations was the first international organization to try to bring the civil war in Bosnia-Herzegovina to an end. The U.S. government was at first hesitant to take an active part in the Bosnian conflict. This began to change in February 1994, when the United States supported an ultimatum issued by the United Nations to the Serbs to withdraw their heavy weapons within 12 miles of Sarajevo or hand them over to the United Nations. The same ultimatum required Muslims to put their heavy weapons under U.N. control. The ultimatum was set for February 21, at 1 A.M. local time, and North Atlantic Treaty Organization (NATO) forces under U.S. command were charged to execute air strikes against targets not in compliance. Despite bad weather with heavy snow, the ultimatum worked. Some credit also went to the Russians, who put pressure on their fellow Christian Orthodox Serbs. Russian U.N. troops were moved into the Sarajevo area, which gave the Serbs additional assurance. Two days after the ultimatum, the *New York Times* published a front-page picture showing residents strolling through the streets of Sarajevo and the caption "A Respite from Fear for Sarajevans."[27]

With this success, the United Nations became more assertive. On February 28, 1994, it took a decisive step to enforce the no-fly zone over

Bosnia-Herzegovina. Such a no-fly zone was supposed to have been in effect from the previous April, but there were numerous violations from all warring factions. As with the ultimatum for Sarajevo, NATO, under the leadership of the United States, was charged with the enforcement of the zone. In the morning hours of February 28, 1994, American F-16 fighter jets discovered six Serbian light attack aircraft in the process of bombing a munitions plant controlled by the Muslims. After ignoring two warnings, four of the Serbian aircraft were shot down, while two escaped. This was the first time in the organization's 44-year history that NATO forces were involved in a military clash.

After these two incidents, in which the international community had threatened and actually used military force, things began to move also on the diplomatic front. The United States brought about an agreement between Muslim and Croatian representatives who had come to Washington. The agreement was that Muslims and Croats in Bosnia-Herzegovina should join in a federation. The federation of Muslims and Croats would be made up of cantons in which the majority of the population would either be Muslim or Croatian. These cantons would have authority over police, education, culture, housing, public services, tourism, and radio and television. The federation would be responsible for foreign affairs and national defense. At the signing ceremony in Washington, DC, on March 18, 1994, President Clinton said, "The agreements signed today offer one of the first clear signals that parties of this conflict are willing to end the violence and begin a process of reconstruction."[28] However, this accord did not address the situation of the Serbs in Bosnia-Herzegovina. For President Clinton this was the next step, and he warned that "Serbia and the Serbs in Bosnia cannot sidestep their own responsibility to achieve an enduring peace."[29]

During March 1994, there were more hopeful signs on the ground. The siege of Sarajevo was lifted to some extent and a few residents could leave the city, although only with special permits. In the city itself, the bridge linking the Muslim and the Serbian neighborhoods was opened again. There was even a soccer game between a local team and a team of the United Nations. However, in other parts of Bosnia-Herzegovina, there were still disturbing signs of violence, and war again broke out on a large scale; it took another year and a half, to the fall of 1995, until an accord could be reached in Dayton, Ohio, to end the war. Massive military interventions by NATO forces were necessary to achieve this result. These interventions came in reaction to a horrendous shelling of the Sarajevo marketplace on August 28, 1995. The reaction of the NATO forces was quick and, this time, very powerful.

On October 5, 1995, Bosnia's warring parties set a cease-fire brought about by the United States, and the leaders of Bosnia-Herzegovina, Croatia, and Serbia were invited for peace talks in Dayton. After fierce negotiations, an accord was signed on November 1, 1995, by Secretary of State Warren Christopher for the United States, Alija Izetbegovic'; for Bosnia-Herzegovina, Slobodan Milošević for Serbia, and Franjo Tudjman for Croatia. The peace accord was formally signed on December 14, 1995, in a ceremony in Paris in the presence of President Clinton and other world leaders.

The highlights of the **Dayton Accord** include the following stipulations:

The warring parties must withdraw their forces behind the agreed cease-fire lines.

Sixty thousand peacekeepers under NATO command, headed by an American general, monitor the cease-fire and control the airspace. About a third of the peacekeepers will be Americans.

Persons indicted by the international tribunal as war criminals cannot hold office.

Refugees have the legal right to reclaim their homes or to receive compensation.

Bosnia-Herzegovina maintains its current borders, and a constitution creates a central government according to power-sharing principles.

Bosnia-Herzegovina is divided into two subentities, the Federation of Muslims and Croats with 51 percent of the territory and the Serb Republic with 49 percent of the territory. Each subentity has its own governmental institutions.

Officials at all levels are to be chosen in internationally supervised elections. Elections in Bosnia-Herzegovina were held on September 14, 1996. They went relatively smoothly, certainly better than many had feared. The elections were supervised by the Conference on Security and Cooperation in Europe. Despite some irregularities, this organization declared the election results valid, which opened the door for the elected officials to assume their duties. The presidency consisted of three members, with one seat reserved for each ethnic group. The Muslims elected Alija Izetbegovic´, the Croats Krešimir Zubak, and the Serbs Momc´ilo Krajišnik. These three men all represented not moderate but nationalistic parties within their ethnic groups. Having received the most votes, Izetbegovic´ chaired the presidency, but this did not give him more power because each member of the presidency had veto power. In the Bosnian national parliament, it was also a victory of the nationalist parties of the three ethnic groups, and here, too, each group had veto power. Another element of power sharing was that a Muslim and a Serb rotate on a weekly basis in the prime ministership and that a Croat was made speaker of parliament. If we add the federalist structure of the country, all formal elements of power sharing were assembled. Does this mean that the international community was able to impose a regime of power sharing on the warring factions? On paper, this was true, but it was altogether another question whether power sharing would work in praxis.

As we remember from the first section of this chapter, successful power sharing is not only a matter of the right institutions but also of the right spirit of accommodation. And in this respect, much was left to be desired. Having gone through a bloody civil war, it was difficult for Serbs, Croats, and Muslims to find trust in each other, an important precondition for successful power sharing. But there are at least two factors that should facilitate power sharing in the long run. Having three major ethnic groups with none of them controlling a majority of the population is considered a good precondition for power sharing. The small size of the country, about 4 million people, also speaks for successful power sharing. For the time being, however, the international presence is still necessary to keep the three groups from fighting again. Elections continue to favor extremist parties in all three ethnic groups, a bad sign for the stability of the country. In 2004, the responsibility for the international troops was transferred from NATO to the EU, and the number of American troops was greatly reduced. And here we have a fourth issue for discussion: Do you consider the military involvement of the United States in Bosnia-Herzegovina as a positive example of American foreign policy, or should the handling of the crisis have been left to Europeans?

In Kosovo, the prospects for power sharing are even less favorable than in Bosnia-Herzegovina. As we remember from Chapter 12, Kosovo did not have the status of a republic in the old Yugoslavia, but was rather merely an autonomous province within the Republic of Serbia. When Communism was toppled, Miloševic´, the Communist leader in Serbia, began to play the nationalistic card and abolished the autonomy of Kosovo. As we have seen in Chapter 12, the most important military battle of Serb history was fought on Kosovo land, and this land is considered sacred by Serb nationalists. Therefore, it was a shrewd move on the part of Miloševic´ to demonstrate his nationalism in bringing Kosovo under direct Serbian control. This control was exercised in a brutal and ruthless way with massacres, rapes, and expulsions against the Albanians, who at the time were about 90 percent of the Kosovo population, the remaining 10 percent being mainly Serbs and also quite a few Roma. In 1999, NATO, under American command, intervened—not with ground troops, but only with air power. It worked, and the Serb armed forces were driven back into Serbia proper. Shortly afterward, Miloševic´ was toppled and brought to the international war tribunal in The Hague; he died before his trial was brought to an end. After the Serbian troops had left, the Albanians in Kosovo committed, in their turn, brutal atrocities against the Serb and Roma minorities. With this background, it is understandable that power sharing is most difficult in Kosovo. The situation was further complicated because the Albanians demanded independence, whereas the Serbs wanted to keep Kosovo as part of Serbia.

In 2008, Kosovo went ahead and without prior international agreement declared its independence (see Box 13.2). Some countries including the United States recognized this independence, but other countries, in particular Russia, refused to accept Kosovo as an independent country. The strongest resistance came from Serbia which continues to consider Kosovo as part of Serbia. Serbs in Kosovo itself act as if they are still part of Serbia, using, for example, Serbian currency in daily life and Serbian license plates for their cars. They get financial and economic support from Serbia. Therefore, the crisis over Kosovo is far from over, although relatively little violence occurs. Serbia renounced to take back Kosovo with military means, but there are sometimes clashes between Albanians and Serbs.

In Macedonia, the situation is the opposite of that in Kosovo, with the Albanians in a minority and the Macedonians (who are ethnically close to the Serbs) in a majority. Although some violence flared between the two groups, it was much less than in Kosovo. Therefore, the chances for successful power sharing are better. A member of the Macedonian parliament brought home the point of what is the criterion for successful power sharing when he exclaimed: "We have improved the constitution to reduce ethnic conflicts, now we must improve the mentality that has caused these ethnic conflicts."[30] This is indeed the crucial point: Power-sharing institutions are necessary in a deeply divided society, but they are not enough; these institutions also need to be filled with an accommodative mentality, what is called a "spirit of accommodation" in consociational theory. In 2009, parliamentary elections in Macedonia were considered by international observers to be free and fair and with almost no violent incidents. The situation, however, is still precarious. There are increasingly fights on school grounds between Albanians and Macedonians, so much so that

▶ BOX 13.2   KOSOVO MARKS "INDEPENDENCE DAY"

Kosovo has marked the first anniversary of its unilateral declaration of independence from Serbia.

Parliament in Pristina held a special session at 1100 local time—the hour at which the declaration was made—while thousands celebrated outside. Prime Minister Hashim Thaci said it had been "a year of historic success." Serbia still refuses to recognize Kosovo and correspondents say parts of northern Kosovo remain tensely divided between ethnic Albanians and Serbs. MPs from the Serbian parliament in Belgrade attended the assembly set up by the Serb minority in protest at Tuesday's celebrations. Ethnic Albanians constitute 90 percent of Kosovo's 2 million people. Kosovo's unilateral declaration of independence last year has so far been recognized by only 54 of the UN's 192 countries, including the US, Japan and all but five of the 27 members of the European Union. Serbia, backed by Russia, has refused to recognise the declaration and has challenged its legality at the UN's International Court of Justice. In a BBC interview, Kosovo's president, Fatmir Sejdiu, said he expected other nations to join those who had so far recognized its independence, even though the government was not yet in control of all of its territory. "Kosovo's independence represents the most rational step of its own time, as it gave its people the chance to live in freedom and peace with its neighbors, and aspirations to integrate into the bigger European family," he said. Mr Sejdiu said Kosovo had paid particular care to safeguard the rights of minorities and wanted to be the "fatherland for all its citizens." As parliament held a special session on Tuesday morning, Prime Minister Thaci told MPs that this was the "biggest and most important holiday for the people of Kosovo." "The year we left behind was a year of achievement and of pride. It was a year of historic success for our country," he said. Outside, thousands of people gathered to mark the anniversary, many waving Kosovo's new flag and banners saying "happy birthday." For ethnic Albanians this is the chance not just to celebrate but also to remember those who died fighting for independence, the BBC's Helen Fawkes in Pristina says. The Serb population, however, is ignoring the

(Continued)

> ### ▶ BOX 13.2 CONTINUED
>
> anniversary—for them, Kosovo's breakaway from Serbia was an illegal act and it is still part of Serbia, she adds.
>
> 'Fragile'
> Albanian leaders say the Serbs are being constantly encouraged by the authorities in Belgrade to boycott and reject any offers coming from Pristina. On Tuesday, in defiance of the anniversary celebrations, Serbian deputies travelled from Belgrade to the northern Kosovo municipality of Zvecan, which is controlled by Serbs, to attend a session of their alternative parliament. Meanwhile, Serbian President Boris Tadic vowed that his country would never recognize the independence of its former province and would defend its "legitimate rights by legal and diplomatic means, not force." "Kosovo is not a country," he said in a statement. The Serb minority and their religious sites are currently protected by a NATO-led force. Also helping to keep order is the EU's largest ever police and justice mission, Eulex, which deployed in December. ■
>
> *Source: BBC News,* February 17, 2009.

school authorities take measures to segregate the two groups of students; for example, teaching one group in the morning and the other in the afternoon.[31]

POWER SHARING AND DELIBERATION

The Macedonian member of parliament quoted at the end of the last section goes to the core issue of the consociational theory of power sharing. It is not enough to have power-sharing institutions; there must also be a **cooperative mentality** among the people who make up these institutions. What concept shall we use to designate such a mentality? The usual concept used in consociational literature, "spirit of accommodation," is unfortunately rather vague. As a consequence, it was never possible to use this concept for empirical investigations in a valid and reliable way. No good measurements were ever developed to get an empirical handle on the concept. Therefore, empirical research on consociationalism was always strong on institutional aspects but weak on the cultural aspects of attitudes and values.

The challenge for future research is to replace the concept of spirit of accommodation with a concept that is theoretically more grounded. In recent years, one of the authors (Steiner) has participated in a research group that has replaced the concept of spirit of accommodation with the concept of **deliberation**. This concept is widely used in the philosophical literature, where initially it has mainly been developed by Jürgen Habermas,[32] although today many other philosophers contribute to the discussion on the deliberative model of democracy. The key aspect of the model is that politics is not seen exclusively as a power game of personal and group interests but also as a place where the force of the better argument has some weight. Thus, it does not only matter who has more power, but also who has the better arguments. What a good argument is, is not a priori given but must first be found out in a mutual discourse. As many people as possible should be involved in such a discourse, including ordinary citizens. Arguments must be logically justified so that a rational dialogue can emerge. All actors should be sincere and truthful in their statements, not misleading and trying to deceive others. Arguments should be framed in terms of the common good, and all arguments should be treated with great respect. In reality, no political debate will ever reach this ideal type of deliberation. The empirical question will always be how close or how far away a particular political debate is from this ideal type.

In our research group, we investigate under what conditions some minimal level of deliberation can be attained in the deeply divided European societies of Bosnia-Herzegovina and Belgium, outside Europe in Colombia. To measure the level of deliberation, we have developed a special index that we call the Discourse Quality Index (DQI).[33] To explain variation in the level of deliberation, we look at psychological factors such as a sense of tolerance. We also investigate whether prior information on the deliberative model has an influence on the level of deliberation. Furthermore, we investigate whether decision rules influence the level of deliberation. As a research method, we use experiments with participants on all sides of the deep cleavages in these societies.[34]

We hope that our research will have a practical impact on the potential for democracy in deeply divided societies. One possibility is to include research results on deliberation in textbooks for schools at all levels, from kindergarten to college. The Organization for Security and Cooperation in Europe (OSCE), for example, is interested to develop new textbooks for Bosnia-Herzegovina that will be used by all groups, Serbs, Croats, and Muslims (Bosniaks). When children learn that politics is not always only a matter of power but that sometimes a good logical argument for the common good counts, too, they may later be willing to listen to the arguments of others. If such a willingness emerges, people from other groups appear also as human beings with reasoning capabilities. Such processes of mutual humanization should reduce the risk that one kills people simply because they belong to other ethnic, racial, religious, or language groups.

NORMATIVE EVALUATION OF POWER SHARING

The concept of power sharing has become very much a part of the everyday political discourse in many countries around the world. Consociational scholars are involved in consulting activities in many places. Thus, we deal with a field of political science that is very much linked to political praxis. This closeness makes it urgent that we reflect carefully on the normative implications of the power-sharing model.[35] One critique of the model is that ordinary citizens have too little say if the elites work so closely together. A common criticism is that power sharing really amounts to an elite cartel. Are the relations among the elites not so cozy and secretive that they are tempted to look out primarily for their own interests, to the detriment of the interests of ordinary citizens? How can citizens hold the ruling elites accountable if they cannot replace them with a set of elites in opposition?

We agree with the critics that there is a danger in consociational countries that the elites are in too cozy a relationship with each other, mutually protecting their respective fiefdoms. In the German language, the term *Filz* ("felt") nicely captures this aspect of a close-knit elite cartel. Power sharing, however, does not necessarily mean that power rests with a closed elite cartel. It is certainly true that in its initial formulation consociationalism meant the making of deals among the elites behind closed doors, but in a modern form, consociationalism can very well be made compatible with a spirited public discourse about the political differences in a grand coalition. If the participants in a grand coalition are willing to respect each other's opinions, an open public discourse may very well occur. Thus, citizens may learn where the various partners in a grand coalition stand on specific issues. If, furthermore, a strong referendum is combined with a grand coalition, the danger of undue elitism can be reduced. With a strongly developed referendum, a competitive element is added to consociationalism. The role of opposition is taken up not by an opposition party like in the Westminster model but directly by the citizens. Citizens can inform themselves about the various policy alternatives discussed in the grand coalition, and then make a final decision on key issues of the political agenda.

We agree with the critique that the concept of democratic stability, so central to consociational theory, is problematic or at least misleading. If democratic stability simply means that democracy is maintained, the concept is not problematic. However, such a definition only begs the question of what exactly is meant by *democracy*. If the essence of democracy is defined as stability in the sense of the absence of political protests and political unrest, the concept becomes highly problematic. Political protests and political unrest such as street demonstrations, sit-ins, and strikes may be signs of a vibrant democracy. This is not to say that deaths and serious injuries resulting from such events are a positive sign for any democracy. All this shows that it is not easy to determine how political protests and unrest fit within a good definition of democracy. Consociational scholars were perhaps not always careful enough in how they defined democratic stability. Sometimes they used the concept too much in terms of an absence of political protests and unrest, and more reflection is needed in this area. Too much tranquility and calm may be harmful for a good democracy. In our view, for the sake of conceptual clarity, the ambiguous concept of democratic stability should best be replaced with the concept of democratic quality. The real question is how good a democracy is. If we put the question in this way, we can arrive at a broad definition of democracy, which should include at least the following elements: civil liberties, citizen participation, competitive elections, absence of severe violence, civility in the political discourse, respect for minorities, and equal opportunities.

A third normatively grounded critique is that consociational scholars have become political advocates of the consociational pattern of decision making and thus to have unduly entered the political arena as actors of their own.[36]

Have consociational scholars with their consulting activities indeed become undue advocates of the pattern of consociational decision making? After the end of the Cold War, the biggest challenge of the world may very well be to keep relations among different cultural groups relatively peaceful. From Rwanda to Bosnia-Herzegovina, we know too well to what atrocities intercultural conflicts may lead. Should political scientists only observe such dreadful events and not try to have a positive influence? In our understanding, political scientists always have some influence, even if they are not conscious of it. Just by teaching and writing, they influence how their listeners and readers think about the world.

The point is that we as political scientists are never purely objective external observers, but always have some influence on the world. A first step is to reflect on this influence. For consociational scholars, this means making explicit to themselves and to the outside world from which normative perspective they make their policy recommendations when engaging in consulting activities. What is, for example, the relative importance they attach to the values of nonviolence and social justice if the two are in conflict? What is also needed on the part of consociational scholars engaged in consulting activities is that they spell out not only the potential but also the limits of their research. If these conditions are fulfilled, there is nothing wrong if political scientists go to Bosnia-Herzegovina and Rwanda to offer advice. To the contrary, through such activities they contribute to a high level of public discourse about the problems of this world. And with this point, we come to our final issue for discussion: How do you view the potential and the limits of consociational scholars giving practical advice based on their research on power sharing?

KEY TERMS

achieved 270	deliberation 298	postdictive 287
ascriptive 270	divisions 269	predictive 287
autonomy 271	favorable 272	proportionality 271
consociational 269	fragmented 270	reinforcing 271
cooperative	Good Friday	sharing of power 269
mentality 298	Agreement 283	social stratification 275
cross-cutting 271	grand coalitions 271	spatial separation 282
Dayton Accord 295	measure 275	veto power 271

DISCUSSION QUESTIONS

1. Is there an alternative to consociational democracy in highly divided societies? Is competitive pluralism such an alternative? How can the rights of minorities best be protected in deeply divided societies?
2. Why is consociational democracy often considered to be "elitist"? Are elites necessarily more moderate than ordinary citizens, or could the opposite be true?
3. Cooperation among the top representatives of the various societal segments often comes at the cost of increasing tensions between the followers of any specific groups and their leaders. Why is this so?

4. In which societal structure is civil war more likely: one that is characterized by reinforcing cleavages, or one that is characterized by cross-cutting cleavages?
5. "Success" for consociational democracy basically means establishing peace and harmony in deeply divided societies. Is such success purely a function of its institutional configuration, or are other supporting elements also necessary? What might such elements be? How important is culture?

NOTES

1. The term *consociational* is derived from Johannes Althusius's concept of *consociatio* in his *Politica Methodice Digesta* (1603), reprinted, with an introduction by Carl Joachim Friedrich (Cambridge, MA: Harvard University Press, 1932).
2. Arend Lijphart. Consociational Democracy. *World Politics* 21 (January 1969): 207–225; Gerhard Lehmbruch. A Noncompetitive Pattern of Conflict Management in Liberal Democracies: The Case of Switzerland, Austria, and Lebanon, in Kenneth MacRae, ed., *Consociational Democracy: Political Accommodation in Segmented Societies* (Toronto, ON: McClelland and Stewart, Carleton Library, no. 79, 1974).
3. Gabriel A. Almond. Comparative Political Systems. *Journal of Politics* 18 (August 1956): 391–409.
4. Arend Lijphart. *The Politics of Accommodation: Pluralism and Democracy in the Netherlands* (Berkeley, CA: University of California Press, 1968, 104).
5. gfs.berne, Sorgenbarometer, October 2004.
6. Based on the national census of 2000.
7. For example, David Earle Bohn. Consociational Democracy and the Case of Switzerland. *Journal of Politics* 42 (February 1980): 179.
8. The only violence that occurred with regard to the language question was in the Jura. The issue was whether the French speakers in the predominantly German-speaking Bern Canton should have their own Canton and where the borders of this Canton should be.
9. Jean Ziegler. *Une Suisse au-dessus de tout soupçon* (Paris: Editions du Seuil, 1976).
10. Ibid., 497.
11. For a broad application of consociational theory to Northern Ireland, see Rupert Taylor, ed., *Consociational Theory: McGarry and O'Leary and the Northern Ireland Conflict* (London and New York: Routledge, 2009).
12. Richard Rose. Northern Ireland: The Irreducible Conflict, in Joseph V. Montville, ed., *Conflict and Peacemaking in Multiethnic Societies* (Lexington, KY: D. C. Heath, 1989, 13).
13. *New York Times,* September 1, 1994.
14. *New York Times,* October 4, 1994.
15. *The Times,* November 17, 1999.
16. *New York Times,* September 27, 2005.
17. Ibid.
18. www.telegraph.co.uk, May 8, 2007.
19. For the data, we consulted the statistical yearbook of Czechoslovakia and various other publications. For help with the translation, we express thanks to Joseph Anderle, a colleague at the University of North Carolina at Chapel Hill.
20. Jiří Musil. Czech and Slovak Society. *Government and Opposition* 28 (Autumn 1993): 480.
21. Ibid., 493.

22. Václav Havel. *Letters to Olga* (New York: Knopf, 1988).
23. *New York Times*, March 28, 1990.
24. For the phenomenon of Vladimir Mečiar in Slovak politics, see Samuel Abraham. Early Elections in Slovakia: A State of Deadlock. *Government and Opposition* 30 (Winter 1995): 86–100.
25. Herbert Kitschelt. The Formation of Party Systems in East Central Europe. *Politics & Society* 20 (March 1992): 7–50.
26. This prediction can be found on page 248 of the second edition of this textbook, published in January 1991.
27. *New York Times*, February 23, 1994.
28. *New York Times*, March 19, 1994.
29. Ibid.
30. *Neue Zürcher Zeitung*, November 16, 2001.
31. *Neue Zürcher Zeitung*, May 14, 2009.
32. Jürgen Habermas. *Between Facts and Norms: Contributions to a Discourse Theory of Law and Democracy*. Trans. William Regh (Cambridge, MA: MIT Press, 1996).
33. Jürg Steiner, André Bächtiger, Markus Spörndli, and Marco R. Steenbergen. *Deliberative Politics in Action* (Cambridge, UK: Cambridge University Press, 2004).
34. Jürg Steiner, *The Foundations of Deliberative Democracy. Empirical Research and Normative Implications* (Cambridge, UK: Cambridge University Press, 2012).
35. More on the normative aspect of power sharing in Jürg Steiner and Thomas Ertman, eds. *Consociationalism and Corporatism in Western Europe. Still the Politics of Accommodation?* (Amsterdam, Netherlands: Boom, 2002; also published as a special issue of *Acta Politica* 37 (Spring/Summer 2002).
36. Ian S. Lustick. Lijphart, Lakatos, and Consociationalism. *World Politics* 50 (October 1997): 88–117.

The European Union

More than 200 years ago, the 13 American states joined together in a single political system—the United States of America. Today, there is a movement toward European integration. Will there ever be a United States of Europe similar in form to the United States of America? Most likely not. The historical circumstances are so different that Europe will not simply copy the American model. The main difference is that the European countries have far **older historical traditions** than the American states had when the United States of America was founded. As a consequence, the European Union has sometimes greater problems than the federal government in the United States to make sure that the member countries fully comply with EU laws. Tanja A. Börzel and her colleagues have discovered that the most powerful countries are least likely to comply with EU laws whereas smaller countries with an efficient bureaucracy are most likely to do so.[1]

Nonetheless, European integration is already a reality to a certain extent. European voters participate regularly in elections for the European Parliament. Other governmental bodies include the European **Council of Ministers,** the **European Council,** the European Commission, and the European Court of Justice (ECJ). What are the functions of these institutions, and how much power do they have? What is the relationship between these European institutions and the political institutions in the member countries of the European Union (EU)? These questions are very important for American students who, later in their professional lives, may be involved in European affairs. With regard to business dealings in Europe, the main responsibilities in many areas are no longer in the national capitals but in Brussels, the capital not only of Belgium but also of the EU. To export oranges, for example, from Florida to Great Britain, the paperwork must be submitted to European bureaucrats in Brussels. Similarly, if an American company wants to sell kitchen tools in France, it must be aware of the safety standards that are set by European authorities. The influence of the EU extends even across the Atlantic. Already as early as 2001, Mario Monti, then European competition commissioner, blocked a merger between General Electric and Honeywell, two American companies that had secured approval from the U.S. Justice Department for their merger.[2] As the chapter will show, however, "The European Union is more than a means to lower economic transactions costs," as Liesbet Hooghe and Gary Marks argue in a literature review of the European Union.[3] They show that besides the purely economic aspect, the EU has much to do with the identity of people in Europe. Some develop a European identity, whereas others insist on their national identity and reject the entire concept of European integration.

HISTORY OF EUROPEAN INTEGRATION

European countries warred for many centuries. A serious effort to stop these seemingly endless wars once and for all was made after World War I. In 1914, European leaders had sent their countries' youths to war fired with enthusiasm. Each side expected a quick and heroic victory. The eventual Allied victory, however, came only after four years of trench warfare and tremendous losses on both sides. After the war, many well-meaning people became active in the so-called **Pan-European movement,** which demanded the unification of Europe so that war could never again break out. Members of this movement urged Europeans to recognize their common cultural heritage. But the time for this movement was not yet ripe. Mussolini's Fascist Party took over Italy in 1922. In 1929, the Great Depression began. In 1933, Hitler became dictator of Germany, and in 1939, another world war began.

World War II was, if such comparisons are possible, even more dreadful than World War I. Aerial bombardment increasingly spread the suffering directly to the civilian population. After the war, the idea of European unification was quickly brought up again. In a famous speech in Zürich in 1946, Winston Churchill called for the construction of a "kind of United States of Europe."

A first step was the foundation of the **Council of Europe** in Strasbourg, France, in 1949. Its members were drawn from the national parliaments of the Western European democracies. The Council of Europe had only a consultative character. It required no surrender of national sovereignty, and its decisions were based on unanimous votes, giving each country a veto power. The Council of Europe still exists today and does important work; its Commission on Human Rights investigates human rights abuses. The Council of Europe also has a Court of Human Rights. Although it has no means to enforce its rulings, they are widely followed by the member states, since there is great moral pressure to do so. In order to increase this pressure, the Council of Europe decided in April 1996 that countries violating human rights may be suspended temporarily from some activities of the council.[4]

There is sometimes resistance to rulings of the European Court of Human Rights, in particular in Great Britain, against which the court has ruled on several occasions. In March 1996, for example, the court upheld the appeal of the journalist Bill Goodwin against the British courts' refusal to acknowledge that he should be entitled to protect professional sources from disclosure.[5]

The Council of Europe has also established the **European Social Charter,** expanding its activities to the area of social rights. The charter guarantees, for example, the right to work, the right to health care, and the right to welfare. Such rights, however, are more controversial than human rights, so in regard to social rights, the Council of Europe has less influence.[6]

After the breakdown of Communism in Central and Eastern Europe in 1989, it was the Council of Europe that offered these countries their first access to a European institution. Compared with the EU, the Council of Europe is much less important. Although the Council of Europe meets in Strasbourg in the same building where the parliament of the EU meets, it is important to differentiate between the two institutions.

The current EU had its institutional beginning in the **European Coal and Steel Community** (ECSC), which was founded by the Treaty of Paris on April 18, 1951. At the time, coal and steel were the crucial elements in any war effort. It was felt that pooling these important raw materials on a European level should prevent future wars in Europe. With this goal in mind, the key aspect was to include both France and the Federal Republic of Germany, which had gone to war with each other three times in the preceding hundred years: in 1870–1871, 1914–1918, and 1939–1945. Also participating in the ECSC were Italy, Belgium, the Netherlands, and Luxembourg. The initiative was made successful through such leaders as Jean Monnet and Robert Schuman of France, Alcide De Gasperi of Italy, and Paul-Henri Spaak of Belgium, who are today counted as the founding fathers of the EU.

In 1954, European integration suffered a painful setback. The six member countries of the ECSC had planned to extend their collaboration to the establishment of a European Defense Community. Five countries had already ratified the corresponding treaty when the French National Assembly voted against it, not wishing to have French troops under a common European command.

After this setback in defense affairs, the economic route to European integration was pursued further. A common market for coal and steel having been established, its six member countries extended their economic collaboration to other areas. In 1957, they signed the crucial Treaty of Rome, establishing the *European Economic Community (EEC).* For the peaceful use of nuclear energy, they created a special organization, the *European Atomic Energy Community (Euratom).* The three communities, ECSC, EEC, and Euratom, were never merged into a single entity. However, there were good reasons to regard them as constituting one unit insofar as their political and legal structure was concerned. In the media and in everyday life, the three communities were commonly called the *European Community (EC).* On February 16, 1978, the European Parliament acknowledged this usage and accepted a resolution that the three communities "be designated the European Community."

Despite Churchill's Zürich speech, Great Britain was not a founding member of the EC. In 1957, the British did not really feel that they were a part of Europe. For the British, Europe was the Continent, and when they crossed the English Channel, they considered that trip as "going to Europe." But by the 1960s, Britain had changed its mind and—mainly out of economic necessity—applied for membership. France, under General Charles de Gaulle, feared for its own leadership position, and it twice vetoed the entry of Britain. It was only in 1973, when de Gaulle was out of office, that Britain was able to join. To this day, many British citizens have strong emotional reservations about the process of European integration. Denmark and the Republic of Ireland also joined in 1973; Greece followed in 1981; Spain and Portugal in 1986; and Austria, Finland, and Sweden in 1995. By the time these latter three countries joined, the EU had been formally established. After the breakdown of Communism in 1989, it took until 2004 for the first formerly Communist countries to join the EU: the Czech Republic, Hungary, Poland, Slovakia, Slovenia, and the three Baltic countries of Estonia, Latvia, and Lithuania. The two Mediterranean islands of Cyprus and Malta joined the EU at the same time. Three years later, in 2007, Bulgaria and Romania joined. Thus, the EU currently has 27 members.

To revitalize the EC, on February 18, 1986, its member countries signed the **Single European Act**. The act's goal was to set up a common market for goods, labor, capital, and services by the end of 1992. These goals were already contained in the Treaty of Rome, but with the Single European Act a fixed timetable was set, and by January 1, 1993, the EC had indeed, with a few exceptions, reached the goal of a common market. Profiting from the momentum of the project, in December 1991 at Maastricht in the Netherlands, the EC countries signed the **Treaty on European Union** (EU). The goal of this ambitious treaty is to strengthen the political and monetary ties in the community. It became effective on November 1, 1993, whereby the EC became the European Union. For the remainder of the chapter, we will adhere to this latter usage, except when we refer to specific events before November 1993, for which we will still use the name *European Community*. In recent years, the EU has attempted to give itself a proper constitution. We will deal with this aspect in a special section later in the chapter.

In addition to the Council of Europe and the EU, some other organizations contribute to European integration. The *European Free Trade Association (EFTA)* was created by Western European countries that did not wish to join the EC. Great Britain was the most important founding member of EFTA, but, like most other founding members, it later changed its membership to the EC. Currently, only four countries make up EFTA: Iceland, Liechtenstein, Norway, and Switzerland.

Then there is the *Organization for Security and Cooperation in Europe (OSCE)*, which met for the first time from 1973 to 1975 in Helsinki and Geneva. This was the first institutional setting for Western, Central, and Eastern European countries to meet. Also included in this institution were the United States, Canada, and the Soviet Union. After the breakup of the Soviet Union, its membership was taken over by Russia. An important function of the OSCE is to supervise elections in countries that are still politically unstable, especially in Eastern Europe and in the Balkans.

COUNCIL OF MINISTERS

When the EC began to operate under the terms of the Treaty of Rome, the Council of Ministers was considered to be its legislature, operating by the unanimity principle. (The name was later changed to Council of the European Union, but since the old name is still widely used in the media, we do the same in this book.) The Council of Ministers still has important legislative functions, but it increasingly shares these functions with the European Parliament. The 27 member countries of what is now the EU each send one minister to the meetings of the Council of Ministers. The particular minister sent depends on the issue under debate. The Council of Foreign Ministers, also called the General Affairs and External Relations Council, is considered to be at the highest level. It deals not only with foreign policy issues but also with general matters, such as changes in the various treaties on which the EU is based. For other matters, the corresponding ministers come together; for agricultural matters, for example, the ministers of agriculture would meet. Meetings also take place at the level of ministers for finance, social affairs, transport, and so on. This list illustrates the broad range of topics discussed by the Council of Ministers. We should remember that the main job of the ministers is in the governmental institutions of their home countries; however, they spend more and more of their time with their EU colleagues.

How are decisions made in the Council of Ministers? With the Single European Act, an attempt was made to give more importance to the majority principle. Although it was not possible to abolish the unanimity rule altogether, it was agreed to use majority voting on matters such as the internal market, the environment, and research and technological development. For politically more sensitive issues, however, such as taxation and rights of workers, each country still can claim its veto power, although this power is rarely used now.

If voting takes place, how is it done? The allocation of votes to each country is roughly proportional to the square root of its population, which obviously favors the smaller countries. Germany, France, Italy, and the United Kingdom each have 29 votes; Spain and Poland 27; Romania 14; the Netherlands 13; Belgium, the Czech Republic, Greece, Hungary, and Portugal 12; Austria, Bulgaria, and Sweden 10; Denmark, Ireland, Lithuania, Slovakia, and Finland 7; Cyprus, Estonia, Latvia, Luxembourg, and Slovenia 4; and Malta 3. On this basis, the total number of votes is 345, and to reach a decision, a qualified majority of 255 (73.9 percent) votes is required. The votes in favor must also correspond to 62 percent of the total population of the EU. Thus, one needs to do quite a bit of math to determine whether the Council of Ministers has made a positive decision.[7]

EUROPEAN COUNCIL

The European Council brings together the chief executives of the 27 member countries. These are the most prominent political leaders in Europe. In the initial phase of the EC, the European Council did not exist. It evolved from the practice, dating from 1974, of regularly organizing informal meetings of the chief executives. Two leaders of the time, the French president, Valéry Giscard d'Estaing and the German chancellor Helmut Schmidt, were instrumental in setting up this tradition. In the Single European Act, the European Council was formally established as an institution of the EC. It meets at least twice a year for short sessions of a couple of days. The chair for these meetings used to rotate among all the member countries every six months, the same system as for the Council of Ministers. Since 2010, however, the European Council has a permanent chair, called European President. The first holder of this important office is Herman Van Rompuy, former prime minister of Belgium. The president of the European Commission, which will be discussed in the next section, attends the meetings of the European Council in his own right. The foreign ministers are also in attendance at these meetings. The European Council is also called European Summit.

If we compare with the United States, the European Council corresponds closely to the Governors' Conference. Imagine if the Governors' Conference were the most powerful political body in the United States! Each governor would probably feel responsible primarily for the interests of his or her own state. This is, indeed, the situation in the European Council. The power base for each participant is in his or her own respective country. To survive politically, the members of the European Council must, first of all, win elections at home. If they lose those elections, they are also out of the European Council. Thus, the members of the European Council naturally view a problem first from their own national perspective and not from an overall European view. Therefore, important decisions can be reached only if all national interests are more or less accommodated. Meetings of the European Council often resemble a "game of chicken," in which each participant tries to wait out all others before making concessions. This leads to hectic, late-night sessions in which some bargain is finally struck out of exhaustion. Quite often, however, such late-night agreements tend to obscure real differences, such that the issue must be taken up again at a later meeting. Observers have grown accustomed to an atmosphere of crisis at European Council meetings, but somehow the European Council muddles through to keep the EU going. After all, the participants know that the demise of the EU would leave every member country worse off. Thus, a solution of some kind is always found, even if it is only to study the problem further. Overall, the European Council has become the most important institution of the EU. It is here that the basic political compromises are worked out. They are usually prepared elsewhere, but the key issues are left to the chief executives. If their power base is weakened in their home countries, this also weakens decision making in the EU.

EUROPEAN COMMISSION

The institution that brings continuity to the operations of the EU is the European Commission. In contrast to the members of the Council of Ministers and the European Council, commissioners work full time for the European Union. There are 27 commissioners, one for each country. The members of the commission are nominated by their respective national governments and appointed by the "common accord" of the governments of the member countries. Under the Maastricht treaty, their appointment has to be approved by the European Parliament. The European Parliament can force the commission to resign *en bloc,* by a no-confidence vote. In fact, in March 1999, following the release of a scathing report issued by the European Parliament, the entire commission resigned amid charges of patronage, cronyism, and financial irregularities. This is quite instructive in that it shows that the powers of the European Parliament and the European Commission are similar to those in the domestic realm of parliamentary systems.

The commission is headed by a president, who is chosen by agreement of the member countries. Once a president is appointed, the member countries appoint the other 26 members of the commission. The president of the European Commission is sometimes labeled by the American media as the "European president." Pictures are published with the caption "Two Presidents," showing the American president and the president of the European Commission standing side by side. The powers of the two offices, however, are quite different. Nevertheless, the duties of the 27 commissioners are clearly not to represent the interests of their national governments. In fact, they must take an oath swearing that they will represent the interests of the EU only and will not take any instruction from their national government or any other body. This is of course difficult in reality, as it is impossible to suddenly distance oneself from one's own national identity and interests. Still, the commission is clearly the most supranational body of the EU.

In assessing the nature of the presidency of the European Commission, we see that there is an intriguing chicken-and-egg problem: What comes first, a powerful office or a powerful officeholder? Must the office be made powerful to attract powerful leaders, or is the first step appointing a powerful leader who can lend power to the office? At first, it was difficult to attract powerful leaders to head the commission, but recently, competition has increased among top politicians wishing to become its president. When Jacques Delors resigned as president in 1994, the prime ministers of Belgium, the Netherlands, and Luxembourg all wanted the job. There was fierce bargaining in the European Council, and at the end, Jacques Santer of Luxembourg was appointed. His predecessor, Jacques Delors, had served under French president François Mitterrand as an influential economic minister but, at the time, had no immediate prospect of becoming president of France. Hence, he was willing to move to Brussels to head the commission. This pattern has not yet changed: To be the top leader in France and the other big countries is still preferable to being president of the commission. As the appointment in 1994 demonstrated, top leaders in the smaller countries are increasingly eager to exchange their jobs for the position of president of the commission. The newest example is José Manuel Barroso, who in 2004 resigned as prime minister of Portugal to become president of the European Commission. After the election of the European Parliament in June 2009, Barroso was appointed for another term. He was the only candidate, and the vote in the newly elected European Parliament was 382 against, 219 in his favor, and 117 abstentions. It is important to note that before this parliamentary vote, Barroso was endorsed by the European Council, which consists of the chief executives of all 27 member countries. This shows that the real power in the EU is still with the European Council rather than with the European Parliament. Without the endorsement of the European Council, no one has a chance to become president of the European Commission.

The European Commission directs a large bureaucracy at the headquarters in Brussels. The commission meets at least once a week. Each commissioner is responsible for specific policy areas, such as external relations, agriculture, social affairs, energy, and transport. The commission is in charge of the EU's routine day-to-day operations. It also has the authority to make certain policy decisions on its own, what Martin Shapiro and Alec Stone call "administrative rule making."[8] Sensitive policy decisions, however, are dealt with by the Council of Ministers and, if they are extremely sensitive, by the European Council. The main task of the commission is to prepare the meetings of the Council of Ministers and the European Council. The commission also has executive functions in the sense that it supervises the implementation of the decisions reached by the Council of Ministers, the European Council, and the European Parliament.

EUROPEAN PARLIAMENT

In the Treaty of Rome, the European Parliament was called an "assembly," but in 1958, it gave itself its current name. Initially, the European Parliament consisted of delegates of the national parliaments, and it met for short sessions in Strasbourg. This led to useful contacts, but the European Parliament had virtually no decision-making power, although it could approve nonbinding resolutions and submit questions to the Council of Ministers. Its only real decision power was to force the European Commission to resign with a no-confidence vote. But as we have seen earlier, this right was not used for a very long time, indeed not until 1999. Thus, for a long time, the European Parliament was not much more than a forum for an exchange of ideas among delegates from the national parliaments.

The real legislature was, as noted, the Council of Ministers, and this arrangement was increasingly seen as a democratic deficiency of the EC. To be sure, the Council of Ministers had democratic legitimacy in the individual member countries in the sense that its members belonged to the respective national governments, and these national governments were selected by the national parliaments, which in turn were elected by the national electorates. However, this was too long a chain to give to the Council of Ministers real democratic legitimacy. It was felt that the European voters should have a direct voice. Thus, on December 20, 1976, the Council of Ministers decided that the European Parliament should be directly elected by the European voters. The first direct elections took place in 1979. The term was five years, and further elections were held in 1984, 1989, 1994, 1999, 2004, and 2009. Voter turnout was 62 percent in 1979, 59 percent in 1984, 58 percent in 1989, 57 percent in 1994, 50 percent in 1999, 45 percent in 2004, and 43 percent in 2009. Compared to national European elections, these turnouts are rather low (see Chapters 3 and 10). It is particularly disturbing that the trend is downward. This raises the question of the extent to which the European Parliament has been able to establish itself as a representative institution of the European voters.

Turnout was lowest in Slovakia (20 percent), Lithuania (21 percent), Poland (27 percent), Romania (27 percent), Slovenia (28 percent), and the Czech Republic (28 percent), all new member countries in Central and Eastern Europe. If voter turnout is a measure of the political involvement of the citizenry and their belief that by participating they can affect various outcomes, the declining turnout rates are disturbing, to say the least. It might very well be that citizens perceive politics in Brussels as too far removed to affect them, or that their voice would not make a difference at all, or both. The low turnout to elections for the European Parliament is one manifestation of the often cited "**democracy deficit**" that plagues the EU. This is paradoxical insofar as the impact of the EU on the daily lives of Europeans is increasing rather than decreasing.

What political parties are represented in the European Parliament? They are basically the same party families that can be found at the national levels, listed as follows (with the 2009 election results in parentheses):[9] Conservatives and Christian Democrats together form a parliamentary group (EPP/ED) (36 percent); Socialists (PES) (22 percent); Liberals (ALDE) (11 percent); and Greens and European Free Alliance (EFA) (7 percent).

Two party groupings within the European Parliament are outspokenly against EU integration: the Independence-Democracy Party (Ind/Dem) (2 percent) and the Union for Europe of the Nations (UEN) (5 percent). The latter states unmistakably that it favors a "Europe based on the freedom of nations to decide, where diversity is the first of all riches, and not a federal Europe which would subject sovereign nations and take away the identity of European peoples."[10] There is even a "regional" party represented in the European Parliament: the European United Left/Nordic Green Left, which received 4 percent of the vote in the 2009 elections. The remaining votes went to various splinter parties.

The MEPs (members of the European Parliament) sit in their chambers in Strasbourg and Brussels not according to their nationality but rather according to their party affiliation. Just like in the national parliaments, party loyalty matters also in the European context, where MEPs who go against the party line may not be placed on particularly influential delegations or committees, or may even be fined, though this rarely happens.

The European Parliament has basically the same problem as the European Commission, in the sense that it is unclear whether a powerful office or powerful officeholders come first. In the first elections, some eminent leaders, such as Willy Brandt of Germany and François Mitterrand of France, were elected. But it soon turned out that, for many, their participation was mostly a symbolic gesture of goodwill. Brandt and Mitterrand, for example, gave up their seats in the European Parliament to continue their careers in their home countries. When the European Parliament was elected for the second time, relatively few prominent leaders entered the race. They considered a seat in the European Parliament an insufficiently powerful position. This still appears to be the case at the beginning of the third millennium.

How powerful has the European Parliament become since its direct election by the voters? A historical analysis of the development of national parliaments all over the world suggests that the crucial step has been gaining control over the **budget**. The U.S. Congress is powerful because it controls the purse. In this respect, the European Parliament still has little power. The budget does not originate in the European Parliament but in the European Commission. It then passes between the Council of Ministers and the European Parliament. The real budgetary power has remained with the Council of Ministers. Parliament can reject the budget but has no authority to draw up its own budget. Nevertheless, it has gained the right to make certain amendments to the budget in certain limited areas. The power of the European Parliament ultimately will be determined in the battle over these budget questions. If Parliament can obtain significant control over both revenues and expenditures, it will be the crucial step in transforming the EU into a truly supranational organization: Essential sovereign power will have been transferred from the member countries to the European level. But many politicians and voters—especially in Great Britain, but also elsewhere—fear such a development and will resist any effort to expand the European Parliament's budgetary power. Seen in this broader context, quarrels over the budgetary rights of the European Parliament are not at all technical in nature but go to the very heart of European integration.

In the parliamentary system of government to which Europeans are accustomed, it is crucial that parliament exercises power in the selection of the executive cabinet. In this respect, too, the European Parliament lacks power; it is not even clear who the executive is and whether the EU has an executive at all. As we have seen in the preceding sections, the European Commission has executive functions for the day-to-day operations of the EU. However, for politically sensitive matters, the Council of Ministers makes executive decisions, although it also has legislative functions. Finally, there is the all-important European Council, which makes the most sensitive executive decisions.

The European Council does not depend on a vote of confidence of the European Parliament, nor does the Council of Ministers. For the European Commission, the situation is ambiguous. Legally, the European Parliament has the right, as we have seen in the last section, to dismiss the commission with a vote of no-confidence, which in fact, as noted, it did in the spring of 1999. But it has no right to select a new commission, so the national governments could simply reappoint the old one. With the Maastricht Treaty, Parliament received the additional right to approve the appointment of a new commission for its five-year term. In 2004, a new commission president and 24 new commissioners needed to be installed for the 2004–2009 legislative period. The European Council nominated a new commission president, José Manuel Barroso, and the Council of Ministers nominated one commissioner from each country. This was followed by hearings by the European Parliament that voted on the whole body (the commission president and the 24 commissioners). The Barroso European

Commission was approved by 449 members of Parliament, with 149 "no" votes, 82 abstentions, 12 who did not vote, and 38 absentees.[11] The European Parliament thus approved the commission by 61 percent. Thus, the approval by the European Parliament was not a formality at all.

After approval by the European Parliament, the new "government of the EU" is appointed by the Council of Ministers. This process is similar to the process of **investiture**, the formal process of government formation that can be found in various national parliaments. Some discussion exists within the EU concerning transforming the Council of Ministers into a second parliamentary chamber called the *Senate*. The institutional construction would be similar to that in Germany, where the Bundestag represents the people and the Bundesrat represents the Länder (states). Under this arrangement, the current European Parliament, as a first chamber, would represent the European voters; the renamed Council of Ministers, as a second chamber, would represent the individual countries. This would allow the European Commission to develop from an "embryo of a European government" (see previous section) into a real European government. As in a regular parliamentary system, it would derive its legitimacy from a vote of confidence in Parliament. With such a development, the European Council would become redundant, because the European Commission clearly would be the executive. Such a construction would be in the interest of both the European Parliament and the European Commission, but certainly not of the political institutions in the national capitals. The strongest resistance against such a plan comes from the British House of Commons, which would be degraded to a local parliament, analogous to an American state legislature. There is also resistance from other national capitals, such as Copenhagen, the capital of Denmark. Thus, it is not likely that the European Union will receive the clearly structured institutions of a parliamentary system anytime soon. The ambiguous relationships among the current institutions will continue for some time. In the context of the present section, it is important to stress once more that the European Parliament is *not* a classical legislature. It shares this function in a complex way with the Council of Ministers. This ambivalence is expressed in the following description in an official publication of the EU:

> The Council of Ministers, which represents the Member States, adopts Community legislation (regulations, directives and decisions). It is the Community's legislature, although in certain areas specified by the Single European Act and the Maastricht Treaty it shares this function with the European Parliament.[12]

This is typical convoluted bureaucratic language from Brussels, which makes it so difficult for Europeans to understand the institutions of the EU. The fault, however, is not primarily with the bureaucrats in Brussels but with the unclear delimitation of the various EU institutions.

If we look at the legislative process in detail, the European Parliament plays four different roles according to the issue at hand: (1) agreement of European Parliament required, (2) European Parliament has no say, (3) cooperation procedure between European Parliament and Council of Ministers, and (4) co-decision procedure between European Parliament and Council of Ministers. We look at each of these in turn below:

1. Based on the Single European Act and the Maastricht Treaty, there are certain issue areas where the agreement of the European Parliament is required, such as the acceptance of new EU members. The agreement of the European Parliament is also required for changes in the rules for the European parliamentary elections, for the introduction of a European citizenship, and for the organization of a European central bank.

2. There are other issue areas in which the European Parliament has no say. This is the case for changes in the existing treaties of the EU and the proposal and ratification of new treaties. Thus, the Maastricht Treaty was ratified only by the member countries, but not by the European Parliament. This is a strong limitation on the power of the European Parliament because the various treaties form the constitution of the EU. The European Parliament is also excluded from most foreign policy and security issues.

3. The cooperation procedure is described in Article 189c of the Maastricht Treaty. It applies in particular to the issue areas of transport, the environment, developing aid, and workplace, regional, and social policies. For these issue areas, two readings in the Council of Ministers and two in the European Parliament are required, but ultimately the views of the council prevail.

4. The co-decision procedure was introduced with Article 189b of the Maastricht Treaty. It applies in particular to the internal market, consumer protection, mutual recognition of diplomas, education, culture, and technology. In these areas, the European Parliament is able to block a proposal of the Council of Ministers. But Parliament is still not able to impose its own will. If, after its second reading, an absolute majority of Parliament rejects a proposal of the council, a conciliation procedure begins. If this procedure fails, Parliament can kill a proposal made by the council if once again an absolute majority of the members of Parliament reject this proposal. Thus, the co-decision procedure gives the European Parliament a veto power in certain areas.

The European Parliament has its regular sessions in the French city of Strasbourg, and France very much insists that it continue to do so. Many committee meetings, however, and some extraordinary plenary sessions are held in Brussels, the seat of the European Commission. To make things even more complicated, the secretariat-general of the parliament is located in Luxembourg. Because the members of the European Parliament, therefore, travel a great deal, one sometimes speaks in this context of a "circus." The elections for the European Parliament are held within the individual countries. The election system in all countries is based on proportionality. Even Great Britain changed in 1999 to proportional representation, although for national elections to the House of Commons it kept the winner-take-all system (see Chapter 3).

Another central institution of the European Union is the European Court of Justice. For more detailed information on the European Court of Justice, see Chapter 5, where we discussed this institution as part of the court system in Europe.

EUROPEAN BUREAUCRACY

Perhaps the best guarantee of the EU's continued existence is the many thousands of bureaucrats it employs. These "Eurocrats," as they are often called, have an obvious career interest in the continuation of EU operations. In addition, many lobbyists working in Brussels have a personal professional interest in the survival of the union. Over the years, all of these people, working directly or indirectly for the EU, have developed some elements of a common cosmopolitan European culture. They tend to live in the same neighborhoods in Brussels, and they attend the same parties and share the same gossip. When the Eurocrats went on strike one day—without regard to nationality—it was said, of course as a joke, that this was the best sign yet that European integration was alive and well. A drawback to the development of this bureaucracy in Brussels is that ordinary European citizens increasingly see the EU as a giant, anonymous organization over which they have no control. And yet, they sense that this distant bureaucracy has an important impact on their daily lives.

WHAT DOES THE EUROPEAN UNION DO?

What the EU can do depends very much on the resources available. This raises a very important question: How is the EU financed? The EU is financed by essentially three elements: first, what is called **traditional own resources** (TOR). These are customs duties and agricultural duties levied on imports coming from countries outside the EU. A small amount is also contributed to the EU budget by sugar producers, who pay levies for exporting sugar. That first element covers about 13 percent of total EU revenue in the 2011 budget. The second resource for the EU budget comes from levies based on the various member states' **value-added tax** (VAT) levels, which accounted for about 11 percent of total EU revenue in 2011. Finally, the third and most important resource of EU budget are the **contributions** made by the various member states measured as a percentage of their gross national income (GNI). This third resource amounts to about 75 percent of the EU budget. The rest represents "other revenue" such as bank interest, repayments of unused community financial assistance, and interest on late payments. The total EU budget is currently capped at 1.24 percent of combined national GNIs, which corresponds to about 293 euros per EU citizen per year on average. There is a widespread misconception that the EU budget is enormous. In reality, it is about 140 billion euro which is smaller than the budget of a medium-sized member state such as Austria or Belgium. Interestingly, not unlike American states, the European budget must be balanced, that is, it is not possible for the European Union to go in debt.[13]

A glimpse at the expenditure side of the 2011 EU budget reveals two major components. Around 42.5 percent goes to the preservation of the environment and natural resources in order to ensure a healthy environment and safe agricultural products. The second major expenditure, around 35.6 percent, goes to working toward cohesion for growth and employment. This is designed to create economic growth and jobs in the member countries and to create more "**cohesion**" among the member states by helping weaker regions of Europe to transform their economies to more successfully compete in a globalized world. Of the remaining 22 percent, 9 percent are used toward "competitiveness for growth and employment." These are funds used for research and education, training, as well as innovation. Almost 5.7 percent are spent on what is called "The EU as a Global Player," which means the "foreign policy" of the EU. Around 5.6 percent are used toward administrative costs to run the European Union, which include the staff salaries and building costs of all EU institutions. Finally, 1.6 percent goes to information sharing in order to fight crime, terrorism, and illegal immigration.[14]

Agricultural Policy

In the 1970s the agricultural policies of the EU amounted to little more than subsidizing farmers. This often led to surpluses of "mountains of butter" and "lakes of milk" that were bought by the EC and then destroyed in order to stabilize prices, while at the same time consumers paid relatively high prices for these goods. This overemphasis on food production had its roots in the postwar food shortages as well as in the strong **influence of farmers** in the EC. However, in 2003 the Common Agricultural Policy (CAP) moved to much broader goals: sustainable agricultural policies, which not only means increasing the competitiveness of European farmers but also achieving this with concerns for the ecological balance and the viability of farming as a respected profession. But the CAP is also concerned about food quality and food safety in addition to animal welfare. There are now precise regulations as to how much space pigs, laying hens, and calves must have in their holding pens; light, temperature, and floor requirements; and how animals must be treated during transport and prior to slaughter.[15]

A well-known point of contention between the United States and the EU is over genetically modified organisms (GMOs). The EU has been very suspicious of gene-spliced crops, termed "Frankenfood" in Europe, particularly in the wake of the outbreak of mad cow disease in the United Kingdom and other European countries. The United States takes the view that the EU uses the health concerns of the European public as an excuse to impose nontariff barriers. Eventually, the EU agreed that some GMOs can be sold in Europe, but only after they are labeled as such and when their traceability (where did they originate?) is ensured. There is a healthy distrust among much of the European public for GMOs, seriously limiting the sales of such products.

Regional and Development Policy

The Structural and Cohesion Fund is designed to promote solidarity among EU countries by reducing developmental gaps among the regions and alleviating disparities among EU citizens. Among the most important elements of the Structural and Cohesion Fund are the development of **infrastructure**, such as roads, railroads, ports, bridges, airports, power lines, and power-generating plants. The fund also provides support to prevent industrial decline, support the development of rural areas, provide training for workers, combat long-term unemployment, and promote research and development.

Since Ireland joined the EU in 1973, it received over 17 billion pounds in structural and cohesion funds. In the past 10 years alone, the funds helped develop major road projects, rail systems, and the construction of seaports. In 1973, Ireland, Greece, Spain, and Portugal qualified for cohesion funds because each country's GNP per capita was less than 90 percent of the EU average. In 2003, Ireland did not qualify for the receipt of funds because it passed this threshold as a result of outstanding economic performance. This shows the remarkable impact of the structural policies of the EU in terms of its ability to shape the infrastructure of a society to such an extent that it can compete on a global level. As these brief examples show, the two main goals of EU policy are agricultural and regional development policy. However, these are such broad definitions that it can be said that literally no policy area is left untouched by the EU.

Common Currency—the Euro

A remarkable feat occurred when, on January 1, 2002, the euro bills and coins were introduced in 12 out of the then 15 EU countries. Sweden, Denmark, and the United Kingdom still use their own national currencies. The European Central Bank described the establishment of the euro as "the biggest monetary changeover in history."[16] Slovenia joined the euro in 2007, Malta and Cyprus in 2008, Slovakia in 2009, and Estonia in 2011. Thus, today 16 of the 27 EU countries are members of the euro zone. Other Central and Eastern European countries hope to join in the near future.

Great efforts have been made by governments to persuade European publics to embrace the euro. As might be expected, it is not easy for any society to give up its currency, because it represents part of the identity as a nation. The economic advantages of having a unified currency across most of the EU area are evident. Anyone who has traveled in Europe before the euro knows the hassles connected with having to change currency (and pay transaction fees and commissions) every time one arrives in a different country. In addition, macroeconomic advantages of the euro range from eliminating exchange rate fluctuations, to price transparency that invigorates competition, to more opportunities for foreign investors. Also, because the economic area covered by the euro is so much larger than the previous individual economies with their own currencies, external shocks to the European economy will have much lower impacts on the euro area than they had when each nation had its own currency and was not economically integrated. Moreover, having a single currency in a market based on the four freedoms of movement (people, goods, capital, and services) and that encompasses about 500 million consumers makes the EU a powerful countervailing power to the economic hegemony of the United States and enhances its impact in international organizations such as the International Monetary Fund (IMF) and the World Bank.[17]

Prior to the introduction of the euro, Germany insisted on the following two criteria: Governments must keep their deficits under 3 percent of their GDP and their national debts under 60 percent of GDP. Germany was concerned that with the introduction of the euro, member states might engage in lavish spending programs leading to inflation—an economic curse with which Germany had a particularly bitter experience in the 1920s. However, in the fall of 2003 both France and Germany experienced economic recessions, forcing them to exceed the 3 percent deficit rule of the convergence criteria. In theory, any member state exceeding one of these criteria would have to pay excessive fines. Alas, neither Germany nor France was punished, to the chagrin of many smaller European countries such as Ireland, Portugal, and Austria, which under heavy political and social costs stuck to the criteria. As a result, the existing rift between bigger and smaller EU members opened even wider, and a perception among the European public grew that there were really two Europes: one for the big, powerful countries that could flaunt rules, and another for the smaller ones that complied with them. Thanks to the improvement of economic conditions in Europe, France and Germany were able to reduce their fiscal deficits below 3 percent. With the global financial and economic crisis of 2008–2009, several countries in the euro zone were forced to increase their budget deficits beyond 3 percent of GDP in order to stimulate their economies. Under these exceptional circumstances, the European Commission allowed these countries quite a bit of time to bring their budgets back to under 3 percent of GDP.

Overall, the euro can be considered as quite a success story. In relation to the U.S. dollar, the euro turned out to be quite strong. One goal, however, was not attained in the euro zone, namely equalization in the international competitiveness of the participating countries. On the contrary, there is a worrisome drifting apart, with Greece and Spain in particular becoming less competitive and Germany and the Netherlands more so. The European Commission sees the reason for this drifting apart in the tendency of countries such as Greece and Spain to spend too much on consumption and not enough on investments.[18] As discussed in Chapter 9, there are great advantages to having a unified currency, but one disadvantage is that a country in the euro zone cannot devalue the euro, which would make exports cheaper and imports more expensive, which presumably would put countries on a path to economic recovery as they become more competitive. Such inability could be considered a serious undermining of national sovereignty. In fact, Greek leaders reportedly considered for a brief period leaving the euro in May 2011 and reintroducing their "old" currency, the drachma. Such a move would have drastic consequences (see Box 14.1). And yet, there is no mechanism of "getting out of the euro." When the common currency was conceived, nobody believed that any country would give it up once the positive aspects of the common currency had been experienced.

BOX 14.1 GREECE CONSIDERS EXIT FROM EURO ZONE

By Christian Reiermann

The debt crisis in Greece has taken on a dramatic new twist. Sources with information about the government's actions have informed Spiegel Online that Athens is considering withdrawing from the euro zone. The common currency area's finance ministers and representatives of the European Commission are holding a secret crisis meeting in Luxembourg on Friday night.

Greece's economic problems are massive, with protests against the government being held almost daily. Now Prime Minister George Papandreou apparently feels he has no other option: Spiegel Online has obtained information from German government sources knowledgeable of the situation in Athens indicating that Papandreou's government is considering abandoning the euro and reintroducing its own currency [...]

One year after the Greek crisis broke out, the development represents a potentially existential turning point for the European monetary union—regardless which variant is ultimately decided upon for dealing with Greece's massive troubles [...]

Sources told SPIEGEL ONLINE that Schäuble [German Finance Minister] intends to seek to prevent Greece from leaving the euro zone if at all possible. He will take with him to the meeting in Luxembourg an internal paper prepared by the experts at his ministry warning of the possible dire consequences if Athens were to drop the euro.

"It would lead to a considerable devaluation of the new (Greek) domestic currency against the euro," the paper states. According to German Finance Ministry estimates, the currency could lose as much as 50 percent of its value, leading to a drastic increase in Greek national debt. Schäuble's staff have calculated that Greece's national deficit would rise to 200 percent of gross domestic product after such a devaluation. "A debt restructuring would be inevitable," his experts warn in the paper. In other words: Greece would go bankrupt.

It remains unclear whether it would even be legally possible for Greece to depart from the euro zone. Legal experts believe it would also be necessary for the country to split from the European Union entirely in order to abandon the common currency. At the same time, it is questionable whether other members of the currency union would actually refuse to accept a unilateral exit from the euro zone by the government in Athens.

What is certain, according to the assessment of the German Finance Ministry, is that the measure would have a disastrous impact on the European economy.

"The currency conversion would lead to capital flight," they write. And Greece might see itself as forced to implement controls on the transfer of capital to stop the flight of funds out of the country. "This could not be reconciled with the fundamental freedoms instilled in the European internal market," the paper states. In addition, the country would also be cut off from capital markets for years to come.

(Continued)

> ▶ **BOX 14.1 CONTINUED**
>
> In addition, the withdrawal of a country from the common currency union would "seriously damage faith in the functioning of the euro zone," the document continues. International investors would be forced to consider the possibility that further euro-zone members could withdraw in the future. "That would lead to contagion in the euro zone," the paper continues.
>
> Moreover, should Athens turn its back on the common currency zone, it would have serious implications for the already wobbly banking sector, particularly in Greece itself. The change in currency "would consume the entire capital base of the banking system and the country's banks would be abruptly insolvent." Banks outside of Greece would suffer as well. "Credit institutions in Germany and elsewhere would be confronted with considerable losses on their outstanding debts," the paper reads.
>
> The European Central Bank (ECB) would also feel the effects. The Frankfurt-based institution would be forced to "write down a significant portion of its claims as irrecoverable." In addition to its exposure to the banks, the ECB also owns large amounts of Greek state bonds, which it has purchased in recent months. Officials at the Finance Ministry estimate the total to be worth at least €40 billion ($58 billion) "Given its 27 percent share of ECB capital, Germany would bear the majority of the losses," the paper reads.
>
> In short, a Greek withdrawal from the euro zone and an ensuing national default would be expensive for euro-zone countries and their taxpayers. Together with the International Monetary Fund, the EU member states have already pledged €110 billion ($159.5 billion) in aid to Athens—half of which has already been paid out.
>
> "Should the country become insolvent," the paper reads, "euro-zone countries would have to renounce a portion of their claims."
>
> *Source: Der Spiegel Online, May 6, 2011.*

Nevertheless, in August 2011, the European Central Bank (ECB) announced that it will buy government bonds from Italy and Spain, two other countries teetering on financial collapse in order to avoid any contagion spreading from Greece to the other Mediterranean countries. This action by the ECB will put Euros into Italy's and Spain's coffers and, combined with austerity measures, will enable these countries to avoid default, or so it is hoped.

Continued Expansion: Where Does "Europe" End?

The process of EU enlargement was negotiated through the treaty of Nice (signed in 2001), which laid the institutional groundwork for future enlargement. It was ratified in all the EU parliaments, except in Denmark and Ireland, which required referenda. The Irish people rejected the treaty in 2001 by 54 percent but in 2002 voted for it. Incorporation of the relatively poor countries from Central and

Eastern Europe raised concerns about large numbers of workers offering cheap labor arriving in the "old" EU countries, that the more developed EU countries will have to pay for the reconstruction of the new Central and Eastern European members, and that investment capital from the richer EU countries will move toward the east, where labor costs are a fraction of those in the west. In fact, the new EU members in Central and Eastern European are already engaged in a "race to the bottom" in order to attract foreign direct investment from the rest of the EU.

In addition, some observers are concerned that the generous **welfare systems** in the "core" EU states such as Germany and Austria might act like a magnet and attract people from the new EU members in Central and Eastern Europe. Just as countries are competing against each other to attract investment by lowering standards, so might welfare states have to begin lowering benefits to deter Central and Eastern Europeans from moving to richer EU countries. Hans Werner Sinn, head of the Institute of Economics at the University of Munich, has argued that competition between states to reduce the generosity of their welfare systems in order to deter immigrants will lead to an erosion of the German welfare state, so that "in 50 years we'll have a situation like that in America."[19] Indeed, many countries imposed restrictions on the eligibility for welfare benefits to members of the accession countries: For example, people from the new EU countries in Central and Eastern Europe have to be employed for a certain time depending on the host country before they can claim welfare benefits.

Although some of these concerns are well founded, similar arguments were heard when Spain, Greece, and Portugal were considered for EU membership. In the meantime, these countries have become trusted members of the EU, have seen dramatic economic development, and have upheld basic principles of democracy and human rights within their borders. The rationale for the 2004 and 2007 expansion was that incorporating the new countries would unite Europe in peace after a history of division and conflict, extending prosperity and stability to its member states, thus making Europe a safer place and stimulating economic and social reform in the new member states. It is very likely that these effects will occur in the long run.

For countries to join the EU, they must meet the "Copenhagen criteria," which state that a prospective member must:

- be a stable democracy, respecting human rights, the rule of law, and the protection of minorities
- have a functioning market economy
- adopt the common rules, standards, and policies that make up the body of EU law

In November 2005, the European Commission presented an "enlargement package" that included potential candidates for further enlargement in the western Balkans, such as Albania, Bosnia and Herzegovina, Macedonia, Serbia, Montenegro, and Kosovo. These countries will be screened in terms of their progress toward fulfilling the Copenhagen criteria. At the time of this writing, the accession negotiations with Croatia have been completed and Croatia is expected to become the 28th member of European Union by July 1, 2013.

Turkey's EU Membership Prospects

One of the most hotly debated countries considered for EU entry is Turkey. In October 2005, membership talks between the EU and Turkey began in earnest, thus securing Turkey's 40-year campaign to become a member of the EU. Though it could take a long time, if ever, for Turkey to become an actual member, fierce resistance was put forth by many EU countries, particularly France, Germany, and Austria. Particularly with the election of Nicolas Sarkozy as French president, the chances of Turkey becoming a member of the EU in the near future have diminished. German chancellor Angela Merkel has also been against full-membership talks.

There are three main concerns voiced against membership of Turkey in the EU: its size, poverty, and religion. First, if Turkey joined the EU in about 10 years, it would have an expected population of around 80 million people. Given the drastic decline of Germany's population, which stands at around 82 million now, Turkey could easily be the most populous country in the EU 10 years from now. It grows seven times faster than the EU average. This could mean that in terms of votes in the Council of Ministers and seats in the European Parliament, Turkey will have at least the same influence as, if not more than, London, Berlin, or Paris.

The second concern voiced against Turkey's membership is its poverty level. In 2009, Turkey's GDP per capita measured in purchasing power standards was about 31 compared to the indexed EU-27 average set to 100. In other words, the per capita value of all goods and services produced in Turkey, controlling for their prices, is less than one-third of that produced on average in the EU-27. Education in Turkey also lags seriously behind all the EU-25 countries. The PISA scores (OECD's Program for International Student Assessment), which were designed to measure the effectiveness of school systems in providing young people with a solid foundation of knowledge and skills, show Turkey to be last compared to the EU-27 in terms of the reading, science, and mathematics skills. Thus, a serious developmental gap exists between Turkey and the EU-27, not to mention that between Turkey and the EU-15, which will require massive amounts of financial assistance over a long period of time. Most of this assistance will have to be provided by the more well-to-do members of the EU.

The third issue, and for many observers the most intractable of all concerns, is the fact that Turkey is 99.8 percent Muslim, 70 percent of which belong to the Sunni sect of Islam. With the horrific attack on the World Trade Center on September 11, 2001, the gruesome assassination of Theo van Gogh in the Netherlands by a radical Muslim, and the growing Islamophobia in Europe since the early 1990s triggered by increasing immigration of Muslims into relatively homogeneous European nations, many observers argue that European citizens will find it very difficult to accept Turkey as a partner in the EU on cultural grounds. One example of the cultural chasm separating Turkish and Western cultures can be found in the **honor killings**, where in countries such as Germany and Italy, Turkish women were murdered by their own family members, mostly their brothers or husbands, because they wanted to end a relationship with their Turkish partners, refused to wear the traditional *hijab* (the Muslim headscarf), or, the ultimate shame, decided to adopt a Western lifestyle. Other observers raise the issue of geography: From a geographical perspective, only a very small part of Turkey is located on the European continent, which is separated from Asia Minor by the Bosporus strait. On which basis, they ask, can Turkey be admitted to the "European" Union?

The religious differences between Turkey and the EU are used by many as an argument against Turkish membership. However, including an overwhelmingly Muslim country such as Turkey into the fold of the EU could help to stave off radicalization in Turkey and even help in the integration of Muslims in Europe. Turkey is one of the very few Muslim countries that has managed to remain secular and pro-Western as a member of NATO (North Atlantic Treaty Organization), and yet is made up of a society with deeply held Muslim beliefs. On this basis, Barack Obama, visiting Turkey in the spring of 2009, encouraged the EU to accept Turkey as a member.

Sweden, Italy, and the United Kingdom are the staunchest supporters of Turkey to join the EU while Austria, France, and Germany are some of the strongest opponents to accession. French and Austrian government officials flatly state that Turkey should not become a member while Germany's Angela Merkel speaks of a "privileged partnership" of Turkey with the EU. According to a Eurobarometer survey, while in 2004, 80 percent of Turks supported EU accession, by 2009 that percentage had dropped to 45.[20]

In fact, even Turkish elites and certainly investors are becoming less enamored with the EU given the debt crises its southern members face and the sluggish economic growth in Europe, combined with growing Islamophobia. While in the first quarter of 2011, the EU economies grew by 2.5 percent, Turkey's economy grew by 11 percent over the same period, making it the highest-growing economy in the world. Turkey's credit rating is one of the few which has actually been upgraded since the economic crisis of 2008 began.[21]

In August 2007, the Turkish parliament elected a new president, Abdullah Gül. He is the first president who outspokenly shares his Muslim conviction and whose wife wears the *hijab,* prompting some nervous moments in Turkey as it was unclear how the military, a staunch defender of secularism, would react. But President Gül's unwavering support for full Turkish EU membership helped to ease the tensions in the wake of his election. Interestingly, the more obstacles the EU presents for full membership talks, the less public support there is in Turkey to become a member of the EU. With Turkey receiving the cold shoulder from the EU for so many years, it is very possible that it reorients its attention from the West to the East, to Iran, Iraq, and Syria—which in Turkey is called the "no problem strategy"—a development that could not be in the interest of the European Union. To be sure, much of the negative reaction by European publics is based simply on racism and xenophobia, which cannot be tolerated, particularly given Europe's past. Yet in the case of Turkey, given the relentless expansion by the EU, many Europeans are asking themselves the question, "What is Europe, and where does it end?" With accession of so many more countries, many of them increasingly diverging in cultures, economic capacities, and religions, on which grounds could a **European identity** emerge?

A CONSTITUTION FOR EUROPE? "NON" AND "NEE"

The purpose of creating a European constitution would be to enshrine in one encompassing framework the multitude of complex treaties that have hitherto governed the EU. Moreover, the union's confusing three-pillar structure would have to be streamlined into one body of law with a single legal personality.

Ratifying the EU constitution could have been achieved in two ways: by votes in the national parliaments or by the politically riskier method of referendum. For the constitutional treaty to come into effect, all 25 EU countries at the time had to ratify it (this was before entry of Bulgaria and Romania). Before the French cast their ballots on the treaty, nine countries (Austria, Germany, Greece, Hungary, Italy, Lithuania, Slovakia, Slovenia, and Spain) had already endorsed the EU constitution. Spain did so in a referendum, with 77 percent of Spaniards supporting the document, although the voter turnout was barely over 42 percent.

The date for the French referendum on the EU treaty was set for May 29, 2005. That date was awaited with much anticipation, since France was the first, large, founding member of the EU to hold such a referendum. Most remarkably, the French national constitution did not necessitate a referendum on this issue. It could have been passed via votes in Parliament. However, a year prior to the 2005 referendum, French president Jacques Chirac had decided to ratify the EU treaty via referendum, confident that it was winnable.

It was not. The night of the referendum brought a debacle for the French president and the "oui" supporters; around 55 percent of the voters rejected the treaty. Voter turnout was a robust 70 percent. This result sent shockwaves across Europe because there was no "Plan B" in terms of what to do in case of a rejection of the treaty. Only three days after the French rejected the treaty, the Dutch held their referendum. The Dutch tend to be very loyal "Europeans," but there the treaty was shot down also, even more decisively—with 62 percent of the voters saying "nee" to the EU constitution with a turnout of almost 63 percent. The people of two founding member states had spoken, and they delivered a resounding slap in the face to the elites who favored passage of the treaty.

The shock of these two referenda was so severe that the ratification schedule was suspended and replaced by an indefinite "period of reflection." The purpose of the suspension of the ratification schedule was to avoid further blows to the EU treaty and allow leaders of countries with wavering publics, such as Great Britain, to extract themselves from the process without having to face a referendum.

Why did French and Dutch voters reject the EU constitution? It is fair to say that very few voters actually read the constitution before they made their decision. Few issues in the EU treaty were part of the public debate, which itself was cleverly orchestrated by the respective "yes" and "no" organizers. In France, section III of the treaty, which dealt with competition policy and market economy principles, became the focus of the "non" campaign, even though many of these principles date back to the Treaty of Rome signed in 1957. Critics of the document argued that section III would undermine social solidarity by favoring the well-to-do at the expense of the working class. In addition, with 10 percent unemployment, public fears were rampant that people from the new EU countries in Central and Eastern Europe would come to France and take away jobs from the locals. The poster child of these fears was the imagined "Polish plumber" who would show up immediately to fix the sink and charge less than the French plumber, thereby driving French plumbers out of business.[22]

The most outspoken critics of the constitution were to be found on both sides of the political spectrum. The former Socialist prime minister Laurent Fabius stirred up a very popular "non" campaign in his party, winning over many skeptics, even though the Socialist Party was officially a supporter of the EU constitution. Fabius feared that the constitution was too pro-market, would undermine the French welfare state, and would leave insufficient protections for workers' interests. The Communists, together with the Greens, unionists, and the antiglobalization movement, made similar arguments about the undermining of the welfare state, the exploitation of the environment, and the loss of French identity should this referendum pass.

On the right of the political spectrum, nationalists such as Jean-Marie Le Pen, leader of the National Front, were also against the EU constitution because they feared that its ratification would allow even easier access of foreigners to come to France. Peasants and farmers remained unconvinced that supporting this document would be in their favor. In addition, the "no" vote on the constitution was as much a referendum on Chirac's policies as it was about the future of Europe, since many parties and movements used this opportunity to strike a blow at the substance of Chirac's policies as well as at his style of government.

In the Netherlands, the people voted "nee" for different reasons. Dutch "no" voters were concerned about "Europe" becoming too powerful and interfering with the traditionally very liberal Dutch policies on gay marriage and soft drugs. In addition, after the murder of filmmaker Theo van Gogh, the Dutch have become much more sensitive to immigration and the challenges associated with the growing heterogeneity of their society (Chapter 12).

Overall, the rejection in both France and the Netherlands of the EU constitution highlighted the general disillusionment of the people with the highly elitist character of the EU. In these two referenda, people voted not only on the EU constitution, but also on what they thought about the introduction of the euro; the enlargement from 15 to 25 EU countries in 2004; the initiation of talks with Bulgaria, Romania, and Turkey to become future members; and the general elitist way in which things are done in Brussels. It is well known that the EU suffers from a "democratic deficit," meaning that decisions are made at very high levels within the EU but also within the respective member states, and do not necessarily correspond to the desires of the citizens. There was remarkably little citizen input when the euro was introduced and when the 2004 enlargement was decided. Once the voters finally had a chance to make their voices heard, they reflected on the totality of their concerns about the EU, and their verdict was a resounding "no" to the direction in which the EU was going. The rapid introduction of the euro and the zeal with which EU elites pushed through enlargement was too quick for many citizens, and with their vote they essentially called for a pause in the fast-paced changes. In their literature review, Liesbet Hooghe and Gary Marks show that indeed the political elite in Europe have a much more positive attitude towards the EU than ordinary citizens, and they admonish that "party leaders in position of authority must look over their shoulders when negotiating European issues."[23] Andreas Follesdal and Simon Hix go in the same direction in their critique when they argue that "the EU is simply too distant from voters."[24]

Oftentimes, critics of the EU integration process underestimate how far Europe has come. Only a little over 60 years ago, the bloodiest battles in the history of mankind occurred in Europe together with the most gruesome genocide ever conceived. Today, Europe, despite some undeniable challenges, is a flourishing, dynamic, modern single market encompassing about 500 million consumers who are at peace with one another. The EU project remains one of the most ambitious undertakings ever devised in which countries voluntarily give up part of their sovereignty in order to reap the fruits that grow on common ground. The challenges that confront individual European democracies in the age of globalization are immense. European integration will ensure that European democracies can successfully compete against other economic superpowers such as the United States and Japan, and the future superpowers India and China.

This positive side of the accomplishments of the EU got a boost on June 23, 2007, when the European Council replaced the sensitive term of a European *constitution* with the narrower concept of a *Reform Treaty*. As American readers are well aware, the term *constitution* has a great emotional and symbolic significance, and many Europeans were not ready to have a constitution at the European level in addition to their national constitutions. "Reform Treaty" expresses better where the EU stands today. The text of this treaty is also much shorter than the initially proposed constitution. At the symbolic level, the European flag with the 12 stars on blue ground is no longer declared as the official flag of the EU; the flag, however, can continue to be used, although without official status.

In terms of substance, the negotiations were very hard, and at several times it looked as if they would break down. Poland wished to have more say in the decision mode for the Council of Ministers. They even brought up the very emotional argument that the Polish population would be much larger today if so many Poles had not been killed by Nazis in World War II. Considering this argument, Poland should get a greater weight in the Council of Ministers. Great Britain was opposed to granting even more power for the EU, in particular in the area of foreign policy where the initial draft of the Reform Treaty planned for an EU foreign minister.

In the first half of 2007, the rotating presidency of the EU was with Germany, so it was up to German chancellor Angela Merkel to preside over the controversial June 2007 meeting of the European Council. She did an excellent job, having separate meetings with the Polish president, Lech Kaczynski, and the British prime minister, Tony Blair, and bringing in other countries if necessary. The full meeting itself took 36 hours, going on long into the night. Finally, there was a breakthrough heralded by everyone. The president of the European Commission, José Manuel Barroso, exclaimed: "The goal for the summit was to reach a mandate for an institutional settlement. We have reached it. This shows that Europe is on the move in the right direction. Reaching agreement was a credibility test for the Union. This Reform Treaty provides the Union with the capacity to act."[25] The EU does not get a foreign minister, but a member of the European Commission with the cumbersome title "High Representative for Foreign Affairs and Security Policy," who will be at the same time the vice president of the European Commission. More importantly, this office holder will preside over the meetings when the foreign ministers of the member countries come together. Thus, in many ways, there will be a EU foreign minister, although not by title, a typical EU compromise. A typical EU compromise was also reached with regard to the decision mode for the Council of Ministers, namely, to extend a deadline. Initially, it was planned to replace the current decision mode described earlier in the chapter by 2009. This deadline was now extended to 2014 and under certain conditions even to 2017, which pleased Poland since the new decision mode will give Poland slightly less weight than the current one; therefore, Poland gets quite a long grace period. Afterward, for a decision to be valid it will need a double majority, 55 percent of the member countries, and the winning side must correspond to 65 percent of the total EU population.

These June 2007 negotiations of the European Council are typical of how the EU often works: compromises with regard to exact titles of particular offices, extensions of deadlines, and exhausting meetings long into the night. Although these are not elegant ways to make decisions, it works for the EU. It muddles through.

The Reform Treaty contains three other important institutional innovations: First, the presidency of the European Council shall no longer rotate every 6 months, but every 30 months, giving more continuity to the office. Second, a majority of the national parliaments can force the European Commission to redraft legislation, which should bring the EU closer to the citizens of the individual countries. A third innovation goes even further in involving citizens at the EU level: It gives 1 million EU citizens with their signatures the right to force the European Commission to begin to draft legislation in a particular issue area.

After all details were worked out, the Reform Treaty was formally signed by the EU leaders on December 13, 2007, in Lisbon; the treaty is thus also called the Lisbon Treaty. It needs to be ratified by all 27 member countries. Since the document is no longer called a constitution, ratification by the national parliaments was considered as sufficient. In Ireland, however, the Supreme Court was of a different opinion and decided that Ireland needed a popular referendum for ratification. In 2008, the referendum failed, with only 47 percent of voters supporting the Reform Treaty, once again throwing the EU in a crisis. One year later, however, with some concessions of the EU, the referendum on the treaty passed with 67 percent yes votes. Contributing to this turn-around in the Irish electorate was also the great deterioration of the Irish economy with the global economic crisis of 2008–2009. The EU helped Ireland with a huge financial package, and the Irish voters realized how much they depended on the EU. Barroso, the president of the European Commission, commented that "Ireland has given Europe a new chance."[26] The Reform Treaty could now go into effect. This means in particular that the presidency of the European Council is no longer rotating but is fixed for two and a half years. Herman Van Rompuy, prime minister of Belgium, was appointed as first permanent president.

KEY TERMS

budget   313
cohesion   317
contributions   316
Council of Europe   305
Council of
   Ministers   304
democracy deficit   312
European Coal and Steel
   Community   306
European Council   304

European identity   324
European Social
   Charter   306
honor killings   323
influence
   of farmers   317
infrastructure   318
investiture   314
older historical
   traditions   304

Pan-European
   movement   305
Single European
   Act   307
traditional own
   resources   316
Treaty on European
   Union   307
value-added tax   316
welfare systems   322

DISCUSSION QUESTIONS

1. What does Europe gain or lose by establishing an "ever closer union"?
2. How would you define "Europe"?
3. Can you foresee a time when there is a "United States of Europe"? Yes or no, and why?
4. What arguments are in Turkey's favor or disfavor in terms of joining the EU?
5. Why is there a "democratic deficit" in the EU?
6. How would you suggest making the EU more responsive to the people?
7. In which policy areas do you think the EU is the strongest? The weakest?
8. What institutions account for the supranational/intergovernmental character of the EU?
9. Compare the EU institutions with those of the United States. What are the similarities and differences?

NOTES

1. Tanja A. Börzel et al., Obstinate and Inefficient. Why Member States Do Not Comply with European Law? *Comparative Political Studies* 43 (2010): 1363–1390.
2. *BBC News*. Q&A: GE's Failed Merger, July 4, 2001.
3. Liesbet Hooghe and Gary Marks. A Postfunctionalist Theory of European Integration: From Permissive Consensus to Constraining Dissensus. *British Journal of Political Science* 39, no. 1 (October 2008): 11.
4. *Neue Zürcher Zeitung*, April 24, 1996.
5. *The Guardian*, April 2, 1996.
6. Philipp Büchler. *Die Entstehung der Sozialcharta des Europarates* (Lizentiatsarbeit: Universität Bern, 1993).
7. http://europa.eu.int/.
8. Martin Shapiro and Alec Stone. The New Constitutional Politics of Europe. *Comparative Political Studies* 26, no. 4 (January 1994): 412.

9. http://www.europarl.europa.eu/parliament/archive/elections2009/en/index_en.html.

10. From the UEN Party Platform: http://www.uengroup.org/home.html.

11. Giacomo Benedetto. 2004 European Parliament Election Briefing No. 22: The European Parliament Election Results and the European Parliament of 2004. European Parties Elections and Referendum Network (EPERN).

12. Ibid.

13. Financial Programming and Budget, EU Budget explained 2011. http://ec.europa.eu/budget/explained/myths/myths_en.cfm.

14. Ibid.

15. http://www.europa.eu.int/comm/food/animal/welfare/farm/.

16. http://www.euro.ecb.int/.

17. http://www.europa.eu.int/.

18. European Commission, Directorate General for Economic and Financial Affairs. Quarterly Report on the Euro Area, vol. 8, no. 1, 2009.

19. Hans Wermer Sinn. Den Sozialstaat gilt es zu schützen. *Netzeitung,* June 30, 2006.

20. Anti Turkey rhetoric undermines Turks' support for EU bid, *Today's Zaman,* December 16, 2009.

21. EU Accession Hurdle no longer a problem for Turkey Property, *Times.com,* July 22, 2011.

22. Laurent Cohen-Tanugi. The End of Europe? *Foreign Affairs* 84, no. 5 (November/December 2005): 355–359.

23. Hooghe and Marks. A Postfunctionalist Theory of European Integration, p. 5.

24. Andreas Follesdal and Simon Hix. Why There Is a Democratic Deficit in the EU: A Response to Majone and Moravcsik. *Journal of Common Market Studies* 44, no. 3 (2006): 536.

25. www.ec.europa.eu, June 24, 2007.

26. *The New York Times,* October 4, 2009.

Globalization and European Democracies

In the first 14 chapters of this book, the central assumption is that countries are **sovereign** policymakers. Particularly in Chapter 10 on policy outcomes, we have argued that a whole host of outcomes, among them unemployment, economic growth, health, education, and environmental outcomes, are the result of idiosyncratic types of election systems, political parties, the processes of cabinet formation, the role of interest groups, and the specific historical experiences of modernization.

In Chapter 14 on the European Union (EU), however, we highlighted the central trade-off that comes with joining the union: In order to take advantage of a common market encompassing about 500 million consumers, the sovereignty of nations becomes **restricted**. How does joining the EU restrict sovereignty? If people can travel across intra-EU borders without any border controls; if goods, capital, and services can freely cross borders without the capacity of states to impose duties; if nations cannot shape exchange rate policies anymore because they all share the same currency (except the United Kingdom, Denmark, Sweden, and some of the new accession countries); if they are limited in the way they can engage in economic policy because they are not supposed to exceed budget deficits of 3 percent; if the quality of products must correspond to certain "harmonized" standards; if there are EU-wide regulations ranging from the environment to how to treat farm animals to labor regulation; if the setting of interest rates is performed by a European-wide central bank; if EU law takes precedence over national law in increasing measure—if these and many other effects of the EU apply, one might say that the capacity of a country to engage in its "own" policies is restricted. These are just a few examples of how the EU limits the sovereignty of countries to engage in their own policymaking. This does not negate our claims in Chapter 10 that policy outcomes do reflect national idiosyncrasies; however, there is no doubt that the maneuvering room for national policymaking is becoming more tightly circumscribed.

But what does "Europeanization" have to do with "globalization"? Both of these concepts are in fact very much related, insofar as they both mean a reduction of the sovereignty of nations. However, from the examples just given and from what we wrote in Chapter 14, it is clear that Europeanization goes much farther and deeper than globalization ever could, at least in the foreseeable future. The difference between Europeanization and globalization is that the former is driven by clearly defined procedures, under the auspices of national elites, and ultimately, at least ideally, by the citizens of the various countries. Through elections, a democratic process, either the people or their representatives vote on whether or not to join the EU, notwithstanding the widespread observations that the EU suffers from a "democratic deficit." In addition, many other decisions are made by the people's representatives in the various nations' parliaments. What makes the EU a unique historical process is precisely the fact that it unfolds against a detailed set of regulations, the so-called "**acquis communautaire**," a document that today encompasses about 170,000 pages.[1] Once the people of a country have, through the democratic process of referendum, decided that they wanted to join the EU, this means that they are then obliged to accept and implement the "acquis," as it is known in short. The acquis, this common body of EU law, covers everything from free movement of people, to competition policy, to environmental issues, to the collection and use of statistics, to external relations, social policy and employment, and many other policy areas.

Thus, the difference between Europeanization and globalization is twofold: First, Europeanization is based, at least ideally, on a **democratic process** that involves either the citizens directly, or their representatives. Second, it spells out in detail what it means for a country to join the EU. Globalization has no democratic impetus, and there is no document that is comparable to the acquis that regulates in such detail every aspect of cross-border relations. Rather, globalization is a process that is "anarchic," that is, market driven without any regulation or oversight. Europeanization is driven by **governments**, whereas globalization is driven by **markets**.

WHAT IS GLOBALIZATION?

Globalization is a process whose origins are directly related to advances in **technology**, particularly transportation technologies. Globalization can be described as the "obliteration of distance" as a result of the development of seagoing ships; the invention of the locomotive, the airplane, and automobiles; the development of other transportation technologies such as the invention of the compass; and the utilization of motorways and containerization. In addition, large-scale transportation projects such as the opening of the Suez Canal and the completion of the Union Pacific Railroad in 1869—and, in more recent times, the Channel Tunnel connecting the United Kingdom with France—aid in the unfolding of globalization.

There is a certain "hype" surrounding globalization, and the media portrays it as if it were a recent phenomenon. "Separate individuals have become more and more enslaved under a power alien to them...a power which has become more and more enormous and, in the last instance, turns out to be world market." This quote could have been gleaned from the sign of any antiglobalization protester who demonstrated at the latest G8 meeting. Yet, these words were uttered over 150 years ago by Karl Marx as he penned *The German Ideology* in 1845–1846![2]

In fact, in 1913, shortly before World War I, world merchandise exports as a percentage of GDP had reached such impressive levels that, after significant drops in the interwar period and also after 1950, it took the Organization for Economic Cooperation and Development (OECD) until the late 1970s to reach similar levels of world trade. Trade, measured as the average of exports and imports as a percentage of gross domestic product (GDP), in the United Kingdom was 27.7 percent in 1913; this level dropped to 13.1 percent in 1950, increased to 16.6 percent in 1970, and reached 21.1 percent in 1987, significantly short of the 27.7 percent the United Kingdom had achieved in 1913.[3] Thus, globalization is an uneven process marked by periods of rapid expansion of trade followed by contractions during the interwar years when many countries, but particularly the United States, took an isolationist stance, and also during the immediate years after World War II.

It is true that the process of globalization has accelerated in more recent years with the development of information and communication technologies. Advances in telecommunications, digital systems, satellite technology, fiber optics, and the Internet have dramatically reduced **transportation** and **transaction costs**, making products and services that were hitherto not tradable ready to be exchanged in the global marketplace. Such products include perishable and seasonal fashion items, as well as the production and interpretation of information itself, such as management consultancy, films, television news, and others. A prime example of how globalization obliterates distance is today's capacity to **outsource** customer service for high-tech products to India, or the Indian physician who interprets via the Internet a patient's X-ray taken in the United States or Europe. These technological advances are complemented by international organizations, such as the International Monetary Fund (IMF), the World Bank, and particularly the World Trade Organization (WTO), the last of which zealously works toward a reduction of tariff and nontariff barriers in order to let the world market deal its "invisible hand" even more effectively.

The consequences of these technological developments and the impact of the WTO on the world economy are staggering: International trade has been growing at a much larger rate than economic output. Between 1950 and 2004, global economic growth increased by a factor of six while trade increased by a factor of 25. The value of global merchandise exports in 2006 was almost 200 times greater than the value of global merchandise exports in 1950 (expressed in U.S. dollars at current prices). One of the most direct effects of technological development on globalization is the capacity of capital markets to move international capital. In his book, *The Ascent of Money*, Niall Ferguson argues that in 2006 the value of all the stock markets in the world (51 trillion US $) was actually 10 percent bigger than the value of the goods and services produced globally (47 trillion US $)![4] Of course wealth held in stocks is risky—stock markets rise and fall and by late 2008 the stock market had contracted by 40 percent. The consequences of globalization not only have an economic dimension, but they also affect communities as international "cultural products" such as music, films, television, and others penetrate into hitherto local areas. For example, in 1996, the TV show *Baywatch* was the most widely viewed show, with 1.1 billion viewers in 142 countries. It was shown on every continent except Antarctica.[5] By 2001, *Buffy the Vampire Slayer* had become the most popular TV show in the world, and today, the Chinese can watch the foibles of *The Simpsons*. In 2009, the world's most popular TV show was *House* and *Desperate Housewives* was the world's most popular comedy show by attracting a global audience of 65 million viewers.[6]

In 2001, the share of U.S. films as a percentage of all films in Germany was 77 percent, and this share is 74 percent in the United Kingdom, 62 percent in Spain, 60 percent in Italy, and 47 percent in France. In all countries, except the United Kingdom, this percentage grew steadily between 1984 and 2001.[7]

Another form of cultural globalization can be observed in the various American traditions that have gained popularity in continental European countries, such as Halloween. Halloween originated with the Celts, is pagan in tradition, and was transferred with Irish immigrants to the United States. It has only very recently been celebrated in continental European countries such as Austria, with the same trappings of jack-o-lanterns and kids disguising themselves as ghosts, witches, or imps and demanding treats—except in Austria kids do not say "trick or treat" but rather "süss oder sauer" (sweet or sour). An Irish tradition thus was transported via migration to the United States, where it became widespread. Today, this tradition is making the trip back to Europe via satellite beams directly into households of Europeans, who eagerly absorb American popular culture.

This little vignette demonstrates that along with technological development and cultural adaptation, **migration** is also a central element of globalization. Since the late 1950s, countries such as Germany and Austria have actively recruited so-called guest workers, first from Italy, then from former Yugoslavia and Turkey, to help in the reconstruction of their countries after World War II and during the years of the economic miracle of the 1960s and early 1970s. After the quadrupling of the oil prices in 1973–1974, however, labor immigration was curbed as economic activity came to a sudden stop. Nevertheless, incentives given to guest workers to return home did not have the desired effects. In fact, despite a stop on labor migration, immigration into European countries continued on the basis of family reunification—the guest workers brought in their wives and extended families, increasing the percentage of the foreign population.[8]

Figure 15.1 shows the foreign population across various European democracies over a 16-year period from 1992 to 2007. In most countries that percentage has increased over time, although it has decreased for the Netherlands. Over time, there is very little movement in any direction of the

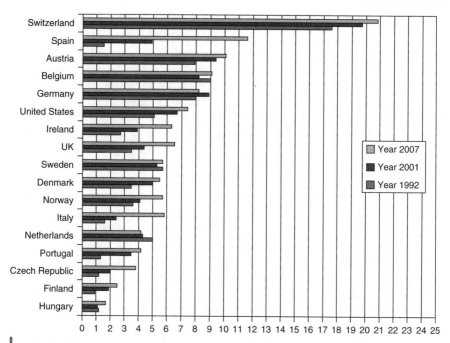

FIGURE 15.1

Percentage of foreign population in selected European democracies in 1995, 1999, and 2007.

Source: OECD Factbook, 2010.

statistics in Belgium, Germany, and Sweden. Switzerland has by far the highest percentage of foreign population among its ranks, which is partly explained by the difficulty of becoming Swiss, followed by Spain and Austria. The largest increases in foreign populations are visible in Spain, Italy, and Ireland. It is important to distinguish between *foreign population* and *foreign-born population*. The latter tends to generate higher percentages of the total resident population because it also includes subjects who are foreign born but have attained national citizenship. The OECD defines *foreign-born population* as follows: "The foreign-born population can be viewed as representing first-generation migrants, and may consist of both foreign and national citizens."[9] In some countries, the foreign-born population is significantly higher than the foreign population, such as in Sweden where in 2007 that percentage made up 13.4 percent of the population, in the Netherlands where it was 10.7 percent, in Norway where it was 9.5 percent, and in Austria, where it was 14.2 percent.

A second major development that led to further increases of migration from the east toward Western Europe was the fall of the **Soviet Union**. This unleashed waves of immigrants into Germany, both asylum seekers and migrants who, on the basis of their "ethnic German" status, were granted German citizenship immediately. Germany is one of the few countries, besides Israel, that allows its citizens who have emigrated to return to their homeland. People with papers indicating their German ethnic origins—regardless of how many generations they lived outside of Germany in Russia, or Kazakhstan, or other parts of Central and Eastern Europe—made use of their privilege and immigrated to Germany. Between 1988 and 2004, over 3 million ethnic Germans immigrated to Germany, many of them ill-prepared in terms of the culture shock and lack of language and other skills. Ironically, the "ethnic Germans" prove to be much more difficult to integrate than the Turks and their descendants. The Turks have lived in Germany for decades, usually speak fluent German, mostly have jobs, and are relatively well integrated, but yet have not been able to become Germans until recently.[10]

The clearest example of globalization, or, in other words, increasing interdependence, is probably the **environment**. For instance, while particular lifestyles are territorially bound (e.g., driving gas-guzzling vehicles in the United States or producing steel in Eastern Europe in the 1970s and early 1980s with coal-fired power plants), the effects of such behaviors or policies are not. The carbon dioxide from fuel-inefficient vehicles traps heat and adds to the greenhouse effect, leading to global warming, while the sulfur emitted in the Czechoslovak steel mills came down as acid rain in Finland, destroying the aquatic life in thousands of Finnish lakes in addition to adding to the greenhouse effect. Polluted air does not recognize borders and will drift freely wherever the winds will carry it. Similarly, when the Chinese push forward with no-holds-barred economic development, this will manifest itself in a corresponding demand for oil; people all around the world will feel the effects of Chinese development in the form of higher oil prices and, again, in the form of increased pollution. As another example, the ancient tradition of cockfighting in Indonesia has led to the jumping of the avian flu virus from birds to humans. Although the avian flu virus has not mutated to the degree that it can be transmitted from human to human, if this does occur, modern transportation methods such as airliners will aid in the rapid dissemination of the virus, as they did in the case of AIDS. Meanwhile, the already-infected birds take flight along their migration routes, carrying the bird flu virus with them to any country in which they eventually settle.

These examples highlight a central feature of both globalization and the environment: the **interconnectedness** of individuals and their lifestyles, regional and national policies, poverty, political development, diseases, wars, environmental outcomes, and many other aspects. Such interconnectedness decreases the capacity of nation-states to tackle such issues on their own while at the same time increases the importance of international organizations, leading some proponents of globalization to proclaim that national borders are becoming obsolete, while others decry this as "globaloney."

Globalization, then, can best be understood as a continuing process of integration and increasing interdependence between countries. In more practical terms, it means that more people worldwide:

- are most likely wearing a shirt made in China,
- have traveled abroad,
- are driving a foreign car and watching more foreign films,

- have jobs with international connections,
- are more aware of events abroad,
- count people from other countries among their friends,
- perhaps think of moving to another country,
- use modern communications technologies such as e-mail and the Internet,
- are affected by environmental outcomes not produced in their country,
- know more about other countries and cultures,
- are concerned about faraway diseases reaching their own country,
- work for an international company,
- are aware of other countries' traditions,
- consume products made abroad,
- invest in companies abroad,
- are affected by economic developments in countries far away from their own,
- talk to people on the telephone or the Internet in another country, or
- use services generated in another country, or both.

It is precisely this global interconnection and interdependence that explains why the economic crisis of 2008, which originated in the United States, made its way so quickly around the world: As advantageous globalization may be in good times, it can be just as disastrous in bad times. As we have seen in Chapter 9, reactions to the global downturn differ between Europe and the United States. Despite our arguments about increasing sovereignty of the EU, when it comes to dealing with the economic crisis, each European nation went its own way. When it comes to fiscal and monetary policy, there is very little cooperation across European countries.

HOW SHOULD GLOBALIZATION BE MEASURED?

There is not one perfect measure to capture the elusive concept of globalization. But our discussion thus far has highlighted various dimensions of globalization, such as economic, cultural, technological, and political dimensions. The Swiss Federal Institute of Technology in Zurich developed a **globalization index** based on economic, social, and political categories. More specifically, the index examines actual economic flows such as trade and foreign direct investments, examines economic restrictions such as the degree to which a country restricts foreign direct investments and trade, and contains data on information flows such as the spread of ideas, images, information, and people, while the political dimension measures spread of government policies.

A central predictor for the degree to which a country is "globalized" is simply its size. For example, trade expressed as imports and exports as a percentage of GDP in Luxembourg is almost 200, whereas in the United States that percentage is around 21.[11] This means that Luxembourg trades around twice as much as it produces, while the United States trades only around a fifth of what it produces. The difference, of course, is that the United States has a gigantic internal market whereas Luxembourg, a very small country, is extremely exposed to the vagaries of international business cycles. Thus, by definition, the smaller a country is, the more "globalized" it has to be, at least in economic terms. Using the Swiss

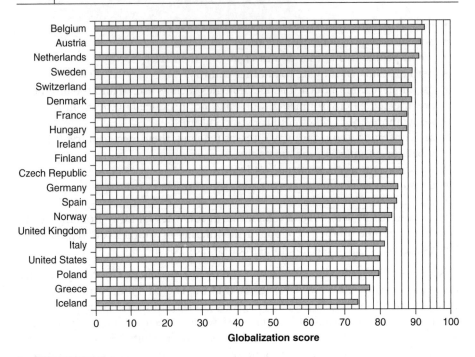

FIGURE 15.2
Globalization score 2011.

Source: Axel Dreher. Does Globalization Affect Growth? Evidence from a New Index of Globalization. *Applied Economics 38*, no. 10 (2006): 1091–1110, updated in: Axel Dreher, Noel Gaston and Pim Martens. *Measuring Globalisation—Gauging its Consequences* (New York: Springer, 2010).

index, Figure 15.2 indicates that in 2011 Belgium followed by Austria and the Netherlands are the most globalized countries, while Poland, Greece, Iceland, and the United States are the bottom of our rankings. This means that the smaller a country is, the more its sovereignty is circumscribed by the forces of globalization It is this fact, which some consider troublesome, to which we now turn.

THE CHALLENGES OF GLOBALIZATION FOR EUROPEAN DEMOCRACIES

If it is true that globalization is driven by the logic of markets, many central elements of European politics should be affected. As a general rule, it is safe to say that governments are more interventionist in European democracies than in the United States and thus should be more affected by the results of globalization. In addition, Europeans generally favor equality over liberty, again highlighting the central role of the state in achieving equality. For these reasons, European countries should be particularly affected by the process of globalization.

How do citizens feel about globalization? Globalization usually becomes an issue when there are violent street protests, as was the case with the "Battle

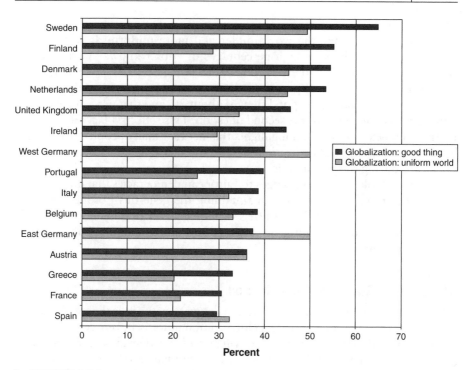

FIGURE 15.3

Percentage of respondents who agreed to the following question: "You may have heard of globalization, that is the general opening up of all economies, which leads to the creation of a worldwide market. Could you please tell me if you tend to agree or tend to disagree with the following statements: (1) Overall, globalization is a good thing for our country. (2) Globalization leads to a duller and more uniform world."

Source: Eurobarometer [EB 61], European Commission, 2004.

in Seattle" in 1999 at the Ministerial World Conference of the World Trade Organization, or during G8 meetings, when the leaders of the richest, most powerful nations come together. However, in the most recent G8 meeting in Deauville, France, in May 2011, no major protests or demonstrations took place. Public opinion surveys indicate (Figure 15.3) that attitudes about globalization are not as negative as some of the headline-grabbing protests suggest.

The graph in Figure 15.3 is ordered from the highest to lowest percentage of those who think that globalization is a "good thing." The Scandinavian countries and the Netherlands show a majority of people who believe that globalization is a good thing for their country, while Greece, France, and Spain are at the bottom of that list, with only around 30 percent of the people believing that globalization is a good thing. When it comes to the cultural dimension (i.e., when the question is asked whether people think that globalization "makes the world a duller and more uniform place"), few Europeans tend to disagree with that statement. In most European countries, more respondents believe that globalization will make the world duller and more uniform. It is important to note, however, the very high percentages of "don't knows" in this survey (for ease of interpretation, these are not shown in Figure 15.3). For example, the average percentage of those people who answered "don't know" to the question of whether globalization is a good thing is about 20, and that percentage rises to about 25 when it comes to the second question. This reflects a lack of reflection on this complex question and highlights the fact that many people are confused about the meaning of *globalization,* despite the fact that it has become such a buzzword during the past decade.

We now look at three challenges to European democracies that directly arise as a result of globalization: first, maintaining the generous European **welfare state**; second, the unprecedented levels of **immigration** into many of the "old" European countries; and third, the sense of loss of **"community"** across many of the same countries.

The Welfare State and Globalization

Globalization's biggest challenge to national governments is dealing with the loss of control over domestic politics. As globalization unfolds and erodes the coveted principle of national sovereignty, who will address the demands of marginalized and dislocated citizens? Where is the locus of legitimate government if that very government is hamstrung by international market forces? To whom do citizens turn when there is mass unemployment, when they become sick, when there is an economic depression, when they get injured on the job, or when they lose their possessions in a natural catastrophe? Will they turn to their elected government for help, or will they turn to the "world market"?

The world market has no address to which concerned citizens could send their petitions. There is no substitute for local politics, which can address the concerns of citizens. Nowhere is this more clearly visible than in the extent to which many European democracies have invested in social insurance schemes to ensure social harmony, provide equal opportunity, and offer protection from unemployment or illness (see Figure 1.1). Sweden, for example, spends over 27 percent of its GDP on such social expenditures, whereas the United States spends about 16 percent.

In Chapter 1, we highlighted the presence of extensive welfare states as one of the distinguishing features of European democracies. Many observers, however, are concerned that globalization will undermine the capacity of European democracies to maintain their social protection schemes. What is the logic of their argument? In order to fund national health care, public pensions, stipends, unemployment insurance, and many other public programs, modern welfare states rely on **tax revenues**. Tax revenues depend largely on a vibrant business sector that invests in the domestic economy, thereby generating corporate taxes as well as personal taxes as a result of people being employed by the company. These taxes, generated as a result of domestic economic activity, enable welfare states to fund their programs.

However, as we have noted, as a result of modern production and transportation technologies, many companies today have an "exit" opportunity, that is, an opportunity to leave their home country and produce in parts of the world where taxes are lower, wages are lower, and regulations such as environmental regulations are less stringent. Such "mobile asset holders" (mobile assets include capital, production facilities, and also highly qualified white-collar workers) will become "footloose," or able move to wherever the possibilities for higher profit are more promising, a process called **business process outsourcing**.

It bears repeating that "outsourcing" is not a new phenomenon. It occurred already in the 1970s when the production of relatively simple products such as textiles, shoes, or assembly processes were moved offshore.[12] The point of offshoring is to protect the company's "assets" by "mitigating" tax payments.

What is "new" is that nowadays, even services, such as financial services, customer services, and software production and support are moved offshore—these activities were previously believed to be very difficult to outsource. For example, New York parking tickets are sorted in Ghana; the data on unemployed New Jersey welfare recipients are handled in India.[13] This does not mean that more traditional forms of outsourcing have stopped. In a most ironic case, the uniforms of American border control agents are manufactured in Mexico.[14]

Nevertheless, the business sector that today shows a strong tendency for outsourcing is the information technology (IT) sector. In the summer of 2003, the board of the German high-tech giant Siemens announced that its software development division, which encompassed a workforce of 30,000, would no longer be able to keep these jobs in "expensive business locations" such as Germany, and was considering moving software development to India and China. Deloitte Consulting estimates that across Europe, 700,000 IT jobs will be moved to cheaper locations in the coming years. The situation is similar in the United States. According to Forrester Research, the American service sector will lose 3.3 million jobs by 2015. One out of four of the 500 biggest U.S. companies are outsourcing jobs offshore.[15]

Capital appears to have a great advantage in this globalized world for two reasons: First, the owners of capital can put significant pressures on governments to provide **inducements** to the companies to stay by promising them lower taxes, fewer social services for their workers, and even help in reducing the influence of unions. Incumbents' reelection chances are seriously reduced if unemployment increases as a result of companies closing their doors and moving to another country. This puts governments in the worst possible position, insofar as they have to deal with rising unemployment on the one hand, and at the same time face a reduced capacity to pay for unemployment benefits as a result of the shrinking tax base on the other. Consequently, incumbents have strong incentives to ensure that capital stays put by giving corporations tax breaks, by reducing the share of labor costs paid for by the employer, and through other economic incentives. For example, in many European democracies such as Germany, Austria, Belgium, and Finland, employers' contribution to social insurance is almost as high as the actual wage they pay their workers. The total labor costs per hour for an average American steelworker in 2005 consisted of about $19 for pay and $5 for social insurance, whereas in Germany, the share of a steelworker's pay is almost the same as in America, around $19, but the social insurance element, in German called *Lohnnebenkosten,* comes out to about $15, for an hourly total of $34.[16] In 2010, the hour labor costs for the EU-27 area was 26.9 euros (about 37 US dollars) with the highest labor costs in countries such as Denmark and Sweden (about $53 and $51, respectively) and the lowest labor costs in countries such as Bulgaria, Lithuania, and Latvia ($4.4, $7.2, and $8.00, respectively).

The second major advantage owners of mobile assets have is when it comes to choosing a new **location** for production. For example, large multinational corporations will often play off one location against another, engaging the governments in a bidding war against each other. Governments will thus be compelled to offer better conditions than their competitor in terms of, again, lower taxes; less onerous regulation; and no costs for such facilities as roads, sewage systems, bridges, and so on that the company needs for production. This will lead to a continuous undercutting by countries of each other's bids to the point where companies will locate in the country with the lowest wages, the least regulation, and oftentimes unsafe working conditions, and where they have to pay the least amount of social services, a process known as the **"race to the bottom."**

In the minds of many observers, these developments threaten the viability of the welfare state. If the tax base shrinks as a result of concessions given to holders of mobile capital to either stay put or to attract more of them, it is questionable whether the welfare state can continue to exist. These are legitimate concerns; yet, empirically, scholars have not been able to find a clear-cut connection between outsourcing and a reduction in the generosity of the welfare state.[17] Others have actually found that the more globalization is taking place, the more prominent the welfare state becomes, exactly the opposite of what the proponents of the globalization thesis assert. How can this be explained? The argument goes something like this: If it is true that modern Western nations cannot compete on the basis of price with less developed societies, they must compete on the basis of quality. Producing high-quality products requires an extremely well-educated populace, which, in turn, can only be achieved through increased public investment into education (human capital) and infrastructure (physical capital). In other words, the more globalization proceeds, the more the welfare state is needed to counteract the adverse effects of globalization.[18] The verdict is still out on these academic issues, but there is no doubt that outsourcing is affecting the daily lives of millions of Europeans.

Immigration and Globalization

The second challenge to European democracies arises with increased immigration into Europe. The nineteenth century saw significant emigration *from* Europe, but since the early 1960s, Europe has become a destination for immigrants. As mentioned above, particularly Germany, but also Austria, aggressively recruited so-called guest workers from Turkey and former Yugoslavia to help in the reconstruction of their war-ravaged countries and during the economic boom, the so-called *Wirtschaftswunder* (economic miracle) that unfolded in the late 1950s until 1973–1974. In addition, as explained earlier, with the fall of the Berlin Wall, millions of asylum seekers and ethnic Germans returned to Germany from far-flung corners of Central and Eastern Europe and Russia during the 1990s.

These were, of course, legal immigrants. However, over the past decade, Europe has been experiencing increasing illegal immigration, in the form of **human trafficking** organized by groups such as the Chinese "snakeheads" and the Italian and Russian Mafia in combination with poorly paid, corrupt border guards whose job is to supposedly secure the eastern borders of the EU. Countries with long sea borders such as Greece and Italy find it exceptionally difficult to patrol their waters, and oftentimes, if they do encounter a ship smuggling illegal immigrants, they are forced to aid women and children who were thrown overboard by the smugglers in order to escape. A second route of illegal immigration is from North Africa. Recently, the Italian government forcibly returned over 2,000 African migrants who had gathered on the small island of Lampedusa, Italy, and who planned to continue their journey farther north. They were returned in military aircraft to Libya, which has become a major staging ground for human traffickers wishing to smuggle Africans into Europe.[19] It is estimated that about 500,000 illegal immigrants make their way into Europe per year.[20]

A large number of the illegal immigrants who make it into Europe are unskilled, do not speak the national language, and find it extremely difficult to adjust to the local culture. A large percentage of women are forced into prostitution in order to pay the smugglers who brought them into Europe. It is estimated that the business of human trafficking is second only to drug smuggling. Human trafficking is a big business, with $7 billion generated by prostitution alone.[21]

European democracies face two separate yet related challenges: first, the political ramifications of legal and illegal immigration; and second, how to integrate those who have been given legal status in a European country. Immigration into relatively homogeneous European societies is fueling resentment by natives—because the immigrants are "different" in race or religion, or they take jobs away from natives, or because natives believe they have come to exploit the cushy welfare state. These motives make for a volatile mix. Racial prejudices fueled the appalling attacks in 1992 and 1993 that involved the firebombing of Turkish families, Vietnamese foreign laborers, and asylum seekers from Kosovo in the towns of Mölln, Hoyerswerda, Solingen, and Rostock.

People with such resentments are fodder for leaders of the radical right, who transform these sentiments of **xenophobia** into political support for their parties. Xenophobia has been an explosive political issue, and explains the electoral successes of Jean-Marie Le Pen in France in 2002, Jörg Haider in Austria in 1999, and the 2004 electoral successes of two German radical right-wing parties in the Länder of Brandenburg and Saxony, located in former Eastern Germany. In Saxony, the NPD (*Nationaldemokratische Partei Deutschlands*—National Democratic Party of Germany) gained 9.2 percent of the popular vote and had

12 members in Saxony's parliament. However, in the 2009 state elections the NPD received only 4.6 percent of the vote and in failing to pass the 5 percent threshold was not entitled to any seats in the Saxony Parliament.

The second challenge immigration presents is the integration of newcomers. Even if they have arrived legally, either as immigrants or asylum seekers, newcomers are often pushed to the margins of society, living in separate worlds, oftentimes referred to as "parallel societies." They tend to gravitate toward larger cities and form ethnic enclaves such as in the Swedish city of Malmø, where almost 40 percent of the town of 250,000 is foreign born. Integration of newcomers who are racially, religiously, and ethnically "different" into the hitherto largely homogeneous European population is challenging enough, but is made even more difficult if "otherness" is reinforced by poverty—in other words, when almost all the poor are minorities and almost all the minorities are poor.

This toxic brew of discrimination, bad schools, prejudice, lack of opportunity, poor housing in ethnic ghettoes, poverty, and hopelessness exploded across France during November 2005, when nightly riots occurred involving the burning of cars and property, perpetrated mostly by second- or third-generation Muslim immigrants of North or West African origin, who constitute about 10 percent of the French population. One of the factors behind these riots was youth unemployment, which had reached a staggering 40 percent in those ethnic enclaves.[22] The riots revealed a wide chasm between the white, well-to-do French citizens and the marginalized citizens.

Although economic deprivation was certainly a major contributor to the French riots, the riots also point out the failings of the French **Republican model** of integration. This model essentially says that all French citizens have the same cultural identity—French. In fact, being French is the only acceptable identity. Everybody is supposed to be equal in this model insofar as all French citizens are the same "children of the Republic," as then president Jacques Chirac declared at the height of the riots.[23] The French model of integration is an **assimilationist** model requiring that everybody speak the same official language and go through a common curriculum in school. This model does not allow any other forms of identity, such as wearing the Muslim headscarf, because such outward symbols would threaten the identity of the nation. The *l'affaire du foulard*, the headscarf debate, has plagued France since 1989, when two schoolgirls, wearing the traditional Muslim headscarf (*hijab*), were expelled from a public school. On March 15, 2004, Chirac signed a law banning the wearing of conspicuous religious symbols in schools, on the basis that such symbols would undermine the separation of church and state (*laïcité*) and national cohesion. Another element of the French Republican model is that the government does not keep official statistics on ethnicity, religion, or social class, as this would "violate the Republican tenet that France is 'one and indivisible.'"[24]

It is a bitter irony that this very model intended to create a sense of French identity based on common Republican principles did exactly the opposite: reveal dramatic differences in life chances between two classes of citizens—the "native" French with French-sounding names, with addresses in the swanky city centers, and with white skin color; and the second- or third-generation

French citizens with dark skin, Muslim-sounding names, and addresses in the dilapidated suburbs.

The second strategy of incorporating new citizens is called **multiculturalism**, which represents the opposite of assimilation. The Netherlands has practiced multiculturalism for the last three decades, but this approach has also been found deficient. Multiculturalism means that the state recognizes the cultural differences of immigrants and actively assists them in maintaining their language—setting up schools for their children with a customized curriculum, exemptions from dress codes, affirmative action policies, or allowing dual citizenship.

The most drastic failure of integration is of course when visible minorities, even if they are citizens of a European country, use violence in the name of a different ideology or religion. Three of the four suicide bombers who killed 56 people and injured 700 others in London on July 7, 2005, were of Pakistani descent and one was of Jamaican descent, but they were all British citizens. In the wake of these bombings, carried out by radical Muslims, then prime minister Tony Blair proposed strict **antiterror** measures, including surveillance of mosques, extremist Web sites, and bookstores, and deportation of radical Islamic leaders who incite anti-Western feelings among impressionable Muslim youths. Blair used strong language to defend his controversial deportation policy: "The rules of the game are changing....We are angry. We are angry about extremism and about what they are doing to our country, angry about their abuse of our good nature....We welcome people here *who share our values and our way of life.* But don't meddle in extremism because if you meddle in it...you are going back out again" (emphasis added).[25] This declaration is not consistent with British multiculturalism policies, and it is likely that political support for such policies is waning in the wake of radical Muslim bombings. In addition to Britain, other nations have also engaged in the deportation of radical Muslim leaders. In the summer of 2005, Italy deported eight radical Palestinian imams, and France ejected 12 so-called Islamic preachers of hate.[26] The latest German immigration law includes explicit deportation measures for those who preach hatred, holy war, or violence (*geistige Brandstifter*).

These episodes demonstrate that incorporation of immigrants, particularly those of Middle Eastern descent, is a significant challenge to European democracies, even if such immigrants have become citizens. There is no doubt that "Islamophobia" is spreading in European democracies. Europe, as opposed to the United States, does not have a "melting pot" identity. In fact, just the opposite is true. As we have seen in the French case, identity is connected to abstract Republican principles. In the case of Germany, until recently, German identity was connected to blood relationships (*jus sanguinis*). These rigid forms of identity make it much more difficult for immigrants to find acceptance and equal life chances among their European host societies as compared to the United States, where upward social mobility among immigrants is more vigorous. **Integration** of immigrants is one of the biggest challenges European democracies will face in the near future because it raises a fundamental question: Who are we?

Nothing illustrates the political and cultural incompatibility between the West and Muslim countries more than the "cartoon controversy," which erupted in January 2006. A Danish newspaper had published cartoons depicting the prophet Mohammed in September 2005. One cartoon showed Mohammed wearing a bomb-shaped turban, the fuse of which was on fire. Muslims around the world reacted angrily against these depictions and organized massive street demonstrations in Egypt, Pakistan, Malaysia, Thailand, Algeria, Afghanistan, and other Muslim countries as well as in many Western nations with significant Muslim immigrants. They attacked the Danish, Norwegian, Italian, and other Western embassies in many Muslim nations either by burning them down or by damaging them otherwise. Many Western nations recalled their ambassadors from Muslim countries for fear of their lives.

Muslims consider depictions of Mohammed blasphemous, and they were particularly offended by the degrading context in which their prophet was shown. Since the riots over the cartoon broke out, over 130 people have lost their lives because of it. The West reacted with claims that such depictions are protected by fundamental rights such as freedom of expression, which finds its origin in Western thought. Muslims, on the other hand, argue that with the right of freedom of expression comes responsibility. This cartoon controversy highlighted that the nature of the conflict between Muslims and the West is **cultural**. While globalization facilitates contact with members of other cultures, it also highlights the differences between peoples, often with dire consequences. And yet, as long as immigration of Muslims into Western countries continues, integration policies will be the only means to increase understanding between two potentially hostile groups of people.

Globalization and the Fragility of Community

The previous section has highlighted challenges to community that are driven by people in motion. But globalization can affect communities even without "others" impinging on host societies. This is particularly an issue when economic interests clash with local cultures or traditions. The competitive pressures of globalization are often described as "inevitable," "natural," or "logical," and it is a common belief that one can do very little against the imperatives of the world market. The central claim here is that economic rationality clashes with deeply held moral or religious principles, and that, "inevitably," the "logic" of the market will undermine these moral and religious tenets, thereby destroying the very sense of community and **identity** of particular groups.

Food is a case in point. In August 1999, José Bové, a French farmer educated at the University of California, Berkeley, together with some accomplices, wrecked a half-built McDonald's in the small French town of Millau, catapulting Bové to instant celebrity status. Bové is a sheep farmer who makes the famous French Roquefort cheese. The United States placed a tariff on Roquefort in retaliation for the French banning American hormone-treated beef. Bové's intent was to show how multinational agricultural companies standardize the production of agricultural products, impose standardized "taste," and, with the help of the World Trade Organization (WTO), undermine small, local agriculture based on "natural" production methods. Food for the French is not only an issue of sustenance, but it is a way of life, a manifestation of culture. McDonald's stands for the opposite of culture—it stands for homogeneity; standardization; sameness; and loss of color, texture, and local identity—at least in the eyes of globalization critics.

The French take "culture" seriously. There is such a thing called *l'exception culturelle française* (French cultural exception), which means that "culture" is not something that can be bought and sold, that it is not a commodity. For the French, culture is not primarily entertainment; it is an artistic expression of what it means to be French. Given this widespread perception, it follows that culture in all its forms, but mostly in terms of films, music, fiction, and food, needs to be protected from outside competition, particularly from the influence of Hollywood filmmakers, who often pander to the lowest of human instincts. French elites believe that the market should not decide what becomes most popular—art needs to be supported for its own sake. Indeed, since the mid-1990s regulations in effect state that 40 percent of all films shown must be of French origin. In addition, for every ticket sold on a foreign film, a certain percentage goes to toward **subsidizing** the French film industry. As a result, the French film industry is rather vibrant as compared to that of other European countries.

IS GLOBALIZATION A THREAT OR AN OPPORTUNITY FOR EUROPEAN DEMOCRACIES?

Europe is "ready" for globalization for the simple reason that Europeanization has already integrated almost all of Europe to a remarkable extent—with free and open borders and unlimited exchange of goods, people, capital, and services. Europeanization is a process that goes much further and deeper than globalization. A thought experiment will help make the case. Take, for example, CAFTA, the Central American Free Trade Agreement: There are no "four freedoms" (free movement of people, commodities, services, and capital) between the United States and Central America. For example, there are no laws governed by CAFTA that take precedence over national laws; there is no common currency across CAFTA; there are no environmental, labor, or social regulations that apply to all CAFTA countries equally; there are no political institutions that give representation to the member states of CAFTA; there is no CAFTA passport; and so on. In fact, such developments seem unthinkable. Thus, what the EU has achieved in integrating 27 countries goes far beyond what even the most convinced proponent of globalization could hope for.

At the same time, globalization challenges the European welfare state, as noted earlier. This is clearly a threat, but also an opportunity: Because European democracies will not be able to compete on the basis of price, they will have to compete on the basis of quality. In order to produce high-quality products, Europe will need a highly educated workforce. Thus, globalization puts tremendous pressures on European education systems to be on the cutting edge. In addition, the welfare state may in fact function like a cushion, protecting the countries from the ups and downs of the international business cycle. It may even be the case that welfare states, for that very reason, will be able to better weather the challenges of globalization than less developed welfare states. It is quite instructive that the populations of Sweden, Finland, Denmark, and the Netherlands, who embrace globalization the most (see Figure 15.3) are also protected the most by very generous welfare states.

Immigration and integration of newcomers represents another threat, but, again, another opportunity as well. Europe must open its borders for newcomers and integrate them in such a way that they have equal chances for social mobility. This will force European countries to move away from their parochial conceptions of identity based on Republican or ethnic principles. Europe is rapidly aging and will need the influx of newcomers to bolster its population and maintain its social security systems. Germany understood these challenges and, in a historic act, changed its immigration law from *jus sanguinis* (where citizenship is based on blood relations) to *jus soli* (territorially based citizenship) in 2000.

It is ironic: Precisely because of the process of EU integration, each EU member country might have a better chance to weather the assault of globalization than if they were exposed to it individually. This is possible for two reasons: First, EU integration is not anarchic. People and their representatives in the member countries do have a say about the most critical decisions the EU makes, despite claims about the elitist character of the EU. Second, the EU represents a mighty economic superpower that can impose itself and withstand pressures from other economic superpowers much more effectively than any individual EU country ever could, without the fear of retaliation. This can most clearly be seen in the recent decision by the EU to prevent Chinese textiles from flooding European markets by holding the shipments at European borders. Since January 1, 2005, Chinese textile products have saturated world markets as a WTO restriction on quotas expired. The EU launched an investigation and concluded that certain types of Chinese imports need to be curbed to protect the European textile industry. It may very well be that in the future, the European Union will be able to shield Europeans from the less desirable consequences of globalization while taking advantage of its benefits.

KEY TERMS

"acquis communautaire" 332
antiterror 345
assimilationist 344
business process outsourcing 341
"community" 340
culture 346
democratic process 332
environment 336
globalization index 337
governments 332

human trafficking 343
identity 346
immigration 340
inducements 341
integration 345
interconnectedness 336
location 342
markets 332
migration 334
multiculturalism 345
outsource 333
"race to the bottom" 342

Republican model 344
restricted 331
sovereign 331
Soviet Union 335
subsidizing 347
tax revenues 340
technology 332
transaction costs 333
transportation 333
welfare state 340
xenophobia 343

DISCUSSION QUESTIONS

1. In what way does globalization affect your personal life?
2. Is it possible to maintain one's sense of community and at the same time embrace globalization?
3. Why do immigrants in Europe seem to have more difficulty integrating into their host societies than in the United States?
4. Can you think of examples where the market imperative does not undermine one's sense of community, but rather fosters it?
5. Why might globalization affect Europe more than the United States?
6. What is the difference between "Europeanization" and globalization?
7. When did globalization begin?
8. What are the central factors that determine the extent of globalization?
9. What might the effects of business outsourcing be on your chance of finding a job?
10. What are the dangers that come with "obliteration of distance"?

NOTES

1. There is quite a debate about just how many pages the "acquis" encompasses, but the latest estimates suggest around 170,000 pages. See: Just How Big Is the Acquis Communautaire? http://www.openeurope.org.uk/research/acquis.pdf.
2. Karl Marx. *The German Ideology* Quoted in Robert Tucker. *The Marx-Engels Reader,* 2nd ed. (New York: Norton & Company), p. 163.
3. Paul Krugman. Growing World Trade: Causes and Consequences. *Brookings Papers on Economic Activity* 26 (1995): 327–377.
4. Niall Ferguson. The Ascent of Money: A Financial History of the World (New York: The Penguin Press HC, 2008).
5. *Guinness World Records Book* (London: Guinness World Records Limited, 2001). http://www.guinnessworldrecords.com/.
6. Pop-confidential, Pop culture de-classified. http://popconfidential.zap2it.com/2009/06/13/desperate-housewives-is-the-worlds-most-popular-comedy.
7. Human Development Report 2004. *Globalization and Cultural Choice* (New York: United Nations Development Programme, 2004), p. 87.
8. Markus M. L. Crepaz. *Trust beyond Borders: Immigration, the Welfare State and Identity in Modern Societies* (Ann Arbor, MI: University of Michigan Press, 2007).
9. OECD, *Trends in International Migration* (Paris: OECD, 2003).
10. Ibid.
11. Markus M. L. Crepaz. Global, Constitutional, and Partisan Determinants of Redistribution in Fifteen OECD Countries. *Comparative Politics* 43 (January 2002): 169–188.
12. Fröbel Folker, Jürgen Heinrichs, and Otto Kreye. *The New International Division of Labour* (Cambridge, MA: Cambridge University Press, 1980).
13. Wolfgang Müller. Ihr seid einfach zu teuer. *Der Freitag,* January 16, 2004.
14. Lou Dobbs Tonight. *CNN,* November 28, 2005.
15. Müller, Ihr seid einfach zu teuer.
16. International Labor Cost Comparisons. *Steel on the Net.* http://www.steelonthenet.com/labour_cost.html
17. Duane Swank. *Global Capital, Political Institutions and Policy Change in Developed Welfare States* (Cambridge, MA: Cambridge University Press, 2002). Another influential book is Geoffrey Garrett. *Partisan Politics in a Global Economy* (New York: Cambridge University Press, 1998).

18. Crepaz. Global, Constitutional, and Partisan Determinants of Redistribution in Fifteen OECD Countries, 2002.

19. Silvia Poggioli. *National Public Radio*, October 13, 2004.

20. *London Daily Telegraph,* February 19, 2004.

21. Immigration: Europe on the Move. *CNN*, 2003.

22. An Underclass Rebellion. *The Economist,* November 12, 2005, 24.

23. France May Extend Government Emergency Powers. *National Public Radio,* November 15, 2005.

24. Alfred Stepan and Ezra Suleiman. French Republican Model Fuels Alienation Rather Than Integration. *Taipei Times,* November 18, 2005.

25. Blair Proposes Strict Anti-Terror Measures. *Washington Post*, August 6, 2005.

26. Colin Randall. France Ejects 12 Islamic "Preachers of Hate." *The Telegraph,* July 30, 2005.

INDEX